Bringing the Passions Back In

Edited by Rebecca Kingston and Leonard Ferry

Bringing the Passions Back In
The Emotions in Political Philosophy

UBCPress · Vancouver · Toronto

16 15 14 13 12 11 10 09 08   5 4 3 2 1

Printed in Canada on ancient-forest-free paper (100% post-consumer recycled) that is processed chlorine- and acid-free, with vegetable-based inks.

Library and Archives Canada Cataloguing in Publication

    Bringing the passions back in : the emotions in political philosophy / edited by Rebecca Kingston and Leonard Ferry.

Includes bibliographical references and index.
ISBN 978-0-7748-1409-6 (bound); 978-0-7748-1410-2 (pbk)

    1. Political science – Philosophy. 2. Emotions – Political aspects. 3. Emotions (Philosophy).
4. Political psychology. I. Kingston, Rebecca II. Ferry, Leonard, 1971-

JA71.B753 2007   320.01   C2007-903467-5

Canadä

UBC Press gratefully acknowledges the financial support for our publishing program of the Government of Canada through the Book Publishing Industry Development Program (BPIDP), and of the Canada Council for the Arts, and the British Columbia Arts Council.

This book has been published with the help of a grant from the Canadian Federation for the Humanities and Social Sciences, through the Aid to Scholarly Publications Programme, using funds provided by the Social Sciences and Humanities Research Council of Canada.

Printed and bound in Canada by Friesens
Set in Fairfield by Blakeley
Copy editor: Sarah Wight
Proofreader: Tara Tovell
Indexer: Lillian Ashworth

UBC Press
The University of British Columbia
2029 West Mall
Vancouver, BC V6T 1Z2
604.822.5959 / Fax 604.822.6083
www.ubcpress.ca

Contents

Foreword: Politics and Passion

Charles Taylor

The idea that democracy is threatened by passion is strange but, in a sense, true. We all know cases where populations carried away by collective passions have done or endorsed terrible things. For example, the sense of national grievance among Germans in the Weimar Republic was played upon by Hitler and other extreme-right demagogues with dreadful results. There are lots of other examples, perhaps not as dire in their consequences, but fearful nonetheless.

But how about positive passions? The way, for instance, in which the sight of suffering people on our television screens, in the wake of a tsunami or a famine, unleashes great waves of generosity and solidarity. Or the way in which thousands of people are ready to demonstrate for hours and days, often in very difficult conditions, to establish their right to vote, or to make their votes count, as in the Orange Revolution in the Ukraine.

These positive cases weigh less with us when we think of passions and politics in general because we have already fixed our basic categories. By "us" here, I mean the philosophy and common sense of our culture – or at least the major influences that set the tone for these. And this view places passion or emotion in another category from reason. It is one thing to be able to think out the best thing to do; it is another to feel strongly that something is good or bad, right or wrong. Everybody agrees that if your feelings are rightly directed, then things will go very much better – which is what happens when we contribute to Oxfam, or stay out in the cold in Kiev.

But the idea is that, if your emotions are aligned with your reason, this is a matter of luck or good management (especially good training); it's not because your feelings have contributed anything to your reasoning. Feeling and thinking are separate. To many people this view is just common sense. Thinking and feeling are different functions and belong to different "faculties," to use the traditional language.

But history shows that this dichotomy is an invention of modern Western culture. It doesn't exist elsewhere, not even in the deep philosophical sources of our culture, among the Greeks. The contributors to this book make this point very clear. For Plato, for Aristotle, and for the Stoics, in different ways, feelings, passions, *pathē* were cognitive states. And there is something obviously right about this. When I'm angry at you for pushing me off the bus, the anger is inseparable from my knowing (or at least believing) that it was you who pushed me off, that you did it on purpose, that you meant harm to me; similarly, when I fear a stock market crash, the fear can't be separated from my apprehending great disadvantage to myself as my pension fund goes up in smoke; and so on.

We know with our feelings. But sometimes what we sense through our feelings clashes with what we know through dispassionate reason. I'm still mad at you, even after I learn that you were pushed from behind when you knocked me off that bus. And so perhaps we can disregard feeling as a source of knowing after all? But this would be a big mistake. In our dealings with others, a completely dispassionate perspective would fail to pick up the nuances, the ambivalences, the resentments, or the hidden sympathies of others. Persons without these emotional sensitivities would be terrible negotiators and bad political leaders, incapable of bringing people together in an important common enterprise.

In particular, we can see in our world how people whose sensitivities are narrow, and only operate within their own home culture, commit tremendous blunders in their dealings with others and remain blind to the damage they wreak in the world. The present world superpower offers daily examples of this kind of (largely involuntary) self-stultifying action, sowing stupefaction and horror in its wake. Knowing through feeling is perhaps even more important when it comes to moral matters. Someone whose view on genocide is only that, upon dispassionate reflection, he thinks it is not a very good idea, doesn't yet "know" what's really wrong with it.

All this clearly shows not just that you can't factor emotions out of politics, which we already knew. More importantly, it shows that we can't factor emotions out of what makes for good politics, grounded in reality and moral truth, nor out of what makes for democratic politics, in which people can be brought together.

The excellent papers in this collection bring these points home, partly in recovering ancient thinking on these matters (for instance, Chapters 2 and 3), partly in showing the ways in which the modern traditions of thought have oversimplified and flattened our understandings of reason and emotion (for instance, Chapters 5 and 9), and partly by reflecting on the nature of modern politics itself. This volume will help to deepen the discussion, and to recruit more people into the debate, on this range of issues, which is essential to our understanding of ourselves and our world.

Acknowledgments

We would like to thank a number of individuals and organizations who have been important to the development of this project. The idea for this book was sparked by a panel we organized for a meeting of the Canadian Political Science Association. We also appreciate the support of colleagues and graduate students of the Department of Political Science at the University of Toronto; many vibrant discussions among us have furthered some of the reflections contained in this book. Thanks are also due to the Social Sciences and Humanities Research Council of Canada, which helped to make this book possible.

Chapter 1 is reprinted, with permission and slight revisions, from The Journal of Philosophy 75, 3 (1978): 139-61. Chapter 3 is reprinted, with permission and slight revisions, from The Review of Metaphysics 56, 2 (December 2002): 267-96. Chapter 10 is reprinted, with permission from Blackwell Publishing, from Midwest Studies in Philosophy, vol. 22, Philosophy of Emotions, ed. Peter E. French and Howard K. Wettstein (Notre Dame, IN: University of Notre Dame Press, 1998).

We owe a tremendous thank you to Katherine Reilly, whose patience has rivalled that of any great Stoic. Whether from Guatemala or Mexico City (global citizen that she is), she has continually ensured that what at first appeared to be a gargantuan task became a manageable one. Great thanks also go to Emily Andrew, our editor at UBC Press, who has been extremely helpful and encouraging, and indeed the very form of what an editor should be.

We also wish to thank our family and friends. Kant suggests that his knowledge of the common man was revealed to him by reading Rousseau. In contrast, we recognize that our partners and close associates contribute most to our learning about the human condition. Rebecca thanks Ronnie, Gabriel, Zimra, and Pauline. Len thanks his grandparents (Leo, Sally, Willis, and Audrey), his parents (Leonard and Phyllis), his children (Lauren and Leonard), and for her patience and her love, his wife (Jenny).

We were greatly saddened to hear of the death of Robert C. Solomon, one of our contributors, while this volume was in preparation. He is, of course, the man most responsible for putting the emotions at the top of our intellectual concerns today. In tribute to his tremendous contributions to our understanding of these issues, and indeed of ourselves, we dedicate this volume to him.

Bringing the Passions Back In

Introduction: The Emotions and the History of Political Thought

Leonard Ferry and Rebecca Kingston

We are well aware that political life is fraught with emotion. This is the case not only for political actors, whose ambitions, loyalties, pride, ideals, et cetera are often reinforced and undermined in quick succession in contemporary liberal democratic societies, but also for citizens whose hopes and fears for their country, as well as for their families and the world, ebb and flow in a complex set of reactions to the events unfolding around them, emotions and passions that can sometimes spur every one of us to political action.

Surprisingly, however, in the academic world and particularly in the normative models commonly debated among political theorists of contemporary liberalism and liberal democracy, there is little serious regard for the important and varied roles that emotion plays and should play within the political arena. The lack of close attention may stem from a deep suspicion of the dangers that unchecked passions have wrought in the political history of the West.[1] Indeed, those who trace the birth of modern liberal democracy to attempts to find a solid basis for social accommodation in the wake of the violence of the religious wars of the early modern period may see good historical cause to sideline emotion in politics.

Still, such sidelining has its costs. The relative lack of positive interest in human emotions in current liberal democratic thinking is deficient for two reasons. First, the traditional rational, normative approach to theory remains an overly ideal and utopian view of political life. Moreover, it risks holding no interest for – indeed, alienating – those citizens directly implicated in political life. Some theorists suggest that such rational, normative expectations increase political apathy and cynicism within our political communities.[2]

Second, and perhaps most importantly in theoretical terms, the rational, normative vision of politics so prevalent today can be said to harbour an incomplete, if not manifestly false, concept of the human subject. This vision is largely derived from Kantian inspiration in our intellectual tradition, and Kant notoriously likened passions to cancerous sores.[3] New developments in the fields of psychology and the philosophy of mind show, however, that we cannot easily compartmentalize the faculties of reason and emotion within the human soul, nor indeed malign so severely our capacities for emotion and passion. While there is no clear consensus on how to understand and explain emotion, there is an acknowledgment that emotional capacities are more complex than previously thought and depend largely, if not wholly, on our cognitive abilities. Furthermore, our capacity for emotion is an essential and positive feature of humanity; our emotional lives, however intense, provide a necessary foundation for the possibility of meaning and human happiness. This recognition also raises the possibility of what we might call "rational emotion."

All the contributors to this volume are aware of these important developments and recognize their significance for the field of political theory. They also acknowledge that existing resources within our own theoretical traditions can help illuminate the consequences of these new understandings for politics.

The first section of this introduction provides an overview of recent developments in the literature devoted to the emotions and philosophy of mind, developments that form a backdrop to this volume. The second section offers some general reflections on the possible implications of these theories for our understanding of politics, as well as highlighting some of the more important themes and points of contention found in this collection.

What Is an Emotion?

Most of the major philosophers in the Western tradition have furnished us with an answer to the question of what is an emotion. Given the diversity and richness of the tradition, of course these answers differ. Some theories of emotion stand in conceptual opposition to one another: compare Chrysippus' identification of the emotions with mental judgments and William James' identification of them with physical feelings, for instance.[4] Other theories, theories with broad family resemblances, still differ over details. Among cognitive accounts of the emotions, for example, there is significant disagreement over the nature of and role played by judgment in the make-up of an emotion: some identify emotions with judgments; some keep them distinct but claim that judgments are components in, causally responsible for, or constitutive of emotions.

Over the last fifty years, there has been an explosion of interest in and a growing consensus around a new[5] family of theories of the emotions.[6] That the emotions are in some manner related to cognition or are themselves cognitive has become a commonplace of contemporary philosophical psychology.[7] Even those who do not accept this as a fully satisfactory explanatory theory find themselves adopting it if only as a temporary measure, thereby acceding to its dominant position. Take the reflections of Robert Nozick as an example:

A large part of how we feel about life is shaped by the emotions we have had and expect to have, and that feeling too (probably) is an emotion or a combination of them. What emotions should we desire – indeed, why should we desire *any* – and how should we think about the emotions we do have? The recent philosophical literature describes the structure of emotions in a way that is somewhat illuminating – I am not completely happy with it, but I have nothing better at present to offer. Emotions, these philosophers say, have a common structure of three components: a belief, an evaluation, and a feeling.[8]

Despite his tentativeness about the theory, Nozick asks us to accept the messy interconnectedness both of human life with the emotions and of the emotions with mental phenomena. To speak of beliefs and evaluations as "components" of an emotion is to indicate that some relation holds between the emotions and the mind. Here the psychophysical "feeling" of an emotion is only one part of a larger whole, incomplete on its own. In addition, for an emotion to be experienced seems to require that the agent make judgments about the facts of the situation or event to which the emotion stands as response. Such judgments must be accompanied by a further relation of the agent to the situation or event with a decidedly normative cast. The supposition of a three-part structure, therefore, introduces into discussions of the emotions several questions about the precise nature of and role played by cognition (we look at some of these more closely below).

Conceiving of emotions in this way also requires that we take a particular normative stance in relation to the importance of emotion in the living of a life. For those who accept even a limited cognitivist account of the emotions, an account that makes beliefs or evaluations integral to the experience of an emotion, emotions cannot be dismissed as an instinct or other natural activity (like digestion) that stands outside of moral concern.[9] So Nozick asks why we should desire to experience emotion and leaves open the question of how the emotions we do have should be assessed. One reason Nozick gives for thinking the emotions not merely ineliminable from normative philosophy but positively contributing to the same is that they model values: they "provide a kind of picture of value ... They are our internal psychophysical response to the external value, a response ... not only due to that value but an analog representation of it."[10]

Interest continues to grow, not only in these theories themselves, which belong chiefly to the philosophies of mind and action, but also in the avenues that these have opened for other branches of philosophy, including especially political and moral philosophy. The papers in this collection explore some of the themes raised by and about this recent philosophical work on the emotions.

Feelings, Beliefs, and Evaluations

What follows is a brief characterization of some of the topics that remain central to conceptualizations of the emotions in some form of cognitive frame, focusing primarily on the insights that cognitive theories have generated. What we do say of noncognitivist accounts amounts to mentioning their criticisms of their cognitivist counterparts. Still, we hope that even by doing so little we manage to convey some of the resources that theories of the emotions have made available to the understanding of human action, individually and collectively, and to suggest some of the paths future work will have to tread. Let's begin with an example of a specific emotion, pride, which will enable us to point to some important distinctions and issues:

At a small campus coffee shop, Bill and a few friends discuss what they've accomplished during the past week. As all are graduate students, a common theme is that they have not done enough – they have neither read nor written what they had hoped, indeed planned, to do. But Bill announces that he has had a great week. He has so managed his time as to be able to read three large nineteenth-century novels: Dickens' *Bleak House*, Eliot's *Middlemarch*, and James' *A Portrait of a Lady*. Unlike his friends, Bill feels good about his work and about himself. He feels a certain swelling, a sense of accomplishment, as his friends acknowledge his achievement. The impression of his own distinction in this regard fills him with confidence, and this self-assurance reveals itself to his friends in his speech and his mannerisms. He doesn't hide his feeling of superiority. He feels flush with energy, and he lets everyone know.[11]

This example suggests several questions that continue to engage philosophers exploring the emotions. We've already said that our example is an instance of the emotion pride. But what is pride? The answer depends on the answer to the often-asked question of what an emotion is. How will we recognize it? "The best signs of passions present," Thomas Hobbes advises, "are either in the countenance, motions of the body, actions, and ends, or aims, which we otherwise know the man to have."[12] Hobbes' list is extensive, but not obviously helpful beyond suggesting some more questions that we might want to ask. Is Bill's emotional experience identical with the physiological changes that he experiences, as William James held? Are these changes unique to this emotion? René Descartes thought that even if they were not unique they were helpful signs: "It is easy to understand that Pride and Servility are not only vices but also Passions, because their excitation is very noticeable externally in those who are suddenly puffed up or cast down by some new occasion."[13] Can we use these occurrences to identify one emotion as distinct from another? And if the physiological changes Bill experiences are not adequate to account for the nature of this emotion, to what must appeal be made? In appealing to something else, are we free to jettison the physical feelings Bill experiences altogether from our descriptions of the emotion – that is, are the feelings associated with an emotion necessary, if not sufficient, conditions of an emotion? Are we compelled to shift our focus from the physical to the mental? Does such an analysis make of the physical expression of Bill's emotion merely a contingent event? Peter Goldie has recently objected to the reductive treatment of many of the feelings of an emotion in the hands of cognitive theories, whether those theories treat the feelings as something added to an emotion experience or as unnecessary.[14]

Uncomfortable with the inability of physiological explanations to account for the specification of discrete emotions, philosophers since Anthony Kenny have indeed turned to the mental (without denying that the same is embedded in physical brain states).[15] Here too questions arise. Just what is required for the experience of an emotion? Is the emotion of pride identical to Bill's belief that he has read three novels last week? Benedict de Spinoza defined pride as consisting in "thinking too much of ourselves, through self-love ... pride is an effect or property of self-love, and it may therefore be defined as love of ourselves or self-satisfaction, in so far as it affects us so that we think too highly of ourselves."[16] To experience pride, then, we need to make a judgment or hold some belief about ourselves and our accomplishments. Bill believes that he has read three books, and his emotion has for its object at least this belief. Talk about emotions having objects, however, introduces into the discussion what is generally referred to as the "intentionality" of an emotion. Emotions are about something. We perceive ourselves threatened *by* some person, thing, or event and experience fear. Someone treats us in a manner we judge as slighting and we become angry *at* the person and the supposed slight. Does Bill's belief that he has read three books cause his emotion? Is this factual belief sufficient to account for the judgment that Spinoza identifies as central to pride?

The mere description – Bill read three books – doesn't seem sufficient. Recall Nozick's three-part structure: belief, evaluation, and feeling. It would seem possible for Bill to have such a belief without experiencing any emotion. Surely Bill can believe that he has eaten three meals on the day in question without feeling proud of it. What else is needed? Many of those who have taken up the cognitive approach to explaining emotions claim that the factual description of a given situation must be attached to a normative or evaluative judgment. Having read three books, or at least these three books, is significant and something to feel proud about. Something like this kind of evaluation seems necessary to the overall claim Bill makes in feeling proud. And, as Charles Taylor has argued, the relevant "import-ascription" cannot merely be subjective, because the import-ascription of an emotion involves "a judgment about the way things are, which cannot simply be reduced to the way we feel about them."[17] Although it may prove difficult to agree on what standard is being deployed, we must agree that this second feature of an emotion requires the invocation of some evaluative standard. Does this mean that the emotion is equivalent to the factual description plus the evaluative judgment? If not, how are they related to the emotion? Are they causal factors, or components? What role do these two mental aspects, factual description and evaluative judgment, play in the experience of an emotion?

That both are necessary conditions of the intelligibility of an emotion is suggested by an argument Nozick makes in *The Examined Life*: "Suppose you say you feel proud that you read three books last week, and I say that you're misremembering; I counted and you read only one book last week. You grant the correction and reply that nevertheless you feel proud that you read three. This is bewildering."[18] The source of the bewilderment is that without the belief that caused or accompanied the emotion, the emotion itself should no longer obtain. A similar conclusion follows, Nozick argues, if the evaluation that goes with the belief fails. If, for example, Bill can be convinced that reading is not good and not something to feel proud about, then for him to continue to feel proud would be equally bewildering. Whatever Bill might be feeling, it wouldn't be pride. Pride requires both a belief about certain facts – that something is or is not the case (that Bill has read three books) – and an evaluation of a specific kind – that pride is felt in relation to having done something to distinguish oneself (Bill's having read these three books seems a real accomplishment given a belief that reading three books of this sort is a genuine achievement and something to be admired.)

When these two requirements are satisfied, Nozick continues, "there perhaps goes a feeling, a sensation, an inner experience." Nozick's inability to assert the necessity of the third component of an emotion, its feeling, highlights the fact that the physiological level of understanding the emotions is the most problematic for cognitivist theorists. Is the feeling of an emotion necessary? What are its sources? Is it also merely a mental state? Or does the feel of an emotion require also an accompanying physiological change? The problem involves how one conceives the relation of the mind (belief and judgment) to the body (physiological reaction). Are there other grounds for believing the belief and evaluation that inform the intentional object of an emotion to be necessary and perhaps sufficient for the emotion?

Imagine that in the above example Bill's friends, instead of bemoaning their idleness, had been exchanging lists of books that they had read. Each list contained the three books mentioned by Bill as well as others. This group of friends would hardly find Bill's achievement something to esteem. Absent their recognition, would Bill himself think that his accomplishment merited his feelings? It's possible, of course, that for Bill this still would represent an accomplishment that the others could acknowledge – perhaps Bill is an athlete who spends much of his time training. In either case it seems clear that the evaluative aspect cannot be removed without changing the nature of the experience.

Can the same be said of the factual description? Assume that Jane, another friend, enters the coffee shop. She notices Bill's behaviour and discovers its source. But she finds herself in a slightly uncomfortable position: she has stopped by the coffee shop hoping to return Bill's copy of *Middlemarch*, which she borrowed at the beginning of the week. How will Bill react if she divulges this fact? If Bill did not deliberately deceive his friends but, rather, misstated the facts in the heat of the moment (or even misremembered them: perhaps he only began the novel before Jane borrowed it), he may simply have to concede that he didn't read three novels. But if the evaluative judgment depends on it being three, allowing that two books is a sufficiently lesser feat, will Bill still feel proud? This question seems to demand a negative answer: how can Bill feel proud of having done something that he didn't actually do? He might alter his evaluative judgment, lowering the standard, as it were, and so feel proud that he read two books; but he could not feel proud of having read three novels while knowing that he had only read two.

Emotions and Evaluations

In addition to these thorny problems, the relationship between emotions and value raises others. For example, Spinoza's definition of pride raises its association with vice. He sees pride on its own as a problematic emotion: "It would take too much time to enumerate here all the evils of pride, for the proud are subject to all emotions, but to none are they less subject than to those of love and pity."[19] Contrast this with David Hume, who acknowledges that his discussion of pride will offend those familiar with "the style of the schools and pulpit" that characterizes pride as exclusively vicious. For Hume, although pride can be vicious, it is potentially virtuous: "I observe, that by *pride* I understand that agreeable impression, which arises in the mind, when the view either of our virtue, beauty, riches or power makes us satisfy'd with ourselves."[20]

For the moment, we want to point out only some of the ways in which the emotions relate to the good life. At least three "conditions of fitting-ness" exist with respect to the emotions. From the supposition that they are cognitive – that they depend upon beliefs and judgments about descriptive and normative states of affairs – it follows that emotions can be fitting or unfitting, locally and in general. By locally, we mean that the belief itself can be mistaken and that the emotion may or may not be appropriate to the belief. Return for a moment to the example of pride. If Bill is wrong about having read three books, or if he is wrong to think that reading is a good to be pursued, the response that he has will itself be mistaken. The first supposition is experiential: either he has or hasn't read this many books. The second concerns evaluation: having read this many books in a week is or is not a matter about which one should feel pride *because* it is or is not something integral to good living. The third condition of fittingness is proportion. If Bill over-reacts, becoming ecstatic about having read three books to the point where his response becomes a nuisance to others who value such an accomplishment differently, then his reaction may be judged inappropriate. Similarly, if, having accomplished something that is recognized as a source of pride, he shows no emotion, he may be faulted for being cold and unfeeling. Emotions are fitting, Nozick writes, when "the belief is true, the evaluation is correct, and the feeling is proportionate to the evaluation."[21]

The emotions can also fit or fail to fit in a larger sense. Generally, one must consider whether or not one should experience emotions or seek to situate oneself in such a way as to prove impervious to them. If a life lived without emotion is determined to be the best sort of life for human beings, then the third condition of fit will never obtain, because and insofar as the fittingness of the prior judgments or beliefs have altered. The Stoics argue forcefully that the elimination of emotion is a precondition of human flourishing, and their analysis of the emotions is intimately tied to this normative conclusion.

Becoming impervious to the emotions is only possible, however, if the emotions are under our control. Conceiving of emotions as cognitive events of a relatively complex order, such that they can be *constituted by* if not *identified with* rational judgments, brings them into the realm of the voluntary, according to Cicero in the third and fourth books of the *Tusculan Disputations*. One need not agree with the Stoic conclusion. Sartre did not expect the emotions to be driven from the human agent, but he did reject excusing agents because of their emotions: "The existentialist does not believe in the power of passion. He will never agree that a sweeping passion is a ravaging torrent which fatally leads a man to certain acts and is therefore an excuse. He thinks that man is responsible for his passion."[22] Others have been far less confident in pronouncing on the responsibility of agents for the emotions. But all have had something to say about the relation of the emotions to the lived lives of agents, to their pursuit of fullness, to their conceptions of value and the good.

Politics and the Emotions

So what are the repercussions of these ways of conceptualizing the interplay and interdependency of emotion, cognition, and reason for our understandings of and possibilities for democratic engagement? Regarding our capacity to reason as inextricably tied to our emotional capacities may do little to change our understandings other than to suggest an alternative phenomenological description of what sort of reasoning is actually taking place. Indeed, it might be suggested that the most dominant theories of our time, such as Rawls' *A Theory of Justice*, already recognize an emotional underpinning, such as an ongoing desire for justice, that makes a normative picture possible.[23] If such is the case, we need only to supplement those established normative visions, on a terrain that they have conceded, with a somewhat thicker understanding of the human subject. And this would not necessitate any real changes to the content and implications of those theories.

But the consequences may not be quite so straightforward. The articles in this volume point to a variety of ways in which, by taking seriously these new accounts of the complexity of the human psyche and the intricate connections between emotion and reason, we must begin to rethink some of our common suppositions. All the authors in this collection recognize that human emotional capacities, given their necessary and sometimes desirable contributions to political life, also present challenges. From among the contributions to this book we can identify at least four ways in which these new theories can have an important impact on contemporary democratic and liberal democratic theory: they can generate a rethinking of our traditional ways of distinguishing between private and public; they can lead us to seek greater clarity on the ways in which emotion continues to sustain current political commitments in liberal and democratic regimes; they can contribute to recognizing better outcomes in democratic practice including democratic deliberation; and finally, in general, they allow us to develop a more realistic set of political expectations.

Public and Private

There is a long tradition of regarding state institutions as guardians of "sober second thought" against the excessive emotional responses of private individuals and even elected legislative bodies. In a recent work, for example, Cass Sunstein highlights the role of government officials in examining public fears in the light of expert evidence and in subjecting citizens' emotive responses and public panics to the sane adjudication of administrative rationality. Such a role supposes a boundary between the higher reason of officialdom and populist unenlightened emotionalism.[24] In addition, we can see that despite Rawls' recognition of a desire for justice as a precondition for a just political community, the distinction between the public domain and the particular interests that remain hidden behind the veil of ignorance in the realm of the private depends on, and indeed is constituted by, a conception of public reason itself.[25] Of course, many feminist critics of the liberal tradition have long been aware of the dangers of these conceptions.[26] Still, many theorists continue to conceive the border between the private and the public within liberal thought as that point where one crosses from unreason and the sentiment of households to rational public justification.

The primordial importance of the emotions at the core of political life could disrupt this distinction between the public and private that has been a common trope of our liberal democratic understanding. Do we not begin to blur the line between acceptable and unacceptable policy justifications if we admit of an emotional grounding to a drive for justice? If we accept current developments in the philosophy of mind, acknowledging a much more complex human psychology including an inextricable connection between emotion and reason, the normative models in political theory that give public legitimacy to reason over and against the emotion of the private sphere must be rethought.

Emotions and Citizenship

Dismantling the reason-emotion divide as one of the proper boundaries of political life may also open up debate on whether the emotional lives of citizens can be regarded as a worthy object of public policy, and in what ways. In Britain, recent reforms have led to a great increase in the availability of cognitive behavioural therapy through the National Health Service, and the government has even embarked on a project to institute a program for emotional literacy in the schools.[27] While liberals may be averse to the idea of directly legislating the emotional lives of citizens, these reforms go some way in promoting certain models of emotional well-being for citizenry. How can they be reconciled with liberal assumptions? A more sophisticated understanding of human psychology than that traditionally acknowledged in political theory will allow us to better come to terms with such new areas of policy. In general, if we are concerned about the failure of contemporary liberal democracies to foster the qualities required for the exercise of responsible citizenship, then these new understandings can be helpful to an educational project to promote the critical yet affective judgment required of a mature liberal democratic citizen.[28]

In addition, an acknowledgment of the relevance of emotions in political judgment and political life may help us better to acknowledge the differences among liberal regimes, even those with similar institutional forms and constitutional ideals. This is crucial to understanding the opportunities as well as pitfalls in building and sustaining democratic regimes worldwide. For example, what general dispositions of the citizenry are necessary for the effective functioning of liberal democracy itself? While certain authors, as we have seen, believe a general desire for justice among citizenry to be indispensable, others have conceptualized this fundamental liberal democratic ethos in competing ways, for example Judith Shklar's fear of cruelty (the liberalism of fear) or Alexis de Tocqueville's love of equality.[29] Most political theorists could agree, however, that the emotions play an important role in assuring the centrality of liberal values in the experience of the liberal democratic citizen. In other words, it is our emotions along with our reason that relay to us the importance of a set of practices that express recognition of dignity and respect for the human person, the importance of freedom, and other key commitments through which liberalism can be defined.

Still, to recognize judiciously the inextricable importance of the emotions for our political lives, we must find some means by which we can adjudicate among them, finding criteria by which we can assess those emotional qualities or associations which can further the cause of democracy and justice and those which can detract from them. Should we accept all forms of emotion and of emotional states as in some way conducive to liberalism or democracy, or should some emotional templates be encouraged (or discouraged) for the sake of maximizing equality and freedom? In either case, how can this be done?

Another approach to examining the place of the emotions in a variety of regimes is perhaps more common to the ancients than among today's political scientists, at least until recent attempts to revive the republican tradition.[30] This approach explores the varying forms of *ethos* across different types of society. On a broad scale, some theorists argue within a cognitivist framework that the emotions are socially constructed, in whole or in part.[31] If emotions are largely the product of our beliefs and evaluations, and if our beliefs and evaluations are in general acquired through cultural transmission, then our emotional experiences can be regarded as a direct legacy of our social experiences and education. For the ancients, this was a matter of differing structures of governance. Can competing forms of government, such as monarchies, constitutional monarchies, republics, and tyrannies, still be associated with distinct emotional patterns among the rulers or the citizenry? Here emphasis can be placed on the patterns by which power is exercised and their possible impact on our political identities. The idea holds that a variety of emotional dispositions are associated with differing political forms, and that these public passions, so to speak, can play an important and positive role in the defining and consolidating of our broader political commitments. This may help us to understand the possibilities and limitations of competing forms of governance, as well as the continuing distinctions that we can see among different forms and practices of regimes.

Emotions and Democratic Deliberation

A third approach explores the particular and often competing passions of people living within liberal democratic states. While traditional theories, as we have seen, have often relied on the emotions to secure broad commitment to core liberal values such as liberty and equality, in more specific political debates the emotions have often been regarded as problematic. The consequent challenge has been to seek a mechanism whereby the competing passions of the public could be neutralized or minimized before or through the process of public deliberation. With the recognition that the idea of a purely rational public debate is founded on false notions of the relationship between reason and the emotions, it is incumbent upon political theorists to seek new means of integrating an appreciation for emotional life into the heart of our theories of public deliberation. The actual workings of deliberation involve a wide variety of motivations on the part of citizens, and one cannot expect outcomes of deliberation in an actual democratic setting to be based on bare rational principles. A new understanding of deliberation that not only incorporates an understanding of the inextricable importance and positive contribution of emotion in the formation of political judgment but also explores the means by which the passions can work in the public sphere to achieve a degree of impartiality will help us become better judges of the democratic process.

One effect of this may be, as recognized by Michael Walzer, an appreciation not only of the passionate commitment that is required in a vibrant democratic community but also of the importance for politics of conflict, both within and among nation states.[32] This appreciation should teach us to avoid a narrow view of politics as the achievement of idealized consensual outcomes through rational deliberation. The centrality of emotion and competing passions in all forms of political action will inevitably mean that some people will feel better than others do about any political outcome.

Emotions and Political Aspirations

A final, and hopefully positive, effect of these rather new questions in political theory is to provide a vision of political life that more clearly conforms to the lives and aspirations of citizenry. Those who take up the cause of "bringing the emotions back in" have often suggested that the decline of citizen interest in the formal political process, as measured by a number of indicators, is in part due to a cynicism bred by an unrealistic model of what the political process should be.[33] While political theorists may be hubristic to think that their models of politics have so much popular impact, nonetheless an important gap is evident between contemporary political theory and the realities of politics in liberal democratic regimes. If our theorizing is to mean something in a world of new challenges to democratic governance, we must first seek a groundwork that conforms more adequately to the experience of citizens. A positive re-evaluation of the emotions in the political realm is one step towards a more meaningful dialogue with our own liberal democratic experience.

Overview of the Chapters

The essays in this volume are arranged for the most part chronologically, seeking to retrieve the importance of the debate on the emotions in political life through a number of thinkers and historical contexts in the Western tradition. Chapter 1, "Explaining Emotions," by the distinguished philosopher Amélie Oksenberg Rorty, is her classic 1978 statement of the need for a more complex approach to emotional life. She shows that no one principle can explain our emotional lives and that along with questions of individual and genetic dispositions we should also consider the social and cultural causes of both our emotions and the perceptions that underpin them. This chapter helps to lay the groundwork for this collection insofar as it provides an important philosophical account of how the emotions are being reconsidered. Rorty also provides us with a new postscript to this path-breaking article.

This volume's historical project begins with a consideration of ancient Athens. In "Plato on Shame and Frank Speech in Democratic Athens" (Chapter 2), Christina Tarnopolsky builds on revisionist accounts of Plato's Socrates. She argues that Plato, through an examination of the workings of *parrhēsia*, was putting forward a model of respectful shame to apply in both philosophy and politics as a corrective to (rather than replacement for) the norms of democratic practice in Athens. Like Sharon Krause and Marlene Sokolon in later chapters, Tarnopolsky suggests that we should reject the temptation to categorize our emotions as intrinsically either helpful or harmful for liberal democracy. Rather, we should embrace the full range of our emotions, acknowledging that they can serve democracy well only if they are manifested in ways that warn us about our vulnerability and mortality.

Arash Abizadeh's "The Passions of the Wise: *Phronēsis*, Rhetoric, and Aristotle's Passionate Practical Deliberation" (Chapter 3) shows that the practical wisdom central to Aristotle's ethics and politics does not function without emotion. Indeed, he argues that emotion (*pathos*), character (*ethos*), and logic (*logos*) are constitutive elements of both Aristotelian rhetoric and *phronēsis*, partly in terms of how the particulars are perceived and partly in terms of how deliberation proceeds in view of that perception. A proper understanding of the place of emotion in Aristotelian *phronēsis* and rhetoric, and an understanding of how the democratic forum can constrain rhetorical practice, allows a more favourable outlook on the possibilities of democratic politics in the absence of what Aristotle would judge to be full virtue on the part of statesmen and citizens.

In "Troubling Business: The Emotions in Aquinas' Philosophical Psychology" (Chapter 4), Leonard Ferry suggests a means to negotiate between those theories that view the emotions as fully conditioned by chemical and neurological reactions and those that suggest that the soul is wholly under our cognitive control. In broad terms, Thomas Aquinas' view of human action allows for a spectrum of possibilities in the human soul ranging from fundamentally physically generated feeling through a gradual range of emotion over which we can be said to hold an increasing degree of control. Ferry maintains that the perspective of Aquinas allows us to understand more fully those aspects of the soul over which we may have a certain command and those aspects that are more a matter of physical reflex. This has important political and legal implications, given the inconsistency in how our institutions deal with individual responsibility for emotional life. A better and more comprehensive understanding of the range of emotional life and the possibilities, though limited, of cognitive control will provide a better basis for informing our political and legal judgments.

In "The Political Relevance of the Emotions from Descartes to Smith" (Chapter 5), Rebecca Kingston argues that an important change occurred in the study of emotions in the seventeenth century. In the effort to apply new scientific methods to the study of the soul, theorists began to conceptualize emotion and passion as not only an internal phenomenon but an individual one. They thus abandoned a whole tradition in political theory that can be traced back to the ancients, a tradition that recognized the possibility of distinguishing social and political communities on the basis of a shared emotional disposition. Kingston maintains that the abandonment of the idea of "public passion" has impoverished political discourse, leading to a contemporary understanding of liberalism that devalues the passions in public life by relegating their legitimate sphere of action to private life. Noting that this decline of the idea of a public passion was an unintended consequence, Kingston calls not only for recognition of this idea as an analytical tool to help make sense of our political lives today but also for a larger and more positive role for the emotions in our normative understanding of politics.

Sharon Krause, in "Passion, Power, and Impartiality in Hume" (Chapter 6), re-examines David Hume's phenomenology of judgment and demonstrates how it is a relevant and realist corrective to theories of modern liberalism. She shows how the central importance of affect for moral judgment does not undermine the possibility of impartiality in Hume, due to the social fabric of moral feeling (which is built on a certain sensitivity to the pains and pleasures of others), the need for a generalized perspective in judgment that mitigates against the imposition of our own individual interests, and, finally, the limits imposed by human nature on what can and cannot be approved of in moral judgment. She acknowledges that, today, the acceptance of a Humean account of moral judgment would need to be supplemented by a commitment to broad forums of democratic deliberation, so as to extend individual sympathies and to provide the conditions for as broad and as generalized a standpoint as possible.

Ingrid Makus explores the place of emotions in the thought of Jean-Jacques Rousseau in "Pity, Pride, and Prejudice: Rousseau on the Passions" (Chapter 7). At the outset she describes the problems for contemporary liberal democratic thought in reviving a theory of the relationship between the passions and politics. Such a theory, she argues, must eschew foundationalist thinking while still holding to features of the ancient account of politics that recognize the centrality of the passions and a tie between reason and emotion secured by virtue. But how can virtue be addressed in a contemporary liberal democratic context that is pluralistic in both theory and practice? She argues that the philosophy of Jean-Jacques Rousseau can help to overcome the impasse, in particular through an understanding of the possibilities for the education of the natural human impulse to compassion.

In "Feelings in the Political Philosophy of J.S. Mill" (Chapter 8), Marlene Sokolon explores some of the tensions evident in Mill's work around the theme of emotions, or what Mill calls "feeling." Mill's reaction to his father's strain of utilitarianism was in part inspired by a need to incorporate a more sympathetic role for the emotions in utilitarian thought and calculation, but he was also suspicious of the workings of certain types of emotions (a tendency reflected in contemporary discussions on the emotions today, which Sokolon calls the "negative-positive polarity"). Mill thought that one could construct a political community in which the undesirable or destructive emotions would be isolated from political and ethical decision making. Sokolon, examining how these tendencies in Mill's thought resonate in contemporary debates on the emotions in public life, argues against this view. She suggests that the whole range of emotional response (including shame, disgust, and other seemingly negative emotions) can, in principle, be valuable in public life. The task of politics is to ensure that these emotional responses are associated with the appropriate objects for public approval and disapproval.

Leah Bradshaw's "Emotions, Reasons, and Judgments" (Chapter 9) evaluates the arguments of various philosophers who advocate a more important role for emotion in democratic judgment and deliberation. She begins with contrasting the views of Aristotle and Kant on the place of reason and emotion in politics, and then shows how more modern developments in political theory, like the work of Richard Rorty, manifest a departure from both. She is critical of Rorty and other thinkers who advocate a full embrace of emotion and passion in politics without some regard for the place of reason, no matter how worthy an emotion such as compassion may seem on the surface. As she states, "For compassion to have any substance politically, it has to be converted to virtue, which is measured by reasoned actions." She argues that only emotion aligned with reason, such as found in modern demands rising from indignation (rather than compassion), constitutes a ground for just political action. As such, she provides what may be regarded as a reconsideration of the arguments of this collection, given her return to the classics to support the centrality of reason for virtue and the need for traditional political and educational reform. Nonetheless, she recognizes that the forceful passions (such as indignation) will always be allied to those virtues (such as courage) that are closely associated with the pursuit of justice. In this regard she thus acknowledges that we cannot develop an understanding of politics without an idea of passion as a potentially positive agent of change.

Chapter 10 is an essay by Robert C. Solomon entitled "The Politics of Emotion." The chapter examines four ways in which the emotions can be considered political: first, emotions should be considered as situated in the world and not just inside individual minds, given their association with actual events and situations; second, emotions are political in their function to sway and persuade others to view a situation in a certain way; third, emotions have a political function in our relation with our own selves, that is, how we shape our own relation to the world and our perceptions of it; fourth, the very description and labelling of emotions carries important political implications. This piece broadens the conversation among the authors in this book by describing a wider scope for the play of politics associated with our emotional lives and our attempts to understand them.

All of these contributions force us to come to terms with a more complex yet more realistic human psychology than has traditionally been acknowledged in political theory. The authors all agree that the history of political thought can shed light on ways of reconceptualizing the place of the emotions and passions in politics. In addition, the chapters in this volume share a tone of caution, insofar as none of the authors call for a reliance on emotional principles alone; rather they seek a better recognition of the importance of emotion and of its links to rationality than is currently found in most contemporary liberal democratic theory.

Matters of Contention

Needless to say, this collection is an overview and does not claim to be a comprehensive treatment of the theme in the history of political thought. Nor indeed do all the authors agree on the way in which the emotions are most relevant to the political process. These disagreements point to a number of areas where there are emerging debates in the field of emotion and politics. For example, can emotion on its own, through the course of deliberation, lead us to just and publicly worthy outcomes in judgment? To what degree, and in what manner, should education be central to the liberal democratic project? Can we acknowledge or indeed find any worth in the process by which our emotional lives are constituted by our social and political context? Should we regard these features of our selves as inherited prejudice and a likely source of misjudgment, or are they a matter of our very identities that must be respected to enable proper political judgment?

The work highlights the differences between those who argue for a key set of emotional dispositions (such as a capacity for shame, indignation, or compassion) as particularly relevant for democratic life, and those who hold that any emotion can be both helpful and destructive in the democratic process. Still, both positions point to a need to explore in greater detail the difference between the potentially positive and negative force of emotion in political life and how precisely this is to be adjudicated. If we are to accept a certain blurring of the distinction between the working of emotion and rational discernment, then how precisely do we determine the vision of the political good by which we can adjudicate helpful and destructive modes of political life? Can such a vision be achieved through democratic consensus? If not, how can it be justified as a normative vision?

In the long run, we hope that the deliberations begun here will encourage those who have developed an interest in these issues and will point out further avenues for reflection both within and outside the Western tradition of political theory.

Explaining Emotions

Amélie Oksenberg Rorty

Sometimes our emotions change straight away when we learn that what we believed is not true. The grieving husband recovers when he learns that, because she missed her plane, his wife did not die in the plane crash. But often changes in emotions do not appropriately follow changes in belief. Their tenacity, their inertia, suggests that there is *akrasia* of the emotions; it reveals the complex structure of their intentionality.[1]

I want to examine the strategies we use to explain cases of unexpected conservation of emotions: those that seem to conflict with a person's judgments and those that appear to have distorted our perceptions and beliefs, making them uncharacteristically resistant to change or correction.[2] I shall begin with complex cases, so that we will be forced to uncover layers of explanation that need not normally be brought into play in what are taken to be the standard cases. When people act or react in ways that can be explained by reasonable beliefs and desires, we tend to suppose that these beliefs and desires are the causes of their behaviour. We then try to construct our explanations of the more complex cases using only what was necessary to explain the simple ones. Not surprisingly, we are often left with bizarre cases at the margins of our theory: self-deception, *akrasia*, and the irrational conservation of emotions. By beginning with fringe cases, we may find the more complex structures that underlie the apparently straightforward cases but which are difficult to discern when everything is going as we expect.

One of the difficulties of our enterprise is specifying the psychological principles that rationalize a person's beliefs and desires, her interpretations and responses. When an emotion appears to be anomalous, and its explanation requires tracing its etiology, identifying the intentional object of the emotion is difficult without constructing its rationale, if not actually its justification. But accurately describing a person's beliefs and attitudes, especially when they involve *akrasia* or the apparently inappropriate conservation of the emotions, often involves attributing false beliefs, apparently irrational intentional sets.[3] Sometimes it is implausible and inaccurate to explain an inappropriate attitude by attributing a belief or desire that would rationalize it, because the apparently anomalous emotion is embedded in a system of other inappropriate attitudes or false beliefs. Yet explaining a person's condition requires tracing its causal history, reconstructing the details of a ramified, gradually changing intentional system of attitudes, beliefs, and habits of attention and focusing. Constructing this causal history often involves reconstructing a rationale: the problem is to determine at what point in that history to apply some modified version of the principle of charity.[4] Often it is accurately applied only quite far back in the person's psychological history, to explain the formation of pre-propositional but intentional habits of salience, organization, and interpretation. These habits, through later intervening beliefs and attitudes – many of them false and inappropriate – explain the conservation of emotions. When so applied, the principle of charity is modified: it accounts for the coherent appropriateness of the *formation* of a person's intentional system without maximizing agreement on the number of true beliefs. It is not the belief or emotion that is rationalized but how a person came to have it.

Emotions do not form a natural class. A set of distinctions that has generally haunted the philosophy of mind stands in the way of giving good descriptions of the phenomena of emotion. We have inherited distinctions between being active and being passive; between psychological states primarily explained by physical processes and psychological states not reducible to nor adequately explained by physical processes; between states that are primarily nonrational and those that are either rational or irrational; between voluntary and nonvoluntary states. Once these distinctions were drawn, types of psychological activities were parceled out *en bloc* to one or another side of these dichotomies. The next step was to argue reclassification: to claim that perception is not passive but active, or that the imagination has objective as well as subjective rules of association. Historically, the list of emotions has expanded as a result of these controversies. For instance, the opponents of Thomas Hobbes, wanting to secure benevolence, sympathy, and other disinterested attitudes as counterbalances to self-interest, introduced them as sentiments with motivational power. Passions became emotions and were classified as activities rather than as passive states. When the intentionality of emotions was discussed, the list expanded still further: *ressentiment*, aesthetic and religious awe, anxiety, and dread were included. Emotions became affects or attitudes. As the class grew, its members became more heterogeneous and the analysis became more ambiguous; counterexamples were explained away by charges of self-deception.

When we focus on their consequences on behaviour, most emotions can also be described as motives; some – but not all – emotions can also be described as feelings, associated with proprioceptive states.[5] The objects of some emotions – exuberance, melancholy – are difficult to specify; such global states verge on being moods.[6] Still other emotions come close to being dispositional character traits: we speak of vengeful or affectionate persons. But when we speak of psychological state as an emotion, contrasting it to motives, feelings, moods, or character traits, we focus on the ways we are affected by our appraisals, evaluative perceptions, or descriptions.[7]

The causal history of an individual's emotions, the significant events that form his habits of response, affects his conception of their objects. That causal history contains three closely interwoven strands: (1) the formative events in a person's psychological past, the development of patterns of intentional focusing and salience, and habits of thought and response; (2) the socially and culturally determined range of emotions and their character-istic behavioural and linguistic expressions; and (3) a person's constitutional inheritance, the set of genetically fixed threshold sensitivities and patterns of response. Because the social and genetic factors were assumed to be shared or invariable, their effects always appearing within a person's psychological history, we have treated them, when we focused on them at all, as fixed background conditions. But they are essential to the full account, and often critical in explaining apparent anomalies: their contribution to that explana-tion does not reduce simply to a variant of individual psychological expla-nation.[8] I shall, however, abstract from the social and genetic factors, and concentrate on the intentional components in the formation of a person's individual emotional dispositions.

Causes, Objects, Targets

Jonah, a news writer, resents Esther, his editor, whom he thinks domineering, even tyrannical. But as bosses go, Esther is exceptionally careful to consult with the staff, often following consensus even when it conflicts with her judgment. His colleagues try to convince Jonah that Esther's assignments are not demeaning, her requests not arbitrary. Jonah comes to believe he was mistaken in thinking her actions dictatorial; he retreats to remarking that she derives secret pleasure from the demands that circumstances require. Where his colleagues see a smile, he sees a smirk. After a time of working with Esther, Jonah realizes that she is not a petty tyrant, but he still receives her assignments with a dull resentful ache; and when Anita, the new editor, arrives, he is seething with hostility even before she has had time to settle in and put her family photographs on her desk. Although many of the women on the secretarial staff are more hard-edged in mind and personality than either Esther or Anita, he regards them all as charmingly endowed with intuitive insight. He patronizes rather than resents them.

To understand Jonah's plight, we need distinctions. We are indebted to David Hume for the distinction between the object and the cause of emotions. But that distinction needs to be refined before we can use it to understand Jonah's emotional condition. In the case of the husband who believed his wife had been killed in a plane crash, the precipitating or immediate cause of the man's grief is hearing a newscast announcing the fatal crash of the plane his wife intended to take. But of course the newscast has such a powerful effect on him because such a news story is itself an effect of the significant cause of his grief: her death in the crash. Often when we find emotions puzzling, it is because we do not see why the immediate cause should have such an effect.

The significant cause of an emotion is the set of events – the entire causal history – that explains the efficacy of the immediate or precipitating cause. Often the significant cause is not in the immediate past; it may be an event, or a series of events, long forgotten, that formed a set of dispositions that are triggered by the immediate cause. Tracing the full causal story often involves more than locating initial conditions or identifying immediate causes: it requires analyzing the magnetizing effects of the formation of our emotional dispositions, habits of thought, as well as habits of action and response.[9] Magnetizing dispositions are dispositions to gravitate toward and to create conditions that engender other dispositions. A magnetized disposition to irascibility not only involves a set of specific low thresholds (e.g., to frustration or betrayal) but also involves looking for frustrating conditions by perceiving situations as frustrating. It not only involves wearing a chip on one's shoulder but involves looking for someone to knock that chip off. Magnetizing dispositions need not by themselves explain actions or attitudinal reactions: they can do so indirectly, by characterizing the *type* of beliefs, perceptions, and desires a person is likely to have. Such traits determine actions and reactions by determining the selective range of a person's beliefs and desires.[10] The genesis of a magnetizing disposition need not always lie in an individual's particular psychological history; such dispositions are often acquired, along with other characteristically culture-specific intentional sets and motives, as part of a person's socialization. It is because significant causes often produce magnetizing dispositions that they are successful in explaining the efficacy of the immediate causes of an emotion: they explain not only the response but the tendencies to structure experience in ways that will elicit that characteristic response.

In order to understand the relation between the immediate and the significant cause, we need to refine the account of the objects of the emotions. The immediate object of an emotion is characteristically intentional, directed, and referring to objects under descriptions that cannot be substituted *salva affectione*.[11] Standardly, the immediate object not only is the focus of the emotion but also is taken by the person as providing its ground or rationale. The immediate target of the emotion is the object extensionally described and identified. I shall refer to a person's emotion-grounding description of the target as the "intentional component of the emotion," to his having that description as his "intentional state," and to the associated magnetized disposition as his "intentional set." Of course a person need not be able to articulate the intentional component of his emotions. Ascriptions of emotions, like ascriptions of belief, are inferences to the best explanation.[12]

A person's intentional set may fail to ground the emotion because the target does not in fact have the relevant properties, or because it does not have them in the configuration with the centrality that would ground the emotion, or because it does not in fact exist: the description does not succeed in referring. The difficulties of ascribing intentional states and of referring in opaque contexts are no more (and no less) devastating in ascribing emotions than they are elsewhere.[13] When an otherwise perceptive and reasonable person widely and persistently misdescribes matters or persistently responds in a way that apparently conflicts with his beliefs, we first try standard strategies for explaining misperceptions and errors. Sometimes, indeed, we persuade a person that her emotion is unfounded; and sometimes this persuasion is sufficient for the emotion to change.

When an emotion remains intractable or an anomalous intentional set persists, we suspect that the emotion is rooted in habits of selective attention and interpretation whose activation is best explained by tracing them back to the significant causes of a magnetized disposition.[14] The causal story of that formation can take several forms. For instance, we might suspect that Jonah resents Esther because he now is, or once was, resentful of his mother. His mother may be the (acknowledged or unacknowledged) target of his emotions, and Esther only the front for that target. But Jonah's mother need not be the explanatory target – acknowledged or not – of Jonah's emotion; she may simply have been a crucial part of the significant cause of Jonah's magnetized disposition to structure and interpret situations by locating some female figure whom he sees as hostile and domineering, a figure who, so seen, grounds his resentment. Which of the various alternatives best explains Jonah's condition is a matter for extended investigation; we would have to examine a wide range of Jonah's responses, interpretations, and emotions under different conditions. In any case, our best explanatory strategy is as follows: when in doubt about how the immediate target and precipitating cause explain the emotion, look for the significant cause of the dispositional set that forms the intentional component of the emotion.[15]

Habits and Intentional Sets

The significant cause can help us reconstruct the rationale of the intentional component of the emotion, once we examine the composition of the significant cause. An important part of the history of Jonah's condition will show us what we need:

Not only does Jonah regard women in high places with resentment and hostility; he also suffers from nightmares and, sometimes, from obsessive terrors.

Both have a recurring theme: his mother is trying to kill him. Moreover, he loathes scarves, refusing to wear them even in the coldest, dampest weather. No matter what wonderful things have just happened to him, he breaks into an anxious sweat when he walks through the scarf section at Woolworth's. His mother, a gruff, brusque woman, used to swathe him in scarves that she knitted herself. But she always bought the itchiest wool imaginable; and when she bundled him up in winter, she used to tie the scarf with a swift, harsh motion, pulling it tightly around his throat. She had never come close to trying to kill him. She was in fact an affectionate woman, but an awkward one. Certainly she was occasionally ambivalent, and sometimes exasperated and angry. It was because Jonah was sensitive to the negative undertones of her attitudes (a sensitivity that had an explanation of its own) that he felt the pressure of the scarf as painful rather than as reassuring or comforting.

To understand what has happened to Jonah, we must examine several components of the significant causes of his nightmares, phobias, and terrors. When children remember events as attacks, they may be picking up genuine undercurrents in the behaviour of those around them. Adults often behave with hostility without attacking, seductively without trying to seduce. Because children are unable to place the undercurrents they discern in the context of a person's whole psychological character, they magnify what frightens them. So the fantasy often rests on something perceived. Perception shades into magnified or distorted interpretation, which shades into fantasy, often in ways that can be distinguished only with the benefit of theory-laden hindsight.

But let us suppose that what Jonah's mother did was not in itself sufficient to form his emotional dispositions. His perceptions of the attitudes that determined her manner toward him are essential ingredients in the causal story of his condition. There were not two events, two significant causes but one: the tying of scarf in a way that pained Jonah. In such situations it is often necessary not only to identify the significant cause by an extensional description (scarf tied at a certain speed and a certain pressure) but also to see it through the eyes of the beholder. When we understand that both components of the significant cause – the scarf tightly tied and Jonah's feeling that tying as painful – are fused in the forming of Jonah's emotional dispositions, we can see how locating the significant cause can help us reconstruct the emotion-grounding description that links the intentional component of Jonah's emotion to its immediate cause and target.

Because the intentional component of the significant cause and the intentional component of the apparently anomalous emotion do not always fall under the same description, the significant cause is not always as easy to spot as, in this post-Freudian age, we have located the significant cause – and even the explanatory target – of Jonah's emotion, almost without stopping to think. Nor need the significant cause involve a particular set of events that fused and formed the person's magnetized dispositions, the patterns of salience and attention. The causal story is likely to involve idiosyncratic beliefs and associations, many difficult to recover or articulate. In any case, our motto can now be made more precise: when in doubt about the rationale of an emotion, look for the intentional component of the significant cause of the dispositional set that forms the intentional component of the emotion.

But we are not yet through explaining Jonah's condition, for we do not yet have an account of his tendency to interpret the minimally harsh manner of his mother's scarf-tying ways as hostile. It might seem as if we have reintroduced our original problem – the problem of explaining an anomalous emotional reaction – at an earlier stage. Jonah's perceiving his mother as hostile is an essential part of the significant cause of his phobias and his troubles with female bosses. Nevertheless, if only Jonah and not his brother Abednego has this intentional set, although Abednego was also tightly swathed in itchy scarves, we have not got the significant cause in all its glory: though our explanation is fuller, it is not yet complete.

To understand why the usually perceptive Jonah so misperceived his mother's attitudes, I must tell you more of his story:

Jonah was the eldest of the children. During his childhood, his father, the Major, was given army leave only to return home for short visits. At an appropriate time after one of these visits, Abednego was born. Since his mother was on her own at the time, Jonah was sent off to stay with his adored grandfather while his mother was in the hospital. Now the truth of the matter is that the adored grandfather loathed his daughter-in-law, whom he saw as a domineering, angry woman, the ruination of his son. Without intending to do so, Jonah's grandfather conveyed these attitudes to Jonah, who at that time was apprehensive of losing his mother's affections. Susceptible to the influence of a figure who represented his absent father, he found in his grandfather's attitudes the confirmation and seal of what might have been a passing mood. His grandfather's perspective became strongly entrenched as his own.

We now have an account of why a reasonable person might, in a perfectly reasonable way, have developed an intentional set that, as it happens, generates wildly askew interpretations and reactions.[16] But have we found a stopping place, thinking we've explained an anomalous attitude simply because we have come to a familiar platitude? Perhaps: that is a risk explanations run; but if we have stopped too soon, at a place that requires further explanation, we can move, whenever the need arises, farther back in the causal story. And indeed, we may want explanations of reactions that are not at all anomalous: we can ask why an accurate perception or a true belief has the form it does, why a person focused on matters *this* way rather than that.

The principle of charity is now seen to be very general in scope. Characteristically, it is best applied to the intentional components of the significant causes of magnetizing dispositions, where it accounts for a range of attitudes and beliefs (without necessarily maximizing agreement on truth), rather than to individual episodic beliefs. Moreover, its use presupposes not only that we have a certain gravitational attraction toward truth but that we are also endowed with a wide range of psychological dispositions that determine the ways in which we acquire and change our beliefs and attitudes. These dispositions are quite varied: some are neurophysiological determinants of perceptual salience (e.g., red being more salient than grey under standard background and contrast conditions); others are psychological in character (e.g., the dominance order of emotions under standard conditions: fear displacing and reorganizing the emotional field in characteristic patterns); still others are psychosocial (e.g., the effects of mass hysteria or the presence of a schizophrenic on a person's schema of intentional sets). In short, when we try to apply the principle of charity where it best explains and identifies the range of our attitudes, its canonic formulation is so modified as to disappear as a special principle.

But having come to the end of Jonah's story, have we come to the end of an account of how we explain emotions? Our questions seem now to multiply: Will we, in tracing the significant cause to an appropriate stopping point, always still introduce an intentional component of the significant cause? Are we to interpret young Jonah's tendency to take on the intentional set of a figure who stands in a certain relation to him as itself an intentional set? Or do significant causes of magnetizing dispositions sometimes have no intentional component of their own? We do not know enough about the neurophysiology and psychology of early learning to know what constraints should be set on our philosophical theory. In any case, an account of the etiology of the intentional components of emotional dispositions is nestled within a general psychological theory and inseparable from theories of perception and theories of motivation. The holistic character of mental life makes piecemeal philosophical psychology suspect.

Since airtight arguments have vacuous conclusions, it would be folly to stop speaking at the point where we must start speculating. There are good, but by no means conclusive, reasons for recognizing a gradation between beliefs or judgments in propositional form, and quasi-intentions that can also be physically or extensionally identified. Let us distinguish:

1. beliefs that can be articulated in propositional form, with well-defined truth conditions
2. vague beliefs in sentential form whose truth or satisfaction conditions can be roughly but not fully specified ("It is better to have good friends than to be rich.")

3 specific patterns of intentional salience that can be formulated as general beliefs (A pattern of focusing on aspects of women's behaviour construed as domineering or hostile rather than as competent or insecure might in principle be treated as a set of predictions about the behaviour of women under specific conditions.)
4 intentional sets that cannot be easily formulated as beliefs (A pattern of focusing on the military defensibility of a landscape, rather than on its fertility or aesthetic composition, cannot be so easily formulated as a set of predictions about the benefits of giving priority to military defence over fertility or aesthetic charm. Nor can such patterns of salience be translated straightforwardly as preference rankings. For instance, a painter can focus on patterns of colour in a landscape rather than on its compositional lines, but the patterns and habits of his attending are quite distinct from his painterly preferences.)
5 quasi-intentional sets that can, in principle, be fully specified in physical or extensional descriptions (e.g., other things being equal, painful sensations are more salient than pleasurable ones).

For such intentional sets – patterns of discrimination and attention – the question of whether the significant cause of a magnetized intentional set has an irreducibly intentional component is an open one. Such quasi-intentional components form patterns of focusing and salience without determining the description of those patterns. A quasi-intentional set (patterns of perceptual salience under standard conditions of contrast and imprinting) can be given both physical and intentional descriptions; in some contexts, the physicalistic descriptions can function in an explanation, without any reference to the intentional description. But in other contexts, particularly those that move from functional explanations toward interpretive or rational accounts, the intentional description is essential. Often the intentional and the quasi-intentional components of the significant cause of magnetized interpretive dispositions are ambiguous in this way: we tend to read the intentional component back into the significant cause when doing so helps rationalize the person's responses. But the intentional set that is introduced at that stage often bears a causal rather than a directly logical relation to the magnetized set produced. (The quasi-intentional set that made Jonah prone to adopt his grandfather's interpretations at just that time bears a causal but not a logical relation to the intentional set he acquired as a result of this sensitivity. But the connections between the intentional set he acquired from his grandfather and the intentional set that leads him to see Esther as domineering are logical as well as causal.)

In such cases there are physiological generalizations about the quasi-intentional states under their extensional descriptions. Although the opacity criteria for intentionality do not yet apply, it is useful to recognize that such selective sensitivities are oriented to a stimulus under a description that later does function in its fully intentional form. Holistic considerations influence us: the wider the range and the greater the complexity of behaviour that is best explained by the intentional set in its fully intentional form, the more likely we are to treat the significant cause as having that intentional component, even though it need not, in its original appearance, have then functioned in its fully intentional form. (For instance, a child can be frightened by a clap of thunder without initially having an intentional set to interpret such sounds as danger signals. If he is ill and feverish, hearing loud sounds is painful, and, if he is generally in a weak and fearful condition, he can develop a fully intentional sensitivity, becoming frightened *of* thunder because he had been frightened *by* it.)

Objections

One might wonder: Why do we need these distinctions descending like a plague to devour every living thing, transforming a once fertile plain into a desert? Why can't we explain intractable, inappropriate emotions more simply and elegantly by specifying the relevant belief that fixes the description of the target? Perhaps what explains Jonah's resentment is that he thinks figures in authority are likely to be, or to become, authoritarian. Although such beliefs or judgments are occasionally interesting and true, the appropriate plausible belief is sometimes difficult to ascribe. Jonah does not resent Abe Zloty, the editor-in-chief, though Zloty is far more peremptory than Esther. It seems more plausible to ascribe to Jonah the belief that when women are in a position of authority, they become insufferably authoritarian. But Jonah is a sceptical sort of fellow, who rarely leaps to generalizations, let alone wild ones. Often when we don't understand an emotion, or its intractability, we also don't understand why the person should have and hold the belief that is its intentional component. The belief "explains" the emotion only by subsuming its intentionality in a more general frame.

But our objector persists, claiming that in tracing the etiology of an emotion, intentional sets and quasi-intentions are unnecessarily complex ways of talking about beliefs or evaluative judgments. If we judge emotions for their rationality, goes the objection, then some belief must either be presupposed by, or embedded in, the emotion. The correction of an emotion generally involves the correction of the mistaken belief. Certainly many cases do follow such a pattern, and certainly some emotions can be identified by the full-blown beliefs that are also a part of their causal explanation. But the issue is whether the intentional component of an emotion is always a belief, and whether there are emotions that are more properly evaluated as inappropriate or harmful than as irrational.

If the intentional component of an emotion is always a belief, then the conservation of an emotion after a change of belief would always involve a conflict of beliefs. This may indeed sometimes occur; but often the only evidence that the person retains the abandoned belief is his emotional state. One of the reasons for resisting the assimilation of all intentional components of emotions to beliefs is the difficulty of stating *what* the belief is. There is sometimes no non-question-begging way of formulating a proposition p, where "inserting p in the sentence 'S believes that —' would express the fact that the subject was in that state."[17]

A person may not only deny having the abandoned belief but (with the exception of the episode in question) consistently act in a way that supports that denial. On the view that emotions always involve beliefs, it becomes necessary to suppose that the person is massively successful in deceiving herself about the conflict between the belief embedded in the emotion and the belief implicit in the rest of her conduct. This is certainly a recognizable and even common phenomenon. It seems implausible, however, to assimilate all cases of the conservation of emotions to cases that involve a self-deceptive denial of such conflicts. No doubt much conservation can be explained by ambivalence, and at least some ambivalence can be understood as involving conflicting judgments, with the person deceiving herself about at least one side of a divided mind.[18] But unless the claim is to raise questions, the conservation of emotions cannot *automatically* count as grounds for attributing self-deception. Characteristically, self-deception involves quite distinctive behaviour: signs of facial malaise, frozen features, and certain sorts of systematic failures in action.[19]

Even if it were the case that – in a much revised and extended sense of "belief" – the intentional components of emotions were beliefs, the distinctions we have drawn would have to be reintroduced to differentiate the ways in which a person accepts or uncharacteristically ignores or refuses counterevidence. The phenomenon of the conservation of emotion would then reappear as the anomalous conservation of belief. To explain such conservation, we would once again have to return to the ravenous hordes of distinctions between the immediate and the significant causes of magnetized intentional states; we would have to introduce beliefs that could not be attributed in propositional form. Explaining the anomalous conservation of belief, or its resistance to considerations or observations that would characteristically change it, would lead us to exactly the same sort of schema of causal explanation that we use in understanding the conservation of emotions.

There are objections from other quarters. Nowhere does the mind-body problem raise its ugly head with a stiffer neck than in the analysis of the thought component of the emotions. In some cases, it might be said, the significant cause isn't significant at all. It casts no light on the rationale of the intentional component of an emotion because there is no rationale. For example, in the narrative epilogue at the end of *War and Peace*, Leo Tolstoy describes the emotional condition of the aged Countess Rostoff. She needs, he says – and he suggests that this is in part a physiological need – to become angry, melancholy, merry, peevish, to express the cycle of her emotional repertoire every few days. Usually the family manages to arrange matters in such a way as to give her emotional life an air of appropriateness. But sometimes this cannot be done, and she becomes peevish in a situation in which she is normally merry. Tolstoy remarks that in infancy and old age – and, we could add, in adolescence – the apparent reasonableness that we believe really conditions our adult emotional life wears thin, and emotions reveal a rhythm and pattern of their own. (Tolstoy does not, unfortunately, go on to speculate whether the independent rhythm of the emotions is merely disguised in our prime, indiscernible beneath our bustling intention-directed activity, or whether what makes the emotional life of infants and the senile different from our own is precisely that their emotions are merely coincidentally associated with the appropriate intentions.) When a person suffers from a hormonal imbalance, his emotions have one target after another, none linked to the intentional component of a significant cause. When we look for the explanation of a recalcitrant inappropriate emotion, there is sometimes no need to look deeply into the etiology of the intention: the state of the person's endocrine system is explanation enough.[20] The best thing to do with this objection is to accept it gracefully. It is, after all, true.

But we must be careful not to conclude too much. From the fact that the best explanation of a person's emotional state may sometimes be glandular malfunction, it does not follow that, under standard conditions, explanations of emotions can be given without any appeal to beliefs or intentional states.[21] Most physicalistically oriented theories fill in their accounts by tracing the interaction among the *sorts* of physical states that are associated with being in an emotionally charged condition (generally metabolic states).[22] Such physicalists do not, however, claim to be able to identify the propositional content of a person's attitudes solely by reference to physically described brain states. On this view, we would not expect to find strict physicalistic laws distinguishing Jonah's perceiving-Esther-as-Slavic and his perceiving-Esther-as-Semitic.

The zealot hard-core physicalists go farther: they propose to identify "psychological" states as states whose descriptions eliminate all reference to intentional states and their propositional content – distinguishing Jonah's believing Esther to be bossy from his believing her to be vain – by specifying the differences in the brain states that constitute the two beliefs. It seems at the very least premature to present the results of what is an extended and only projected program of research as having provided the explanations we need, especially as zealot hard-core physicalists have yet to give us an account of how to proceed with the reductive analysis. So far, all we have are science-fiction stories about possible worlds in which the reductive analysis has taken place, where what scientists somehow discovered is already part of the popular culture. Until the theory is established, all the physicalist account of the emotions adds to the intentionalist account is the important observation that, when the best explanation of a person's emotional state is primarily physiological, then raising questions about the causal force of the intentional object may produce arbitrary, ad hoc answers. There may be a revealing pattern in the immediate causes or objects of an adrenally charged person's various aggressive angers, but sometimes that pattern is best explained by tracing the effects of chemical changes on perception and attention.

This suggests that, for at least these sorts of cases, the physicalist and the intentionalist accounts of anomalous emotions are perfectly compatible and perhaps even complementary, physicalist theories explaining why a person is in *that* state, while intentionalist theories explain why the emotion has *that* intentional object. The theories appear to be at odds only when both get reductionally ambitious: when, denying overdetermination, each tries to explain all phenomena at all levels. Certainly if the intentionalist accounts deny that a person's hormonal state ever enters into the explanation, and if the physicalistic accounts deny that intentionality is ever required to explain or identify the emotional states, the two approaches will clash in an unilluminating struggle whose sterility will be masked by the parties goading each other to dazzling displays of ingenuity.[23]

Does it follow that both levels of explanation, the physiological and the intentional, are necessary while neither is sufficient? The situation is (un)fortunately more complex. Physiological and intentional aspects do not enter into all emotions in the same way. The difference between a distaste for malicious gossip in departmental politics and the terror of waking after a nightmare whose drama one has already forgotten, the difference between nostalgia-for-the-lilacs-of-yesteryear and fear in the face of a powerful danger, are differences in kind.

Some emotions are primarily associated with physical states largely affected by metabolic imbalance: for example, malfunctions of the pituitary or adrenal glands are associated with highly specific emotional disorders, leaving the rest of a person's emotional dispositions relatively intact. Other, quite different sorts of emotional disorders are associated with some types of brain damage.[24] Still other sorts of emotions – such culturally variable ones as nostalgia or Sunday melancholy – seem difficult to associate with any particular physical condition. While the introduction of intentional apparatus seems forced in some cases, the introduction of physiological determinants is forced in others.

Explanation, Change, and Rationality

We can expect three things from the study of history: the sheer pleasure of knowing particulars; useful precepts for the important matters of life; and

> furthermore because the origins of things recur in the present from the
> past, we acquire the best understanding of all things from a knowledge of
> their causes.
>
> – Gottfried Leibniz, Preface to *Accessiones Historicae*

The conservation of emotions has its explanation in the conservation of habit, especially of those magnetized dispositions involved in selective attention and focused interpretation. We have concentrated primarily on that aspect of a person's psychological history which explains the formation of his characteristic intentional habits. But social and genetic factors also contribute to the causal story; the full account of the conservation of emotional habits would have to include these determinants as well. The three layers of explanation – the individual, the social, and the genetic – are closely interwoven. A person's constitution – his threshold to pain and to various sorts of stimuli, the structure of his glandular and nervous systems – affects the development of his intentional sets, his habits of interpretation and response. Constitutional factors (for instance, metabolic rate) influence the social roles and settings in which a person is cast; this in turn affects the formation of his intentional sets. Sociocultural factors structure the interpretations of a person's experiences: a range of emotional responses is formed by such interpretations.[25] The full explanation of a person's emotions requires not only an analysis of the causal contribution of each of the three strands but also an account of their interactions.

(What goes without saying may need to be said: we should not be misled by talk of interaction, layers, or strands to suppose that we are dealing with distinct variables whose causal interaction can be traced. What is variable in a theory need not be independently variable in fact. At this stage, we are still using metaphors; we are not yet entitled to suppose we have detached them as a technical vocabulary. "Biological limits" or "constraints" to sociocultural variation, physiological "determinants" of psychological or intentional processes, cultural "forms" of biological "givens": all these expressions are borrowed from other contexts. Our vocabulary of the interrelation of these "domains" is crucially in the formative stage; talk of separate but interwoven explanatory strands must be treated as provisional to a developing explanatory scheme – heuristics without ontology. We have here a clear example of the encroaching constitutive character of early terminological raiding. Perhaps eventually, by tracing these sorts of borrowings, we shall be able to see the rewards – and the costs – of theft that cannot be distinguished from honest toil without the benefit of a program.)

My suggestion that emotions are not only explained but often also identified by their causal histories may appear either trivial or exaggerated. No one would deny that we require more than the immediate occasion to understand the exact shades of Jonah's resentment: the images and thoughts, the sensations and anticipations, the evocation of associated emotions that constitute just *that* condition. But it doesn't follow that we need a causal account to identify his condition as a case of resentment, and to explain it by his perception of Esther.

Certainly emotions are often identified in a rough way without tracing their causal histories; one need not always know why a person is angry to recognize her condition. The contexts in which emotions occur and their expression in speech and behaviour are sufficient to identify them; their immediate contextual causes are often quite sufficient to explain them. There is, however, a rough and unexamined but nevertheless quite specific folk psychology that stands behind and informs such standard explanations.[26] The explanatory strategies that I have sketched make explicit the stages and assumptions embedded in our ready and quick contextual identifications of emotions and their intentional objects. It is because we supply the standard causal history of emotion-types that we readily identify tokens of that type.

But instances of emotion-types differ markedly from one another in their origins, their expressions in speech and action, and in their psychodynamic functions. To bring order to these heterogeneous classes, we need a much finer taxonomy of the varieties of, for example, anger, melancholy, and envy. Such taxonomy can be constructed by distinguishing varieties of causal histories of the intentional component of these emotions. Differences in the characteristic causal histories of their intentional components helps to explain why different instances of the same emotion-type often have different tonal and behavioural expressions. But we have been too impressed by the multiplicity of instances of emotion-types, and so have tended to distinguish different instances of the same type by the differences in their particular intentional objects. Certainly if we want an account of their individuation, especially in cases of overdetermination, this is necessary.[27] When we identify and explain a particular emotion without tracing its etiology, however, we are implicitly classifying it as a standard instance of a *variety* of the emotion-type; in doing so, we are relying upon the characteristic causal story that distinguishes that variety from others. If we thought that the causes of a person's condition conformed to none of the standard histories, we would doubt the attribution.

If this analysis is correct, then an account of how people succeed in changing emotions that they judge inappropriate or irrational closely follows the more general explanation of how people change their habits. The difficulties involved in bringing about such changes – the deep conservation of emotional habits – make claims that emotions are choices or voluntary judgments seem implausible.[28] Sometimes (rarely) some people (a happy few) are able to take steps to restructure their intentional sets and revise their emotional repertoire. Sometimes secondary emotions – emotions about emotions – play a crucial role in such transformations. For instance, someone who thinks that the objects he fears are indeed dangerous may nevertheless reasonably judge that he is too afraid of being afraid. He may think that he should not go as far as he does in order to avoid situations where the possibility of danger is only remote. It is this secondary fear ("We have nothing to fear but fear itself") that impels the responses the person might judge inappropriate; and it is this, rather than the first-level fear, that he might wish to change. Or it might go the other way: a person might underwrite a second-level emotion, and wish to change its first level.[29]

Shifts in emotional repertoires can often take quite subtle forms: someone might wish to check the standard expression or behavioural consequences of either a first- or a second-level emotion without wishing to change the habits or intentional set of having it. Although some tendency to action, often taking the form of posture or expression, is "part" of many first-level emotions, it is often possible to restrain or mask the behaviour without changing the emotional set.[30] One of the ways of doing this is to distinguish more sharply between the varieties of instances of an emotion-type. A person might learn to discriminate between appropriate and inappropriate responses by coming to see that different instances of the same type cluster together because they have the same causal history. They form a variety defined by its etiology. If he tackles his problem of identifying and overcoming inappropriate resentments separately each time, Jonah is unlikely to make much headway by learning not to resent Esther, and then learning not to resent Anita, and then Sarah, ... and each and every woman in authority. Because he thinks some cases of resentment are perfectly justified by their causes and objects, he is unlikely to solve his problem by setting himself the task of avoiding resentment altogether. But by understanding the special etiology of the variety of resentments of which his resentment of Esther is a particular instance, he can at least begin to be alert to the situations that trigger magnetized dispositions he regards as inappropriate.

The analysis of the causal history of our emotions suggests that judgments of the appropriateness of the emotions must be made on a number of different levels. It may be not only irrational but inappropriate for someone to be frightened of lions in a zoo, but it is not inappropriate to be frightened before one has had time to be reasonable, so constructed that one's fear is not immediately eradicated by one's more considered reactions. It may be irrational for Jonah to take on his grandfather's attitudes without testing them, and irrational for him to reinterpret all the evidence that might correct his attitudes. But it is also beneficial for children to tend to absorb the intentional dispositions of the crucial figures around them, even at the cost of generating confusion and conflict. What is maladaptive in a particular case need not be so typically; it may be highly beneficial for habitual responses to dominate rational considerations, and for them to be changed by rational considerations only with considerable difficulty. It is part of the discomforting character of our emotional life that the genetic programming and social formation of emotional dispositions do not respect the rationality or the comfort of individuals.

Thirty-Five Years Later: A Postscript

When and how do we voluntarily act – and continue to act – from emotions that we judge undesirable or inappropriate, all things considered? Most explanations of *akratic* emotions focus on the scope and structure of individual psychology. Attempting to understand the dynamics of what happens when someone apparently ignores or forgets what she seems to know or believe, most explanations of *akratic* emotions bracket their social sources and reinforcement. As long as such deviant emotions were classified as species of culpable irrationality, the ultimate culprit was typically thought to be motivational: the agent's considered judgments were deflected by emotions or desires that were, all things considered, less solidly justified but more pressing or powerful. We need to go farther to ask when and why this happens. When we understand the social, political, and economic sources of emotional *akrasia*, we shall also see that these sources stand behind a person's ordinary, standard-issue emotional repertoire. Once again, the fissures of *akratic* pathology reveal the structure and dynamics of ordinary psychological functioning.

Akratic emotions rarely occur as isolated events. As signs of psychological disorders, they are typically habitual and patterned; and they are frequently sustained and reinforced by sociopolitical and economic arrangements. Envy is supported by economic structures that generate consumer desires; anger is prompted and enforced by the social and cultural value placed on aggressive responses to perceived slights. Like other intentional activities, emotional responses are endorsed by sustaining social support. As standard beliefs and motives are elicited and reinforced by social patterns and political institutions, so too are the standard issue dispositional patterns of our emotional repertoire.

A familiar case study may help: the members of a president's cabinet can collectively act aggressively from grandiose indignation that they would not endorse in solitary reflection. Influenced by their collective power and eminence, and by the luxurious appointments of the cabinet room, supported by the army of their secretaries and assistants, solicited by lobbyists and consulted by the media, they so collude in magnifying one another's tendencies to the pretensions of self-importance that the policies on which they consensually agree are stronger than their individual attitudes, in *foro interno*. They will collude in expressing – and acting on – indignant aggression that they would check if they were acting as individuals. The forms of such aggressive responses are modelled by social images and practices of admiration and contempt, by sports and the media, by popular films and biographies: "We must respond promptly with massive force and strength."

William Ruddick and Rom Harré have called our attention to the ways that psychological habits are enhanced and entrenched by social collusion.[31] Their analyses of these social processes extend to emotional *akrasia*. Social norms and institutional practices provide models for the development of the sources and expression of emotions and motives. Greed is prompted by envy; envy is used to prompt consumer activity. An ambitious stockbroker learns to wear emotional blinders when she follows the ethos of the market in selling junk bonds; she models her approach to her clients by imitating other brokers; her friends envy and enthusiastically admire her aggressive initiative and ingenuity; they manifestly delight to share in her bounty. Although the stockbroker is moved by her pastor's description of the plight of the elderly who are bilked by junk bond trading, his impact does not compare with the weight and ramification of the social rewards of her hard-hearted chicanery. Carefully selective emotional blindness is as much the result of social conditioning as is carefully selective aggression.

We can extend Ruddick's and Harré's insights. Social institutions and economic systems encourage and foster the very actions that they also condemn. While promoting the emotions that prompt habits of co-operation, they also reward radical independence; while condemning aggression, they also praise "aggressive initiative." While admiring selfless devotion, they also reward canny self-interest. Except in extreme cases, rewards and sanctions do not form a clear and guiding pattern. Recent theories of the social construction of psychological phenomena present examples and analyses of the self-fulfilling effects of linguistic and categorical frameworks that channel and model psychological and behavioural patterns. A redescriptive turn of phrase, rather than a clear objective difference, distinguishes *akrasia* from acceptable normal behaviour. The difference between one stockbroker's "envious greed" and her colleague's "assertive initiative," or between the rage of a veteran suffering from post-traumatic stress and his officer's politically aggressive indignation, expresses widely ramified ideological and political interests.

Laws, economic institutions, civic associations, moral and religious ideals, and public culture express and model the formation of social habits. Conflicts among them provide some of the major sources of emotional *akrasia*. Early childhood experience – patterns of family behaviour, their motives and habits, preoccupations and expectations, the tonality of interactions – is affected by patterned pressures that are not always discerned by the people formed by them. Status, occupations, and the extent of a family's disposable income profoundly affects the ambitions, opportunities, and expectations of its members. Chronic unemployment, the reversal of stereotypic gender divisions of labour, laws affecting primogeniture – all these manifestly affect the tonal stress and tensions within family configurations. Class and ethnic patterns frame legitimate or forbidden outbursts of anger; they provide criteria for justified claims to power and property; they affect the emotional specifications of generic desires.

While officially condemning envy as a socially undesirable trait, most societies use, and even induce, envious traits to encourage the development of useful talents and abilities. Market-based, consumer-oriented economic systems generate invidious comparisons as a way of increasing consumption. We are bombarded by images of women who are admired for their expensive cars and clothes, who take exotic vacations with desirable men. The public is systematically presented with alluring images of svelte bodies and junk food, power and junk bonds. The mass media, television dramas, songs, and advertisements present riveting and reigning models of desirability and success. They are brilliantly designed to affect patterns of consumption, through images of satisfied desire, all providing some of the structural, social, and political sources of systematically focused characterological *akrasia*.

Workplaces, banks, courts, armies, and hospitals all stream, direct, and constrain citizen motives. They define flow charts of duties and virtues, rights and obligations whose infractions carry severe costs and sanctions. Nonconformists are regarded with suspicion and charged with irrationality; they have difficulty eliciting co-operation and suffer pressure that is intended to produce guilt, or at the very least, shame. Social institutions provide the models for public deliberation and accountability, setting norms for the tenor of broader social interactions, finely attuned for status and power, formality or intimacy, empathic tact or aggressive confrontation. They form the patterns and the habits exercised in resolving ordinary conflicts, and they define the terms of utility and fairness.

Our struggles against emotional *akrasia*, our attempts at integration, reflect conflicts among the larger social and economic institutions that structure our motives. *Akrasia* of envy and greed could express the tension between a person's ideals of social service and the attractions of an expensive, lively style of life, but could just as well express tensions between cosmopolitan urbanity and a suburban country-club enclave or between personal and impersonal social service. The canny emotional *akrates* puts herself in situations where her emotions and the actions they prompt will be socially supported. The increasingly overt and sharp conflicts among the objective social interests, and the presumptive separation of public and private domains, block the possibility of integration. This disarray is no accident; it is deeply embedded in our economic arrangements and in our cultural self-presentation and self-understanding. For us, the most powerful and effective moral influence on the possibility of integration is the economy ("It's the economy, stupid"). Our psychology, our emotions, and our habits are profoundly influenced by the way that economics drives civic politics. Both, taken together, pervade absolutely every nook and cranny of our lives. We must fashion ourselves, form our abilities and habits in such a way as to make ourselves employable; worse, we experience and enact the economy's need to generate the inexhaustible and unsatisfiable desires that define and direct our activities.

Our role – our place – in the economy shapes our lives, determining our security and pleasures as well as the kind of recognition we receive. Domestic economy is fixed in a closed pattern that sets the generations at odds: what we give to our children is no longer available for our parents; what we give to our parents diminishes what we have for ourselves.

To the extent that any part of the population is hopelessly and structurally excluded from an economically driven civic life, they have no objective reason to follow its principles and ideals, realistically having no stake in the life they serve and express. Whatever a society may say and promote in the way of the emotional habits of social cohesion and co-operation, however it may assert the interdependence of citizen welfare, it perforce also confronts the harsh realities of the economic formation of emotional and motivational structures. To be sure, social and economic institutions also structure and promote the sentiments of fairness and justice – and the generosity and kindness on which they depend – when they are exercised at some cost to individual interests. The persona that strives to integrate the diverse and often conflicting directions of socioeconomic habit-formation only succeeds in adding yet another voice to the cacophony that is the endeavouring self. Integration is admired as an intrinsic good because it frequently brings little else. The call to integrate motives and habits is all the more fervent because it involves effort, risk, and loss.

A policy of astute compartmentalization appears to evaporate emotional *akrasia* by justifying what would otherwise present itself as dis-integration or dis-association. It does so all the more effectively and securely when socio-economic institutions separate "distinct" domains: work, family, recreation, citizenship. The habits and mentality of severe cost accounting that govern many occupations are cordoned off from those that govern affectional rela-tions. Ironically, sometimes the very attempt to integrate habits – to import business practice cost accounting into friendships, for instance – may supply the occasion for emotional *akrasia*. It can also go the other way: a judge who finds herself importing the emotional habits and mentality of her personal life into the courtroom can violate the principles she thinks ought to govern her judicial decisions.

So far, we've concentrated on the *akrasia* of envy and greed. Let's turn to the darker and more troubling case of a veteran who suffers from post-traumatic stress syndrome. His difficulties in readjusting to civilian life, his anxiety, depression, and rage are often acted out in ways that further deepen his alienation and dis-integration, setting an ever-enlarging pattern of erratic action. These disorders often arise from the shock of combat experience, but they extend beyond them. Having been trained to violate some of his deepest civilian habits, he must set aside a good deal of that training on his return to civilian life. The humiliations of military training, the arbitrariness and tyranny of superior officers, their willingness to risk the safety of their men – contribute to PTS. As well, combat veterans' families and friends are unable to envision their experiences – and, after a time, they do not even wish to hear about them. To make matters worse, veterans return to a changed and often straitened economy. Unlike their friends who avoided the draft, they have lost crucial years of professional training; they have difficulty finding the kind of employment – constructing the kind of life – that recruitment posters led them to expect. All this, taken together, magnifies their sense of alienation. It provides the sources of the kind of lashing *akratic* rage that they do not condone and that extends their sense of alienation to self-alienation.

The distress of combat veterans extends to equally far-reaching but less narrowly traumatic cases. An increasingly large part of the population suffers chronic and structural unemployment. They see themselves as permanently excluded from the satisfactions that continue to be ideologically and economically publicly broadcast to form standard life expectations. Like veterans, they may suffer the disintegration of deeply entrenched, socially formed attitudes, emotions, and motives. They find themselves confounded and confused by the tensions within their attitudes, and they suffer the further damaging effects of blaming themselves. Not even the most hardened cynic can magically shed the ideals and desires that fuel his cynicism. The injurious conflicts that arise from difficult readjustments of this sort are fertile ground for *akrasia*, depression, and other forms of emotional disintegration.

Whether the stockbroker or the veterans or the chronically poor succeed in resisting the lure or pressures of emotional *akrasia* is largely a matter of political and economic luck. The success of their integrative efforts depends on the extent to which their economic situation and social environment systematically supports rather than undermines those efforts. They cannot be so situated that their capacities for effort are only notionally postulated.

Plato on Shame and Frank Speech in Democratic Athens

Christina Tarnopolsky

Plato's *Gorgias* abounds with references to famous Athenian democratic leaders, such as Themistocles and Pericles (455e, 472b, 515e, 519a), and to specific Athenian democratic practices such as delivering speeches, voting, calling in witnesses to one's reputation, and ostracism (456a, 471e, 472c, 473e, 516d).[1] In fact the dialogue contains Plato's most explicit thoughts and harsh criticisms of the institutions and practices of his native city.[2] And for this reason the *Gorgias* has been interpreted as Plato's own "Apology," in which he outlines his reasons for forgoing a career in Athenian democratic politics in favour of opening a school of philosophy.[3] This interpretation of the *Gorgias*, which I summarize in the first section below, poses a significant challenge to the kind of project to which this book is dedicated. Why turn to an antidemocratic thinker like Plato in order to reconceptualize the place of the emotions in our contemporary democratic life? Perhaps more importantly, why turn to a dialogue that focuses on the emotion of shame when this very emotion has historically been one of the most efficient means of preventing certain groups from participating in democratic politics and preventing certain topics from even entering the public realm of deliberation?

The first step in answering these questions involves challenging the characterizations of Plato as an antidemocratic theorist and of shame as an antidemocratic emotion. Plato's theories have historically been co-opted by conservative thinkers, first to denigrate the Athenian experience of direct democracy in favour of rule by elites or distant governments, and, more recently, to support an American regime of secrecy and "noble lies" in response to the new worldwide threat of terrorism.[4] But these uses and abuses of Plato have often been achieved by totally abstracting his canonical texts from the living Athenian democratic tradition "to which they owe substantial debts, even in critique."[5] In recent years, a number of classical and political theorists have begun to investigate and reconstruct the classical Athenian democratic ideology and to reinterpret Plato and Aristotle's texts within this context in order to challenge the co-optation of these classical theorists by contemporary conservatives.[6] This chapter builds on this work in order to reformulate Plato's relationship to democratic Athens with specific reference to the issues of shame (*aidōs/aischunē*) and frank speech (*parrhēsia*), recapturing these Platonic insights for contemporary theories about the role of emotions in democratic politics.

In what follows I show that Plato contributes to our contemporary theories in four ways. First, he reminds us that emotions are not virtues, and therefore that no emotion can be designated negative or positive for democratic deliberation without investigating the various forms of each emotion, and the different ways in which these various forms interact with reason.[7] (See Sokolon, Chapter 8 in this volume, for a critique of the negative-positive polarity of emotions in John Stuart Mill's political philosophy and in current theories.) As Leah Bradshaw writes in Chapter 9 of this volume, "Emotional responses in themselves do not warrant our praise or blame." The point for Plato was not to banish shame from democratic deliberation but to understand the different ways in which this emotion could endanger or facilitate this deliberation.

Indeed, by Plato's time the Greek verbs *aideomai* and *aischunomai*, occurring with an accusative referring to another person or persons, could mean either "I feel shame before" or "I respect" or some combination of both.[8] And, in the *Gorgias,* Plato builds upon these existing and differing meanings, even while going beyond them, in order to articulate the differences between Gorgianic "flattering" shame, which endangers democratic deliberation, and Socratic "respectful" shame, which is meant to enhance this deliberation.[9] (See Abizadeh, Chapter 3 in this volume, for the argument that Aristotle's notion of passionate political deliberation also entailed the risk of flattery and demagoguery even while allowing for the possibility of a rhetoric that could instil virtue in both the speaker and the audience, and thus actually change the character of the deliberators.)

My second point is that this dual structure of shame meant that speaking openly and frankly about one's views in the public realm was similarly dual. Such speech was not a virtue unless it was done in a specific manner and was harmonized or combined with the emotions in specific ways. For Plato, to speak with *parrhēsia* (frankness or outspokenness) was not to speak *without* the emotions of shame or fear (even though the mistranslation of *parrhēsia* as "fearless speech" tends to suggest this) but rather to speak with a particular kind of shame or fear in the absence of which *parrhēsia* became rashness, rudeness, obscenity, or flattery.[10] Again, in the *Gorgias*, Plato builds upon contemporary debates in Athens concerning a form of *parrhēsia* that facilitated democratic deliberation and a form that actually endangered it because the person said "the most stupid or dangerous things for the city."[11] Although Callicles accuses Socrates of rudeness and obscenity at one point in the dialogue (494e), the dialogue as a whole illustrates that it is Callicles' brand of frankness (*parrhēsia*) that most endangers democratic Athens because of his particular kind of ignorant self-pretence and flattering shame.

Third, I argue that Plato shows us why we need to look at the complex entanglements between reason, the emotions, *and the imagination* when talking about the role of emotions in politics. (For different accounts of the important role of the imagination in emotional perceptions or judgments in Aquinas and Hume, see Ferry, Chapter 4, and Krause, Chapter 6 in this volume.) One of the ways in which emotions can become pernicious for democratic politics occurs when the specific object to which they are directed consists of the fantastical projection of our all-too-human desire for godlike omnipotence. In what follows, I argue that this is precisely what Plato found problematic about the type of flattering shame that motivates Polus and Callicles in the *Gorgias* and, by extension, his tyrannical democratic contemporaries. Again, the point for Plato is not that we ought to banish the imagination from our democratic deliberations, but that we need to investigate the kinds of imaginative identification and projection that can either facilitate or endanger these deliberations. More specifically, Plato shows us how flattering shame can disrupt our deliberations by projecting a fantastical ideal of the omnipotent political actor who never has to feel any pain or experience any limitation of his desires. And he shows us how Socratic respectful shame involves the imaginative ability to take on the perspective of the other in ways that actually announce our mortality even while disclosing new possibilities for action.

Finally, I argue that instead of construing frank speech (*parrhēsia*) and shame (*aidōs/aischunē*) in terms of the modern Kantian dichotomies between autonomy and heteronomy, activity and passivity, self-assertion and conformity to norms, Plato shows how the two always point simultaneously in *both* directions and thus have an inherent social and political structure.[12] (For an account of the political character of Plato's theory of emotions more generally, see Kingston, Chapter 5 in this volume.) In fact I believe that the canonical picture of Plato and the modern distrust of shame owe far more to these problematic modern dichotomies than to what Plato and his contemporaries actually thought about the role of shame in democratic politics. So before developing Plato's view within the context of Athenian democratic politics, I need to reconstruct some of the central aspects of the Platonic "Apology" allegedly offered in the *Gorgias* in order to clarify the canonical image of Plato that I wish to contest.

Plato contra Democratic Athens

Plato's critique of the institutions of democratic Athens first comes to light in the repeated distinctions Socrates makes between the true political art, which he alone pursues, and the flattering practices of Gorgianic rhetoric, which his interlocutors pursue (462b8-466a5). In his discussion with Polus,

Socrates twice contrasts his style of refutation with the style of refutation that Polus and "all Athenians and foreigners, save a few" think is the correct one to be used in law courts and political gatherings (471e1-472d1, 473e6-474b3).[13] Here Socrates argues that calling in many false witnesses of good repute to support one's arguments "is worth nothing in regard to the truth; for on some occasions someone would be borne down by the false witness of many who seem to be something" (472a1-3). He goes on to tell Polus that he is not one of the political men because he does not agree with nor is he skilled at the procedure that counts the votes of all present. Instead, he tells Polus, "I know how to provide one witness for what I say, the man himself to whom my speech is directed, while I bid the many farewell; and I know how to put the vote to one man, while I don't converse with the many either" (474a7-b1). Statements like this certainly seem to render Socrates' method antidemocratic, especially in light of the fact that the phrase used for determining resolutions in the Athenian assembly was "it appeared right to the citizenry." Finally, in his discussion with Callicles, Socrates launches what appears to be an all-out attack on the famed democratic leaders: Pericles, Cimon, Miltiades, and Themistocles, for failing to practise either the true art of rhetoric or the flattering one (517a8), and for making the Athenian citizens worse than they were before these leaders came to power (515d1-519b3).

Now, a significant part of this critique is explicitly stated by Socrates and displayed by him in his refutations of all three interlocutors: Gorgias, Polus, and Callicles. This is the fact that each man's sense of shame causes him to "contradict himself in front of many human beings, and this concerning the greatest things" (487b6). In each refutation Socrates seems to skilfully refute his opponent's thesis by getting that individual to consider how an Athenian audience would view his remarks. As I mentioned above, Socrates professes to Polus that he is incapable of utilizing the method of the rhetoricians and politicians that involves compelling someone to agree to a thesis by calling in the testimony of "many false witnesses" or "most Athenians." But the dialogue itself shows that Socrates is in fact *better* at this form of refutation than any of his interlocutors. Socrates emerges as a master of the psychological compulsion involved in the phenomenon of shame (*aidōs/aischunē*) who manipulates his interlocutors' fear of disgrace or dishonour before others.[14] "Might makes right" does not translate simply into the physical strength of the many, but also into the psychological strength of social conformity, which works through the sense of shame.

But if this is the case, and Socrates truly is the popular speaker that Callicles accuses him of being (494d1), then Plato would seem to be dramatically illustrating just why this democratic oratory and the emotion of shame are worth nothing in regard to the truth. Such democratic rhetoric works through the love of honour and the fear of disgrace rather than through a love of truth and a fear of untruth.[15] By skilfully manipulating their sense of shame,

Socrates is able to get his interlocutors to contradict themselves by asserting not what they believe to be true but rather only what they think convention requires of them. Plato's rejection of a life in Athenian democratic politics thus depends on the fact that it deals only with appearances, with the images that one must project to the many, who are themselves like children demanding pastries and sweets instead of beneficial medicines (464d8, 518b8). His whole philosophy rests on the fundamental distinction between appearance and reality, convention and nature. And the sense of shame comes to light as precisely that emotional barrier to truth that prevents people from seeing beyond the conventions of their own society. The search for reality and truth can thus take place only between a few close philosophic associates in those spaces outside of politics where shame is discarded and replaced by philosophic *eros*. (Hence the setting of the *Republic* in the home of a resident alien, Cephalus, and the setting of the *Phaedrus* outside the walls of Athens.)

Disrupting the Canon

Of course, if this is Plato's criticism of shame (*aidōs/aischunē*), then he is not really articulating anything novel for either his contemporary audience or modern readers. By Plato's time the notion that shame could dispose one to be overly concerned with one's external reputation or honour (*timē*) in the eyes of others was a significant theme both in Greek tragedies and in oratorical speeches. Euripides' *Hippolytus* examines shame more than any other tragedy, and one of its themes, articulated in Phaedra's great speech (373-430), is that shame can dispose one to take pleasure in and base one's conduct on the external rewards and sanctions of honour and disgrace in opposition to what is noble (*kalon*).[16] In his *Electra*, Euripides favourably contrasts the shame of the Farmer, which consists of a proper regard for others, with that of Electra and Orestes, which is ultimately selfish and concerned only with their prestige in the eyes of, and ultimately at the cost of, others.[17] Sophists and orators such as Antiphon and Democritus also take up this problem with a form of shame that is overly concerned with external sanctions, honours, and conventions.[18] For modern readers, this characterization of shame as concern with one's reputation in an ultimately selfish way resonates with Kant's disparagement of this emotion for being non-moral, egoistic, and heteronomous.[19]

The real problem with the canonical interpretation of Plato's view of shame, however, is not that it is completely wrong and not that it lacks novelty in relation to his contemporaries. And I will not turn this canonical Plato on his head and argue that he was actually an avid supporter of Athenian democracy or that he advocated dishonouring and disgracing others as part of a philosophic hazing ritual necessary to become a disciple of Socrates. Nor do I want to argue that contemporary democracies require more of this type of shame. I believe that the *Gorgias* does illustrate what Plato took to be serious difficulties with Athenian democracy and with the kind of shame that often motivates Socrates' three interlocutors. But the canonical view oversimplifies what for Plato amounts to a much more complex understanding of the place of shame in political life.

Moreover, as I stated earlier, Plato's views on these matters rely on debates and discussions about different forms of shame (*aidōs/aischunē*) and frank speech (*parrhēsia*) that already existed among his fellow Athenians. So before proceeding to develop Plato's own complex views on shame, I will reconstruct this rich Athenian democratic context. A number of political theorists and classicists have recently begun to examine the ways in which Plato's dialogues utilize or develop various Athenian democratic ideals and institutions, often alongside or even within his criticisms of Athenian life and politics. A new reading of Plato's treatment of democracy is enabled by first reconstructing various aspects of the Athenian "democratic imaginary" or "normative imagery," and then juxtaposing these to Plato's (or Socrates') account of his own philosophical practice.[20] Such a strategy has shown that there are significant similarities between Socratic dialectic and the pre-liminary scrutiny (*dokimasia*) and final accounting (*euthunai*) that Athenian citizens had to undergo before assuming administrative offices and stepping down at the end of their tenure.[21] And while Plato notoriously attacks certain democratic institutions, such as the ideal of freedom (*eleutheria*) in Book 8 of the *Republic* and the institution of majority rule in the *Gorgias*, he often does so because they threaten certain other ideals or institutions shared by Platonic philosophizing and Athenian democratic politics.

In this vein, and for the purposes of this chapter, important similarities exist between Plato's depiction of philosophic activity and the *parrhēsia* (frankness/openness) that was expected of anyone addressing the Athenian assembly.[22] And this connection between philosophy and the practice of *parrhēsia* is characteristic of Plato's depiction of philosophy in his early (*Laches*), middle (*Gorgias* and *Republic*), and late (*Laws*) dialogues.[23] It thus eludes being explained simply by the distinction between a democratic Socrates (depicted in Plato's early dialogues) and an antidemocratic Plato (elaborated in his middle and late dialogues). This connection therefore suggests that we see Plato not as an enemy to democratic Athens but as an immanent critic of a corrupt Athenian democracy calling this community "to its own best possible self without romanticizing what a rigorous pursuit of that best self would entail."[24]

A second strategy employed for this new reading of Plato's dialogues involves distinguishing between the representations of democracy and democratic leaders in the dialogues and the actual institutions and theories of democracy that were prevalent in Athens at the time. This distinction is especially important for understanding Socrates' criticisms of democracy and its slide into tyranny in Book 8 of the *Republic*, and Socrates' criticism of the democratic leaders Pericles and Themistocles and the democratic citizen Callicles in the *Gorgias*.[25] In these instances the "democracy" and "democrats" Socrates criticizes are those that fail to live up to certain ideals explicitly espoused in Athenian democratic discourse.[26] Both of these criticisms mention the Athenian practice of *parrhēsia* as a normative ideal shared by democratic debate and Socratic dialectic, which Socrates (and Plato) think aren't actually being practised by those who profess to be democrats or friends of democracy.[27] Thus, Socrates and Plato emerge not as antidemocratic but rather as sympathetic critics recalling their fellow citizens to the true practice of democracy. And the very things which Socrates sarcastically praises Callicles for possessing – wisdom, goodwill, and *parrhēsia* (487a) – are put forward as democratic ideals that are meant to counter the tyrannical impulses of "Calliclean democrats" who flatter the *demos* in hopes of gaining power over them.

Following the first strategy, I shall reconstruct the Athenian democratic ideal of *parrhēsia* and highlight those elements that are common to this Athenian ideal and to the respectful shame exemplified in Socrates' elenctic activities. This comparison shows that Socrates' distinctions between the flattering practice of Gorgianic rhetoric and his own painful method rely on distinctions that were already being made by democrats in fifth and fourth century Athens. Plato's accomplishment in the *Gorgias* is not that he articulates an ideal of discussion that is completely alien to his Athenian democratic audience but rather that he shows how the co-operative ideals of justice and moderation can be made consistent with the more traditional heroic ideals of courage and self-assertion in the figure of the just and courageous *parrhēsiastēs*, Socrates.[28] In the *Gorgias*, it is Socrates who consistently maintains the democratic ideal of *parrhēsia,* because he alone is able to continue speaking frankly about his view of the good life, even when his views seem strange and dissonant to most human beings (482c1). And this practice requires that he be without the kind of flattering shame that often motivates his interlocutors, who contradict themselves because they fear the pain and criticism that their views would elicit from an Athenian audience.[29] In contrast, Socratic respectful shame requires participants who are willing to suffer the pain of critique in the ongoing and reciprocal investigation of their collective ideals.

Following the second strategy, I show that Socrates' attacks in the *Gorgias* are directed at supporters or leaders of democracies who dream of being tyrants while falsely professing to be concerned with the common good. His critique is therefore levelled not just at the corrupt democratic practice of flattering rhetoric but also at the fantasies of those who engage in this practice. If the occurrent experience of shame involves the recognition that we don't actually live up to our own ideals or self-image, the experience can also show us that we don't live up to the corrupting image of the tyrant. (For a full discussion of the difference between the occurrent experience of shame and the disposition or sense of shame, see "The Structure of Shame," below). A certain type of shaming might then play a positive role in preventing these democrats from becoming the tyrants they secretly (or not so secretly) admire.

As will be seen below, both Polus and Callicles think that they want to be tyrants, but the life they have chosen and the fact that they continue conversing with Socrates reveals that they have not fully actualized this ideal *in their own lives*. Socrates' interlocutors might be speaking "frankly" when they admit their admiration for the tyrant, but if they are themselves deceived about how much their actions conform to the ideal, then they are in fact "false witnesses" for the tyrant. Their words might correspond to their self-image, but this self-image might not correspond to their actions. If Socrates can get them to feel ashamed by some of the actions that the image of the tyrant entails, then he might get them to recognize the gap between their selves and this image. In this case, their occurrent experience of shame would be closer to what Socrates means by knowledge of his own ignorance: knowing that you are not identical to the tyrant might be a necessary step towards knowing who and what you are.

Parrhēsia as an Athenian Democratic Ideal

I will turn first then to an account of the Athenian practice of *parrhēsia* in order to reconstruct the rich democratic context of the *Gorgias*. *Parrhēsia* is often translated as frankness, openness, or free-spokenness, but its literal meaning is "to say everything" – from *pas* (everything) and *rhēsis* (a saying, speaking, speech).[30] More specifically, it referred to the practice of frankly speaking one's own mind, "especially uttering a deserved reproach."[31] *Parrhēsia* was an essentially democratic ideal for two reasons. First, "it forcefully articulated some of the meaning of the Athenian conception of freedom (*eleutheria*)," which was itself articulated in part through its contrast to tyranny, in both its Athenian and Persian forms. Under tyranny one had to flatter the tyrant and could not speak one's mind without being put to death. In contrast, *parrhēsia* was part of the democratic practice of holding those exercising power accountable through exposing lies and abuses of power, and demanding change.[32]

Second, *parrhēsia* expressed one of the substantive ideals of democratic assembly debate, that the decisions rendered by the majority be wise and not simply democratically legitimate. In this respect *parrhēsia* was a necessary complement to the more procedural ideal of *isēgoria*, which meant literally "equality of public address."[33] *Isēgoria* allowed all citizens to be actively engaged in the deliberative process by allowing them to present their views of the public interest for consideration by everyone.[34] At the same time, however, *isēgoria* also produced one of the greatest threats to the discernment of a public interest and the production of wise decisions. This threat consisted of "manipulative and deceptive oratory in the service of a speaker's personal ambitions rather than the public interest. By pandering to the whims and desires of the people, a clever orator could elevate himself to a position of leadership."[35] Indeed, the danger of deceptive and flattering rhetoric was a major reason for the deep ambivalence that the Athenians exhibited towards the arts of rhetoric and sophistry. Because the right to speak was an essential part of the Athenian political identity, learning to speak well was seen as crucial to becoming a successful citizen and leader. Yet the art of rhetoric also supplied the means by which demagogues could rise to power by appealing to the interests, pleasures, and desires of the lower classes.[36]

The critical ideal of *parrhēsia* was thus utilized to counter this threat through its opposition to deceitful and flattering rhetoric. An appeal to the ideal of *parrhēsia* was meant as a way of affirming the speaker's personal integrity, freedom of thought, commitment to speaking and exposing the truth, and commitment to placing the public interest over personal interests and pleasures.[37] *Parrhēsia* also entailed a certain amount of danger and a degree of courage on the part of the speaker, who risked heckling, humiliation, fines, and even punishment for offering insincere or unwise advice to the assembly or criticizing it.[38] This danger was linked to the critical character of the truth, which was always "capable of hurting or angering the interlocutor."[39] Finally, *parrhēsia* implied a close connection between the speaker and his words.[40] Speaking with *parrhēsia* meant that a person's cares and convictions were on display, and it was not to be confused with "mere audacious speech, with playing the devil's advocate, or even with bold speculation."[41]

The practice of *parrhēsia* was, however, not linked simply to the virtue of the speaker, but also required a certain virtue on the part of the audience or hearer: "To the extent that the hearers willingly suffer criticism, reflect on their opinions and generally listen to others, their public-spiritedness (that is, their placement of the public good before that of personal pleasure) is on display as well as that of the speaker."[42] Thus for the Greeks, democratic deliberation involved a complex and reciprocal process of activity and passivity, speaking and listening, that required participants willing to suffer harsh rebukes, fines, and even imprisonment. Speaking with *parrhēsia* ensured that proposals before the assembly were rigorously scrutinized and criticized, and that the will of the *demos* was itself interrogated.[43]

Parrhēsia and Shame

This presentation of *parrhēsia* bears a striking resemblance to Socrates' own model of the true art of rhetoric, which he professes to practice in the *Gorgias*. The term *parrhēsia* occurs six times in the *Gorgias* (487a3, 487b1, 487d5, 491e7-8, 492d2, 521a6) and indicates the psychological disposition required of an interlocutor in order for Socrates to discover the "true things themselves" and "to make a sufficient test of a soul's living correctly or not" (487a2). In these same contexts, Socrates consistently and explicitly opposes *parrhēsia* to shame. Immediately after Callicles delivers his defence of powerful and superior rulers, Socrates tells him that he will serve as a "touchstone" for Socrates to test his own soul because he possesses three things: knowledge, goodwill, and *parrhēsia* (487a3). And he goes on to state that Gorgias and Polus were inadequate interlocutors because they lack *parrhēsia* and are too sensitive or inclined to shame: "and these two foreigners here, Gorgias and Polus, are wise and friends of mine, but rather too lacking in outspokenness and too sensitive to shame [*endeesterō de parrēsias kai aischuntēroterō mallon*], more so than is needful. And how could they not be? Since indeed they have advanced so far into the sense of shame [*aischunēs*] that – on account of feeling shame [*aischunesthai*] – each one of them dares to contradict himself in front of many human beings, and this concerning the greatest things" (487a-b).

As indicated earlier, the Athenian democratic ideal of *parrhēsia* required that a speaker frankly and boldly utter his own sincere thoughts on a subject, instead of flattering or deceiving the audience by tailoring his remarks to their views. It seems then directly opposed to the psychological disposition of shame, which is attuned to the ways that an audience views one's utterances and which can inhibit one from saying anything that audience will deem inappropriate or shameful. Indeed, Socrates' remarks that shame prompted both Polus and Gorgias to contradict themselves concerning how one ought to live suggest that shame is a hindrance not just to good political debate but also to Socratic dialectic. One of the requirements of Socratic *elenchus* is that the interlocutors always be frank about what they really believe, and Socrates reminds Callicles of this when he is on the verge of uttering an insincere remark: "You are corrupting the first speeches, Callicles, and you would no longer be sufficiently examining with me the things that are, if you're going to speak contrary to how things seem in your own opinion" (495a6-8). Here, again, it is Socrates and not Callicles who extols the democratic practice of frank and open speech, but now for the purposes of engaging in a philosophical discussion.

This opposition, however, does not mean that Socrates or any person speaking with *parrhēsia* is altogether without shame. As I mentioned above, *parrhēsia* requires that the speaker and the audience possess the courage, respectively, to utter a deserved reproach or to suffer the pain of critique. Yet this kind of reciprocal relationship is also integral to the shaming experience of the Socratic *elenchus*. In each case the participants must be willing to suffer the pain of critique that is integral to the experience of being shown that they (i.e., either individuals or the collectivity) do not live up to the very ideals they have set for themselves. (In Attic Greek, the word *elenchus* means both a reproach, disgrace, or dishonour, and a cross-examination or test for purposes of disproof or refutation.)[44] In each case, both parties to the debate must be able and willing to experience the painful cognitive-affective recognition of the gaze of an other that reveals an inadequacy in the self. But what can be positive about the experience is that it can reveal a truth common to the agent and patient, the speaker and audience: one can feel ashamed before an other *because* one shares with that other the judgment that one's behaviour violates some ideal or standard of morality or propriety. Thus, the recognition inherent to the feeling of being ashamed before an other can consist in the acknowledgment that a deserved rebuke or reproach has been given by this other. And this kind of respectful relationship to the other is manifested in both the democratic ideal of *parrhēsia* and in the Socratic *elenchus*. In this way shame and *parrhēsia* can be intricately connected to the positive attempt "to reconstruct or improve oneself," either as an individual or as part of a collectivity.[45]

What endangers the discovery of this common truth and the project of reconstruction is precisely the person's reaction to the experience. While the experience can be both painful and beneficial for the discussion participants, either party to the debate may fixate solely on the pain of critique as something bad to be avoided in the future. Their sense of shame will then inhibit them from any future situations in which they will have to feel this pain or make others feel it. A false consensus can then form wherein "debate" becomes a kind of reciprocal exchange of pleasures or pleasantries, such that neither party has to endure the pain of critique. Instead of respectfully showing each other just how and why they have fallen below a certain ideal or exemplar of action, each party to the debate merely flatters the existing prejudices and opinions of the other in order to avoid the pain of rebuke. This is not to say that Plato advocates a politics of feeling bad rather than one of feeling good, for this alternative would itself fixate only on the *pain* of critique rather than the *benefit* that is inherent to it. Rather, Plato wants the Athenians to avoid a politics of flattery wherein the person delivering the message and the audience receiving it aim only at the pleasant and not at the good (465a1).

The Structure of Shame

The occurrent experience of shame, as articulated in the democratic ideal of *parrhēsia* and the Socratic elenchus, can thus lead to two very different reactions and two very different senses of shame: either the flattering shame that is involved in the Gorgianic model of politics and rhetoric, or the respectful shame that is required for Socratic self-knowledge. In order to make these distinctions clear, I will analyze more carefully some of the elements of the phenomenon of shame and some of the ways in which shame words are used in both English and Greek.

First, the other that judges the self to be inadequate in the occurrent experience of shame can be real or imagined, that is, it can be an actual audience or an internalized one.[46] In either case, this other can be more than just the fact of being seen: it can be the repository of very specific attitudes, ideals, and behaviours.[47] One might feel ashamed only before the contemptuous eyes of one's friends or those one respects, and one might even feel proud if the "wrong" people – those one doesn't admire – express contempt for one's actions.

Second, the emotion of shame involves physiological and behavioural as well as cognitive elements.[48] The physiological and behavioural elements of shame consist of a number of things: the feeling of pain, certain physiological symptoms (e.g., blushing) and such behavioural responses as averting one's gaze, squirming awkwardly, and bowing or veiling the head. The Platonic dialogues abound with examples of blushing interlocutors.[49] Although no one in the *Gorgias* is described as blushing, Callicles' response to Socrates' final line of questioning vividly illustrates the kind of painful squirming exhibited by someone who is feeling ashamed: "I don't know what you are saying Socrates, so ask someone else ... How violent you are, Socrates. But if you're persuaded by me, you'll bid this argument farewell, or else you'll converse with someone else ... Couldn't you go through the argument yourself, either speaking by yourself or answering yourself?" (505c-d).

But the cognitive elements of the emotion of shame are just as important. Indeed, certain emotions are difficult if not impossible to differentiate by virtue of bodily changes, whether in terms of the experience of the subjects or the observations of others.[50] A person can flush red and experience a certain amount of pain when she is ashamed, embarrassed, humiliated, angry, or afraid. In order to differentiate these emotions, one needs to consider the cognitive elements: these emotions involve different appraisals or evaluations of different situations.[51] When we see someone flush red in front of a person wielding a gun, he might be afraid, or angry ("That's my gun and I told him not to touch it"), or ashamed ("That gun reminds me of my previous life as a mobster"). That is, the person's explanation of his emotion will refer to the circumstances to differentiate the emotion. In order for someone to be afraid of a person wielding a gun, the first person has to be in a certain cognitive state that involves specific intentional attitudes directed to circumstances in the world: that the gun is loaded, that guns can harm people, that the other person intends to pull the trigger, and so on.

What I have just outlined very schematically refers only to the occurrent experience of shame. However, just like English speakers, the ancient Greeks used emotion words in a dispositional sense as well.[52] Emotional dispositions are propensities to have occurrent emotions. So, for example, a person who is quick to become angry is described as irritable, and a person whose anger, when triggered, is extremely strong is referred to as irascible. But an angry person need not be characterized by either of these two dispositions, so occurrent emotions and emotional dispositions are distinct phenomena.[53] In fact, what is said about shame in the *Gorgias* often refers to the second-order disposition or sense of shame, rather than to the occurrent feeling of shame. The problem is that the second-order disposition and the occurrent experience can be expressed identically. At this level, especially with painful emotions such as shame, the shame-word refers not to our feeling ashamed but to our disposition to avoid situations in which we feel shame.[54] Thus one's sense of shame is supposed to enable one to avoid actions and situations that one judges to be shameful (*aischron*). These second-order dispositions are more likely to be described as character traits than feelings or emotions, and are sometimes (though not in the case of shame) designated by different words, such as irascibility or timidity rather than anger or fear.[55] Quite often English speakers distinguish the second-order disposition from the occurrent emotion by distinguishing between the sense of shame and the feeling of being ashamed. Yet even the words "shame" and "ashamed" can each refer either to the inhibitory disposition or to the occurrent emotion. Thus when we say, "Have you no shame?" "the 'shame' whose absence is being decried is a second-order disposition regarded as a desirable character trait."[56] We might also say, "He felt ashamed to say what he thought in front of her," meaning not that he felt the occurrent emotion of shame but rather that he felt inhibited to say something that would have made him feel the occurrent emotion. Similar ambiguity can occur in the Greek as well, adding to the complexity of the *Gorgias*.

Flattering versus Respectful Shame

I now want to utilize a number of these concepts to articulate what I consider to be Plato's critique of the flattering shame that is involved in Gorgianic rhetoric. First, it is important to note that in order to develop a second-order disposition or sense of shame an individual must first experience the occurrent emotion of being ashamed. Parents care for their children through shaming as well as loving, and anyone who has ever cared for infants can attest to the fact that they often take great pleasure in doing the most disturbing and tyrannical things. Yet when they are rebuked for engaging in these shameful activities, this pleasure is replaced (or at least accompanied by) the painful recognition of the disapproving gaze of the parent. The pain and awkwardness the child feels in shame is not a result of direct physical punishment but rather of the psychological punishment of disapproval and criticism. As human beings, we feel very intensely how we are judged or viewed by others. The blush is the physiological manifestation of this recognition of the gaze of the other.[57] Even if we are aware of no inadequacies in our self and walk into a room where everyone turns and expresses contempt, the painful pangs of embarrassment or shame are hard to avoid. Similarly it is extremely hard not to feel good about ourselves if we walk into a room where everyone looks at us admiringly. This good feeling can occur even if we were thinking disparaging thoughts about our self upon entering the room. Human beings can and often do orient their lives to pursue the pleasures of recognition, admiration, and honour and to avoid the pain of derision, contempt, and dishonour. Our sense of shame can thus orient us to avoid contempt or derision *as such* rather than orienting us to avoid the actions that were originally judged to be bad and thus worthy of derision. And this is part of what happens in the case of flattering shame. One fixates on the *pain* that is inherent to the cognitive-affective recognition of the gaze of an other that reveals a certain inadequacy in the self, and this painful recognition becomes the "shameful" situation that one tries to avoid in the future. As Douglas Cairns points out, the Greek verbs *aideomai* and *aischunomai* could refer to the experience of feeling shame before an other *whose status was irrelevant except as a potential source of criticism.*[58]

I believe that this kind of shame is what Socrates critiques in the Gorgianic model of rhetoric and politics. Here the democratic orator pursues his own interests by flattering others in order to gain power over them. The goal seems to be the avoidance of the occurrent experience of shame for both the orator and the audience. As a way of ensuring their support and thus satisfying his own desires, the orator never says anything that will cause his audience displeasure or dishonour. But in order to do this successfully, his sense of shame must be attuned to what his audience considers shameful and admirable, so that he can tailor his speech to their views and gain their admiration. (Flattering shame therefore does not refer to the occurrent emotion produced in the audience or experienced by the orator but rather to the disposition or sense of shame that reciprocally motivates both the audience and orator to avoid saying anything that might be painful to their respective audience, even when this involves the truth.) Like a chef who offers children pastries instead of bitter medicines (464e), the orator offers the audience flattering images of themselves so that they never have to hear anything that is painful or displeasing to them. Taking on the perspective of one's audience makes this audience the final arbiter of what can and cannot be said. The speaker thus attempts to conceal any "deficiencies or deviations from the group ideal," and in order to do so he "addresses [himself] directly to the onlooker and is oriented to the objectified public image."[59] The speaker's sense of shame thus attunes him to the view of the other, but in such a way that this other can never again reveal any inadequacies or criticisms of his self. Nor is the speaker oriented to revealing any inadequacies in his audience. Instead, both parties to the debate engage in the pleasure of reciprocal recognition as such.

In contrast to this model of politics and discussion, Socrates' allusion to medicine (464d5) reminds us that the structure of care involved in the relationship between doctor and patient may require painful procedures or bitter pills.[60] The analogy for Socrates is that caring for the health of someone's soul may similarly require the painful cognitive-affective mechanism involved in the feeling of shame. One of the central debates in the *Gorgias*, which is made most explicit in the confrontation between Socrates and Callicles, is whether the pleasant and the good are identical and whether the pursuit of maximal pleasure is indeed the best way of life for human beings. Insofar as Socrates argues against the equivalence of the pleasant and the good, the painful and the bad, then it is certainly not the case that shame is a bad thing *because* it is painful. Socrates' interlocutors in the *Gorgias* draw this conclusion, however. They equate the pleasure of recognition and esteem with the good, and the pain of critique and dishonour with the bad. But when Socrates describes the true art of rhetoric to Polus, he says it does not take into account what is painful:

> For speaking in defense of one's own injustice, therefore, or that of parents or comrades or children or fatherland when it does injustice, rhetoric will be of no use to us, Polus; except if someone takes it to be of use for the opposite purpose, supposing that he must most of all accuse himself, and then whoever else of his relatives and friends happens at any time to do injustice, and not hide the unjust deed but bring it into the open, so as to pay the just penalty and become healthy, and compel both himself and others not to play the coward but to grit his teeth and submit well and courageously as if to a doctor for cutting and burning – pursuing what's good and fine, *not taking account of what's painful*, … and using rhetoric for this purpose, so that, their unjust deeds having become manifest, they may be released from the greatest evil, injustice. (480c1-d9, emphasis added)

Socrates' description of the true art of rhetoric in this passage bears a striking resemblance to the kind of courage and daring *parrhēsia* requires of both the speaker and the audience. As was shown earlier, *parrhēsia* was intricately related to the practice of uttering a deserved reproach and entailed the risk of heckling, fines, and punishment. But a rhetoric that consists of *accusing* oneself and one's friends is very different from one that consists of *flattering* oneself and one's friends. It requires that one remain open to the possibility that the other with whom one is conversing might show one something painful about oneself that one was unaware of or had concealed from oneself in the past. In other words, it requires that one remain open to the possibility of being rightfully shamed out of one's conformity and complacent moralism by an other in the ongoing and mutual project of reflective self-examination. Only thus do we come to truly respect this other, and through the insights of this other come to new possibilities of self-respect.

Unsurprisingly, it is Callicles who thinks that philosophy is appropriate only during one's youth and that it should not get in the way of the more important education regarding the customs and pleasures of one's city (484c-d2). He ends up being the interlocutor least capable of submitting to Socrates' shaming refutations and least willing to learn anything new about himself or his city (505c1-5). Socratic *elenchus* and democratic debate require participants who are willing to recognize the gap between themselves and their idealized self-images and who can make this recognition the necessary first step towards the ongoing project of reconstruction. A respectful shame is thus necessary to constrain or inhibit the flattering shame that prompts participants to slavishly mimic the viewpoints of another, while concealing the fact of this slavish imitation both from themselves and from this other. A person like Socrates might well be unabashed (lacking in flattering shame) without thereby being shameless (lacking in respectful shame).[61]

Indeed, my Platonic typologies of flattering and respectful shame are in part meant to address a prevalent modern misconception about whether Socrates (and philosophers and democrats more generally) are or ought to be shameless.[62] I think that there are many instances in the early, middle, and late dialogues where Plato is careful to show that Socrates is not shameless and to point out just what kinds of people are shameless. For instance, in the *Apology*, Socrates is careful to point out that his accusers are the shameless ones (17b) and that he himself is eventually convicted only because he refused to *shamelessly* wail and lament, and thus pander to the spectators, in order to ensure his survival and acquittal (38e). For Socrates such a shameless act would have been completely discordant with his respect for philosophy. In Books 8 and 9 of the *Republic*, Socrates argues that the *tyrant* is shameless (560d-e, 571c, 571d) and that only the tyrant mistakenly calls his shamelessness courage (561a). In Book 10 of the *Republic*, Socrates says that he himself does have a certain shame before Homer (595b), and in the *Phaedrus*, Socrates says that his first speech was shameless (243c) and that he must recant it in front of a person who is of noble breeding and gentle in character, and before whom he does feel shame (243d). Finally, in the *Gorgias*, Socrates repeatedly tells Callicles that he would be ashamed of not being able to help prevent either himself or his friends or relatives from committing an injustice towards human beings or the gods (509b-c, 522d).[63]

So I do think that there is an other before whom Socrates felt respectful shame and that this was, as he asserts in the *Gorgias* (481d) and the *Apology* (28d), related to his love of philosophy. As Socrates puts it, his obedience to the god means that he will remain in his philosophic station and not "take into account death or anything else compared to what is shameful" (*Apology* 28d).[64] That Socrates had a certain shame before philosophy also means that he might well have felt ashamed before a noble and gentle character like Plato, whose own philosophizing was both similar to and different from his own (hence the above-mentioned *Phaedrus* passage). For Plato and Socrates, the *agon* of philosophic discussion and democratic debate did not consist of shameless self-assertion but rather of a complex negotiation and contestation between the self and others, both real and ideal.

Plato contra Tyrannical Democrats

But is Callicles not equally as unabashed and courageous as Socrates in his frank praise of tyranny? I have tended to treat Callicles as the slavish flatterer of the *demos* that Socrates accuses him of being (481e1). I might therefore seem to be overlooking his first speech about the powerful, unjust, and immoderate life of the tyrant who tramples on the conventions of the many. Here Callicles certainly appears to courageously reject the democratic ideals of Athens rather than mimicking or flattering them. His speech could be seen as an example of democratic *parrhēsia* because he boldly asserts a critique of the *demos* and of the democratic principle of equality. But I shall end this chapter by suggesting why this is not the case: Callicles is not really voicing a view that is alien to his Athenian democratic audience. As Socrates suggests, Callicles' praise of tyranny is actually consistent with "what the others think but are unwilling to say" (492d3). Callicles might be frank about his wish or dream of becoming a tyrant, but this wish may have been shared by many other "democrats" who covertly admired the tyrant while condemning his actions as unjust. Callicles at his most shocking is still only flattering his beloved *demos*, and the moral indignation that the many direct toward the tyrant may be possible only because they envy the goods that he attains through his acts of injustice.[65] Thus, part of Socrates' distrust of the many, which he expresses in the Polus section, rests on the view that they *do* all secretly or unconsciously think that tyranny and indiscriminate hedonism are the best way of life. I believe that Plato felt this was indeed the case in the "democratic" but imperialistic Athens that he so vehemently criticizes in the *Gorgias*.

Moreover, as I mentioned earlier, in critiquing Callicles' particular brand of *parrhēsia*, Plato is relying on debates that were already taking place in democratic Athens. By the fourth century BC a number of orators had begun to distinguish between a critical kind of *parrhēsia*, which was important for good democratic deliberation, and a kind of *parrhēsia* that was reckless and ignorant, and that merely pandered to the desires of an audience drunk on their own lawlessness and lack of self-restraint.[66] This context is extremely important for understanding Plato's criticisms of democracy in both the *Republic* and the *Gorgias*. In Book 8 of the *Republic*, Plato initially characterizes democracy as being a city filled with freedom and free speech (*kai eleutherias hē polis mestē kai parrhēsias gignetai*, 557b2-4). His harshest criticisms of democracy, however, occur in the section where he describes democracy's slide into tyranny (564a-569c). Here, Plato argues that the tyrant eventually does away with anyone who continues to speak frankly to him and to others (*parrhēsiazesthai kai pros auton kai pros allēlous*) in order to fully establish himself in the city and to enslave the citizenry (567b1-3). Plato's criticism of the tyrannical democrat thus focuses on the fact that he banishes the good kind of critical *parrhēsia* from the city and kills anyone who continues to practise it. As Plato dramatically illustrates in the *Apology* and predicts in the *Gorgias,* the gadfly or critical frank speaker, Socrates, is eventually put to death by just such a tyrannical *demos* because he refuses to follow Callicles' advice to gratify and flatter them (521a-b).

In the later sections of the *Gorgias*, Plato articulates what lies at the heart of Callicles' own brand of *parrhēsia,* and his analysis illustrates why this kind of frankness amounts not just to flattery but also to a very dangerous type of ignorance. Socrates sarcastically praises Themistocles and Pericles for being "terribly clever" at supplying the Athenians with ships, walls, and dockyards, all potent symbols of Athens' imperialism (517b-c). But he accuses them of never "leading the desires [of the citizens] in a different direction" (517b8). And Callicles, the product of this imperialistic Athenian democracy, exemplifies this in his own "frank" praise of tyranny and indiscriminate hedonism, i.e., the pursuit of any and all desires (492a-b). For Plato, the problematic desire that lies at the heart of both Athenian imperialism and Calliclean hedonism is the desire for a godlike omnipotence and immortal glory that allows the evasion of pain, suffering, and the ultimate danger – death of the person or the polity. As I mentioned earlier, in flattering shame one equates the shameful with the painful and therefore attempts to avoid all situations in which one has to feel pain and suffering. But since avoidance of pain and suffering is simply not possible for mortal and needy human beings, flattering shame can dispose them to construct a fantastical image of omnipotence as a way of satisfying this desire. We can thus aspire to and be motivated by unreal images and exemplars of action that are not predicable of our human experience of pain and suffering.

For Plato, then, shame becomes a problematic emotion when it is linked to this kind of imaginative projection and desire for omnipotence, which hides rather than illuminates our mortal and needy natures. At the end of the *Gorgias*, Socrates criticizes the Athenian imperialistic democratic leaders, Themistocles and Pericles, for feeding precisely this fantasy of the Athenians by turning their attention only to fortifying the city with countless ships, walls, and arsenals (517c). Such projects, according to Socrates, transformed Athenian democratic politics into a collective endeavour to secure mere life rather than the best life. All deliberations centred on the ultimately fantastical desire to preserve Athenians and their city from every danger, including death, and trying to live as along as possible (511b-c). This fantastical desire for omnipotence is on display not only in the *Gorgias* but also in the fantasies and dreams that haunt Glaucon and Adeimantus when they first encounter Socrates in the *Republic*. Both of them ask Socrates to defend a type of justice that will make its possessor completely invulnerable to chance and to those around him, so that he can live like a god among human beings (358b-366a).[67]

We moderns engage in the same kind of flattering shame when we flatter ourselves that our contemporary democratic practices are completely free of this pernicious form of shame. As Martha Nussbaum has recently argued, this kind of fantastical denial of neediness and vulnerability is *particularly* likely to be true in contemporary societies where "the acceptance of mortality and failure [are] especially shaky, and in which illness and death are all imagined as potentially eliminable by the right kind of scientific and technical effort. Combine these fantasies with the equally prevalent American fantasy that a real man is a self-sufficient being without deep needs for others, and we have the ingredients of some painful social tensions."[68] Contemporary liberal democratic societies are haunted by the same dreams of omnipotence that motivated Socrates' Athenian interlocutors, only now they have more techniques for translating these nightmares into reality.

But Plato's *Gorgias* also teaches us that these possibilities do not mean that the imagination can or ought to be banished altogether from our emotional and political lives. Just as the *elenchus* is used in dialogues such as the *Euthyphro* and the *Crito* to show Socrates' interlocutors that they are not as just as they think they are, in the *Gorgias* it shows his interlocutors that they are not as unjust as they think they are. What Socrates attempts to do in his shaming-refutations of a "democrat" like Callicles is to show him that he doesn't fully identify with the tyrant because he can still be ashamed of some of the actions entailed by the tyrannical life of indiscriminate hedonism. Callicles is ashamed and angry when Socrates points out that his doctrine of indiscriminate hedonism is consistent with a life of constantly scratching itches (494e7) and running away from battles (498e8). The second example shames Callicles into retracting his thesis of indiscriminate hedonism, as Socrates makes Callicles look upon that part of himself that admires tyrants from the vantage point of that other part of himself that admires courageous warriors bravely facing their death in battle (498e7-499b7). Or, as Socrates rather awkwardly describes it, Callicles retracts his thesis "when he himself looks on himself correctly" (495e2). In this moment, he is at least momentarily able to use his imagination to take on the perspective of an other in order to gain insight into his own false pretences. The image of the warrior facing his death in battle announces the contingency of human existence to Callicles even while it discloses the falsity of his own professed doctrine of indiscriminate hedonism. As Callicles blurts out, "As if you thought that I or any other human being did not consider some pleasures better and others worse!" (499b7-8). At this moment the salutary doubleness of the psyche inherent to the experience of shame actually disrupts Callicles' merger with his beloved but tyrannical *demos*. Plato's respectful shaming of Callicles is thus meant to save him, and by extension, his Athenian and future democratic audiences, from "a corrupting vision of [themselves]," thus making Plato an ally rather than an enemy of democracy.[69]

Conclusion

In this chapter I have tried to show just how Plato's complex treatment of shame (*aidōs/aischunē*) and frank speech (*parrhēsia*) in the *Gorgias* can contribute to our contemporary theories of the emotions in democratic politics by offering a nuanced understanding of the complex entanglements among reason, the emotions, and the imagination. As Plato reminds us, no emotion can be classified as simply positive or negative without an investigation of the complex structure of the emotion itself and of the various criteria that ought to determine our acceptance or rejection of this emotion. Every emotion can be pernicious for democratic deliberations when it manifests itself in certain forms or contains certain problematic content and attitudes towards the self or others. In other words, the object of the emotions of love, pity, compassion, disgust, and shame can all consist of either the fantastical notion of the omnipotent citizen or nation, or the much more realistic notion of vulnerable and needy human beings and nations that are mutually and reciprocally implicated in the world order. If the normative content of our ideals is mistaken, fantastical, or unrealistic, then this content will make our emotions negative in their effect regardless of whether they are painful, pleasurable, relational, non-relational, hierarchical, egalitarian, directed towards the self, or directed towards imaginary or actual others. And if respectful shame doesn't open us up to our vulnerabilities in an uncertain world and jolt us out of our false desires for omnipotence, then our love, joy, pity, and compassion can do little to assuage the situation.

The Passions of the Wise: *Phronēsis*, Rhetoric, and Aristotle's Passionate Practical Deliberation

Arash Abizadeh

In contradistinction with views that characterize the emotions primarily as a hindrance to practical reasoning, contemporary moral philosophers have become increasingly impressed with the Aristotelian insight that good practical reasoning systematically relies on the emotions. Moreover, accounts of practical reason have become important for political philosophers seeking to theorize the regulative principles governing democratic deliberation. My intention in this chapter is to demonstrate that Aristotle shows how an account of practical reason and deliberation that constructively incorporates the emotions can illuminate key issues about deliberation at the political level. First, I argue that, according to Aristotle, character (*ēthos*) and emotion (*pathos*) are constitutive features of the process of phronetic practical deliberation: in order to render a determinate action-specific judgment, practical deliberation cannot be simply reduced to logical demonstration (*apodeixis*). This can be seen by uncovering an important structural parallel between the virtue of *phronēsis* and the art of rhetoric. Second, this structural parallel helps to tease out the insights of Aristotle's account of practical deliberation for contemporary democratic theory – in particular, the ethical consequences that follow from the fact that passionate political deliberation and judgment are both unavoidable in democracy and always susceptible to straying from the path that will issue properly ethical outcomes.

Determinate Judgment

Aristotle's critique of democracy rests on his fears about demagoguery, a regime led by popular leaders who, by appealing to the people's passions, are capable of ingratiating themselves with a majority that is thereby led to tyrannize a helpless minority – even to the detriment of the majority itself. Of course, modern liberal democracies have developed various responses to alleviate some of the risks that Aristotle, and in other ways Plato, articulated so long ago. One of liberalism's most significant counters to the threat of the tyranny of the majority has been constitutional constraint on democratic decision making.

[handwritten margin notes: "demagoguery – fear of / Aristotle regineled / by people's passions" and "il"]

Yet Aristotle himself anticipates the limits of such a response. Obviously, the application of abstract laws to particular circumstances cannot be carried out by the laws themselves. The problem this introduces is what we might call the indeterminacy of written *nomos*. I say "written *nomos*" because Aristotle makes a fundamental distinction between written and unwritten *nomos*: the former refers to the codified written laws legislated by a particular *polis*, and the latter refers to the unwritten tacit norms that seem agreed upon by all and that invariably cannot be codified as abstract rules.[1] The indeterminacy of written *nomos* refers to Aristotle's thought that the abstract rules that constitute the written laws are never sufficient to issue forth in a determinate injunction in the face of particular circumstances.

Why? Because the answer to the practical question of what ought to be done in particular circumstances can never, for Aristotle, be fully codified in human speech or writing as a series of abstract rules specified before the fact – there is always a remainder not captured in or by abstract *logos*. In other words, the indeterminacy of written *nomos* is simply a political manifestation of a more general condition: the indeterminacy of universals when employed in practical reason, or what I shall call the indeterminacy of abstract *logos* (and here I mean to evoke connotations of both reason and speech). This indeterminacy refers both to (1) the fact that abstract reason is insufficient to issue in determinate normative injunctions in particular circumstances, and (2) the parallel fact that practical philosophy, whether ethical or political, can never be fully codified in language as a series of antecedently specified, set general practical principles.[2] The ubiquitous requirement for *in situ* judgment and the impossibility of final abstract codification arise from at least three interrelated features of practical philosophy that render it inexact.[3] (1) Abstract rules developed *ex ante* cannot cover every particular contingency that may arise in the future.[4] (2) What is good unconditionally (*haplōs*) may not necessarily be good for me (or good for this or that person or people).[5] (3) Abstract rules, sound as they may be in general, turn out sometimes to be inapplicable in particular cases; in politics, this means that decency or fairness (*epieikeia*) requires that written *nomos* be occasionally overridden, for the sake of justice itself.[6] One might add to Aristotle's reasons that (4) abstract rules cannot also determine the rules of their own application. Consequently, it is unreasonable ever to demand of moral and political philosophy (*politikē*), and the written laws, that they be exact (*akribēs*) in the way that mathematics might be. We cannot remove the deliberating agent from ethics and politics, reducing *politikē* to a passive application of universal principles to particular circumstances. Judgment is required.

But how does the individual render a determinate judgment? We get an indication of Aristotle's answer to this question when he deals with the indeterminacy of abstract codification in the specific instance of the laws. Here he appeals to the *epieikeia* (decency or fairness) exercised by the moral agent, by which the individual may override the written laws for the sake of justice:

> What is decent is just, but is not what is legally just, but a rectification of it. The reason is that *all law is universal,* but in some areas no universal rule can be correct; and so where a universal rule has to be made, but cannot be correct, the law chooses the [universal rule] that is usually [correct], well aware of the error being made. And the law is no less correct on this account; for the source of the error is not the law or the legislator, but the nature of the object itself, since that is what the subject-matter of action is bound to be like. Hence whenever the law makes a universal rule, but in this particular case what happens violates the [intended scope of] the universal rule, here the legislator falls short, and has made an error by making an unconditional rule. Then it is correct to rectify the deficiency; this is what the legislator would have said himself if he had been present, and what he would have prescribed, had he known, in his *legislation* … This is the nature of what is decent – rectification of law in so far as *the universality of law makes it deficient.* This is also the reason why not everything is guided by law. *For on some matters legislation is impossible,* and so a decree is needed. For the standard applied to what is indefinite is *itself indefinite.*[7]

When Aristotle uses the term *nomos* (law) in this passage, he evidently has in mind written *nomos,* as indicated by the frequent reference to the legislator and the fact that he uses *nomos* here interchangeably with matters of legislation. That *epieikeia* is making up for the deficiencies of – and is being contrasted to – written *nomos* and not to *nomos* as a whole is made more clear in *On Rhetoric,* where he speaks of *epieikeia* as an instance of unwritten *nomos.*[8]

But what might the *epieikeia* of the particular, deliberating agent be providing that written *nomos* does not, and that allows the proper treatment of particulars? The answer emerges in Aristotle's discussion of written laws in the *Politics.* He addresses the argument that "to rule in accordance with written [rules] is foolish in any art" because "laws only speak of the universal and do not command with a view to circumstances." The written law is insensitive to the particular circumstances because "the passionate element … is not present in law, but every human soul necessarily has it." On the one hand, Aristotle notes, it might be argued that "what is unaccompanied by the passionate element is superior to that in which it is innate." On the other hand, the existence of this "passionate element" in the human soul means that "he will deliberate in finer fashion concerning particulars [or: in particular cases]."[9] The rule of written law, then, is identified with the "rule of the intellect," which in turn is contrasted with the passionate element found in the human soul.[10] What the written laws lack in comparison with a deliberating agent is the passionate element found in his soul: different parties might cite this lack as advantageous or disadvantageous, but the upshot is that "to legislate concerning matters of deliberation is impossible."[11]

Now, if it is the lack of a passionate element that renders written *nomos* insufficient for matters of deliberation, then how could the practical deliberations of an individual render a determinate action-producing judgment if deliberation itself were solely a matter of (passionless) *logico*-deductive reasoning from premises? The answer is that it could not. But Aristotelian deliberation is not simply a matter of logical demonstration.

In order to make good this claim, in the following section I will examine Aristotle's account of rhetorical deliberation in order to demonstrate the constitutive role of *ēthos* and *pathos* there. Then, in the third section of this chapter, I will uncover a structural parallel between the art of rhetoric and the virtue of *phronēsis*, a parallel suggesting that *ēthos* and *pathos* are constitutive of phronetic deliberation as well.

The Elements of Rhetoric

One might expect that the function of the art of rhetoric is to persuade;[12] but Aristotle says that "its function is not to persuade but to see the available means of persuasion in each case" – and to identify fallacious sophistry where it arises. He defines rhetoric as "an ability [*dunamis*], in each [particular] case, to see the available means of persuasion."[13] The fact that the rhetorician does not aim directly at the end of persuasion is precisely what renders rhetoric a *technē* (art or craft): it has not just a given end or external good but also guiding ends or internal constitutive goods.[14] The given end of the practice of medicine, to cite another example of an Aristotelian *technē*, is to maintain the life and health of its patients, but the guiding end of the doctor qua practitioner of medicine is to perform his *technē* well, which involves, for instance, following certain standard procedures and rules. A doctor can thus perform the *technē* well – that is, fulfill its guiding ends – via a masterful application of its procedures and rules, even if the patient dies. Of course a *technē* with no reliable relation between its guiding and given ends would fail to be viable; the necessity for *technē* arises because some given ends are best achieved by not pursuing them directly. Persuasion is one such end for Aristotle.[15]

Aristotle identifies three means of persuasion through speech: the proofs (*pisteis*) of *ēthos*, *pathos*, and *logos*: "Of the *pisteis* provided through speech [*logos*] there are three species: for some are in the *ēthos* of the speaker, and some in disposing the listener in some way, and some in the argument [*logos*] itself, by showing or seeming to show something." He explains, first, that *ēthos* persuades insofar as the speech of the rhetorician gains the trust of the audience, and that "this should result from the speech [*logos*], not from a previous opinion that the speaker is a certain kind of person." Second, persuasion occurs "through the hearers when they are led to feel *pathos* by the speech [*logos*]." And third, regarding logical demonstrations via paradigm or enthymeme, Aristotle says that "persuasion occurs through the arguments [*logoi*] when we show the truth or apparent truth from whatever is persuasive in each case."[16]

Two comments are in order. First, I have included the word *logos* from the original text quoted above in order to flag an important feature of Aristotle's discussion of the *pisteis*. Although, following Aristotle, commentators refer to the tripartite *pisteis* of *ēthos*, *pathos*, and *logos*, in fact all three *pisteis* for Aristotle occur in *logos*. In other words, when we call the third *pistis* "*logos*," we are using the word in a restricted sense meaning logical demonstration (*apodeixis*), as an instance falling within the broader sense of *logos*.[17] Aristotle's broader notion of practical *logos* or discursive rationality is not constructed in contrast to *ēthos* and *pathos* but rather includes them. The restricted sense of *logos*, as the third *pistis*, refers to strict demonstration or logical persuasion via the use of paradigms and enthymemes: "I call rhetorical *sullogismos* an enthymeme, a rhetorical induction a paradigm. And all [speakers] produce logical persuasion by means of paradigms or enthymemes and by nothing other than these."[18] In one place Aristotle calls enthymeme a "*sullogismos* of a sort," and in another a "rhetorical demonstration [*apodeixis*]."[19] The reference to *apodeixis* is key here because, as M.F. Burnyeat notes, for Aristotle "*apodeixis* is the term that suggests logical stringency."[20] It is this restricted sense of *logos*, as a series of logico-deductive demonstrations that are thereby codifiable, to which the notion of the indeterminacy of abstract *logos* refers.

Second, these passages could be interpreted disjunctively: one might take Aristotle to be saying that persuasion operates via *ēthos*, *pathos*, or *logos* on different occasions. In fact, however, Aristotle understands the role of the three *pisteis* conjunctively: the art of rhetoric requires that *ēthos*, *pathos*, and *logos* operate every time. Important here is that Aristotle advances the conjunctive account by explicitly linking the insufficiency of *logos* (in the restricted sense) to the fact that the given end of rhetoric is not just to persuade but to persuade in producing a determinate judgment:

> Since rhetoric is concerned with making a judgment (people judge what is said in deliberation, and judicial proceedings are also a judgment) it is necessary not only to look to the argument [*logos*], that it may be demonstrative and persuasive [*apodeiktiktos kai pistos*] but also [for the speaker] to construct a view of himself as a certain kind of person and to prepare the judge; for it makes much difference in regard to persuasion (especially in deliberations but also in trials) that the speaker seem to be a certain kind of person ... There are three reasons why speakers themselves are persuasive; for there are three things we trust other than logical demonstrations [*apodeixeis*]. These are *phronēsis* and virtue [*aretē*] and good will [*eunoia*].[21]

As he goes on to elaborate, "goodwill and friendliness" are matters of the *pathē*, which "are those things through which, by undergoing change, people come to differ in their judgements."[22]

A host of commentators have noted that Aristotle's broader notion of *logos*, in the context of practical reason, is not constructed in opposition to *pathos* or to the *ēthos* that the *pathē* help constitute.[23] The main problem such an interpretation faces is found in Chapter 1 of *On Rhetoric*. As is well known, in that chapter Aristotle appears to deprecate rhetorical proofs appealing to *pathos* (he says that "verbal attack and pity and anger and such emotions of the soul do not relate to fact but are appeals to the juryman"), and makes no mention of proofs of *ēthos*.[24] Following Jacques Brunschwig, however, I would argue that far from undermining the claim that *logos* is related to *pathos*, Aristotle is specifying that relation.[25] For the *pathē* he deprecates are those that draw "attention to matters external to the subject" at hand. In other words, the kind of *pathos* that forms a legitimate *pistis* is "entechnical," or found in the speech (that is, *logos*) itself.[26]

A second problem is to specify the relation between *logos* and *ēthos* or *pathos* in Aristotle's thought. Martha Nussbaum argues, for example, that for Aristotle the emotions are constituted by cognitive beliefs that individuate the different emotions; Nancy Sherman too sees cognitions as constitutive of emotions; John Cooper argues that *logos* can persuade desires (*orexeis*) in general because the desires raise cognitive validity claims; Stephen Leighton argues that emotions affect perception, which in turn affects judgment; and Robert Wardy argues that in rhetorical contexts the proper *pathē* "enhance our receptivity to truthful *logos*."[27] I will try to show that Aristotle's view of the relation is importantly clarified by a structural parallel between rhetoric and phronetic practical deliberation.[28]

Parallels between Rhetoric and *Phronēsis*

Since for Aristotle the *telos* of the *polis* is *eudaimonia*,[29] the legitimate political role he assigns to rhetoric implies a belief in at least the possibility that rhetoric can yield ethical judgments consistent with the right reason of a phronetic person (*phronimos*). This possibility is indicated when Aristotle follows his characterization of rhetoric as a capacity to prove opposites – the rhetorician "should be able to argue persuasively on either side of a question" – with the immediate ethical admonition that it is "not that we may actually do both (for one should not persuade what is debased)."[30] But since rhetoric is a *technē* and not itself a virtue like *phronēsis*, the standard for the rightness of its outcomes must be supplied by a source external to the art itself. This is perhaps why Aristotle's parenthetical ethical admonition is not repeated elsewhere in *On Rhetoric*:[31] the admonition is not internal to the art of rhetoric itself but is given externally by ethics to rhetoric. Ethical rhetoric must be rhetoric governed by *politikē*, the architectonic discipline.[32]

But since for Aristotle the legitimacy of political institutions is a function of their contribution to the realization of the *telos* of *eudaimonia*, the mere possibility of yielding ethical outcomes is not enough. To give rhetoric such a prominent and legitimate political role, as the art governing collective practical deliberation in the *polis'* institutions, requires that deliberation so governed have a propensity to issue forth in judgments consistent with *phronēsis*.[33] Aristotle does indeed think that rhetoric has a propensity to yield correct judgments. How can we explain Aristotle's well-known optimism here?[34]

What, in other words, would explain the possibility for, and the propensity of, the art of rhetoric to yield outcomes consistent with the ethical requirements of right reason as embodied in the *phronimos* and his deliberations? My thesis is that the possibility and propensity for this consistency are furnished by the structural similarity in the argumentative process in both types of deliberation. That is, I explain Aristotle's optimism by reference to the internal constitution of the *technē* itself rather than to external ethical constraints not constitutive of the art of rhetoric, because the external strategy fails to explain Aristotle's optimism about the *technē* itself. At the same time, however, Aristotle's optimism cannot depend on collapsing the category of *technē* into that of virtue; rather, my suggestion is that the structural constitution of the art of rhetoric internally generates the propensity to induce judgments consistent with the outcomes of phronetic deliberation. If this is correct, then we have another reason Aristotle assigns rhetoric such a central role in politics: not only is rhetoric a means for generating outcomes with a propensity to be consistent with right reason, but it potentially bypasses the onerous standard of full virtue required in monological phronetic deliberation.[35] By providing structural-technical incentives that substitute for the full virtue required in the monological deliberations of the *phronimos*, rhetoric could enable political institutions to reach correct outcomes despite the ethical shortcomings of the polity's members. In other words, rhetoric might be a way for Aristotle to lower the virtue bar for successful politics.

I have already identified the key structural feature of collective, rhetorical deliberation: it is constituted by the three means of persuasion *ēthos*, *pathos*, and *logos*. Whether a speaker persuades a council or court to render a particular judgment depends on these three species of *pistis* and not just the demonstrative reason embodied in argument. Thus the process of rhetorical persuasion is not constituted solely by *logos* in the restrictive sense of the third *pistis*. In collective deliberation, whether the audience finds the conclusion of the rhetorician persuasive depends on the *ēthos*, *pathos*, and *logos* embodied in the argument leading to it.

I want to argue that, similarly, when engaged in monological practical deliberation, whether the individual phronetic person finds a particular practical conclusion persuasive depends on the elements of *ēthos*, *pathos*, and *logos* involved in the deliberative process that lead (or do not lead) to that conclusion. In other words, the key reason why rhetoric has an internally generated propensity to yield outcomes consistent with the practical deliberations of a *phronimos* is that the structure of the deliberative process is similar: in both cases, *ēthos* and *pathos* combine with *logos* to lead the "argument" to its conclusion.[36]

Indeed, *ēthos* and *pathos* are, along with logical demonstration, constitutive elements of *phronēsis*: all three are necessary and individually insufficient guides that lead practical deliberation to its conclusions. The practical deliberations of the *phronimos* leading to a particular conclusion cannot be reduced to a series of logico-deductive demonstrations that fit into a self-sufficient theory of ethics: Aristotle is precisely the thinker who tells us that ethics can never be fully captured by a theoretical system constructed and codified by abstract *logos*. The proper ethical deliberation characterized by *phronēsis* is, therefore, further constituted by the proper *ēthos* and *pathos* of the *phronimos*. This, of course, is reflected in what I called the indeterminacy of abstract *logos*.

The position I am attributing to Aristotle has important limits. I have argued that what accounts for the possibility and propensity of consistency between the outcomes of rhetorical and phronetic deliberation is the fact of their structural similarity. But of course structural similarity is neither a sufficient nor a necessary condition for securing similar outcomes. It is not sufficient: structural similarity furnishes only the possibility and, at best, an internal propensity for rhetoric to secure phronetic outcomes. But this propensity can be undermined: as we shall see, rhetoric has problems that stem precisely from the possibility of variance from *phronēsis*. Nor is structural similarity a necessary condition for consistency: two structurally very different processes could systematically yield similar outcomes. So the claim here is only that the possibility and propensity for consistent outcomes require an explanation, and that the most plausible explanation to be found in Aristotle is the structural similarity of their respective modes of procedure.

Possible Objections

The most obvious objection to my claim that the practical deliberations of a phronetic person require *ēthos* and *pathos* to render determinacy – the determinacy of an "ought" judgment required for action – would be to counter that, according to Aristotle, it is not *ēthos* or *pathos* but perception (*aisthēsis*) that renders judgment determinate. Indeed, Aristotle states that one reason ethics is inexact is that its application in particular circumstances relies on perception: "Nothing perceptible is easily defined, and [since] these [circumstances of virtuous and vicious action] are particulars, the judgement about them depends on perception."[37] This objection can be formulated as follows: (a) it is perception, and not deliberation itself, that renders determinacy; therefore, (b) insofar as I have relied on the assumption that practical deliberation must issue forth in determinate judgments or actions, in order to demonstrate that deliberation must be constituted by *ēthos* and *pathos* (without which practical deliberation would remain indeterminate), my argument rests on a faulty premise.[38]

Against claim (a) I argue that perception itself is constitutive of the deliberative process and not a separate, discrete moment. If I am correct, then even if the role of *ēthos* and *pathos* were restricted to perception, they would still be constitutive of deliberation. This rejoinder, if successful, addresses claim (b) as well. But I further argue that in any case both the excellence in deliberation and the excellence in perception that are necessary to *phronēsis*[39] are partly constituted by the proper *ēthos* and *pathos*.

Nancy Sherman's argument is relevant here. She argues that one important way in which the proper *pathē* help constitute *phronēsis* is that perception itself can occur via the emotions. What is required is a person of a certain character, who has the kind of emotional makeup that makes her sensitive to the relevant moral features of the particular situation. Without the proper virtues of *ēthos*, and the concomitant *pathē* that constitute those virtues, the agent may simply fail to see what the occasion, in its particularity, calls for. For Sherman, seeing properly via the emotions, and subsequent action accompanied by the proper emotional responses, is part of exercising *phronēsis*.[40]

It might be objected that Sherman's point can be conceded while still restricting the role of *ēthos* and *pathos* in *phronēsis* (that is, the role, which cannot be fulfilled by abstract rules, of rendering the agent sensitive to the particularity of the situation) to perception without extending it to deliberation per se. One might concede that *ēthos* and *pathos* play a role in rendering determinacy but not that this has to do with deliberation. If the import of *ēthos* and *pathos* enters only at the level of perception and not deliberation, then they are simply instrumental to, and not constitutive of, practical deliberation. Indeed, Sherman herself suggests this restriction, saying that when an agent "fails to notice unequivocal [ethical] features of a situation ... [it] is not that she has deliberated badly, but that there is no registered response about which to deliberate."[41]

Two things must be shown to complete the argument that the proper *ēthos* and *pathē* are constitutive of the process of deliberation itself – that is, that the practical deliberations of the phronetic person are led in part by the right ethical emotions and character and not simply by right logical demonstration (which, being indeterminate, would fail to issue forth in determinate practical actions). First, it needs to be shown that *ēthos* and *pathos* make a difference to the outcome of deliberation, that is, that they help to render determinate judgments (for example by determining the range of viable arguments). Second, it needs to be shown that they also make for a different process of deliberation. I propose to show this by deepening the analysis of the parallel between rhetoric and *phronēsis*.

How Ethos and Pathos Function in Deliberation

I have already cited passages in which Aristotle indicates that in order to achieve the guiding end of rhetoric (finding the means of persuasion), the speaker must gain the trust of the audience.[42] According to Aristotle, gaining this trust requires the speaker to have quite extensive knowledge of the audience's particularities of his. To find the means of persuasion, the speaker must be intimately familiar not just with the common subjects of deliberation and the customs, legal usages, and constitution of the particular regime, but also with the audience's particular character or *ēthos*, its circumstances, and its emotional makeup, which includes its state of mind, the object toward which its emotions are directed, and for what reasons. That is why Aristotle spills so much ink on these matters.[43]

Recall that *phronēsis* required sensitivity to, and proper perception of, the morally salient particular features of the circumstance at hand. Now it appears that in aiming at rhetoric's guiding end of finding the means of persuasion, the speaker must demonstrate, via his arguments, an adequate grasp of salient particular features of the situation – namely, the constitution, customs, *ēthos*, and *pathē* of his audience. So in seeking to persuade, the rhetorician is required to emulate the virtuous dispositions of the good seer envisaged by Sherman. The point is that the constitutive structure of the *technē* imposes on the rhetorician the necessity to acquire, as a matter of artful skill, what is in the *phronimos* a matter of internally generated virtue; this constitutive feature of rhetoric is one important reason why it has the propensity to yield outcomes consistent with *phronēsis*. Thus the structure of the public deliberative process itself,[44] and the incentives that structure imposes on the rhetorician, constrain the arguments articulated in deliberation such that the arguments must demonstrate an adequate perception of (what turn out to be ethically relevant) particulars.

So the council does not first deliberate and then render a determinate judgment by the subsequent application of good perception of particulars; rather, the process of deliberation itself proceeds via a perception of particulars that is good enough to enable the speaker to persuade.[45] We have thus uncovered two ways in which *ēthos* and *pathos* are constitutive of the process of rhetorical deliberation: we are dealing with both (1) the character and emotions of the speaker/persuader, and (2) the character and emotions of the audience/persuadee.

In the first case, the character and emotions of the speaker enter the deliberative process via perception. As I have just argued, in order for the rhetorician to find the arguments that persuasively use the *pisteis* of *ēthos* and *pathos*, he must adequately perceive the particularities, such as character and emotions, of the audience. But the adequate perception of these relevant contextual features involves, as Sherman has shown, the emotions and character of the speaker himself. In the second case, the *ēthos* and *pathos* of the audience are directly constitutive of the deliberative process in two ways. First (2.1), in the way just shown, the emotions and character of the audience combine, as *pisteis*, in part to determine the trajectory of arguments the speaker can successfully advance in the process of deliberation, and thereby shape the final outcome. Second (2.2), these particular characteristics of the audience are invariably ethically relevant data that can also buttress premises in the strict logical demonstrations of the *pistis* of *logos* within practical deliberation.[46]

So, in rhetorical deliberation at least, perception cannot be separated from the process of deliberation because the arguments that are persuasive in deliberation itself require demonstration of that perception – and note that this is true because *ēthos* and *pathos* are two sources of *pistis* in rhetoric.[47] My suggestion is that the same holds in the case of monological phronetic deliberation. If, as I have argued, Aristotle's optimism about rhetorical deliberation hinges on a structural parallel with phronetic deliberation – specifically, that both are constituted by *ēthos*, *pathos*, and *logos* – then our account of how *ēthos* and *pathos* constitute rhetorical deliberation can be expected to illuminate their role in phronetic deliberation as well. Of course to demonstrate this is not to "prove" that *phronēsis* and rhetoric share a parallel structure; but if Aristotle's account of *phronēsis* is exclusively and plausibly illuminated by reference to this proposed parallel, then we have further grounds for favouring the proposed interpretation. But how could the account of rhetoric just given translate into an account of monological deliberation and *phronēsis*? Obviously here the persuader and persuadee are one and the same person.[48] But the distinctions just drawn with respect to rhetoric do help analyze the different aspects of *phronēsis*.

Parallel to the first case above (1), the emotions and character of the deliberator qua persuader (or proposer of arguments) enter the deliberative process via their role in adequate perception. The analogy with the rhetorical context suggests that part of what must be adequately perceived with the help of *ēthos* and *pathos* are the particular emotions and features of character of the agent himself ("know thyself"; this is part of point 2.2 below).

Parallel to the second case, first (2.1), the emotions and character of the deliberator qua persuadee might be said partly to shape the trajectory of arguments that the deliberator adduces to himself by helping to determine which validity claims he finds persuasive and which not. For example, a man of cowardly character may find it difficult to persuade himself that the monstrous apparition is in fact an illusion, or that the ugly insect is harmless. Second (2.2), the emotional makeup and character of the deliberator may be ethically relevant as premises in logical demonstrations the individual considers. For example, feeling great affection for a friend may be a good reason to give special consideration to the friend's welfare.

More generally in this case (2.2), the emotional makeup and character of the person can be said to be something like a repository or memory of the wisdom of past experience (*empeiria*), which the agent may consult during the course of practical deliberation. Why? This brings us full circle to the original point with which this chapter began. Faced with the indeterminacy of abstract *logos*, not all considerations that are ethically relevant to a particular situation can be gleaned from a set of codified abstract principles (as discussed in the first section above). Now we can see another reason why for Aristotle *ēthos* and *pathos* help render determinacy in particular practical circumstances. One's character and emotional dispositions may embody the uncodifiable wisdom of past experience, experience necessary to enable practical deliberation to take account of particularities. Consider the following: "Nor is *phronēsis* about universals only. It must also come to know particulars, since it is concerned with action and action is about particulars. Hence in other areas also some people who lack *epistēmē* but have *empeiria* are better in action than others who have *episteme*"; and "*phronēsis* is concerned with particulars as well as universals, and particulars become known from *empeiria*."[49] Consulting how I feel about taking a course of action may provide me with important insight about its ethical validity if my character and emotions are virtuously formed – insight based on my previous experience that is unavailable in the form of an abstract set of principles codified in *logos*. Consequently, *logos* in the broad sense includes both *ēthos* and *pathos*. This is why Aristotle says that the existence of the "passionate element" in the human soul means that "he will deliberate in finer fashion concerning particulars [or: in particular cases]."[50] The parallel with *nomos* is almost exact. For just as the *ēthos* and *pathos* of a *phronimos* form a repository of the uncodified wisdom of past experience, which supplements his abstract *logos* in the narrow sense, so too unwritten *nomos* and the *epieikeia* associated with it represent a repository of uncodified experience that supplements the written law.[51]

This suggests why the perception objection is misguided. Perception and deliberation are not discrete events: perception is constitutive of the deliberative process, and the *ēthos* and *pathos* of the deliberator qua persuader are constitutive of that perception, and thereby of the deliberative process. Furthermore, the *ēthos* and *pathos* of the deliberator qua persuadee are directly constitutive of the deliberative process, in providing *pisteis* that determine the range of potentially persuasive arguments.

Subjectivism and Deception

Should we celebrate or should we fear the role that Aristotle assigns to *ēthos* and *pathos* in practical deliberation, and in *logos* more generally? I want to take this question up specifically with reference to two issues: first, the problem of subjectivism that seems to loom behind this account of phronetic practical reasoning; and second, the problem of deception that arises in the case of rhetorical-political deliberation. Having up to now made an exegetical argument about the logic of Aristotle's position, I want to shift gears and show why the position I attribute to Aristotle is philosophically interesting.

First, the question of subjectivism. Imagine a phronetic person engaged in practical deliberation, deciding whether to chastise severely a friend for a wrong he has committed against her. Let us also assume that, among other things, the phronetic person must balance the chastisement demanded by righteous justice with the forgiveness that friendship demands. My argument has been that on Aristotle's account, the phronetic person cannot, in the heat of the moment, settle matters for herself by a purely logical demonstration appealing to abstract principles. Ultimately, her decision of whether to chastise will rightly be informed in part by what she feels emotionally is the right course of action, and since the dispositional nature of those emotions will be shaped by her virtuous character, those feelings provide an invaluable ethical guide. This sort of account invites the charge of subjectivism: to the extent that the Aristotelian deliberator relies on how she feels in order to decide the ethical course of action, and is incapable of coming to the same conclusion by strictly logical deduction articulable in language, to that same extent "ethical" action seems to lack articulable, intersubjectively contestable (rational) grounds. It appears to register simply the subjective preferences of an individual subject.[52]

But to say that the phronetic person in these particular circumstances is incapable of deciding and acting solely on the basis of logical demonstrations is not to say that she is incapable, after the fact, of articulating a retrospective justification for the emotions that contributed to her decision or action. She is, and this reflexivity about one's emotions is an important part of being an ethical being. Hence the subjectivism charge falls short. But if, furthermore, the appeal to the emotions is retrospectively translatable into a rational-codifiable account, then it would seem that the phronetic person has relied on her emotions to fill out her practical deliberation not because *logos* in the restricted sense is indeterminate per se, as I have argued, but rather because the abstract principles that were available to her were simply incomplete. After having had this practical experience, and having provided a retrospective rational justification, the phronetic person can revise and fill in her abstract principles to cover the offending case, which shows that, contrary to the thesis advanced above, practical deliberation need not in principle rely on the emotions.

This second objection misses the spirit of the Aristotelian account. First, to say that the emotions are rationally justifiable is not to say that all their content is fully translatable into a rational account. Second, by rational justification I mean intersubjectively contestable in discourse – "rational" does not collapse into logical demonstration here. In other words, rational justification is rational in the broad sense that includes *ēthos* and *pathos*. The point is that the emotions themselves are not purely "subjective" but intersubjectively communicable, criticizable, defensible, and so on – in part thanks to the *ēthos*- and *pathos*-dimensions of language – even if not fully articulable in the propositional form of a logical demonstration. Third, the reflexive appeal to reason may never be complete; the retrospective justificatory narrative may be in principle interminable, for there may always be more to say. Fourth, and most important, when I say that the phronetic person can now retrospectively provide a rational justification for her emotions, this is not because she has simply filled out the details of her previously underspecified, but in principle fully specifiable, set of abstract principles. Rather, her retrospective rational justification is now possible because her ethical vocabulary has changed to account for the recent practical experience. But this change in vocabulary may also result in a loss: some ethically relevant features previously covered may be obscured by the new ethical vocabulary, features whose ethical import can subsequently be covered only by the lingering emotional dispositions that the phronetic person's character maintains as a reminder of the now-distant experiences that partly informed her previous ethical vocabulary. Ethics does not collapse into mere subjectivism; nor can it be reduced to an abstract theoretical system of general laws codified in language.

The second question is that of deception, which has ramifications for theories of democracy, especially ones that emphasize deliberation. A deliberative conception of democracy privileges the conditions of communication in the polity for analysis and locates the legitimacy of democracy in free and unfettered communicative processes of political discourse, open to participation by all citizens and meeting various normative criteria.[53] In part, the problem to which Aristotle's account alerts us arises from the limitation of the comparison between rhetoric and phronetic deliberation: structural similarity, it will be recalled, is not sufficient to ensure a consistency of outcomes.

In Book 1, Chapter 2 of *On Rhetoric*, speaking of *ēthos* as a *pistis*, Aristotle explicitly says that the persuasive effect "should result from speech, not from a previous opinion that the speaker is a certain kind of person."[54] This raises the issue of whether the apparent *ēthos* presented in speech is the real *ēthos* of the speaker. This is in part the question of the rhetorician's ability to deceive the audience and falsely gain its trust by simply creating an appearance of *phronēsis* and virtue, even when the rhetorician's character actually lacks these qualities. Indeed, the artful or rhetorical *ēthos* and the real or practical *ēthos* of the speaker may be quite at variance.[55] What persuades is not the *phronēsis* and real *ēthos* of the speaker but the *phronēsis* embodied in the argument itself. As Eugene Garver argues, "The *Rhetoric* licences inferences from argument to artificial *ēthos* but bars further inferences from artificial *ēthos* to real *ēthos*."[56] The problem is that by playing on the *pathos* of the audience, the rhetorician might be able to deceive the audience about not just his own real *ēthos* but the *ēthos* embodied in the speech, and so persuade in a way contrary to ethics and right reason.

In fact, the *ēthos* of the speaker is not the only problem; equally at issue is the *ēthos* of the crowd. The character of the audience and its emotional makeup help dictate what sorts of argument will be persuasive. Political deliberation proceeds by persuasion, and if what will be persuasive depends on the *pisteis* of *ēthos* and *pathos*, then the particular *ēthos* and *pathos* possessed by the audience will in part determine the course of the argument. The problem with the unvirtuous crowd is that a popular leader (*dēmagōgos*) can persuade it via flattery, since "tyranny is friendly to the base, for they delight in being flattered."[57] Hence Aristotle associates the growth of rhetoric with demagoguery[58] – and demagoguery is dangerously similar to a tyrannical regime. Recall that the goodness of rhetoric must be judged by the external standard that the architectonic discipline of *politikē* provides; if rhetoric is not ethical, then it fails to contribute to the proper ends of the *polis*.

These two problems of deception, which form the basis of Aristotle's critique of democracy as demagoguery, bring into full view the dilemma faced by democracy. On the one hand, the *pathos* constitutive of deliberation helps the proper treatment of particulars,[59] and because of the insufficiency of abstract rules, deliberation is an inevitable and necessary component of political life. Moreover, by turning collective deliberation over to an art of rhetoric, political institutions can capitalize on the art's internally generated technical propensity to yield outcomes consistent with phronetic deliberation, in order to lower the virtue bar necessary for successful politics. On the other hand, leaving matters open to deliberation risks abuse – in part because deliberation is a matter of *pathos*, and *pathos*, though beneficial for the treatment of particulars, may nonetheless lead the argument astray. The problem is particularly acute for rhetorical deliberation if rhetoric bypasses the demanding ethical requirements of *phronēsis*: at least the virtue of *phronēsis* requires the right kind of *pathē* constitutive of the right kind of *ēthos*.

At this point, Aristotle appears to suggest another institutional-political remedy: a multitude of persons deliberating is less susceptible to being led astray by *pathos*. He writes, "The multitude is more incorruptible than the few. The judgment of a single person is necessarily corrupted when he is dominated by anger or some other passion of this sort, whereas it is hard for all to become angry and err at the same time." But he qualifies this remedy in the next sentence, seeming to take back what has just been given: "This is certainly not easy for many, but if there were a number who were *both good men and good citizens,* is the one ruler more incorruptible, or rather the larger number who are all good? Is it not clear that it is the larger number?"[60]

The implication seems to be that the multitude must be virtuous to be preferred. The locution "both good men and good citizens," where both coincide, is Aristotle's way of referring to aristocracy: rule of the virtuous. So now it looks as if unless the multitude engaging in deliberation – both the rhetorician and the audience – possesses virtue, the propensity of rhetoric to yield outcomes consistent with *phronēsis* will be effectively undermined, i.e., the virtue bar is not being lowered after all. If the multitude's *ēthos* is not virtuous, then the pursuit of the guiding end of rhetoric, to find the means of persuasion, will not serve the ultimate end of the *polis* identified and elaborated by *politikē: eudaimonia.*

I submit that this requirement is in part the reason why *phronēsis* is, for Aristotle, the paradigm virtue of the individual qua ruler.[61] It is important to note here that it is not just the speaker who is a ruler – "ruler" refers to the entire deliberative body. In other words, ethical rhetoric appears to require that *phronēsis* obtain not just in the rhetorician but additionally in the audience that also makes up the ruling body. The audience must be phronetic not because this enables them properly to infer the real character of the speaker from the artful character embodied in his speech – this possibility is barred – but because the audience's virtue or lack thereof dictates the nature of the available means of persuasion (and whether or not they provide the speaker with incentives in favour of ethical rhetoric).

Unfortunately, the need for a phronetic audience appears to undermine the possibility of a political form of deliberation that can bypass the onerous ethical requirements of *phronēsis* while still yielding good outcomes. The political implications would not be heartening for democratic theory if ethical political deliberation were to depend on the entire body's possessing virtue. "This is certainly not easy for many," as Aristotle lamented.

Liberalism's proposed response to this problem is to impose constitutional constraint on democratic majorities; but Aristotle's argument demonstrates why this proposal falls short: deliberation is ubiquitous. Aristotle's ideal solution to the dilemma is aristocracy. There is much reason to doubt that Aristotle thought that this solution was available in practice, and it is certainly not available to the democratic theorist who rejects the hierarchical aspects of Aristotle's worldview. Liberalism's answer has been judicial review (by "virtuous" aristocrats called judges?), which itself serves to highlight the tension between democracy and liberalism. Yet the dilemma – between the need for deliberation and the threat of de facto tyranny where the deliberators lack virtue – remains, and tyranny is not an acceptable alternative for modern democrats either. So Aristotle's critique cannot be ignored.

Virtue and Democracy

Nonetheless, an analysis of the Aristotelian notion of rhetoric also provides resources for lowering the virtue bar for successful, ethical rhetoric. Although at first blush it appears that rhetoric cannot be ethical unless everyone who is engaged in political deliberation – speaker and crowd – is of virtuous character to begin with, this severe conclusion is attenuated by several Aristotelian considerations.

First, Aristotle mitigates the conclusion that everyone in the audience must possess full virtue accompanied by *phronēsis*, by appealing to the notion of *sunesis:* a capacity to judge well "on a question that concerns *phronēsis*" when someone else speaks.[62] Stephen Halliwell rightly says that "*sunesis* is of general political importance; it provides a broad ground of civic deliberation. Although, on a normative view, *phronēsis* too is called for by the whole apparatus of political deliberation and judgment, a realistic appraisal of actual constitutions will presumably conclude that this is a virtue to be expected more in exceptional practitioners than in typical audiences of rhetoric."[63]

Second, a phronetic rhetorician can, when faced with an unvirtuous crowd, attempt to persuade the audience by appealing not to the virtues that the crowd actually holds now but to an ideally virtuous image of the crowd which the orator rhetorically paints and inspires the crowd to emulate. Thus, the creative act of persuasion would both persuade the audience of an ethical outcome and simultaneously inspire the listeners to become an audience who would indeed choose that outcome.

Similarly, the structure of the rhetorical situation may serve to mitigate, to some extent, the fully phronetic virtue required of the rhetorician himself. Where the speaker simply has goodwill (*eunoia*) toward the audience, he already has a motive to attempt to secure a right outcome. But the structure of the rhetorical situation requires such a speaker, in order to deploy the *pistis* of *ēthos*, to represent himself in his speech as virtuous – a creative representation which in turn can inspire the good-willed speaker himself to rise to his own rhetorical model. Thus the internal requirements of the *technē* of rhetoric itself can serve not just to impose an emulation of virtue, as I have argued up to this point, but also actually to instil virtue in both the speaker and the crowd to a degree not previously realized. The creative act of rhetoric has the potential both to produce the good reasons for a particular course of action and also to change the character of the deliberators. Of course, this is only a potential.

The problem that an Aristotelian analysis of political deliberation identifies admits of two solution-seeking strategies, both of which have their resonance in Aristotelian thought. An institutional response looks to the ways in which the structuring of discursive incentives may help to overcome some of the shortcomings of the virtues of the deliberators themselves – for example, by placing institutional constraints on the types of discourse that enjoy legitimacy in political deliberative settings. (The law courts provide perhaps one of the most institutionalized examples of a structured setting for deliberation.)[64] Such an institutional approach is necessitated by the fact that the problem of deception, while admitting of attenuation, can never be fully resolved. But Aristotle's critique also suggests that an institutional response, by itself, is insufficient, just as constitutional constraint is insufficient.

The second, perhaps complementary, strategy must address the virtues of the deliberators.[65] An analysis of rhetoric highlights the role that a phronetic leader qua rhetorician can potentially play in instilling such virtue. If democracy is committed to the universal participation of all citizens in the political process, then Aristotle's critique makes the virtues a central component of citizenship and points to the fundamental importance of education in political life. For Aristotle, this education is not limited to a purely "civic" education but must be an ethical one. This, of course, raises a host of thorny problems, such as who will be granted the power to determine the nature of that education and how such an education could be philosophically compatible with liberal freedoms, but Aristotle's critique shows that these problems cannot simply be bracketed.

In the end Aristotle tips his hat in the direction of the institutionalists by pointing to the importance of the laws themselves in the education of the citizenry, and in securing leaders inclined to use the creative powers of rhetoric to transform themselves and their audience for ethical ends. So Aristotle's ethical and political thought suggests that, contrary to the assumptions of many commentators today, institutional constraints on the citizenry are an insufficient basis for democracy.

Troubling Business: The Emotions in Aquinas' Philosophical Psychology

Leonard Ferry

Most of us will agree that the emotions are troubling business. Our everyday intuitions about the moral value of emotion seem confusingly contradictory. On the one hand, the grammar of emotion is riddled with expressions that suggest both the passivity of agents *before* and the limited nature of their control *over* their emotions. We speak of being "overcome" with anger, of lurching "unthinkingly" at another in a rage, and of ranting "uncontrollably." Fear "strikes" us suddenly and we freeze.[1] Despair "washes" over and "overwhelms" us. Lovers are said to have "fallen" into that most happy of states. And when things go awry, they can be "drawn" toward jealousy. Indeed, their jealousy might prove so powerful as to manufacture its own warrants with the aid of imagination. However strange it may sound, such descriptions conceive of the emotions as external forces that act on or through us. They threaten to undermine rather than underwrite those parts of the self that we see as securing our moral identity, such as judgment, belief, and rationality.

On the other hand, talk of praise and blame extends in ordinary language not only to those actions we designate as rational but also to those we see as intimately tied up with the passions. We blame the cad who is oblivious to the suffering of others for not experiencing that most basic of passions, compassion. We admire those whose hope encourages them to aspire to greater achievements; but we are critical of those who we believe are sentimentally attached to a groundless hope. Similarly, although there are moments where levity is simply uncalled for, at other times associates who fail to have it strike us as "boorish and stiff."[2] The overbold are thought foolish, as are those who delight in trifles. In cases such as these, the emotions appear to be parts of the self that can be summoned or restrained in response to the specific circumstances of the agent. More importantly, emotions seem to speak to the overall character of the person, inasmuch as the person who fails to respond appropriately is understood to be somehow defective. The person who fails to see when a joke is inappropriate is the type of person whose judgment is untrustworthy. Seen from this point of view the emotions appear internal to, controllable by, and constitutive of the self. Thus the emotions seem, even if only indirectly, to belong to that class of things (actions, beliefs, judgments) that are up to us in the sense that we accept responsibility for them.

Matters are equally complicated when emotion enters into the assessment of the acts and characters of others in a legal framework. In criminal law, for example, agents are often described as having acted under the compulsion of an emotion, such as anger or jealousy. And, because we think of the emotions as happening to us as opposed to things over which we exercise control, they are allowed to enter into sentence deliberations as mitigating factors. Underlying this practice is a conviction that the emotions are somehow external to or other than and different from the agents they afflict. Normally, we reason, X would not have acted in such and such a fashion. It was out of character, something for which X cannot be held fully responsible. Emotions are, therefore, excluded from the normative model of human behaviour assumed in legal reasoning, where culpability is linked closely with rationality. To act out of or under the influence of an emotion is to fall short of that ideal and to merit the imputation of limited culpability. Yet we expect juries to be persuaded not only by the so-called facts of a case but also by appeals to their emotions. Each of the passions is examined in detail in Aristotle's *On Rhetoric* precisely to understand how to dispose an audience to be favourable to arguments about the facts. Arousing the emotions of the audience affects how those arguments are judged: "The emotions are those things through which, by undergoing change, people come to differ in their judgments."[3] Indeed it appears possible to arouse in an audience a sufficient amount of indignation toward one's opponent that her or his appeals to pity will go unheard (2.9.1387b16). So it seems the emotions ought to be included in the making of normative judgments, even to the point of determining what is and what is not acceptable. Perhaps no one has been more consistent, and unfortunate, in rejecting such inclusion in favour of exclusion than Socrates.[4]

Given the confused condition of our ordinary language and everyday practices (including those of the law) where the emotions are concerned, the reticence of some philosophers to accord a significant place to the emotions in moral and political thought is certainly understandable. No wonder René Descartes adopted as the third maxim of his "provisional morality" "to try always to overcome myself rather than fortune, to change my desires rather than the structure of the world and, in general, to get used to believing that there is nothing that is completely within our control apart from our thoughts."[5] So too one can understand, even without accepting, Immanuel Kant's absolute division of the moral law from the passions: "Either there is no higher faculty of desire at all or *pure* reason alone must be practical. What this means is that reason must be able to determine the will by the mere form of the practical rules without supposing any feeling."[6] Admittedly, Kant seems less rigorous than either Descartes or the Stoics before him. For

Kant does not argue that the passions must be extirpated. On the contrary, in *Religion within the Limits of Reason Alone* Kant allows that the "inclinations" are not only not evil but can be considered good – though he does not think "good" the source of or relevant to determining the moral law – if "tamed" so as to "be brought into harmony in a wholeness which is called happiness."[7]

More and more, however, philosophers are calling for the inclusion of the emotions in moral and political discourse. From the side of political philosophy, consider the following:

> I contend that passion is, and should be, an important part of political life: it should therefore be established as a central category of analysis in political theory, alongside other key concerns. Rather than questioning whether and how politics can be purified of passion, or perhaps ignoring it altogether, political theorists need to focus our attention on what *kinds* of passion are at play in a given political context, and what the political consequences of people's various passionate desires are. In particular, we need to look not just at how passions for different goods can be fairly and peacefully maximized, but also at the role that the capacity for passion plays or can play in politics. Finally, we need to develop theories about what would constitute politically just and beneficial forms of passion, and how better to attain them.[8]

From the side of moral philosophy, Michael Stocker argues that modern moral philosophy remains unhealthily schizophrenic in its exclusion of emotion from the determination of what we value.[9] Overcoming such schizophrenia is necessary for those of us interested in revaluing earlier ethical traditions, traditions that look to agents as wholes rather than focusing on the morality of their separate acts whether from the perspective of deontology or consequentialism. Inasmuch as these calls to re-examine the emotions have opened dialogues about moral psychology, philosophical anthropology, and traditional moral and political philosophies, they are welcome. But much remains to be determined before we can accept, without due caution, the ambition to have the emotions take up a *central* role.

The immediate danger, it seems to me, is that in attempting to recover the emotions, to rescue them from the margins of normative discourse, we will be tempted either to exaggerate our understanding of them as phenomena in their own right or to ignore our intuitions about the risks involved in the emotions, as registered both in our practices and in our ordinary language. What is needed is further work both at the level of understanding the emotions themselves and at the level of assigning value to them. To those ends I take up the specific problem of our responsibility for the emotions by looking to the rich moral psychology of Thomas Aquinas for guidance.

There are four major sections to the chapter. First, I frame the argument by suggesting that for Plato and Aristotle it was taken for granted that nonhuman animals experienced emotions. This would later become questioned by Stoics, who held the emotions to be identifiable with judgments that only human animals were thought capable of making. Aquinas is closer, in his psychology, to the position of Plato and Aristotle, which means that any account of the emotions will have as one of its truth conditions that the account must explain both human and nonhuman animal experiences of emotion. Second, I examine the components of an emotion that Aquinas identifies, paying particular attention to the apprehensive or cognitive component. Third, I focus on the distinction in Aquinas between the apprehensive and appetitive components of an emotion. I argue not only that the distinction is defensible but that the appetitive component of an emotion allows us to explain the noncognitive or bodily aspect of emotion. Finally, I suggest how Aquinas' analogous use of emotion terms or concepts to describe experiences with similar effects that are caused by different appetitive powers (that is, the sensitive and the rational appetitive powers) illuminates the seemingly contradictory normative intuitions that we have about the emotions by allowing us to distinguish between those that are under our control and those that are not. Many of the disagreements between cognitive and noncognitive accounts of the emotions can be overcome by distinguishing between emotions properly so called and those that are only analogously so.

I aim to furnish a detailed exposition of what an emotion is, in Aquinas' view. Without a relatively clear answer to that question we cannot begin to address whether or to what extent we are responsible for them. The principal finding here is that in Aquinas there is a hierarchical scale of cognitive activities – with mere sensation at its lowest point, understanding at its highest, and perception falling between the two – causally related to the emotions. This cognitive-function scale may then be mapped onto a graduated view of responsibility for the emotions – graduated, that is, in the sense of marking increases in our responsibility for an emotion as the complexity of the cognitive functions involved therein increases. The third section tentatively explores some of the insights into responsibility that can be drawn from the psychology posited in the second section. I suggest that we generally, in speaking of the emotions, treat them univocally when it makes more sense to think of emotion terms as signifying analogous experiences that participate to a greater or lesser extent in rational thought and judgment. Indeed, I find in Aquinas a division of emotions into those, properly speaking, that belong to the sensitive appetite, and those, where a similarity of effects is evident, that belong to the rational appetite or will. Much more work will need to be done on this specific point, but it does seem to offer distinct advantages. First, whether or not we find that the Thomistic psychology is available to us, we might yet hold it worth exploring distinctions within and among the emotions that map onto differences in the cognitive credentials of the emotions themselves. Second, the usefulness of the distinctions we draw within and among emotions might themselves tell in favour of returning to Aquinas' thought as a source of arguments for justifying the same.

Framing the Debate:
What Do Human and Nonhuman Animal Emotions Share?

We can begin by asking ourselves what may at first appear a simple question: what has to be true about the emotions for Aquinas to be able to attribute them to both human and nonhuman animals? To this question, we will need to describe those characteristics of both that are similar and those that are different. Given the nature of the inquiry, the similarities are of uppermost importance, specifically those similarities required to account for the experience of the emotions.

Few indices of the difference between premodern and modern approaches to problems in moral philosophy are quite as clear as is the approach taken toward nonhuman animal emotions. Many contemporary philosophers are eager to ascribe human emotions to nonhuman animals. Much is at stake in the ascription: Jeffrey Masson and Susan McCarthy use it to argue against animal experimentation; S.F. Sapontzis argues from the fact that animals behave in sympathetic and compassionate ways to their capacity for moral activity; Lawrence Johnson takes care shown by monkeys toward other monkeys as a sign of their ability to act from compassion; and Tom Regan argues that the capacity for emotions is yet another mental capacity shared by human and nonhuman animals that entitles the latter to the protections afforded by moral rights.[10] The analogical argument employed by these philosophers is sufficiently clear: if and insofar as nonhuman animals experience human emotions, they are entitled to claims and protections similar to those enjoyed by humans inasmuch as those claims and protections derive from or are related to the emotions.

Not surprisingly, such a top-down argumentative strategy problematizes the relationship of human to nonhuman animals with respect to the emotions, insofar as it assumes an intellectual-evaluative facet to the emotions. Beth Dixon phrases the problem succinctly: "If we settle on an evaluative theory of emotion as the most viable for characterizing emotions as they occur in humans, then questions about the rationality of animals, and their ability to engage in more highly cognitive forms of thought, become central to determining whether or not they share emotions with humans." She faults theorists who put the alleged emotions of animals to use in moral and political contexts for failing to appreciate the complexity of the problem and for relying "on an uncritical or implausible theory of the emotions." Convinced, as she seems to be, that "the most plausible theory of emotions in humans is either an evaluative or social constructivist theory,"[11] Dixon argues as follows: suppose that x is a necessary condition for any emotion experience; now suppose that x is a cognitive activity of a relatively high or complex order, so high that it is indefensible to impute x to animals; it follows that it is also indefensible to impute any emotion experience to them. This disquieting conclusion gives the lie to all of the moral and political arguments that begin by ascribing to animals a capacity for emotion and arguing from that capacity, one that the animals share with humans, to an analogous sharing of rights that humans enjoy. This problem is not quite as new as Dixon seems to imagine, however.

The ancient philosophers did not speak univocally of animal emotions. The Stoics infamously denied nonhuman animals the experience of the emotions, even though they conceded that animals behave in emotion-like ways.[12] In this regard, the Stoics take a much more rigorous approach than does Plato, as indicated by the following passages from his *Laws* and *Republic*:[13]

> If it is the general viciousness which has brought us to a standstill – I say that it is the law's simple duty to go straight on its way and tell our citizens that it is not for them to behave worse than birds and many other creatures which flock together in large bodies. Until the age for procreation these creatures live in continence and unspotted virginity; when they have reached that age, they pair together ... and they live thereafter in piety and justice, steadfastly true to their contract of first love. Surely you, we shall say, ought to be better than the beasts. (*Laws* 840d-e)

> *Socrates:* Then do you think that our future guardian, besides being spirited, must also be by nature philosophical?
> *Glaucon:* How do you mean? I don't understand.
> *Socrates:* It's something else you see in dogs, and it makes you wonder at the animal.
> *Glaucon:* What?
> *Socrates:* When a dog sees someone it doesn't know, it gets angry before anything bad happens to it. But when it knows someone, it welcomes him, even if it has never received anything good from him. Haven't you ever wondered at that?
> *Glaucon:* I've never paid any attention to it, but obviously that is the way a dog behaves.
> *Socrates:* Surely this is a refined quality in its nature and one that is truly philosophical.
> *Glaucon:* In what way philosophical?
> *Socrates:* Because it judges anything it sees to be either a friend or an enemy, on no other basis than that it knows the one and doesn't know the other. And how could it be anything besides a lover of learning, if it defines what is its own and what is alien to it in terms of knowledge and ignorance? (*Republic* 375e-376b)

Not only does the Athenian, in the first passage, attribute emotions to animals; he also allows that they can act in ways that merit terms of praise demarcating specific virtues, like piety and justice. Moving from the lesser to the greater, the Athenian argues from the bottom up: if even animals are capable of such control, then think how much more capable humans should prove. But what matters most for our purposes is the willingness to attribute the emotions to animals without any overt hesitation. Similarly, in the second passage, the wonder Socrates expresses at the behaviour of dogs highlights two features in that behaviour: that dogs act in ways that resemble what we normally describe as the behaviour of an angry *person,* and that the behaviour follows from a *judgment* of the type that Dixon believes cognitive theories are bound to deny to nonhuman animals.

Dixon does not refer to either of these passages,[14] but she does refer, perhaps with consternation, to Aristotle's ascription of emotions to animals: "Curiously, in Books 8 and 9 of the *History of Animals*, Aristotle quite freely attributes to animals a wide range of emotional states, and likens animals to humans in this regard."[15] For example, he writes, "The anthus, the acanthis, and the aegithus are at enmity with one another; it is said that the blood of the anthus will not inter-commingle with the blood of the aegithus. The crow and the heron are friends."[16] Some of these remarks and accompanying explanations seem to be more the stuff of legend and folklore than one expects from Aristotle, but the attributions of hatred and amiability are undeniable. More importantly, the attributions are less of a casual or figurative excess than Dixon's argument seems to require. Dixon holds that (a) if some variation of the cognitive-evaluative theory of emotion is true, and (b) if Aristotle's "moral theory requires a cognitive analysis" of emotions, then (c) Aristotle ought not, in the name of consistency, to have ascribed *human* emotions to animals. Her argument assumes that (d) Aristotle would be as willing to attribute to animals the appropriate and necessary cognitive abilities ("a subject's beliefs, judgments, knowledge, or cultural context"). Yet Aristotle seems less reticent in this regard than Dixon will allow.[17] Early in Book 8 Aristotle asserts that "the great majority of animals [exhibit] traces of psychical qualities or attitudes, which qualities are more markedly differentiated in the case of human beings" (588a18). These "resemblances" extend beyond mere physical structures to specific affections: "in a number of animals we observe gentleness or fierceness, mildness or cross temper, courage or timidity, fear or confidence, high spirit or low cunning" (588a21-3). No less explicit is the extension of something resembling human intelligence: "With regard to intelligence, [animals possess] something equivalent to sagacity" (588a23-4).[18] Aristotle is careful to indicate that the similarities between human and nonhuman animal intelligence are "analogous and not identical qualities: for instance, just as in man we find knowledge, wisdom, and sagacity, so in certain animals there exists some other natural potentiality akin to these" (588a28-30). But he does allow that some of the higher animal forms are capable of "giving and receiving instruction" (608a17).

Framed in starkly oppositional terms as a choice between either attributing emotions *and* the highest levels of human cognitive activity (such as beliefs and judgments) to nonhuman animals or denying them both, the current debate must look on such attributions as those by Aristotle as unfortunate *aporias*. Dixon's argument strikes me as somewhat backwards. She begins with identifying a property unique to human experiences of emotion that makes it impossible for nonhuman animals to share in similar experiences. Aristotle, however, tends to begin with what humans and nonhuman animals have in common, arriving at key differences only after accounting for such commonalities. Assuming as Dixon does that the emotions are cognitive in the sense of being highly complex acts, she must argue that recent attributions of emotion to animals vary considerably in terms of their convincingness. She concludes: "The thesis that animals have emotions may well be a more difficult case to make than has been recognized thus far."[19] Beginning with the assumed rationality of emotion, she is forced to inquire whether animals possess the required cognitive powers to enable them to experience emotion. She finds, quite reasonably, that they do not, and so she refuses to ascribe to them the emotions.

Dixon's curiosity at Aristotle's attribution of emotion to nonhuman animals is, therefore, ignited in part by her reading of Aristotle and in part by her acceptance of a cognitive theory of emotions. She believes that all cognitive theories demand that the emotions be denied to animals – that is, she places a very high intellectual or rational threshold on what is entailed by cognition. She nowhere argues that animals are incapable of forming judgments, but she deems such judgments "essential" to cognitive theories of the emotion. And she claims that Aristotle's account of the emotions is cognitive in just this sense. "In the case of fear," she writes, "Aristotle says that the efficient cause of fear is the thought of imminent danger ... the thought of imminent danger [is] not just contingently associated with these emotions, [it] constitute[s] part of the essential definition" of fear. By "essential" she means to establish that "without the presence of such a judgment the psychological state in question" could not be the emotion. The judgments specified for each of the emotions are their necessary conditions. Since her intention is to question the propriety of imputing the emotions to animals, the missing or assumed premise of her argument, therefore, must be that animals are incapable of forming judgments.[20]

Given that Aquinas, like Aristotle, starts from the common experiences of emotions between human and nonhuman animals, the principal question that the Thomistic account of emotions must answer is, therefore, whether the powers possessed by nonhuman animals that are analogous to human judgment are capable of furnishing nonhuman animals with intentions about the objects that are apprehended through their senses. Stephen Loughlin remarks that Aquinas' attribution of emotions to nonhuman animals is "striking," specifically in the light of contemporary accounts of the emotions, whether evaluative, constructivist, or both, that ascribe rationality to the emotions.[21] In Thomist terms, however, recent concern with whether the emotions can be properly attributed to nonhuman animals must appear irremediably confused. To clarify this, we need to sketch several features of that account in general terms and also look at how these apply to particular emotions. What must be clarified is not how animals got it into their heads, literally, to experience emotions, but how it is that humans and nonhuman animals experience emotions. What property or properties do they share that accounts for the fact that they have the emotions in common? Granting that they have the experience of emotions in common thus requires Aquinas to assign the emotions to a power that human and nonhuman animals also have in common, which he does. Like Aristotle, Aquinas takes for granted that both humans and nonhuman animals experience the emotions.

A simple outline of how Aquinas describes the emotions proves no easy task once one begins to unearth his philosophical psychology. To anticipate the detailed discussion to follow, Aquinas conceives of the emotions as natural and elicited appetitive movements that follow the apprehension of an undesirable or desirable object. Aquinas distinguishes between appetition and apprehension. All created being has an appetite (a tendency, or inclination) to some end that derives from its form. The end of an appetite is its object. For lesser types of being, the appetite is determined by the form, as is true of fire's tendency to rise. But for those types of being that "participate knowledge" [sic] there is a further appetitive power that depends on the apprehension of the object: "This superior inclination belongs to the appetitive power of the soul, through which the animal is able to desire what it apprehends, and not only that to which it is inclined by its natural form."[22] Human appetites divide into sensitive and rational appetite. The former is located in a bodily organ, and is affected or moved by the impression on it of a sensible object; the latter is not so located, nor so dependent on a sensible object. Both are, however, dependent on an object: "What is apprehended and what is desired are the same in reality, but different in aspect: for a thing is apprehended as something sensible or intelligible, whereas it is desired as suitable or good" (ST I 80, 1ad2). The sensitive appetite is further divisible into concupiscible and irascible powers, which are distinguished by having as their objects present or future goods respectively.[23]

Aquinas' Philosophical Psychology:
Human and Nonhuman Animal Emotions
The Soul, Its Powers, and the Passions in General

The account of emotion that I set out here draws primarily on texts by Aquinas, as well as neo-Thomist work. My aim is not to defend my readings as being closer to Aquinas, either in letter or spirit, though there are times when I think this is true, but to construct what appears to me a more adequate explanatory account of the emotions. I turn to Aquinas because his philosophical psychology enables us to differentiate degrees of cognitive activity, not all of which are humanly rational but which furnish an explanation of how both human and nonhuman animals can experience emotions without forcing us to resort to descriptions of the emotions as *either* cognitive *or* not, or to eliminating altogether the difference in kind between human and nonhuman animals. The either/or alternative pays too little attention to the different roles played in cognition by a triad of cognitive powers: sensation, perception, and understanding. Consequently, the either/or alternative forces explanations of the emotions into what cannot but be a frustrating search for evidence that will finally disprove one side of the disjunction. No such evidence can exist if the emotions are, as I believe, properly speaking movements of the sensitive appetite, which is materially embodied, that depend on immaterial *intentiones* within the internal sense powers, particularly the *vis estimativa* (in nonhuman animals) and the *vis cogitativa* (in humans). Speaking analogously, the effects of emotions often are, in Aquinas, used to describe movements of the rational appetite, with the understanding that these effects are not caused in the same manner in the rational as in the sensitive appetite.[24] Furthermore, the search should prove dissatisfying to any Thomist inasmuch as its terms seem to require either a mind-body dualism (assuming the emotions are cognitive rather than not) or a materialistic reductivism (assuming that the emotions can be accounted for without invoking non-material or cognitive properties).

I want to begin simply by spelling out how Aquinas describes an emotion. Let's take hope as an example. In the *Summa Theologica* Aquinas devotes eight articles to the exposition of hope and despair. He begins by pointing out that the species of emotions are determined by their objects. The object of hope is a (a_1) possible (a_2) future (a_3) good that is nevertheless (a_4) "arduous and difficult to obtain."[25] These four aspects are definitive of the emotion, and they help to distinguish it from despair (non-a_1, or unattainable), joy (non-a_3, or present), fear (non-a_4, or evil), and desire (non-a_4, or the good taken absolutely). Since its object is a good under the aspect of what is future and difficult, hope like fear is a passion of the irascible rather than the concupiscible power. All animals move "for the purpose of realizing [their] desires and intentions" (ST I 78, 1). The soul's appetitive powers refer it "to something extrinsic as to an end." The sensitive appetite is divided into two species: the concupiscible and irascible. The concupiscible inclines the natural agent to seek its good and avoid what is apprehended as harmful to it, and the irascible inclines the agent to resist those things which interfere with either of these "concupiscible inclinations (ST I 81, 2). The irascible passions have as their object "something arduous." They are to be conceived of as "the champion and defender of the concupiscible." This entails that the passions of the irascible appetite begin and end in concupiscible passions.

Aquinas illustrates this fact with reference to anger, which "rises from sadness, and having wrought vengeance, terminates in joy." In the third objection to the article, a_i is said to be accidental rather than specificative, but Aquinas replies: "Possibility and impossibility are not altogether accidental to the object of the appetitive power; because the appetite is a principle of movement; and nothing is moved to anything except under the aspect of being possible." That hope as a whole belongs to the appetitive rather than the apprehensive power is addressed directly in the second article. Aquinas undertakes the demonstration by distinguishing the proper objects of each power. The object of the appetitive power is the good and that of the apprehensive power is the true. Movement is characteristic of an appetitive power, and "hope denotes a certain stretching out of the appetite towards good." In contrast, the activity of the apprehensive power is accomplished when "things known are in the knower" rather than when the knower is attracted to or repelled by the object. Still, it is the apprehensive power that actuates the appetitive power by presenting to it its object under its various aspects (a_1, a_2, a_3, etc.), which means that "hope is a movement of the appetitive power ensuing from the apprehension of a future good, difficult but possible to obtain." The object as apprehended must be seen not only to be what it is but also as bearing some value to the agent apprehending it. But Aquinas asserts only a causal relation between cognitive and appetitive powers rather than a relation of equivalence: "The movement of the appetite takes its name from the knowledge that precedes it, as an effect from a cause" (I-II 40, 2ad3).

In the third article, Aquinas comes to attribute hope to nonhuman animals. He begins with the empirical evidence: "The internal passions of animals can be gathered from their outward movements: from which it is clear that hope is in dumb animals. For if a dog see a hare, or a hawk see a bird, too far off, it makes no movement towards it, as having no hope to catch it: whereas, if it be near, it makes a movement towards it, as being in hopes of catching it." Observe the steps undertaken here: Aquinas begins with what he takes to be experientially undeniable – that is, that nonhuman animals experience the emotions – and proceeds to explain how that can be the case. To account for such activities the sensitive appetites of nonhuman animals, just like those of human animals, are to be understood as responding to "the apprehension of an intellect."[26] Since the experiences are the same, the structures that account for them must also be.

Two features of animal psychology, therefore, call for the attribution to animals of powers outside of and superior to more sensation: (1) the fact that animal activity follows apprehension, and (2) the fact that animals pursue or avoid objects because they are apprehended as being either advantageous or disadvantageous. For Aquinas mere powers of sense are insufficient to account for the second feature, and mapping the apprehensive or cognitive powers of both human and nonhuman animals requires distinctions among sensation, perception, and understanding. Failure to take notice of these distinctions might lead one to attribute to Aquinas a noncognitive theory of emotion. William Lyons makes such a mistake: "Aquinas' account of emotion [is] in terms of impulses or desires, and the accompanying physiological changes and feelings, rather than in terms of cognitive evaluations."[27]

Sensation properly so-called occurs when a sense organ is in the presence of a sensible object to which it is physiologically adapted. The sense of hearing hears the formal object to which it is adapted, i.e., sound, and the sense organs of different species are obviously variously adapted to sense different aspects of the environment. "Analytically precissed [sic] and strictly taken," writes John Deely, "sensation reveals an aspect of passivity wherein mind is open to, dependent upon, and even, as it were, at the mercy of specific elements within the physical ambience wherein it exists."[28] But the experience of phenomena characteristic of sensation (through the five exterior sense powers: sight, hearing, touch, taste, and smell) is only the first level of cognitive activity.[29]

The move from sensation to perception involves the organism in an active ordering of its environment through its interests:

> Mind takes an interest in what is there according to the preferences of the substance of which it is a dimension. These preferences are initially determined by the organism's biological heritage or nature. For what is different between food for a dragonfly and food for a dragon, beyond the difference between a real and mythical animal? The same as the difference between food for a cow and food for a dog, food for a lion and food for a mouse: the biological constitution of each animal determines what, in the whole range of physical surroundings, will provide nourishment and what will not, just as the biological constitution of each animal determines what, in the whole range of physical surroundings, will constitute a threat to the animal and what will not. At this moment the mind begins to *interpret* what the senses reveal. Here is the beginning of perception in its difference from sensation.[30]

Unlike sensory experiences, the percepts that organisms actively form enable the organism to ensure, with at least limited success, its preservation in a largely indifferent physical order. These percepts give a structure and relevance to the external world as revealed through the senses: "Perception adds to sensation's web ... the specific needs and interests of the perceiving lifeform."[31] So the levels of cognitive activity are not discrete and wholly isolated from one another, but perception does involve an increasing abstraction from the particularity involved in sensation proper.

The extent of cognitive functioning at the level of perception is quite broad. From the fact that animal motion seems to follow perceptive apprehension, for example, Aquinas concludes that if animals were incapable of "retaining and preserving" the "species of sensible things," they would be incapable of pursuing those same objects when absent (ST I 78, 4). And animals do pursue absent objects. For reasons that we need not go into here, Aquinas holds that a separate power from the sense organs must be responsible for retaining the species or formal objects of these sensations. In a similar way, Aquinas observes that we cannot explain animals avoiding or pursuing each other and other objects solely in terms of the effects of these objects on the senses: "The sheep runs away when it sees a wolf, not on account of its color or shape, but as a natural enemy; and again a bird gathers together straws, not because they are pleasant to the sense, but because they are useful for building its nest" (ST I 78, 4). To explain such behaviour Aquinas attributes to animals the ability to form intentions. All higher forms of animals, human and nonhuman alike, are capable of perceiving intentions. If it were true that the pleasure and pain of mere sense experience were sufficient to account for the behaviour of the sheep or the bird, it would be unnecessary to add further powers. But intentions – the seeing of the wolf *as* a threat or of the straw *as* useful – cannot be accounted for by the immutation of a sense organ that Aquinas thinks explanatory of sensation. Indeed, he explains the need for the "common sense" by pointing out the inability of the exterior senses to handle more than their proper forms, "Neither sight nor taste can discern white from sweet: because what discerns between two things must know both" (ST I 78, 4*ad*2). In short, the common and proper senses are sufficient to account for the reception of sensible forms, but insufficient to account for their retention or for the formation of intentions. Aquinas attributes to the higher forms of nonhuman animals the powers of phantasy, imagination, memory, the *vis aestimativa*. To phantasy and imagination he assigns the "retention and preservation" of sensible forms, and to memory and estimative power the preservation and apprehension of intentions. The higher animals are therefore said to possess five interior senses.

With respect to the functioning of the exterior senses, Aquinas denies that there are significant differences between human and nonhuman animals.[32] Although the specific sense organs distinguish different properties in the sensible object, both human and nonhuman animals are similarly dependent on the immutation of the extrinsic sensible object at the level of sensation. He does distinguish between the estimative power of animals and the cogitative power (*vis cogitativa*) of humans, without making the transition from perception to understanding or from sensitive to intellective apprehension, inasmuch as the former are able to "perceive these intentions only by some natural instinct." For humans the ability to perceive intentions consists of a "coalition of ideas" (ST I 78, 4). Yet it is dangerous to overstate the difference that Aquinas hopes to capture here. In fact, he describes this power of human animals as the "particular reason" to distinguish it from "intellectual reason," which "compares universal intentions." The full import of this further distinction is revealed in the reply to the fifth objection. The objection argues that, since the estimative power of nonhuman animals is equally distant from both the cogitative power of human animals and the imaginative power of human and nonhuman animals, consistency requires us either to (1) include the cogitative power (whose operation "consists in comparing, adding, and dividing") as fully distinct from the estimative or to (2) rescind the distinction posited between the estimative and imaginative power. In his reply, Aquinas insists not only that what accounts for the "excellence" of the cogitative power is its "affinity and proximity to the universal reason" but also that this affinity does not amount to a "distinct" power from the estimative power of nonhuman animals. Rather, the cogitative is "the same [as the estimative], yet more perfect than in other animals" (I 78, 4ad5). The greater perfection stems from the "overflow" of intellective apprehension into the human "estimative" power, but the overflow does not create a new power. Aquinas denies, therefore, that the *vis cogitativa* is as relevantly different from the *vis estimativa*, as the latter is from the imaginative power, and so he is not compelled to make the choice between disjuncts suggested by the objection. We need not yet make the leap from the level of perception to that of understanding, even though in human animals the highest level cannot but overflow onto and affect the lower level. Indeed, in his *Commentary on the Nicomachean Ethics* Aquinas likens the estimative power to prudence in humans: "Prudence, which perfects particular reason rightly to judge singular practicable relations, pertains rather to this, i.e., the inner sense. Hence even dumb animals who are endowed with an excellent natural estimative power are said to be prudent."[33]

This similarity between the estimative powers of nonhuman animals and the cogitative power of humans helps to explain how both human and nonhuman animals can experience emotions without either (a) having to resort to a noncognitive theory of emotion or (b) having to attribute to nonhuman animals intellectual powers, powers that Aquinas will want to reserve to, as specificative of, human animals only. What I am attempting to demonstrate thus far is that the "judgment-like" component of an emotion may be accounted for in Aquinas' philosophical psychology without attributing to nonhuman animals the highest of cognitive abilities. It is also the case, however, that Aquinas is able to emphasize the commonalities that obtain between human and nonhuman animals at lower levels of cognitive functioning.

For humans, the intellectual nature, that which distinguishes the human species, enters into and colours even those powers that are common to human and nonhuman animals, including perception:

> Our affective nature is not impressed or swayed by the mere vision of things brought about by imagining; but only by things regarded as good or evil, useful or harmful; and this, in man, presupposes opinion with its positive or negative judgments as to the evil and terrible or the desirable and encouraging. Mere

imagining passes no judgment on things. In brute animals, however, the affective power is swayed by natural instinct which plays the same part in them as opinion in man. (CDA 635)[34]

I hesitate to retain the notion of "instinct" because it suggests an absolute determination of the behaviour of the animals in question. This seems untrue to the nature of the types of cognition that Aquinas attributes to nonhuman animals, and, in context, seems uncalled for: he has, in fact, just remarked that Aristotle "allows wise judgment to 'a few animals,' and not exclusively to man, because even certain brute animals have a sort of prudence or wisdom" (CDA 629). However one might account for Aquinas' reticence in this particular passage, what is essential is that his philosophy of mind is able to account for the similarities between the experiences of emotion without denying such experiences to nonhuman animals *because* they lack the judgment-like components of an emotion and without attributing to nonhuman animals the highest level of human cognitive functioning *in order to* account for the judgment-like component. He does this at the level of perception, rather than understanding, through the operation of the *vis estimativa* (in nonhuman animals) and the *vis cogitativa* (in humans):

> [The passions of the sensitive appetite] obey the reason in their own acts, because in other animals the sensitive appetite is naturally moved by the estimative power; for instance, a sheep, esteeming the wolf as an enemy, is afraid. In man the estimative power ... is replaced by the cogitative power, which is called by some *the particular reason*, because it compares individual intentions. Wherefore in man the sensitive appetite is naturally moved by this particular reason. (ST I 81, 3)

I will have even more to say in a moment about the connection between the sensitive (perceptual) judgment and the response of the sensitive appetite to the same: But first I want to consider briefly a concrete example of an emotion, and for this I turn to another irascible emotion, one intimately related to hope, daring: "Daring, being a movement of the sensitive appetite, follows an apprehension of the sensitive faculty. But the sensitive faculty cannot make comparisons, nor can it inquire into circumstances; its judgment is instantaneous" (ST I-II 45, 4). According to Aquinas, daring, which emboldens one to face danger, is the contrary of fear, in which the agent is overcome by the threat (ST I-II 45, 1). The passion in question is not, however, merely a bodily reaction to some physically present object. On the contrary, it involves, on the part of the organism, an assessment of the object, situation, or events in relation to the organism's flourishing. So the charge that Aquinas' account of the emotions is noncognitive cannot be sustained. Yet Aquinas is careful not to identify the judgment-like component of an emotion – what I am referring to as its *perceptual* apprehension – with the higher level of cognitive functioning of human intellect. In fact, in the discussion of daring, Aquinas distinguishes the passion of daring from the virtue of fortitude, inasmuch as the latter does while the former does not include human intellect. Unlike daring, which requires one "to take note in an instant of all the difficulties of a certain situation," fortitude follows the "one deliberation" of "reason [which] discusses all the difficulties of a situation." Given the limited nature of the cognitive component of an emotion, it is more likely to be mistaken, and the agent flush with daring may find the threatened danger too overpowering. Courageous individuals will act in a more enduring and stable manner "because they face the danger on account of the good of virtue which is the abiding object of their will, however great the danger may prove: whereas men of daring face the danger on account of a mere thought giving rise to hope and banishing fear" (ST I-II 45, 4).

However extensive the similarities are between human and nonhuman animals, the difference in kind is not at issue for Aquinas: "The nature of each thing is shown by its operation. Now the proper operation of man as man is to understand; because he thereby surpasses all other animals. Whence Aristotle concludes that the ultimate happiness of man must consist in this operation as properly belonging to him. Man must therefore derive his species from that which is the principle of this operation. But the species of anything is derived from its form. It follows therefore that the intellectual principle is the proper form of man" (ST I 76, 1). Similarly, in the *De Anima* commentary, Aquinas makes two points central to the contentions advanced here: "If you take away that by which things differ, they are left the same; and if rationality is removed from man he is left simply an animal. Now the difference between intellectual and sensuous cognition is that the latter is corporeal" (622). The specific difference in kind between human and nonhuman animals is determined by rationality; human and nonhuman animals both experience the emotions, though for the latter the appetitive movements are never in response to an act of understanding. The point of these distinctions is that both human and nonhuman animals share powers that enable them to experience the emotions. In the case of the sensitive appetite these powers are identical. With respect to the powers of apprehension by which each forms intentions, however, the powers are similar rather than identical, and at the highest level there is no comparison.[35]

The Necessity of Apprehension

Thus far I have shown only that it is possible to conceive of the emotions as shared by human and nonhuman animals and as natural and elicited appetitive movements that follow the apprehension of an undesirable or desirable object. It remains to determine whether the distinction between appetitive and apprehensive powers is necessary. To take a step back for a moment: "To seek the nature of the soul, we must premise that the soul is defined as the first principle of life in those things which live: for we call living things *animate*, and those things which have no life, *inanimate*" (ST I 75, 1, emphasis in original). In short, living things have souls and nonliving things do not. Put in this manner, the proposed definition seems little more than a tautology. The problem, according to Aquinas, lies with the difficulty of the subject matter itself:

> We should note that when we find things differing both by clear and understandable differences and by differences that are still obscure, we must assuredly take the former as a means to arrive at knowledge of the latter. This was the method used by the philosophers in their study of the soul. Living things differ from nonliving in having "souls"; but because the nature of the soul was not evident and could not be investigated except by way of certain more obvious notes which differentiate animate from inanimate things, the philosophers first took these more evident characteristics and tried, through them, to come to knowledge of the soul's nature. These evident notes are two: sensation and movement. Animate things seem to be characterized chiefly by movement, in that they move themselves, and by having sense-awareness or perception. So the ancients thought that if they could discover the principle of these two factors they would know the soul; hence their efforts to discern the cause of movement and sensation. They all agreed in identifying the soul with the cause of movement and sense-perception. But just at this point also their differences began; for some tried to arrive at the soul by way of movement and others by way of sense-perception. (CDA 32)[36]

When in the second book of the *De Anima* Aristotle restates the distinguishing characteristic of animate beings – that of "being alive" – he increases the complexity of the initial division of sensation and movement by differentiating two types of each: "To live, however, is predicated in several ways; and even if one only of these is present, we say there is life; as, for example, intellection, sensation, or movement and rest in place; as well as the movement and rest involved in nourishment, and growth and decay" (413a20-25). In his commentary on this passage, Aquinas applies the new divisions to the various kinds of plant and animal life: "Some living things, i.e., plants, only take nourishment and grow and decay; some have also sensation, but are always fixed to one place – such are the inferior animals like shell-fish; some again, i.e., the complete animals like oxen and horses, have, along with sensation, the power to move from place to place; and finally some, i.e., men, have, in addition, mind" (CDA 255). Any one of these powers is sufficient for the existence of a soul, and in any conjunction of the different powers each separately constitutes a part of the soul (CDA 270).[37] Additionally, Aquinas notes that, though it does not constitute a "distinct degree of living being," the appetitive power is another form of "vitality" because appetite "always accompanies sensation" (CDA 32). The "higher animals" that have the powers of internal sense experience the passions of the soul in a manner similar to human animals (CDA 32).[38] For Aquinas they are equipped to do so because and to the extent that they are capable of forming intentions to which appetitive movements respond. The intentions are necessary conditions for these movements, but they are not sufficient conditions nor are they identical to the movements.[39]

To recapitulate the argument thus far: Aquinas locates the passions in the appetitive, and so, because he distinguishes the appetitive from the apprehensive, he denies to the passions themselves the highest forms of rationality that recent cognitivist philosophers attribute to them. This denial is despite his view of the passions as intentional, one of the primary properties that contemporary philosophers advance in favour of seeing the emotions as cognitive.[40] Yet my reading of Aquinas' theory of emotions is also "cognitive." By that term I intend to draw attention to those levels of cognitive activity, some of which are shared by humans and higher-order animals and one of which is exclusive to humans (a distinction that allows me, I hope, to preserve the difference in kind without turning the emotions into forces that are wholly unrelated to cognitions).[41] Much, therefore, hinges on the separation of the apprehensive from the appetitive if my theory's characterization is to prove an acceptable account of the emotions at the descriptive level.

Consider now the problem that Aquinas faces with respect to the distinction of appetitive and apprehensive powers. It is objected that the appetite is not a special power of the soul because the powers are enumerated by the difference of their objects, and the appetitive power has the same object as the apprehensive power (ST I 80, 1ad2). Contrary to this argument, Aquinas proposes that these powers are differentiated as a result of the different aspects of the object to which they pertain. In "reality" the object of the powers *is* the same, but as apprehended a thing is either "sensible or intelligible," while as desired it is "suitable or good." This difference with respect to the object as term distinguishes speculative from practical intellect: "The intellectual power which reasons to some purpose in view, and is practical, differs in its end from the speculative" (Aristotle, *De Anima* 433a14). So the "object of desire is always the practical reason's starting point," which means that the practical reason and the appetite share the same object; with respect to movement, however, "since a single effect implies always a single cause of precisely that one effect," the "intellect only moves anything in virtue of appetition" (CDA 821-24). The reason is that practical reason of itself does not bring about movement: it is "essentially balanced between alternatives," unless and until "appetition fixes it exclusively upon one alternative" (CDA 825). Similarly, speculative reason does not move, though particular reason, that power linked with the estimative powers of nonhuman animals in the sensitive soul, is capable of moving (CNE 1132).

Unless some reason can be given for separating powers that (a) relate to the same object and (b) house such similar acts, this separation might prove little more than another infamous scholastic distinction without a difference. The separation is sometimes stated in Aquinas as if it were self-evident: "The cognitive faculty does not move except through the medium of the appetitive: and just as in ourselves the universal reason moves through the medium of the particular reason ... so in ourselves the intellectual appetite, or the will ... moves through the medium of the sensitive appetite" (ST I 20, 1). Apart from the repetition of the fact that the universal does not bring about movement, there are other hints at an explanation. Motion is tied, for example, to inclination, a property that is assigned to the appetitive power (CNE 1134). From a different angle, since the emotions are said to involve bodily change, they are placed in the sensitive appetite, rather than the rational, because only the former is realized in and through a bodily organ (CNE 869 and 1351).

Moreover, in his *Nicomachean Ethics* commentary Aquinas acknowledges that both the intellect and the appetite are passive powers. He quickly points out, however, that properly speaking the passions are more correctly predicated of the appetitive power, and the explanation he offers sheds real light on the necessity of the separation (CNE 291). In the case of perception the thing known "is in the knower according to the state of the knower." The object in this case is drawn to the knower, whereas in the case of appetition it is the appetite that is drawn to the object known, "as the one desiring is inclined to the thing desired." Because passivity is more properly denominated of patients drawn to their agents, the appetitive powers are called passions more so than are the acts of the intellect. The key distinction thus concerns the relation to the object. Two further texts will help to illuminate this point. The first concerns that which the apprehensive power requires over and above the appetitive:

> Something is required for the perfection of knowledge, that is not requisite for the perfection of love. For knowledge belongs to the reason, whose function it is to distinguish things which in reality are united, and to unite together, after a fashion, things, things that are distinct, by comparing one with another. Consequently the perfection of knowledge requires that man should know distinctly all that is in a thing, such as its parts, powers and properties. On the other hand, love is in the appetitive power, which regards a thing as it is in itself: wherefore it suffices, for the perfection of love, that a thing be loved according as it is known in itself. (ST I-II 27, 2ad2)

Although the issue addressed in this passage may appear outside of the scope of our interests, the text points out that the appetitive power alone is incapable of treating the object of the apprehensive power as fully as that object needs to be treated in the order of intellection. The second text proves the need for the separation:

> The natural appetite is that inclination which each thing has, of its own nature, for something; wherefore by its natural appetite each power desires something suitable to itself. But the animal appetite results from the form apprehended; this sort of appetite requires a special power of the soul – mere apprehension does not suffice. For a thing is desired as it exists in its own nature, whereas in the apprehensive power it exists not according to its own nature, but according to its likeness. Whence it is clear that sight desires naturally a visible object for the purpose of its act only – namely, for the purpose of seeing; but the animal by the appetitive power desires the thing seen, not merely for the purpose of seeing it, but also for other purposes. But if the soul did not require things perceived by the senses, except on account of the actions of the sense, that is, for the purpose of sensing them; there would be no need for a special genus of appetitive powers, since the natural appetite of the powers would suffice. (ST I 78, 2ad3)

For example, I want to be able to say of any given object that a person, *P*, is capable of considering the object without necessarily being moved by it. To be able to say this is to create an important space for issues of responsibility to enter the discussion. Note that I do not hold of the nonhuman animal, where human understanding is not possible, that this same freedom exists. But with respect to humans it is possible that *P* could consider a loss suffered by her without experiencing the sorrow that normally accompanies the thought of the loss. *P* can say to herself, "X was someone I loved dearly and someone that I have lost," without necessarily feeling the grief and sorrow that must accompany such a thought in a strongly cognitivist account. And if it is possible to have the requisite apprehension without at the same time experiencing the emotion, the apprehension cannot be a sufficient condition for the emotion. *P* might be interested in thinking about not only her loss but the emotion that her loss normally summons for her, and a great period of time need not have elapsed before she wants to think of the loss as emotional experience, but not as causing the emotion all over again at the moment she thinks through it. That is, she may want to assess the experience that she recently underwent. Though this will not always be possible, even one case is enough to prove that the apprehension is not a sufficient condition. The separation of apprehension from appetition should also help explain how the reverse of this hypothetical situation might arise. Say, for example, that *P* decides to think about her loss as part of working through an essay on the emotions. Though from the Thomist perspective, she should be able to do so without re-experiencing grief, perhaps thinking about the loss causes her to feel it sufficiently to be moved to tears. For the strong cognitivist – the theorist who identifies emotions with judgments[42] – this scenario is impossible: once P makes the thought her own that she has lost someone close to her, she cannot but feel the emotion, for the thought is the emotion. I want to be able to say that what has happened is that the emotion has overcome her, that she has failed to carry out her intention. Again my point is to preserve the passivity that the emotions so often make us feel, without reverting to a noncognitive, mechanical conception of the emotions as exclusively physico-chemical changes.

The aim of these reflections is to suggest that a strong cognitivist account of the emotions – one that identifies the emotions as judgments – will have a difficult time accounting for the fact that, at least with respect to human emotions, the apprehension involved in an emotion does not always prove sufficient to cause the emotion. This furnishes us with a justification for treating the appetitive and apprehensive aspects of emotion as separate, just as the discussion in the preceding section of the chapter gave us reasons to believe that a cognitive or apprehensive component is a necessary condition of emotional experience. Yet Aquinas advances an argument that seems at odds with even a minimally cognitive account of the emotions: "Appetition, on the other hand, can move to action independently of reason, as we see in the case of the concupiscible desire which is a sort of appetite. [Aristotle] mentions this desire rather than the irascible because, unlike the irascible, *it has no admixture of rationality*" (CDA 825, emphasis added). Just before I try to clarify why such a statement does not justify the conclusion that Aquinas is a noncognitivist, let me indicate briefly the context and larger relevance of the passage. The text comes from the *Commentary on the De Anima* at that point at which, as Aquinas says, Aristotle leaves off discussing the mistaken opinions of other philosophers on the topic of "the principle of local movement in *animals*" to present his own theory (CDA 818). Two explanations – "mind" (under which we are to include "imagination" in nonhuman animals) and appetite – seem possible. For human animals mind must mean the practical reason rather than the speculative because these have a "different finality": "[Speculative reason] regards truth for its own sake and nothing else[;] the practical reason relates its knowledge of truth to some deed to be done" (CDA 820). But practical reason is neither necessary nor sufficient for all types of local motion, the point Aquinas makes in the passage quoted, because, as a rational potentiality, it is "essentially balanced between alternatives" (CDA 825). If it were sufficient to cause local motion, it would cause contrary motions, which is an impossibility because agent A cannot move away from and toward object O at the same time. If it is true that only two principles seem capable of explaining local motion, and if it is true that one of these, practical reason, must be eliminated, then we have a further reason to concede the necessity of distinguishing apprehension from appetition.

For clarification, Aquinas refers his reader to the following text in the *Nicomachean Ethics*:

For, first of all, emotion would seem to hear reason a bit, but to mishear it. It is like over-hasty servants who run out before they have heard all their instructions, and then carry them out wrongly, or dogs who bark at any noise at all, before investigating to see if it is a friend. In the same way, since emotion is naturally hot and hasty, it hears, but does not hear the instruction, and rushes off to exact a penalty. For reason or appearance has shown that we are being slighted or wantonly insulted; and emotion, as though it had inferred that it is right to fight this sort of thing, is irritated at once. Appetite, however, only needs reason or perception to say that this is pleasant, and it rushes off for gratification. (1149a25-37)

From the normative perspective there is much in this passage that I want to preserve: the emotions do seem to work in just this way, hastily, with an immediacy that may ensure survival in one situation but may equally lead to remorse in another.

But how does it clarify the descriptive claim that Aquinas has made? The first thing to note is that the structure has not changed in its essentials: both what Terence Irwin in the translation refers to as appetite (concupiscible emotions in Aquinas' terminology, which seems closer to the context than Irwin's translation here) and emotion (irascible emotions, specifically anger, for Aquinas) are appetitive movements elicited by an apprehension. For humans, who seem to be the only species being considered in this passage, the apprehension may be the result of either "reason" or imagination ("appearance"). In both cases a "reason or appearance" brings into the cognitive field an object of desire or aversion *as* desirable or undesirable. In the case of anger, from that appearance a further "inference" is made. Aquinas explains: "The reason for this difference is that the pleasing object has the nature of an end desirable in itself and is like a principle in reference to the conclusion. But damage to be inflicted on another is not desirable in itself as an end having the nature of a principle but as something useful to the end, and has the nature of a conclusion in things to be done. For this reason sensual desire does not move by reasoning but anger does" (CNE 1389). That is, because the irascible passions concern future actions, some inference must be drawn that brings a future state of affairs to bear on the activity elicited by the object: the angered individual must conclude in some sense that exacting revenge will restore justice, and the restoration of justice is the end or term of activity. In other words, with emotions like anger, hope, and fear the immediate activity has the character of means to an end. With the concupiscible appetite there seems to be no need for any further inference, because these emotions are concerned not with possible objects but with those actually present, whether the presence of a loved one or his or her loss. Note, however, that Aristotle continues to speak analogously here ("as though it had inferred"). If when we say that the emotions are cognitive we mean that they require an apprehended object (apprehended as desirable or undesirable), then Aquinas' assertion that the concupiscible passions lack rationality does not undermine my contention that his theory of emotion is a cognitive one.

There is one final reason to distinguish the apprehensive from the appetitive. Another feature of the emotions as they are traditionally conceived is preserved by the Thomist account – that is, the belief that the emotions are significantly connected to the body, especially in terms of the physical changes associated with specific emotions (such as tears with sorrow or heat with anger). From Avicenna's conviction that matter is "more obedient to separate substances, in the production of a certain effect, than it is to the contrary agencies within matter," Aquinas takes the opportunity to not only rebut the position but to clarify the union of matter and form, body and soul: "No change in the body results from an act of apprehension unless there be attached to the apprehension some sort of emotion, such as joy or fear, or lust, or some other passion. Now, passions of this kind occur along with a definite motion of the heart, from which there results later a change of the whole body, either in the way of local motion or of alteration."[43]

In that part of the *Summa Theologica* dedicated to the exposition of the emotions, Aquinas begins the discussion by attempting to map out directly the location of the passions with respect to the soul. The question is divided into three articles that progressively specify the location of the passions in the sensitive appetite. The first article asks whether the passions are properly attributed to the soul at all. Two of the objections allege that the passivity of the emotions is such as to exclude them from the soul. First, whereas the soul is not a composite of matter and form but form only, passivity properly belongs only to matter. Second, since the soul is not moved, it is inappropriate to predicate movement (or passion) of it (ST I-II 22, 1ad1, 2). To resolve the dispute Aquinas offers three definitions of "passivity." Something is said to be passive insofar as it receives something for which it had a potentiality. Properly speaking, however, passive receptivity of this sort, unaccompanied by any form of loss, belongs to the order of perfection. When the thing received occurs alongside the loss of something "unsuitable" to the nature of the subject (as when health displaces disease), the subject is more properly said to be passive. But, when the thing lost is "suitable" to the nature of the subject (as when disease displaces health), the subject is most properly said to be passive. The explanation for this hierarchical relationship among these senses of passivity is explained thus: because passivity consists in a subject "being drawn to the agent" – that is, the object responsible for bringing about the change – that which loses what is appropriate to it appears to be more obviously drawn to the agent affecting it. In other words, in the case of reception accompanied by loss, the passivity must be greater if its actualization results in the loss of what is appropriate to the subject.

Understanding is passive in the first of these three senses, "as implying mere reception, [which] need not be in matter," inasmuch as it is a "potentiality" of the soul (ST I-II 22, 1ad1). In contrast, the passions of the soul are in the soul only *accidentally*, insofar as soul is used to refer to the composite of matter and form, because they involve a "bodily transmutation" – that is, a change in matter – as a necessary condition. That the distinction between appetites and apprehensions enables us to account for the embodied feel of an emotion, its physiological component, provides not only further justification of that distinction but also further reasons to believe the Thomistic theory of emotion a more adequate account of the emotions than either merely cognitivist or merely noncognitivist accounts. I turn now to determine whether it can also shed light on the intuitions about our responsibility or lack thereof for the emotions with which I began this chapter.

Aquinas on Responsibility for the Emotions

The issue of responsibility is intimately connected to the evaluation of the emotions. It is through some conception of responsibility that we generally attach to actions their moral weight – that is, praise and blame are reserved for those actions that are characterizable as involving responsibility, where it entails some form of voluntary activity.[44] For example, I praise Jane for taking the time to carefully prepare for her doctoral exams just as I fault Jim for failing to do the same. Both this praise and this blame presuppose that each had the power to decide how to spend their time. Were I to discover that Jim was disabled by an acute illness before his exams, I would alter my judgment of his conduct. I may even find in his determination to sit the exam, despite the adverse circumstances he had faced in preparing for it, a resoluteness that demands admiration. The illness acts as a constraining condition, to invent a term of art for this occasion, on his freedom to act like Jane, and as such it requires me to re-evaluate his act. With the emotions, it is less than clear how one would apply a similarly skeletal picture of ethical assessment, because and to the extent that the emotions are often conceived of as constraining conditions in themselves.

It is possible for the strong cognitivist theorist of emotion to treat the emotions as similarly constraining activity, but only in a much weakened sense. In "Emotions and Choice" Robert C. Solomon argues that the emotions are judgments. Solomon advocates a very strong cognitivist position, in which the bodily experience, which he calls the feeling component, of an emotion is not necessary. To explain why emotions often lead to actions that we regret later, Solomon argues simply that emotions are "rash judgments" that are summoned in times of "urgency" and therefore tend to be less than satisfactory. This does not make them irrational or bodily, just a limited type of judgment. Because emotions are judgments, the problem of responsibility seems easy to resolve: "Since normative judgments can be changed through influence, argument, and evidence and since I can go about on my own seeking influence, provoking argument, and looking for evidence, I am as responsible for my emotions as I am for the judgments I make. My emotions *are* judgments I make."[45] To insist that the emotions excuse bad behaviour is simply to traffic in self-deception and rationalization.

It does seem plausible that I can avoid some of the actions called for by an emotional response. In my anger I can decide not to lash out. This does not mean that I can decide not to be angered, only that I can decide to control the types of behaviour that are subsequent to and urged by my anger. I can also control the dispositions of my character so as not to be the type of person who feels anger strongly at the wrong times or freely gives vent to anger regardless of the consequences. It is not clear how far we can run with this, though. Is the category of the continent individual a real (or natural) category, not merely a result of poor education? If not natural, is it a habituated category, but no less real for that? If the answer to either of these is affirmative, then controlling our emotions indirectly through remoulding the types of people we are reaches a limit that leaves much out of the account. For some, that is, whether by nature or by long habituation, self-transformation may prove impossible. If it is impossible for some to transform their desires so fully as to live in accordance with virtue, we can at least expect these people to fight against their ingrained (whether habituated or natural) opposition to such a life by acting contrary to the emotions that they feel. Certainly their effort to act in a manner contrary to their passions demands admiration, even if of a lesser kind than that accorded to the temperate person. Again, however, what they would be responsible for or in control of would be the actions consequent to the emotions they feel, not the emotions themselves. To deny to their successes any accolades would be inconsistent (unless we can consistently claim that z, as only an apparent good, is to be avoided and that an agent who denies to herself the hope she has of and the joy she anticipates in experiencing z does not deserve to be praised). And to deny the reality of their experience of emotions that contradict their knowledge of good and evil would be to deny that which calls for explanation.

Striking a balance between viewing the emotions as threats to agency or as intrinsically valuable is only one among the many difficulties that arise where the moral worth of emotions is concerned. Don't we want to praise the individual who is justly angered? That we can speak of someone "justly" angered by a slight suggests that we do, in fact, think of the emotions as integral to evaluations of persons. Yet we have a hard time denying that the emotions at times appear to operate at a level where control over them is out of the question. And, to the extent that our evaluations of actions depend on attributing to agents the freedom to have chosen to act otherwise, the emotions seem somehow just beyond the scope of evaluation.

Aquinas reflects this complex of attitudes to and judgments of the emotions. "Opinion," he writes, "has an immediate effect on our affective nature; so soon as we opine that anything is disagreeable or frightening we feel sad or frightened" (CDA 634). This point is made more effectively in a distinction that Aquinas draws from Aristotle:

It should be said that, although the irascible and concupiscible, considered as such, are acted upon and do not act, however, insofar as in man they participate somewhat in reason they also in a way act and are not wholly acted upon. Hence, in the *Politics* the Philosopher says the reason's dominion over these powers is political, because such powers retain their own activities and do not obey reason completely. The soul's dominion over the body is not royal but despotic, because the members of the body instantly obey the soul so far as their activities go.[46]

In other words, the sensitive power, as Aquinas elsewhere remarks (ST I 81, 3ad2), has in the constitution of the human soul the position of a free person over whom only royal rule is justified. There will be opposition between ruler (reason) and ruled (sense appetite). It is a mistake to deny this source of tension in human action. The powers of the sensitive appetite can be commanded by reason, but they can also subvert reason's command. They can be commanded because they "participate" in reason, but they are not to be identified with reason. The relations are complex, as this next passage suggests:

Since there is in man a twofold nature, intellectual and sensitive; sometimes man is such and such uniformly in respect of his whole soul: either because the sensitive part is wholly subject to his reason as in the virtuous; or because reason is entirely engrossed by passion, as in a madman. But sometimes, although reason is clouded by passion, yet something of the reason remains free. And in respect of this, man can either repel the passion entirely, or at least hold himself in check so as not to be led away by the passion. (ST I-II 11, 3ad2)

The identification of emotions with judgments by strong cognitivists, including Solomon, achieves responsibility by denying this complex interplay of stances toward the emotions. In so doing they sacrifice too much of our intuitive understanding of the dangers lurking *in* the emotions to our equally powerful sense of the importance of the passions to the quality of our lives. Noncognitive theories err in the opposite direction by eliminating the emotions from moral discourse as events over which we cannot exercise any control.

But to establish that the evaluation of emotion is a complex problem is not of much practical use. I want to suggest that in Aquinas we find someone whose moral psychology respects this complexity, while suggesting alternative ways of placing the passions in our ethical understanding. Chief among the ways of making sense of the emotions is seeing them as names for experiences that for all their similarity are also very different.

The Difference in Degree

In Aquinas, there is a scale of emotions. At the bottom of this scale are emotions most properly so-called, which are closest to those experienced by nonhuman animals. But there is never an absolute identification, for human emotions are always to be conceived of in relation to reason. It is impossible, in other words, for humans to fully free even their sense experiences from the influence of reason. At the top end of the scale we move, I suggest, beyond emotions altogether into experiences that (while they have similar structures, particularly with respect to the objects of the emotion-experience) differ in kind. At best, then, we must admit that we use the term "emotion" analogously. This is no small admission, however: it should help to clarify not only what we mean by emotion but also how emotion enters into and informs normative discourse.

The difference in degree leaves room in Aquinas' account for emotional responses to be caused by facets of our psychology that are only indirectly, if at all, under our control, as well as by those that we feel are wholly under our control. At the lowest level of mere sensation, the pleasant and painful seem to be experienced by us as they are by any other animals: immediately and without choice. Higher up on this scale of causes of emotional experiences are the perceptions. These may allow for greater control in the sense that the types of ordering that inform the human organism's perceptions of the world include normative judgments. This is not true of all perceptions, however: there remain judgments of fearful situations that will not be up to the human animal. I do not mean the immediate judgment that x (whether x refers to a person, a thing, or a situation) is threatening. Such judgments are likely always to be prone to error, but they may be such merely because they are, as Solomon contends, made in situations where and at times when most judgments are likely to be hasty and short-sighted. I mean that over and above the hastiness of emotion-judgments (if such there be) lies the structure of animal psychology into which these judgments fit – a structure that requires from us responses for which it seems plausible to deny our responsibility. Some physiological experiences that accompany the emotions cannot be avoided at will, and so are not matters open to moral evaluation. When Aquinas remarks that the precepts of the law do not forbid "first movements of concupiscence," he seems to have this point in mind (ST II-II 122, 6ad3).

The Difference in Kind

At the highest level of the hierarchical ordering that I am attributing to Aquinas, there are passion-like experiences that result from judgments and happen in the will, not the sensitive appetite. It is important to remember that we are speaking analogously: Aquinas' use of the terms denoting the passion-like experiences that are not truly emotions is similar to his use of the terms denoting emotions. He makes this point explicitly in his commentary on Aristotle's *De Anima*:

> Note too that, as desire and cognition are both found in the sensitive part, the same division appears in the intellectual part also. Hence love, hatred, delight and so forth can be understood either as sensitive, and in this sense they are accompanied by a bodily movement; or as exclusively intellectual and volitional, without any accompanying sensuous desire; and understood in this sense they are not movements, for they involve no accompanying bodily change. In this latter sense they pertain even to immaterial substances. (CDA 162)

Consider in relation to this doctrinal point Aquinas' response to the suggestion that the will must be divided into the concupiscible and the irascible – as the sensitive appetite is – because charity is sometimes characterized as concupiscible. He argues that while the will moves toward an object just as does the sensitive appetite, the will moves in response to a "judgment of the reason" (ST I 82, 4*ad*2). Thus there are some passions (passion-like) responses in the will whose causes can be identified with explicitly rational judgments. Aquinas makes the division he has in mind explicit in the response to another objection:

> Love, concupiscence, and the like can be understood in two ways. Sometimes they are taken as passions – arising, that is, with a certain commotion of the soul. And thus they are commonly understood, and in this sense they are only in the sensitive appetite. They may, however, be taken in another way, as far as they are simple affections without passion or commotion of the soul, and thus they are acts of the will. And in this sense, too, they are attributed to the angels and to God. But if taken in this sense, they do not belong to different powers, but only to one power, which is called the will. (ST I 82, 4*ad*1)[47]

So for Aquinas there can be two senses to each of our emotion terms. Each term denotes that passion proper common to human and nonhuman animals, and yet the same emotion term or concept also denotes that experience unique or proper to the human animal, rooted in the will, where the appetitive power takes its inspiration not from the particular judgments of the sensitive apprehension but from the universal judgments of understanding. These latter experiences are wholly up to us, while the former are not. Animals, then, can experience "enjoyment" – the fruition of a task – but only imperfectly; humans experience it perfectly through the will and its choice, for which we are responsible (ST I-II 11, 2).

We see this applied earlier in the *Summa* where Aquinas has to explain the attribution to God of passions, in particular that of love (ST I 20). In response to an objection, he asserts that the cognitive faculty mirrors the appetitive faculty of powers. In the former there is universal reason and particular reason; in the latter there is will and sense appetite. The eventual point of the analogy is to distinguish the use of common terms for acts of both types of appetite. That distinction enables Aquinas to refute the objection, which holds that since love is a passion and since there are no passions in God, love cannot be predicated of God.

The chief point seems to be, however, that sense appetite "is the proximate motive-force of our bodies" (ST I 20, 1ad1). That entails that a bodily change accompanies such movement, which allows Aquinas to distinguish between intellectual and sensitive appetites in terms of whether their acts are accompanied by a bodily change. Acts of the sensitive appetite, accompanied by bodily change, are called passions. Acts of the will are not. Yet the same emotion terms (such as love, joy, and delight) describe the acts of each of the appetites, intellectual and sensitive. This means that we use such terms analogously, not univocally.

Thus love as a passion, an act of the sensitive appetite, is not in God, since God has no sensitive appetite (God has no body); but love as an act of the intellectual appetite, or will, is in God.[48] Obviously God never experiences an emotion. But I want to argue that, insofar as humans straddle the ontological divide between beings, human acts that originate in the will rather than the sense appetite can have the character of the emotions without actually being emotions.

Conclusion

Conceiving of emotion as an analogous term enables us to have the best of both worlds, in a sense. Emotions at the lowest end of the scale, emotions most closely approximating the cognate experiences of nonhuman animals, allow for the least amount of control. They are more closely tied to the body and more difficult to govern in an immediate sense. In contrast, those emotion-like experiences that belong to the will are completely under our control. The bulk of human emotions fall somewhere in the middle to lower end of the scale.

What I am trying to get at is suggested by Aquinas' remarks on passivity in the first article of the first question of the "Treatise on the Passions." The passivity of the passions is regularly regarded as a problem for trying to understand agent responsibility over them. Passivity generally contrasts with activity, and it is with activity that notions associated with responsibility, notions like control and mastery, are usually linked. To say that Barbara is responsible for her actions is to say that she is actively controlling or giving shape to what she is doing. In contrast, when we think of Barbara as being controlled by something external, we use passive sentence structures: for example, "She was blown into the wall *by the wind*." The grammatical structure of the sentence makes clear that Barbara is the patient of the wind's agency. The same seems to be the case with at least some of our passion-descriptive expressions. If we say, for example, "Barbara was driven to despair," the emotional object, here unspecified but readily specifiable, seems to be exercising agency rather than Barbara herself. This is true of those emotions that fall beneath the threshold of the rational appetite. Above that threshold we have emotion-like experiences that follow on rational judgments and do not command but are commanded by the free choice of the will. Only at this level is there sufficient indifference for the will to exercise its freedom and for the agent to lay claim to being wholly responsible. We find, I have argued, the resources to enable us to make sense of our seemingly inconsistent intuitions about the emotions in moral and political philosophy. What needs much greater exploration at this level of argument is Aquinas' characterization of rational appetites in terms of emotion; I have made only an initial step. Equally in need of further exploration is Aquinas' theory of emotion itself. More needs to be said about the theory and its relation to current theories. More also needs to be said about its experiential adequacy. I hope that in this chapter I have provided enough to suggest why those future efforts should be undertaken.

The Political Relevance of the Emotions from Descartes to Smith

Rebecca Kingston

In recent years the discipline of political theory in North America has seen renewed interest in the emotions and passions.[1] In particular, there is concern that liberal theory and democratic theory in general, particularly as it has developed within the Anglo-American tradition, have not given the passions their due place or appreciation in collective life.[2] This inadequate consideration of the passions is said to lead to false understandings of how human beings will act in a political setting, and thereby to false normative expectations of politics and to an unduly critical perception of contemporary political behaviour.

This general line of commentary encompasses at least three differing, though sometimes complementary, views of the relation between contemporary political theory and the emotions.[3] Some share what we can call the neglect thesis, that is, that traditional liberal and democratic theory does not incorporate any discussion at all of the emotions and passions of the citizenry. George Marcus, for example, argues that the lack of theoretical attention to the emotions has led citizens to be cynical of democratic politics and led political observers to make misguided criticisms of the vulnerability of citizens to emotional appeals.[4]

Another line of argument, which we can call the marginalization critique, suggests instead that theorists today have focused almost exclusively and excessively on the dangers of emotions in public life, trying to limit their place in the public forum. For example, some deem legitimate only those passions that can be moderated and sublimated in the form of personal interest. Others regard even this sublimation as a starting point for deliberation and compromise that, in the end, manages and transforms the passions, through either concrete constitutional mechanisms or thought experiments that neutralize to a certain degree the conflict of interests.[5]

The third stance views the passions as indispensable to the foundational commitments of liberalism, while denying their centrality for the procedural requirements of liberal politics. Both Judith Shklar and John Rawls, for example, have recognized that collective passion motivated by public concerns is central to establishing the primacy of liberal democratic commitments. Beyond this, however, the passions are perceived as dangerous to the day-to-day workings of liberal democracy.[6]

How one characterizes the relation between the emotions and liberal and democratic theory may have much to do with the historical perspective through which one understands their development. A longer historical perspective may incline one to deny the unity of liberalism and recognize a vast array of positions that share similar commitments to basic values of liberty and equality but with a wide variety of foundations and justifications. Nonetheless, the perspectives presented above all illustrate that in normative terms liberal and democratic theorists in general have often not had an adequate appreciation of the positive role that emotional motivation can and does play in an ongoing way in public life.

For those who acknowledge this weakness, there is no consensus as to the proper solution.[7] Some argue for the need to reorient ourselves with a new view of liberal democracy that incorporates and appreciates all emotional life.[8] Others look at particular emotions and show how we could improve our understanding or practice of politics by recognizing the potential worth of these emotions in our public lives.[9] Still others, such as Michael Walzer and Martha Nussbaum (and Leah Bradshaw in this volume), suggest that while we need to develop a greater appreciation and understanding of the role of the passions in politics, first and foremost as a necessary foundation for the strength of liberal and democratic commitments, we also need to recognize that some emotions should be considered more cautiously with an acknowledgment of their lethal potential to undermine liberal and democratic values.[10]

When we consider the long history of political theory in the West, it is extremely curious that we find ourselves in such a predicament, because the foundational thinkers of our tradition had a sophisticated appreciation and understanding of the role of emotion in political life. Plato in the *Republic* recognizes the fundamental place of sensibility and desire in all aspects of the human soul, and in Book 8 shows a keen understanding of the public dimension of emotions as key in distinguishing types of political regime. Similarly, Aristotle throughout his ethical and political writings recognized the fundamental place of emotions in politics.[11] It is perhaps incumbent upon us, before prescribing a solution to the problem or even adjudicating among the various solutions offered, to look back on the trajectory of our theoretical tradition. How and why did the passions come to be largely discounted – or at least delegitimized and marginalized – with regard to what is expected of citizens in their public actions and to the standards by which we judge the appropriateness of political outcomes? How did the passions in their public manifestation become so suspect in our tradition?

This question touches on a number of different though interconnected facets, such as the changing understandings of the relation between reason and passion, the changing (and arguable impoverishment) of the moral vocabulary through which we make sense of our emotional lives, and competing paradigms for explaining emotions. In this chapter, I focus on the idea that the rational normative ideal that dominates contemporary liberalism and liberal democracy in the Anglo-American world could only be successful on the foundations of prior suppositions about the political relevance of the passions. Indeed, I suggest that at least three major intellectual moves in our tradition help to account for the current situation: first, the effacing or problematizing of the idea of a passion, shared by a political community, whose cause and object is political life; second, a greater tendency to ascribe the causes of all passion to physiology; and third, a modern emphasis on Kantian rational norms as the sole acceptable framework for political science. The third of these moves in intellectual history was made possible largely through the success of the first, against the background of the second. The purpose of this essay is to explore the intellectual dynamic behind the first two of these moves.

As we will see, by the time of Adam Smith, the discourse of the passions had been reoriented towards a consideration of their social causes, through a linguistic and conceptual framework that drained its previous important positive, collective, and public implications. This helped to cement what I regard as the marginalization of the passions vis-à-vis matters of collective importance and political life. Indeed, an intellectual trajectory leading to the denial of the political relevance of the passions was a necessary condition for the subsequent developments of liberal theory. What I mean by political relevance is not only that a matter of public importance might be the object of emotion from one individual to the next, but that there are discernible patterns in the *type* and *quality* of emotional reaction or disposition towards such matters that are shared by citizens or participants in a political community.[12] I suggest the possibility of a "public emotion" or "public passion" that is largely shared by members of a political community with regard to matters of importance to the whole community, often hinging on questions of their collective identity. Examples include the collective feeling of repentance and republican pride in self-renunciation during Savonarola's reign of influence in fifteenth-century Florence, the public fear felt by the French in the wake of 1789, the fear and anger felt by Americans in response to 9/11, and the public jubilation during the Orange Revolution in the Ukraine. With the fall of this notion of the "public passion" in our intellectual history, the passions became regarded as mere projections of largely internal individual and idiosyncratic causes. This redefined them as a challenge, rather than a contributing factor, to our ideas of political community.[13]

This chapter is divided into two sections. In the first section, I discuss

René Descartes' *Les Passions de l'âme* as an important text for the historical evolution of understandings of the passions, because the text differs in
its basic premises from what I will call "the classical view" on the political
and public relevance of the passions. In particular, Descartes' discussion
of emotional life narrowed the focus to the individual person, as body and
soul, as the central locus for the causes and effects of various emotions. In
consequence, emotions became more and more regarded as mere reflections
of individual states of affairs. This shift serves as an important precursor to
the historical decline of the idea of a public passion. In the second section
of the chapter I sketch this decline in general terms through comparisons of
Thomas Hobbes, Lord Shaftesbury, and Adam Smith.

The Political Significance of Descartes' Les Passions de l'âme

Albert Hirschman has given political theorists a well-known narrative on the
taming of the passions in the Enlightenment period.[14] He highlights the rise
of, first, a theory of countervailing passions as a means for taming the passions
and, second, the notion of interest. But if we review the period of intellectual
history covered by Hirschman's analysis, we can see that in terms of political
life, there was an equally significant move away from exploring the public
causes and objects of the passions toward a focus on their manifestations
within the individual soul. Perhaps the best expression of this new orientation in early modern thought is Descartes' work *Les Passions de l'âme*.

The idea of exploring the political significance of Descartes' treatise on
the passions (written in the final years of his life) may seem puzzling given
that there is no mention in the treatise of matters of public significance.
Indeed, Descartes seems to take great pains to disassociate his discussion
from general matters of jurisprudence by insisting that he is exploring the
passions as a matter of science (i.e., "en physicien") rather than as a matter of
moral philosophy.[15] I will argue that it is precisely this analytical disposition,
as well as the analysis that flows from it, that sowed the seeds of the ideas
that the passions can be thought of as separate from reason and that they are
idiosyncratic, unique to each individual, and therefore not a suitable subject
for broader social analysis.

In the opening articles of his treatise, Descartes takes on the ancient
philosophers by challenging their understanding of the animating soul as
the basis for human psychology. He provides an alternative idea of the soul,
one that is conceptually distinct from the body, though clearly functionally
in union with it.[16] In article 2 he foreshadows the main contribution of his
treatise, which is to suggest that we must look to the agitation of the animal
spirits as the most proximate and external source of passionate motivation,
rather than to the soul itself (or in particular, to the lower part of the soul
as the seat of appetites and passions as well as the more general disposition
that allows the lower part of the soul to dominate the higher) as argued by

ancient and medieval thinkers and their early modern heirs.[17] In article 29 Descartes emphasizes the distinction between passions and the will: while both are excitations of the soul, volitions are caused within the soul itself, in contrast to passions, which remain within the broader category of sensations, or things received into the soul. That said, it is sometimes possible to cause a passion by conceiving of a certain object, but in this instance it is the object and its effects on the senses which are of most importance, rather than the means by which it is brought to the senses (art. 51).

This understanding of the strong physiological component of passionate feeling is why Descartes must abandon a strict Stoic doctrine and recognize the impossibility for human beings to attain full self-command and eradication of the passions (arts. 45-46, 212). The conclusion is almost inevitable that while one set of passions remains common to all humankind, the varying disposition of the bodies within which the animal spirits operate dictate varying responses to the same occasion:

> The same impression that the presence of a frightful object forms on the gland which causes fear in some men may excite courage and boldness in others. The reason for this is that all brains are not disposed in the same manner, and that the same movement of the gland which in some excites fear, in others makes the spirits enter the brain's pores that guide part of them into the nerves that move the hands for self-defense, and part of them into those that agitate the blood and drive it toward the heart in the manner needed to produce spirits suitable to continue this defense and sustain the volition for it.[18]

Factors such as social standing, emotional predispositions, maturation, and education will also ensure that both our susceptibility to passion in terms of its emotional force, as well as the particular passion felt in any given situation, will differ widely from one individual to the next.[19] Still, while Descartes does not consider passions as caused by the soul, they are in some sense attributed to it insofar as we cannot be mistaken about emotional feelings in the way that we can about other sensations. That is, we are angry when we feel angry (though this may impair our judgment in other ways), but we can think we perceive some external object when we are merely dreaming.[20]

Desmond Clarke has argued convincingly that the main impetus for Descartes' new depiction of the human mind and the emotions was Descartes' radical attempt to apply a standard seventeenth-century model of scientific explanation, previously applied to the natural world, to the very centre of concerns in moral philosophy and the philosophy of mind.[21] The dualism attributed to Descartes, in this view, is less an endorsement of a doctrine of two substances in the human person, than Descartes' attempt to articulate the clear limits to his efforts to provide a fully naturalistic account of human thinking and feeling. From this perspective, his concern over the inadequacy of traditional scholastic explanations of human experience and his conviction that the new science was equipped with a better model of explanation were primarily responsible for ushering in a radically new and influential understanding of the nature of the passions.[22]

What is the consequence of Descartes' framework for the early modern understanding of the nature of human passion? For Descartes, human beings are opposed to animals in that humans alone are subject to both reason and passion.[23] In this text Descartes does not explore what intrinsic connection, if any, there is between these two capacities, although his neo-Stoic recognition of the need to manage the passions through a form of cognitive defence does acknowledge a form of judgment linked to passion. Nonetheless, Descartes conceives the capacities for passion and reason as quite distinct.[24] There is a connection between the use of reason to manage the passions autonomously, and the exercise of free will, that Descartes identifies in article 17 as the actions, or active principle, the soul. By his understanding that the will is a force distinct from the passions that can move us to act, Descartes was in a sense upholding a traditional view.[25] But his view that the passions were motivated by forces outside the soul obliterated the possibility of rational affection, that is, the uniting of reason and passion in reasonable emotion.[26] Passion and reason were now not only different phenomena, but stemmed from wholly different features of the human person. Only the assent of the rational will could make them coexist, but never could they be seen as synonymous.[27]

So how is this view a real challenge to the classical view and to the premises of scholasticism which grew from it? In contrast to their seventeenth- and eighteenth-century counterparts, Plato and Aristotle in their analyses of the passions share two fundamental principles: that passions must be understood through their motivational causes in the world, rather than through internalized dynamics, and that passions can be understood as collective and as individual phenomena. First, they recognize that the differing causes or objects of the passions, such as love of honour, money, or truth, are more significant in understanding the nature of the soul and the individual than are physiology and the effects of passion within the person. Indeed, for both Plato and Aristotle the moral worth of the cause or object of the passion determines the moral worth of the passionate feeling itself. In both there is a deep understanding of the passions as ways of experiencing the world. On this basis, John Cooper and Charles Kahn have suggested that interpreters of Plato often have been misled by reading Descartes and Hobbes into Plato's discussions (in particular of his middle period) of the parts of the soul. For both Plato and Aristotle, appetite and spirit are distinguished not by the essential mechanics of motivation (for all parts are recognized to have their own kinds of pleasure); rather, they are distinguished by the objects of their impulses, whether they be truth, honour, or bodily pleasure.[28] As Plato himself writes in the *Republic*: "When someone's desires incline strongly for one thing, they are thereby weakened for others ... when someone's desires flow towards learning and everything of that sort, he'd be concerned ... with the pleasures of the soul itself by itself."[29] Similarly for Aristotle the ethical life involves the proper training of the feelings towards the appropriate objects or appropriate actions. Aristotle's interest in rhetoric stems from an awareness of the central importance of speech in shaping our perceptions and feelings with regard to persons and events in the world around us. So in general terms, for both Plato and Aristotle the cause or object of the emotion perceived in the world is most significant, and we judge passions by assessing the worthiness of those objects.[30]

Pierre-François Moreau suggests that the focus on the nature of passions in the context of the individual soul as objects of knowledge in and of themselves was something very new in the history of ideas in the seventeenth century, starting with Descartes and continuing through Hobbes and Benedict de Spinoza.[31] Moreau notes that the interest of the ancients in the workings of the human soul was always circumscribed by a larger agenda such as the work of persuasion (in the case of Aristotle's *Rhetoric*) or political and social organization (Plato's *Republic*). One can broadly characterize the ancient analysis of the passions in terms of what links them to events and situations in the world rather than wholly internal dynamics.

Another point of historical discontinuity relates to the second principle shared by Plato and Aristotle, that the various possible causes of passion can have a strong collective component and work beyond a face-to-face context. Both Plato and Aristotle recognized that the movement of souls towards or away from certain objects or causes helped to distinguish not only individuals but whole regimes. For these classical thinkers the objects of emotional life worked on populations as a whole. In other words, passion had a public component that helped to identify the social life of the regime with a particular emotional quality and particular hierarchy or set of values. This characteristic can in part be attributed to the Greek term for regime or constitution, *politeia*, which in one of its various connotations refers not mainly to the legal structure of a state but rather to the way of life (or the sociological features, to use modern parlance) by which a community distinguishes itself. This way of life included the manner in which citizens related to each other in affect.

Of course, the ideal regime laid out in Plato's *Republic* is geared toward the fostering of the philosophical life, that is, the love of wisdom. In Books 8 and 9 Plato outlines the four imperfect constitutions, from the honour-loving timocracy through the money-loving oligarchy, the freedom-loving democracy, and the tyrannical regime characterized by the pursuit of the lowest pleasures and desires (544c-d).

Many commentators have taken for granted that Plato saw a clear correspondence between the nature of a regime and the same type of individual soul. Nonetheless, the exact nature of this correspondence seems crucial. Traditional commentators such as Alexandre Koyré take the analogy at face value and suggest that Plato is saying as much about the courage- and honour-based nature of timocracies as he is about timocratic man.[32] In this view the principles that inform the types of soul, whether timocratic, oligarchic, democratic, or tyrannical, also inform the politics of the corresponding types of regimes. More recent commentators, however, have raised questions about the city-soul analogy. Bernard Williams suggests that the analogy is a failure because of its inability to account for the complexity of soul of individuals within regimes, and in particular within the ideal regime; Julia Annas suggests that the political side of the analogy is meant to be illustrative and without any deep significance for the study of politics.[33] More recently, G.R.F. Ferrari has claimed that the analogy of city and soul is a loose metaphor, in the sense that both the city and soul illustrate the same general pattern of internal harmony or discord, but without any intended correspondence between the parts of one and the parts of another.[34] It would seem that if one is to take any stance at all on the lessons of Book 8 one must first clarify the nature and status of the city-soul metaphor in this work.

Is it possible that the political rhetoric of Books 8 and 9, in which Plato discusses the cycle of regimes and the descent from justice of Kallipolis through timocracy, oligarchy, and democracy to tyranny, is purely instrumental, meant to do nothing more than present equally discredited variants of individual injustice? A positive response to this question, as suggested by Annas and others, seems puzzling. While one could argue that the dialogue *as a whole* has more to do with the individual soul than with the city as an analogy for the individual soul, the amount of detail devoted to the peculiar institutional setting of the regime throughout the work, complete with eugenic practices and gender considerations, is completely superfluous if the dialogue has no political message or meaning beyond that meant for the cultivation of the self. This is not to say that a political message need be a full endorsement of the just city as a practical political project.

Furthermore, by Book 8 Plato had no need to carry on with the city-soul analogy if it were merely for purposes of illustrating individual soul formation. In Books 6 and 7 he had already abandoned the analogy to embark on his famous metaphors of the sun, the line, and the cave and thereby to provide his readers with a more solid illustration of the nature of his principles of education and truth. One of the main lessons of Books 6 and 7 is that we should not be content with the rule of reason in the soul as a sufficient condition for justice (as argued in Book 4). Rather, exacting epistemic conditions require the just individual to grasp the underlying foundations of value; the study and mastery of philosophy as the knowledge of the Forms will suffice for the understanding and hence the practice of true justice.[35] From this account, it can only be concluded that all individuals who do not love true wisdom must be equally corrupt, deficient, and therefore unworthy of our interest and attention

So why return to an analogy which he no longer requires to talk about the capacities of the individual soul? The unhappiness of the unjust soul can be clearly deduced from the lack of harmony it will exemplify. Still, in Book 9 our attention is drawn precisely to the politics of these deficient and corrupt souls and the regimes they inhabit, and indeed to a certain hierarchy of corruption among them. What does Plato mean by this? The cycle of corruption can make sense only if the political side of the analogy is more than just an illustration writ large. Indeed, if one looks closer, a logic unique to communities and states is evident from the start of the *Republic*. Despite the analogy between the individual and the city on which most of the argument of the text is based, we are presented with two different frameworks for making sense of the place and need for concord in the city and the soul. The dichotomy between the just soul of the philosopher who alone can see the truth and the unjust souls who are not philosophers is not matched by a similar dichotomy in the realm of politics.

So in returning to the discussion of full cities, Plato was doing more than just suggesting that individuals can be distinguished by the objects of their desires. Plato goes to surprising lengths to explore the class dynamics that shape the various political transformations of the cycle of regimes. Socrates states, "And do you realize that of necessity there are as many forms of human character as there are of constitutions? Or do you think that constitutions are born 'from oak or rock' and not from the characters of the people who live in the cities governed by them, which tip the scales, so to speak, and drag the rest along with them?" (544d), suggesting that there is an important collective dimension in the formation of character and in the ordering of desires in the soul.[36] Book 8 can be best understood as an analysis of this process through which the souls of all are transformed by the character of those who govern.

A similar understanding of the link between the conditioning of desire in the soul and the broader social and political context can be found in Aristotle. As Aristotle suggests in the *Rhetoric*:

[A deliberative speaker] should not forget the "end of each constitution; for choices are based on the "end." The "end" of democracy is freedom, of oligarchy wealth, of aristocracy things related to education and the traditions of law, of tyranny self-preservation. Clearly, then, one should distinguish customs and legal usages and benefits on the basis of the "end" of each, since choices are made in reference to this. Now, since *pisteis* [means of persuasion] not only comes from logical demonstration but from speech that reveals character (for we believe the speaker through his being a certain kind of person and this is the case if he seems to be good or well disposed to us or both), we should be acquainted with the kinds of character distinctive of each form of constitution; for the character distinctive of each is necessarily most persuasive to each.[37]

If we remember that for Aristotle character is as much a matter of feeling as of judgment, we will acknowledge that these communities of character or *ēthos* are largely distinguished by a form of collective emotional consensus on what is to be desired and what is to be feared. Furthermore, as suggested by Aristotle in this text, this consensus is not always the product of rational deliberation but can also emerge through a community of affect in a shared emotional response to an action or event. This concordance is not just a matter of similar outcomes, or a fortuitous coming together of those of a similar disposition; it is a matter of shared identity that shapes public institutions and political judgments and in turn directs public responses as to the appropriateness of those institutions and judgments.

It is the two principles shared by Plato and Aristotle and identified above (i.e., passion as understood through its relation to things in and of a common world, and passion as having a possible collective manifestation) that I wish to argue constitute the classical notion of the idea of a "public passion." Despite divergences between the two thinkers as to how they conceptualized the actual cycle of regimes and how revolutionary change occurred, they both adhered to the idea that political communities could be identified in general ways by a common emotional disposition on the part of the participants in the regime. That is not to say, of course, that Plato and Aristotle felt that in principle this was a good thing. There was a clear hierarchy among the different types of regimes identified by each, and only those regimes that could foster the proper sorts of reason and affect (arguably different for each philosopher) were deemed worthy.

By drawing attention to the shared idea in Plato and Aristotle of a public passion, I am not arguing for a return to the Platonic and Aristotelian ideals of the best political communities. Instead, I am exploring how the more general notion of distinguishing political communities on the basis of shared dispositions, involving in part common emotional qualities as a matter of public identity, came to be less central in our understanding in politics in modern liberal communities.

Although scholastic thinkers were also much concerned with the question of the internal workings of the soul and the relative influence of will, reason, and desire, all these thinkers in the end shared the notion of an important connection between the objects and events in the world and the emotional reactions we are subject to. The radical vision of Descartes engendered more scepticism regarding how objects and events in the world might affect us, and thereby made the possibility of broad patterns of emotional response more difficult to conceive. His vision was a first important step in fashioning a theory of politics that paid no heed to the public force of the emotions.

As a consequence of Descartes' analysis, the categories and concepts through which the passions became conceived made the notion of a public passion more difficult, thereby dismantling a powerful tool of social and political analysis and self-understanding. In the first instance, Descartes posits a method of rigorous internal introspection as a new basis for knowledge about the passions. The foundation for his self-proclaimed new science of the passions is an exploration of the internal dynamics of feeling, in terms of both bodily reaction and patterns of thought. The objects giving rise to a passionate response are reconceived as matters that are filtered through perception, and the external occasions for emotional response are considered less important than the individual perceptions, as well as the individual's ability to manage and possibly modify those perceptions. Thus, the method for this new science limits the scope for considering the importance of passions as an integral component of public life, whether as a collective factor shared by a community and helping shape social and political life, or as a product of that life.

In the second instance, Descartes' claim that the passions are largely shaped by bodily disposition, personal habits, and individual strength of soul renders the possibility of a shared common passion among citizens less likely. The public is divided into those who have the strength of soul to man-age their passions (rather than eliminate them, as the Stoics advised and thought possible) for their own well-being (with varying degrees of success based on a myriad of factors), and those who through ignorance, stupidity, or dullness of soul have no need of or no inclination to self-management. Because individuals are solely responsible for policing and moderating their own emotional states, the life of the passions came to be regarded as a mere projection of individual characteristics. Still, as we will see with Hobbes, this approach did not rule out completely the possibility to manage broad patterns of shared emotional dispositions across broad populations for public purposes.

From Hobbes to the Last Rites for Political Emotion

Of course, the notion of a public passion was not limited to the classical philosophers. The idea that there were patterns of emotional reaction in populations and that these patterns were directly related to the type of polit-ical regime was also taken up in various ways by thinkers such as Augustine and Machiavelli.[38] Indeed, although we can associate Thomas Hobbes with the early roots of liberalism and the individualism of the Cartesian approach, Hobbes continued a classical sensibility through a central concern to define a regime by a shared emotional disposition on the part of its subjects. It is important to show how Hobbes carried on this classical notion, which was progressively abandoned through the latter seventeenth century and early eighteenth century despite an attempt by Montesquieu to revive it.

Hobbes is an interesting example because he is driven by an acute interest in the internal dynamic of emotional life, through his own materialist and reductivist lens, all the while maintaining a preoccupation with the need to manage the workings of passion in social and political life. His work recognizes the importance of collective responses to public matters that elicit similar emotional responses and lead communities to engage collectively in actions of fundamental public importance and scope. Indeed, the workings of the covenant in *Leviathan* can be read as largely a psychological manipulation through which the fears motivating each individual in the state of nature are transposed into a shared and collective fear of the Leviathan itself.[39] Without this public passion, the collective agreement to submit would be impossible. Many readers, including John Locke, criticized Hobbes' supposed solution to the problem of political order as a regime based on the principle of fear.[40] It would be of great interest, though beyond the broader purposes of this study, to see how Hobbes is able to combine a modern methodology that highlights an initially private orientation and study of the effects of passions within the individual soul with a continued emphasis on the public significance of the passions.

In criticizing Hobbes, Shaftesbury also continued to uphold the idea of shared public passions. Furthermore, Shaftesbury noted that these passions could work for both the benefit and the detriment of society. The dynamic of sympathy, or conveying the emotional state of one person to another by identification and contact, is called "panic" when passion is spread through the multitude. As Shaftesbury notes, it can be particularly noxious in the case of religious enthusiasm:

> Popular fury may be called "panic" when the rage of the people, as we have sometimes known, has put them beyond themselves, especially where religion has had to do. And in this state their very looks are infectious. The fury flies from face to face, and the disease is no sooner seen than caught. They who in a better situation of mind have beheld a multitude under the power of this passion, have owned that they saw in the countenances of men something more ghastly and terrible than at other times is expressed on the most passionate occasions. Such force has society in ill as well as in good passions, and so much stronger any affection is for being social and communicative.[41]

In contrast to his classical counterparts, for Shaftesbury, these social passions or affections (his term for an emotion tempered in a rational and appropriate way) do not derive from authority or the quality of leadership. They have an independent dynamic and, as a collective phenomenon, test the worth of any leader who has to manage such reactions:

There are many panics in mankind besides merely that of fear. And thus is religion also panic when enthusiasm of any kind gets up as oft, on melancholy occasions, it will. For vapours naturally rise and, in bad times especially, when the spirits of men are low, as either in public calamities or during the unwholesomeness of air or diet, or when convulsions happen in nature, storms, earthquakes or other amazing prodigies – at this season the panic must needs run high, and the magistrate of necessity give way to it. For to apply a serious remedy and bring the sword or fasces as a cure must make the case more melancholy and increase the very cause of the distemper. To forbid men's natural fears and to endeavour the overpowering them by other fears, must needs be a most unnatural method. The magistrate, if he be any artist, should have a gentler hand and, instead of caustics, incisions and amputations, should be using the softest balms, and, with a kind sympathy, entering into the concern of the people and taking, as it were, their passion upon him, should, when he has soothed and satisfied it, endeavour, by cheerful ways, to divert and heal it.[42]

The polemic against Hobbes shines out forcefully here as Shaftesbury notes the ineffectiveness of fighting fear with fear.

Throughout most of his writings, however, Shaftesbury highlights a more positive side of collective passion, what he calls the "social affection." He sees this sense of public good shared by certain communities as a necessary component of moral virtue.

While this idea of social affection is considered by Shaftesbury as an important continuation of the classical view concerning the centrality of emotion in political life, it may inadvertently have had contrary effects. In his most famous essay, "An Inquiry Concerning Virtue or Merit," Shaftesbury discusses the foundations of moral virtue as well as its relationship to religion. In the course of his discussion he places great emphasis on the natural sociability of humankind and argues that all human beings share a natural sense of right and wrong, prior to all social conventions. Reason for Shaftesbury is the human faculty that allows us to recognize and approve of the good. The social affection evokes a devotion to the good of one's fellow human beings, and it is a central component of virtue, along with the natural affection a person must have towards herself: "To stand thus well affected and to have one's affections right and entire not only in respect of oneself but of society and the public: this is rectitude, integrity or virtue."[43]

In conversation with the moralists of his day, Shaftesbury contemplates but ultimately rejects the possibility that there might be an intrinsic conflict between the virtues relevant to the self and those relevant to society as a whole. He argues that each natural affection can be carried to excess and that the art of virtue consists in balancing the interests of the self and those of society, as can be seen naturally in communities of animals.[44] The public authorities also have an important role, in terms of both establishing laws that encourage virtuous behaviour and setting good examples for the community by their own behaviour.[45]

So when Shaftesbury limits the proper scope of the social affection to those things that show devotion to the public good without undermining the good of the self, he appropriates but modifies the classical view. In the course of highlighting the role of social affections and passions for a proper understanding of moral virtue and political theory, Shaftesbury also narrows their characterization to shared devotion to the community. Collective passions such as fear, disgust, shame, and others are here put aside in the effort to show the primacy of social affection. The public passion in Shaftesbury has become the narrow and ideal devotion to the common good, an ideal so distant from many of the views of his contemporaries that it became an important target of intellectual criticism.

In the late eighteenth century, Adam Smith offered another attempt to come to terms with the role shared emotional responses play in our understanding of politics. As with Shaftesbury, the initial impulse to appropriate and preserve aspects of the classical view ended in further repudiation of the older paradigm and its replacement by a new model through which to understand social and political life. For our purposes we will focus on Chapters 3 and 4 of part 1, section 1 of Adam Smith's *Theory of Moral Sentiments*.[46]

Smith sets up his analysis by suggesting the perspective we must take in exploring the nature of the passions or sentiments, and by stating how his analysis relates to his inherited tradition of philosophic reflection. He maintains that sentiments can be understood in terms of either the cause that excites them, or the end or effect they tend to produce. He also states that we tend to judge sentiments in two similar ways: first, in terms of the appropriateness of the affection in relation to the cause (by which we judge sentiments in terms of their relative propriety and decency); and second, in terms of the nature of the effects the sentiment aims or tends to produce, whether they be hurtful or beneficial.[47] He then goes on to suggest that philosophers of his own time have chiefly considered sentiments in the second aspect and ignored the first, despite the fact that, according to Smith, most people consider them under both these aspects.[48] As he explains, "When we blame in another man the excesses of love, of grief, of resentment, we not only consider the ruinous effects which they tend to produce, but the little occasion which was given for them. The merit of his favourite, we say, is not so great, his misfortune is not so dreadful, his provocation is not so extraordinary, as to justify so violent a passion. We should have indulged, we say; perhaps, have approved of the violence of his emotion, had the cause been in any respect proportioned to it."[49] So Smith's intent is evidently to provide his readers with a fuller account of the passions, that is, to complete the modern account of the effects of the passions on the individual soul and their social utility with an account of how we can ascertain their appropriate connection with concrete circumstances. It would seem, at first glance, that Smith would have sympathy for those ancient accounts that depicted the passions and emotions as having an intrinsic connection with the object of feeling, feelings that could be shared among social and political communities. As we will see, however, Smith approaches this point with an underlying scepticism that ultimately undermines the classical view.

Smith is right when he says that philosophers of his time tended to focus on the effects of the passions. Whom does Smith implicate with this remark? Clearly among them, or a primary influence among them, is Descartes, who, as we have seen, looked to physiology and to the effects of the passions on the body and soul. The valuable and painstaking study of Susan James reconstructing the seventeenth-century debate on the passions shows how this general orientation was carried through in the work of Nicolas Malebranche, Hobbes, and Spinoza.[50] Still, James places these thinkers in a narrative that emphasizes a continuity of reflection with the ancients on the passions. While she strives to show the degree to which the seventeenth-century thinkers departed from traditional Aristotelian and Thomistic ways of thinking, she maintains that both the ancients and moderns were primarily concerned with the idea of passion as it had an effect on the soul. Smith suggests another reading of this history that I think is useful in terms of exploring the political consequences of these debates. In seeking a fuller account of the passions, he sought to chart new territory in modern debates about the passions by exploring the causes of sentiment.

Smith's doctrine of sympathy is an important grounding for his broader theory of moral judgment. For Smith, the first rule of thumb in the process by which any person judges the appropriateness of a sentiment is a comparison with the "correspondent affection in ourselves." In other words, we arrive at our own response through an imaginative appropriation of the situation of the person being judged: "If upon bringing the case home to our own breast, we find that the sentiments which it gives occasion to, coincide and tally with our own, we necessarily approve of them as proportioned and suitable to their objects; if otherwise, we necessarily disapprove of them, as extravagant and out of proportion." Our own faculties of sentiment or capacity for emotional response give us a basis for judging the emotional appropriateness and worthiness of the reactions of our compatriots: "I judge of your sight by my sight, of your ear by my ear, of your reason by my reason, of your resentment by my resentment, of your love by my love. I neither have, nor can have, any other way of judging about them."[51]

By this move, Smith reconceptualizes what was at the basis of the classical view. As Plato saw it, a shared moral outlook, in part shaped by the character of political authority itself, gives rise to shared aspirations and shared evaluations on the part of the public. In other words, judgments that are already set through a common moral framework and instilled through education engender a common psychological outlook and thereby a shared emotional life with regard to matters of public importance. In contrast, while Smith is cognizant of the possibility of some degree of shared evaluation, it is developed between individuals, rather than across large numbers in a community, and it is a process in which participation in the sentiment precedes the development of moral judgment. For Smith, the possibility of sympathy does not inevitably result in a shared moral outlook.

Smith did take great pains to assure that this self-referential character of judgment had some ultimate grounding that differentiated it from a simple moral egotism. Indeed, due to his understanding of the social embeddedness of individual moral judgment, some regard Smith as on the ancient side of the divide. According to Glenn Morrow, Smith provides a more radical rendition of Humean sympathy that, in contrast to the methodological individualism characteristic of his age, grounded an inherently social ethics.[52] He argues that Smith's idea of the internalized norm for individual behaviour (or the infamous impartial spectator) was in fact a social construct, based on the individual's sense of concrete others.[53] Further evidence of the impartial spectator as a social construct can be found in Smith's discussion in Chapter 2 of part 5, concerning the effects of custom on the content of the moral sentiment: "The different situations of different ages and countries are apt, in the same manner, to give different characters to the generality of those who live in them, and their sentiments concerning the particular degree of each quality, that is either blameable or praise-worthy, vary, according to that degree which is usual in their own country, and in their own times."[54] Accordingly, one should interpret the impartial spectator not as merely a projection of subjective standards into a fictitious personality but rather as a distillation from the acting and real principle of sympathy that exists among all individuals. Morrow writes:

> The impartial spectator is the personification of that which is permanent, universal, rational, natural in the phenomena of sympathy. Since sympathy is the principle which makes life in society possible, the normal sympathies which the impartial spectator personifies can only be those sympathies which best further the existence of men [sic] together in society ... As the guardian of these rules of morality, the impartial spectator is in a sense representative of the welfare of society; hence to appeal to the sympathies of the impartial spectator is by no means to abandon the social reference.[55]

But Smith begins Chapter 2 of part 5 by asserting that the influence of custom on the moral sentiments is limited. For Smith, these limitations are at least threefold: one, by the issue of proximity (in other words, one's sympathy, not to say one's approbation, will most often be greater with one's closest circle of family and friends); two, by Smith's view that the enlightened disposition of modern commercial times should tend to resist bending to shared patterns of behaviour, as recently highlighted by Emma Rothschild; and three, by the nature of the moral sentiment itself, which limits what can be consented to ("the characters and conduct of a Nero, or a Claudius, are what no custom will ever reconcile us to, what no fashion will ever render agreeable").[56]

While Smith may adhere to the idea of a social ethics in principle, it is (1) largely divorced from actual custom and indeed seen as a device by which custom can be judged;[57] and (2) adjudicated privately. The impartial spectator for Smith is a way to ground social and political judgment in the context of modern societies where sympathies are unequally distributed and passionate responses quite diverse. This spectator represents an idealized or internally normative ideal of social interaction (though derived from concrete experiences) and remains a means for disengagement from existing custom and shared patterns of judgment and emotional response.[58] It is meant to be not plainly or merely a social reference but in many ways an alternative one, as is implied in Smith's invocation of the notion of impartiality.[59] Thus, Smith's analysis of sentiment, while in principle trying to reincorporate the ancient understanding of the social causes of emotion, transforms its political potential and significance. Smith's emphasis on localized face-to-face encounters and the importance of self-command makes it more difficult to conceptualize and appreciate shared patterns of emotional response to matters of public relevance. The idea that communities can be distinguished by a common ordering of desires is absent from Smith.

Although Smith uses the term "public passion," through the intellectual legacy of Shaftesbury this is no longer the idea of shared affect among members of a political community, but rather unique and rare examples when an individual is driven by a sense of the greatness and glory of the country.[60] In other words, passions must be distinguished by their object, as in Smith's view they can rarely be predicated of more than a single individual; when they can it is a matter in need of psychological and philosophical explanation.

The full significance of Smith's conception is that while he claims to be providing a more full account of the passions than that offered by his contemporaries, and one that gestures to ancient ideas by incorporating a strong sense of the social embeddedness of ethical judgment, he puts his account to the service of discriminating among behaviours and a certain disengagement from custom. While the dynamic of sympathy may explain some communication of sentiment among citizens, its force depends on close proximity and the serendipity of personal encounter. Indeed, the workings of sympathy suggest that despite common subjection to similar principles of public authority and historical tradition, little else identifies or holds communities together in terms of emotion. And once the idea of a public passion was laid to rest in this manner, it was only a matter of time before shared rational norms became the sole possible basis for understanding the creation and shaping of political community.

Conclusion

This admittedly schematic history does not do full justice to the breadth of the transition from a robust idea of a public passion to a largely emaciated one. More documenting of the period and the various works implicated remains to be done. This chapter serves only as a broad and initial investigation into an important shift in Western intellectual history.

Moreover, a project to revive the importance of collective passions in politics is not without risks. A feature of the modern project to marginalize the passions in the realm of politics appeals to the very best in us, given the unpredictable and sometimes destructive nature of the passions as they have played themselves out in collective and brutally evil ways through the course of history, ways almost as deadly as coldly rational leadership has been. But a revaluing of the passions does not preclude proper judgments about the right and wrong sort of passions, or objects of passions, in public life. And some degree of emotional understanding and intelligence about ourselves as political beings is a necessary condition for any suitable project of political emancipation.

One might also object that the idea of a "public" passion works against the centrality of individualism in contemporary liberal assumptions. Does the idea not imply some hidden component of required or expected consensus, like Rousseau's famous dictum of forcing citizens to be free through some vague notion of the general will? I recognize that this idea of a public passion does not and cannot exhaust the domain of the public under any account, and that any liberal democratic community will encounter many issues on which citizens have differing and competing emotions. I also hold, however, that at times in contemporary experience there are shared passions within a political community and that these are crucial to our ongoing sense of being a political community. Contemporary political theory is often blind to or dismissive of such manifestations.

The intellectual history presented in the chapter allows us to see more clearly why there is renewed interest today in reviving a notion of passion suitable for the public sphere, for it appears that the marginalization of the passions was not initially the result of a concerted project to redefine politics, but an unintended consequence of other intellectual concerns. How we navigate the return of the passions is certainly an ongoing matter of dispute, but there is a definite need to retune our normative understandings of politics so as to correspond more suitably with the complexity of political life as we experience it. This project is not merely a matter of scientific urgency but, more importantly, democratic urgency, insofar as a normative project that does not incorporate a proper understanding of political passions will never be equipped to do justice to the majority who experience their political life on a different plane than that defended by a large number of liberal democratic theorists today.

shared passions

Passion, Power, and Impartiality in Hume

Sharon Krause

How should citizens evaluate the laws and public policies that bind them? How do we distinguish between laws (either proposed or existing) that are worthy of our allegiance and those that should be rejected or resisted? The courts play an important role in this regard, but as citizens in a liberal democracy we share in this responsibility. The relationship of democratic citizens to the law ought not to be one of blind obedience, after all, but should reflect critical engagement and sound judgment. Indeed, we have a political obligation as democratic citizens to evaluate the laws and to resist, or work to reform, those that violate civil liberties or obstruct social justice. How do we carry out this evaluation? What faculties of mind and heart do we use? In particular, what is the right combination of thinking and feeling, of reason and passion, of cognition and affect, within deliberation? The common response to this question is to insist that there is *no* right combination of reason and passion, at least when it comes to deliberation about important political questions and matters of justice. The only way to achieve good deliberation, in other words, is to excise our passions, emotions, and desires because they impede the impartiality that is needed for sound moral judgment, equitable adjudication, and fair political deliberation. This common opinion is echoed in the theories of democratic deliberation and liberal norm justification that predominate within political theory today, which associate impartial judgment with forms of reason that abstract from the passions.

This essay challenges the predominant view by elaborating David Hume's theory of judgment as a form of impartial passion. Hume treated moral judgment as a reflective passion, a form of sentiment in which thought and feeling are integrated at the deepest level yet structured in highly specified ways. Although he rejects the rationalist's faith in the power of reason to motivate action, he gives reason an important role in judgment. He also takes pains to establish the objectivity and impartiality of judgment. In fact, Humean judgment achieves its impartiality through the mechanism of a generalized perspective, and in this respect it bears a striking affinity to contemporary rationalist accounts of public deliberation and norm justification. Yet Hume shows us why it is important to achieve impartiality in judgment without sacrificing affect, and how it is possible to do so. The generalized perspective of judgment, as he conceives it, grows out of rather than abstracts from the usual sources of human agency as they are found in our common attachments and desires. Indeed, Humean judgment gains both motivational efficacy and normative authority from its footing in these affective concerns. It is a naturalistic account, but one that recognizes the social and cultural dimensions of human nature and makes a place for moral agency.

Hume has much to teach us today, for his account of affective judgment offers a powerful corrective to the rationalism of current liberal and democratic theory. Drawing mainly on his *Treatise of Human Nature* and *An Enquiry Concerning the Principles of Morals*, I elaborate the operations of judgment as moral sentiment, showing show how this concept of judgment achieves impartiality and avoids narrow subjectivism without sacrificing affective engagement. At the same time, I offer a critical analysis of the ways in which the structure of the political order permeates the passions on which affective judgment rests. Insofar as the moral sentiments are socially constituted and hence affected by existing laws and political practices, they will tend to reflect prevailing social inequalities and exclusions, thus perpetuating rather than correcting prejudice. The natural limits of sympathy in Hume's account exacerbate this danger. For all its value in showing the importance of affective modes of consciousness within evaluative judgment and deliberation, then, Hume's sentiment-based theory of judgment is incomplete on its own terms. The irrepressible political dimensions of moral sentiment mean that Hume's account must be supplemented by a commitment to democratic equality, liberal rights, and contestatory public deliberation, a commitment that takes us beyond Hume. To achieve its great promise of affectively engaged but impartial judgment, the Humean approach needs liberal-democratic politics.

Impartiality and the Feeling of Judgment

Hume's account of the affective sources of moral judgment follows from the conviction – shared by men such as Lord Shaftesbury and Francis Hutcheson, his predecessors in the Scottish Enlightenment – that reason on its own cannot motivate action.[1] The "inferences and conclusions of the understanding" can "discover truths," Hume says, "but where the truths which they discover are indifferent, and beget no desire or aversion, they can have no influence on human behavior."[2] Since he is convinced that morality influences behaviour, he concludes that moral judgments must not be conclusions of reason, or must not derive from reason alone (T 457). Insofar as they direct our actions, moral judgments must incorporate affective concerns and desires. As Hume puts it, "Where the objects themselves do not affect us, their connexion can never give them any influence" on our actions (T 414). Moral judgment – which consists in making distinctions between good and bad, right and wrong, virtue and vice – rests on the sentiments of approval and disapproval that we feel on contemplating particular actions and types of character. For "when you pronounce any action or character to be vicious," Hume insists, "you mean nothing, but that from the constitution of your nature you have a feeling or sentiment of blame from the contemplation of it" (T 469). To judge someone virtuous "is nothing but to *feel* a satisfaction of a particular kind from the contemplation of a character," he says; "the very *feeling* constitutes our praise or admiration" (T 471, original emphasis). And our praise or admiration forms the judgment.

Critics of moral sentiment theory often worry that grounding moral judgment in affective modes of consciousness means subjecting judgment to the arbitrariness commonly associated with passions and emotions. This was certainly Kant's view, and similar concerns lie behind contemporary rejections of Humeanism as "subjectivist" and "emotivist."[3] Hume was very much aware of this danger, and he set out to show how moral judgments might achieve a significant measure of impartiality and yet remain sources of personal engagement. This impartiality is established in several ways: first, through the social fabric of moral sentiment; second, through the generalized perspective of moral sentiment; and third, through the mechanism of human nature that underlies moral sentiment.

The Social Fabric of Moral Sentiment

The social fabric of moral sentiment as Hume conceives it means that our judgments always reflect more than merely private responses to the world. What could be more obvious than the fact that feelings of approval and disapproval – our habits of evaluation – are in large part socially constituted? But Hume's point goes beyond the simple assertion that individuals tend to adopt the norms of their society or social group. Indeed, he denies that a truly individual evaluator can ever exist. Judgment is a social phenomenon because moral feeling has an intersubjective basis. The faculty of sympathy is the key. Sympathy communicates the sentiments of others to us so that we feel their pleasures and pains, and our judgments are built upon this communication (T 316-17). Communication is facilitated by the fact that the same range of passions affects us all, although the objects of these passions may differ. Nothing that one person can feel will be totally unfamiliar to another, for no one can "be actuated by any affection, of which all others are not, in some degree, susceptible" (T 575-76).

Note that "sympathy" in Hume, in contrast to contemporary usage of the term, is not a disposition or a virtue but rather a faculty of the mind with an informational function, much like imagination or memory. Like them, it operates automatically within consciousness rather than as the result of individual will or character.[4] It should therefore be distinguished from benevolence or pity, passions that move us to act out of concern for another. Sympathy is not a passion at all and entails no desire; hence it is not itself a source of action. And it need not involve a care for the well-being of the person whose sentiments it conveys. As Hume says, "My sympathy with another may give me the sentiment of pain and disapprobation, when any object is presented, that has a tendency to give him uneasiness; tho' I may not be willing to sacrifice any thing of my own interest, or cross any of my passions for his satisfaction" (T 586). In this sense, the account of judgment Hume offers, although grounded in sympathy, by no means assumes or entails that people will behave benevolently. Yet even where the effects of sympathy are too weak to motivate concern for the well-being of another, the sentiments conveyed still provide the grounds of judgment (T 586).

The key point is that in assessing the phenomena that confront us in the world, human beings are continually responding to the responses of others, and sympathy gives us access to these responses. "As in strings equally wound up," Hume says, "the motion of one communicates itself to the rest; so all the affections readily pass from one person to another, and beget correspondent movements in every human creature" (T 576). Sympathy reverberates within and between people in complex ways to generate moral sentiments of approval and disapproval: "Thus the pleasure, which a rich man receives from his possessions, being thrown upon the beholder, causes a pleasure and esteem; which sentiments again, being perceiv'd and sympathiz'd with, encrease the pleasure of the possessor; and being once more reflected, become a new foundation for pleasure and esteem in the beholder" (T 365). Money is a primary pleasure for the rich man because of the security it brings and the goods it makes available. When I contemplate my rich neighbour, sympathy makes present to me his pleasure in this regard, which causes me to approve (or, as Hume says, "esteem") his condition, or to value wealth. Being rich seems to be a good thing. My esteem then becomes a new source of pleasure to my neighbour, who enjoys his riches even more knowing how much they are generally valued. Pride adds a secondary pleasure to the primary one, increasing it and making it more complex. It also gives me further cause for valuing wealth, as sympathy conveys to me the additional enjoyment that pride generates for him.[5]

Through such layered reverberations of sentiment, sympathy gives rise to judgments of value, which are thus intersubjective at the deepest level.[6] The social character of moral sentiment mitigates the danger of narrow subjectivism raised by treating moral judgment as a feeling, for our judgments (like our feelings) are never solely our own. This intersubjectivity also makes moral judgment a political phenomenon. If our feelings of approval and disapproval arise partly in response to the reactions of others, the nature of our social relations will have a significant impact on these feelings. Imbalances of power that are a function of the political order exaggerate the perceived distance and differences between people and may disrupt the operation of sympathy. In this sense, the political order inscribes the prevailing relations of power into moral sentiment and the judgments that arise from it.[7]

The Generalized Perspective of Moral Sentiment

Although moral judgment is grounded in feelings, only certain kinds of feelings count. It is only "when a character is considered in general, without reference to our particular interest, that it causes such a feeling or sentiment, as denominates it morally good or evil" (T 472). Through sympathy and the exercise of imagination we experience the pleasure or pain that a given character trait generates for the person who possesses it or for those affected by it. Only sentiments arising from such a perspective, which is detached from private interests, can establish virtues and vices. Just as we habitually (even automatically) correct for the impressions of our physical senses, so we adjust our moral judgments to prevent them from being distorted by circumstances and self-love (T 581, 583; E 63n1, 64, 65n1). Despite appearances, I know that the houses I observe from an airplane at twenty-nine thousand feet are not actually the size of ants. Similarly, although I want my candidate to win and her opponent to lose, I can recognize (perhaps even admire) the brilliance of her opponent's well-run campaign. We compensate for distortions in judgment (whether perceptual or interest-based) all the time; the impartiality of moral judgment is not unique in this regard. On the basis of this impartiality Hume can distinguish, as one commentator puts it, between what people do approve and what they should approve.[8]

This distinction, which implies that people sometimes fail to approve what they should, suggests that the generalized perspective may not come to us as automatically as do corrections of the physical senses. Hume offers it as an ideal rather than as a fact. Yet one of the appealing things about Hume's moral theory is that his ideals always have a footing in the facts about who we are as human beings. In this case, the generalized perspective builds on and extends the automatic but minimalist operation of sympathy, which is a natural feature of our moral psychology but is not naturally as extensive or as free from self-love as impartial judgment requires.[9] For one thing, sympathy does not naturally extend equally to all affected parties but tends to privilege one's nearest and dearest. It also may be distorted by self-interest and obstructed by perceived differences among people, or by the faculty of comparison, which reverses sensations and accounts for envy and malice (T 376-77). The generalized perspective therefore must be learned and cultivated. It needs the support of common social virtues, including compassion and self-restraint. Education and socialization are important here. The pressures attendant on living together with others also help to foster the development of corrected judgment: "When we form our judgments of persons, merely from the tendency of their characters to our own benefit, or to that of our friends, we find so many contradictions to our sentiments in society and conversation, and such an uncertainty from the incessant changes of our situation, that we seek some other standard of merit and demerit, which may not admit of so great variation" (T 583). Judgments based on self-love and limited sympathy turn out to be poor guides for action because we cannot operate successfully on this basis in a world characterized by interdependence. So although the generalized perspective is not automatic, it does have a basis in the natural operations of sympathy and a motive in the natural desire to fulfill our settled purposes. Consequently, "experience soon teaches us this method of correcting our sentiments" (T 582).

The sentiments that give rise to moral judgment within the generalized perspective respond to the perceived usefulness and agreeableness of the object under consideration (T 590-91). The pleasing sensation of approval arises when we perceive some action or character to be either useful or agreeable to the person who has it or to those affected by it (T 591). When I make a judgment about Martin Luther King Jr's courage, for instance, the faculty of sympathy allows me to register the pleasures and pains of King himself and those affected by his courage in light of its usefulness and agreeableness. Their (imagined) feelings are made lively in my mind in the form of impressions, and on this basis I experience the sentiment of approval.[10] Although Hume does not emphasize this point, the danger of misidentification always exists. In recent years democratic theorists have pointed out that what feels like empathetic understanding can sometimes be little more than the projection of one's own sentiments onto others.[11] So the faculty of sympathy may convey inaccurate information. The best protection against this danger is to foster the democratic social and political practices through which the exchange of sentiments among citizens transpires, thus facilitating the correction of sympathy where necessary. The notion that we need to embed moral sentiment in democratic social and political practices takes us beyond Hume's own model of judgment, but it is crucial to the viability of the moral sentiment account of judgment, as we shall see presently.

In appealing to usefulness and agreeableness, Hume emphasizes that we evaluate actions and characters based on their general rather than their particular effects. For example, a benevolent person is esteemed virtuous because benevolence is normally useful to society, even though in a particular case some accident may "prevent its operation, and incapacitate him from being serviceable to his friends and country" (T 584). This is another aspect of the generalized perspective that gives rise to moral sentiment. The imagination generalizes the effects of benevolence, thereby allowing us to pass "easily from the cause to the effect, without considering that there are still some circumstances wanting to render the cause a compleat one" (T 585). Because we respond to the general effects of certain actions and characters, we need not be personally familiar with those involved in order to form a judgment in any particular case. Hence we "blame equally a bad action, which we read of in history, with one perform'd in our neighborhood t'other day" (T 584). Without ever having known Pol Pot or the victims of his abuses we have cause to disapprove of him, and if we adopt Hume's generalized perspective we will do so.

Perceptions of usefulness and agreeableness have a cognitive dimension because they involve reasoning about matters of fact and relations of cause and effect. Hume even remarks in the *Enquiry* that "it is requisite to employ much reasoning, in order to feel the proper sentiment" in moral matters (E 5-6, and 125-26). One is likely to feel very differently about a man who has just shot one's neighbour when reason alerts one to the fact that the man acted in self-defence. Moreover, part of what accounts for the difference in feeling here is the *thought* that wanton violence is not generally useful. Without being able to reason, we could not feel in the appropriate ways. And the key to moral judgment in Hume is this right feeling. In achieving impartiality, judgment never abandons the affective mode of consciousness. Consequently, moral judgment operates by means of "engagement and captivation," as one interpreter puts it, rather than dispassionate calculation.[12]

Because the generalized perspective incorporates the sentiments of those who are affected by a given character or action as well as the sentiments of the person whose action or character it is, the possibility of divergent inputs always exists. What happens, then, when the sentiments of the relevant parties, as communicated by sympathy, conflict? The sentiments that figure as inputs in the generalized perspective are themselves subject to moral evaluation.[13] Hume had little patience with sentiments coloured by prejudice, ignorance, and superstition. The sentiments "are perverted" in a person who "never sufficiently enlarges his comprehension, or forgets his interest as a friend or enemy." Prejudice, Hume says, "is destructive of sound judgment" and generates sentiments "which may be pronounced erroneous." Hence "the taste of all individuals is not upon an equal footing" in moral matters as much as in aesthetic ones.[14] He mentions in this regard "the want of humanity and of decency" found in characters drawn by ancient poets such as Homer. Their objectionable character discredits the moral force of their pleasures and pains. Consequently, "we are not interested in the fortunes and sentiments of such rough heroes." Indeed, "we cannot prevail on ourselves to enter into [such a poet's] sentiments, or bear an affection to his characters, which we plainly discover to be blameable."[15] So the normative force accorded to particular feelings within the generalized perspective depends in some measure on the character that stands behind them, specifically on whether this character can itself be endorsed from within a generalized perspective. It also depends on whether the sentiments in question are consistent with what empirical experience tells us about human nature, as we shall see in a moment. Thus in some cases there will be grounds for weighting opposing inputs differently. If we find that we can approve one set of sentiments but not the other, then we have grounds to weigh them differently, which may resolve the conflict and facilitate a determinate evaluation in the matter at hand. In this sense, moral evaluation is often an iterative process. Any one act of evaluation may call for (and build on) other evaluations.

There are nevertheless bound to be some cases in which a conflict of inputs cannot be resolved by iterations of evaluation and differential weighting. Sometimes the sentiments of those affected by a given character trait or action will conflict without there being grounds for us to disapprove any of them. Here we face irreducible moral conflict, which makes a singular determinate evaluation impossible. This indeterminacy may be thought regrettable, but not as constituting a flaw in the Humean approach to judgment. Instead it reflects a real and ineradicable feature of moral life, which is that human goods are irreducibly plural. The things that matter to us do not always (or perhaps ever) fit together into a single harmonious whole. Sometimes the soundest moral judgment is a mixed one. Likewise, when a given quality is agreeable but not useful, or vice versa, a determinate evaluation will be difficult. Courage is a quality that Hume thinks we tend to find immediately agreeable (E 90), but it may be put to ill purpose, as when brave military conquests bring misery to many people. In this case the generalized standpoint should represent feelings of both pleasure and pain. And what could be more familiar than the experience of finding that, on reflection, our moral evaluation of some phenomenon is mixed? The suicide bomber is a figure who inspires a certain uneasy fascination for many of us today because our revulsion for his act is mixed with the fact that we cannot help but be impressed by his courage. We can and should deplore the act, but our disapproval does not say all that may legitimately be said on the matter. There is a moral remainder here, which consists in our common response (however uncomfortable it makes us) to the agreeableness of courage. Hence it is not surprising to hear someone remark that it is sad, and a waste, that the suicide bomber (or the despot, or the conqueror, or the traitor) used his admirable courage to such barbarous purpose. This judgment reflects a suitably dual evaluation. A model of moral judgment that would generate a single, perfectly determinate evaluation in such cases could never be true to the complexity of human experience and the plurality of human goods. Making room for this complexity is a virtue, not a vice, of Humean judgment.

It is worth noting that the generalized perspective of moral judgment never reaches to the level of genuine universalism because sympathy is limited in its effects. Much as we feel our immediate interests more powerfully than those that are remote, so we are most strongly moved by the sympathetic communication of sentiment among those who are closest to us, in terms of both physical proximity and perceived likeness (T 318). Sympathy makes the happiness and misery of others "affect us," but only "when brought near to us, and represented in lively colors" (T 481). So the faculty of sympathy allows us to generate abstract principles of right and wrong, which transcend the narrowness of self-interest and personal prejudice, but it does not lead to a perfectly universal point of view. The limits of sympathy in this regard make Humean judgment vulnerable to distortions arising from the biases of one's society and social group. Inequalities exacerbate this dynamic because sympathy is less likely to register the sentiments of the powerless in the judgments of the more privileged. Here again moral sentiment will reflect the relations of power fostered by the prevailing political order. Hume's relatively unambiguous account of esteem for the wealthy offers an example. Our more democratic political order, which gives a stronger voice to the poor and thereby extends the reach of sympathetic communication, makes for more mixed judgments of the rich.

These considerations suggest that for moral judgment to be fully impartial, given its ineradicable affective content, an egalitarian political order will be called for. Indeed, the fullest realization of affective impartiality may require a political context structured by liberal rights, social equality, vigorous public deliberation, and active democratic contestation, as I will argue presently. Hume himself was insufficiently attentive to the political nature of judgment in this regard. He saw that sympathy was limited in its reach, but he did not explore the ways in which the natural limits of sympathy interact with inequalities and exclusions established by the political order to mar the impartiality of moral sentiment. True, he disapproves of radical inequality on the grounds that "a too great disproportion among citizens weakens any state" and is not "suitable to human nature."[16] Yet he never connects the political structures that foster and protect inequality to the structure of moral judgment. Still, he was committed in his way to showing how our judgments could attain the greatest measure of impartiality. To mitigate the limits of sympathy and enhance the impartiality of judgment, he looked to human nature.

The Role of Human Nature
Hume's writings are full of references to human nature as shaping our responses to the world and thereby providing some common ground of moral feeling (and hence judgment) even across societies (T 183, 287, 318, 469, 547n1, 619; E 47). He does admit that human nature is "changeable," or diverse in many of its particular manifestations. Yet he insists that some needs and purposes are common to human beings, and that these help shape our responses to the world. Consequently, human nature dissuades us from approving certain things. Both domestic and civil slavery, for instance, "trample upon human nature" and this gives us cause to disapprove them, if we are judging from the generalized perspective informed by human nature.[17]

Conversely, qualities such as friendship, mutual attachment, and fidelity are valued everywhere because they answer to basic human needs and capacities.[18] Human nature thus further mitigates the danger of subjectivism in moral judgment.[19]

To be sure, human nature offers minimal guidance. It does not yield determinate decisions on numerous moral questions, as well as matters of social and political policy (T 533).[20] On the basis of human nature some policies will turn out to lack normative authority and motivational force, but the range of policies legitimately claiming authority will be quite broad, and here custom, legal convention, and the inclinations of the individual will rightly have a role. So long as they do not contravene the (minimalist) logic of human nature, Hume sees no reason to object to this diversity.[21] In fact, we should expect diversity given the intersubjective quality of moral sentiment, which entails that variations in the political conditions structuring social interactions will find expression in our judgments.

The appeal to human nature may seem to sit uneasily with Hume's scepticism, and this concern has some merit. If human nature is conceived in terms of an invisible set of final ends or a standard of human perfection, then the quest to know it is indeed at odds with Hume's scepticism and with his empiricist method more generally. Seen as a collection of common, empirically verifiable needs, responses, and purposes, however, human nature turns out to be compatible with his larger philosophical project.[22] In fact, the study of human nature properly conceived is the heart of his project. In discussing his own philosophical purposes in Book 1 of the *Treatise*, Hume says that he aims to "contribute a little to the advancement of knowledge" by steering philosophers to "those subjects, where alone they can expect assurance and conviction." First among these subjects is human nature, including the needs and purposes that experience reveals to be common among human beings, for "human nature is the only science of man" (T 273). Indeed, Hume continues, "the conduct of a man who studies philosophy in this careless manner, is more truly skeptical than that of one who, feeling in himself an inclination to it, is yet so over-whelm'd with doubts and scruples, as totally to reject it" (ibid.). To reject the concept of human nature out of hand, to turn away from the guidance it may offer, would be its own kind of dogmatism. Hume gives human nature a central place in his epistemology and moral philosophy, although he leaves its content open to revision based on what empirical observation reveals.[23]

In addition to human nature, Hume suggests that good judgment is guided by features of the external world. To be sure, he denies that moral sentiments simply respond to moral value inhering in things themselves. In this respect, he differs markedly from Aristotle. Aristotle also envisioned an affective dimension to moral evaluation, holding that the virtuous person's love of the good is a mark of his excellent judgment.[24] But for Aristotle moral feeling is a response to the inherent moral order of the natural world itself. The feeling of moral approval arises (or arises appropriately) when real goodness is on display. The moral feelings of the virtuous person are an index of qualities existing independently in the world. In Hume's view, however, the feeling of approval is not a report about the intrinsic moral status of phenomena in the external world. Instead of reporting value, moral sentiment expresses it, although in an impersonal way. Hume regarded his sentiment-based approach to judgment as a great advance over existing moral philosophy, as it allowed him to explain the "origin" of any action's "rectitude or depravity" without recourse to "incomprehensive relations or qualities, which never did exist in nature, nor even in our imagination, with any clear and distinct conception" (T 476). His approach located the sources of moral and political right on the naturalistic terrain of human needs and purposes – rather than tying them to external standards – and opened them to the light of scientific understanding.

So affect figures in judgment in two ways: in the horizons of concern that orient judgment with respect to a particular set of values (the conditions of judgment), and in the sentiments of pleasure and pain communicated by sympathy within the generalized perspective (the inputs of judgment). Reason contributes by enabling us to perceive relations of cause and effect as well as those of identity or resemblance. It also allows us to ascertain relevant matters of fact, and it identifies the most effective means to our ends. Judgment arises as our affective (but not unreasoned) responses to the world are filtered through the generalized perspective and informed by the facts. Our judgments reflect the social fabric of moral feeling as well as responses that have a footing in human nature. Together, these features establish a measure of impartiality in the moral sentiments and the judgments they generate.

The Justification of Norms and the Cultivation of Character

The discussion thus far has treated Hume's analysis of judgment from the phenomenological perspective, or the perspective of how we experience it. Hume has been criticized for what some readers see as the *merely* phenomenological character of his account. These critics believe that he fails to provide a normative theory of judgment, or a process by which we could assess the validity of the judgments we happen to have. Some even accuse him of psychologizing morality. Yet Hume does go beyond psychology and phenomenology in his treatment of moral judgment. Although the bulk of his analysis is concerned with explaining the experiential facts of judgment, he introduces a normative perspective in the concluding passages of the *Enquiry*. These passages even suggest a general method of norm justification, or the evaluation of prevailing standards of right.

After having explained "the moral approbation attending merit or virtue" in the first part of the *Enquiry*'s conclusion, Hume turns in part 2 to what he calls "our interested *obligation*" to virtue (E 118, original emphasis). The earlier analysis of judgment has revealed the process by which we come to value what we call "virtues" and are motivated to act in accordance with them. But this earlier analysis did not tell us why we ought to value virtue, or why virtue is obligatory for us. How can we be sure that the qualities we consider to be virtues are worthy of our approbation? To establish the basis of this obligation – to justify the norms that virtue entails – Hume asks us at the end of the *Enquiry* to look to "the true interests of each individual" (E 119).[25] Are the virtues useful or agreeable to the person who has them and to those who are affected by them? Do they support rather than thwart common human needs and purposes? Do our standards of right have a basis in fundamental human concerns or natural human responses? If we can answer in the affirmative, then our virtues and the standards they entail are justified.[26] In so considering, we employ the same generalized, sentiment-based perspective involved in moral approbation, but here judgment operates at a higher order of complexity. For now judgment is asked to evaluate itself: what do we feel when we contemplate the prospect of a life lived according to our existing moral judgments?

The notion of human nature thus plays an important role in norm justification. As we have seen, human nature refers to the empirically verifiable responses to the world that observation tells us are common among human beings. People commonly abhor being enslaved, for instance, and commonly feel the power of the religious impulse; they typically find tyranny and cruelty disagreeable; they see promise-keeping as generally useful and mutual attachments as sources of pleasure. Human beings are psychologically and physiologically constituted so as to (largely) share such responses, so that the intersubjective dimension of judgment intersects with its basis in human nature. Hume's idea is that moral approbation and disapprobation, as well as the higher-order judgments involved in norm justification, track these common responses. He regards them as "intrinsically normative," as one commentator says, in the sense that aside from human needs and purposes "there is no normative point of view from which morality can be challenged."[27] Yet it is fair to say that Hume understates how difficult it can be to see and feel human nature operating in us, and to distinguish it from the social customs and legal conventions with which it always interacts. In part, this difficulty reflects the fact that power imbalances and social exclusions may distort our perception of human nature. What we feel to be "common" depends on whose experience we take into account. But even leaving aside the effects of inequality, the difficulties of knowing oneself (and distinguishing the natural from the artificial in one's responses) are impossible to deny, especially in light of the fact that moral sentiments are always also intersubjective.

This is another place where liberal-democratic politics can help to fill out the Humean account, as we are about to see, by incorporating democratic contestation into higher-order judgment and allowing our sense of human nature itself to be challenged and revised in light of wider experience. Yet the difficulties of clearly identifying human nature do not reduce Hume's account of norm justification to mere conventionalism. Although the guidance human nature offers is minimalist and allows for significant diversity, it is not the case that anything goes. Moral sentiment may be intersubjective at the deepest level, and hence shaped by social life, but Hume suggests that with respect to some basic human concerns the responses of different persons regularly coincide. On the basis of such concerns, one can say that a political system that established slavery, or obstructed mutual attachments, or systematically thwarted the religious impulse, or made promise-keeping untenable, would be morally objectionable. By violating these common needs and purposes it would fail the test of Humean justification. Thus when people disapprove of tyrants or slaveholders or liars, we can say with Hume that "from the constitution of [their] nature [they] have a feeling or sentiment of blame from the contemplation of it" (T 469).

Hume's account of norm justification introduces an element of reflexive agency that may otherwise seem to be missing from his moral philosophy. That is, Humean judgment often appears to be merely reactive, emphasizing retrospective evaluation of other persons' character traits rather than deliberation about one's own future action.[28] One commentator has even argued that "the priority the Humean gives to spectatorial-based judgment evaluating character and action effectively displaces the deliberative process engaged in by agents."[29] Certainly Hume himself did not work out all the implications that his sentiment-based approach to evaluative judgment might have for future-oriented practical deliberation, especially in the political context.[30] Yet in describing how we come to affirm the "interested obligation" to virtue, Hume attributes to the judging subject an active, quasi-deliberative role. Judgment still takes the form of a sentiment of approval or disapproval, and this sentiment is in effect a reaction to the prospect of a life lived according to our first-order judgments. But the perspective of this second-order judgment is unmistakably that of a moral agent, one who is asking herself whether or not she should go on living by the standards that have guided her in the past. To be sure, in Hume's example the agent is endorsing her sentiments, not reforming them. Hume was somewhat sceptical about the individual's ability to radically transform her character, and he had no desire to encourage the internalized war on vice that he associated with "the monkish virtues" (E 108). Still, in the very act of asking whether she can approve her character, Hume's moral agent treats herself as responsible for determining her future actions and authorizing the judgments that will guide them. In this respect Hume's concept of norm justification points in the direction of practical deliberation.

As we have seen, Hume insisted upon grounding moral evaluation in sentiment because he was convinced that such evaluation guides action. It is "impossible that the distinction betwixt moral good and evil, can be made by reason," he says, "since that distinction has an influence upon our actions, of which reason alone is incapable" (T 462). Moral evaluations "have an influence on the actions and affections"; they "excite passions, and produce or prevent actions" (T 457). When we decide what we ought to do in moral matters, our decisions incorporate evaluations of moral sentiment as these emerge from the generalized perspective and are tested against what empirical experience tells us about human nature.[31] In other words, moral deliberation for Hume consists in bringing the evaluations of moral sentiment to bear on one's choice of action in a particular context. The sentiment of approbation I feel when contemplating the virtue of courage gives me grounds to seek the courageous path rather than the cowardly one when faced with a choice. Indeed, the sentiment provides a normative basis for the obligation to do so. The affective dimensions of moral sentiment do not make moral action automatic. But the fact that our evaluative judgments are themselves affectively engaged, grounded in the same passions that normally generate action, means that deliberation guided by these judgments is constitutively connected to the animating sources of human action. In this way, the Humean approach to deliberation differs from the Kantian, rationalist model, which posits a deep divide between the psychological factors that regularly motivate action (passions and desires) and the normative basis of moral evaluation (a form of reason that abstracts from passions and desires).

The sentiment-based account of deliberation can, importantly, accommodate moral criticism and the possibility of reform. We are capable of reflecting on the concerns that shape our judgments, and these concerns may change in the light of new considerations. Reason has an important role here: it can point out cases in which our concerns are premised upon false beliefs about matters of fact or incorrect perceptions of causal relations (T 416, 459). If I oppose gay marriage because I think it leads to the erosion of traditional marriage, then evidence to the contrary gives me reason to change my view. The effects of reason in this regard are framed by the larger collection of desires and commitments that constitutes our horizon of concern, however. Evidence about the causal effects of gay marriage on traditional marriage will influence my judgment only if I care about traditional marriage. This concern, too, is subject to revision based on new considerations introduced by reason, provided that these new considerations are related in some way to other concerns that I already have. Thus we can reflect on our ends and not only on the means to these ends, although such reflection always transpires on the terrain of our existing concerns and beliefs. In some cases our existing concerns may be less than fully conscious. Media coverage of black civil rights demonstrators being abused by Southern police officers galvanized the American majority in the late 1950s and early 1960s, in many cases because the anger people felt on seeing this made them aware for the first time of the strength of their commitment to, or concern for, justice.[32] Through this type of critical engagement, Humean internalism allows for an agent, as one interpreter puts it, to "come to see that he has reason to do something which he did not see he had reason to do at all."[33]

Even though Hume is somewhat sceptical about the individual's ability to transform her character, he clearly believes that the education of sentiments is possible: "Let a man propose to himself the model of a character, which he approves: Let him be well acquainted with those particulars, in which his own character deviates from this model: Let him keep a constant watch over himself, and bend his mind, by a continual effort, from the vices, towards the virtues; and I doubt not but, in time, he will find, in his temper, an alteration for the better."[34] He insists, however, that the way to improve one's character is to reform the passions and desires that constitute it. To diminish "or augment any person's value for an object, to excite or moderate his passions, there are no direct arguments or reasons, which can be employed with any force or influence."[35] We cannot reform our sentiments through rational will alone. Reform of this kind arises only in connection with other concerns and affective aims that we have.

This conviction helps explain why Hume teaches us about the distinctions between better and worse sentiments mainly in his literary and historical writings rather than through the philosophical venue of the *Treatise*. One teaches the higher desires by showing their attractions and thereby engaging our affections. Thus Hume's *History of England* portrays Alfred the Great, whose character he describes as "perfect," as an attractive figure not only to others but also to Alfred himself. As one interpreter puts it, the ultimate test of Alfred's merit and virtue is that "we must want to *be* Alfred as much as we would want to be in any other relation to him."[36] The narratives and moral exemplars that populate Hume's literary and historical writings educate the deliberative faculty by engaging our affections for higher and more noble desires, that is, desires that can be endorsed as useful or agreeable from within the generalized perspective and that answer to human nature. The main point for present purposes is that even though we always deliberate in light of our desires, moral deliberation is not thereby made prisoner to unreflective appetites or merely private concerns. Our desires can be revised in light of procedures and standards that are neither idiosyncratic nor random. Indeed, we can deliberate not only about what we ought to do but also about who we ought to be, and on the basis of this kind of deliberation we are fully capable of making changes in ourselves.

Still, our capacity for critical self-reflection and the cultivation of an extensive moral sentiment will be constrained by the limits of sympathy. If there is a basic human interest in morality, as Hume insists, then there must also be a basic interest in the fullest cultivation of moral sentiment. Consequently, this cultivation is something we should strive for.[37] It would be foolish to demand perfection of anything human, including moral sentiment, but we can do better in this regard than what Hume's own model allowed. Since judgment and deliberation cannot do without the passions, the best hope for impartiality lies not in trying to transcend the passions but in reforming the political context that helps shape them. To avoid the distortions that follow from sympathy in its untutored form and to extend the limits of the human imagination, we need political conditions of freedom and equality. As Alexis de Tocqueville said in reflecting on the differences between old-regime Europe and modern democracy, sympathy flows more freely among citizens who are equal.[38] The result is that citizens of democratic societies know one another's sentiments more clearly than do those who live under the conditions of relative inequality that marked Hume's own society. Formal liberty and equality are not enough, however. Sound moral judgment and deliberation also require a significant measure of social equality and a continuing practice of public discussion, both of which expand the individual's horizon of sympathy by exposing her to the sentiments of those outside the familiar terrain of her family and social group. The path to a more truly impartial – but still *affective* – deliberation thus runs through liberal-democratic politics, although Hume himself did not look in this direction. If we are serious about the Humean approach we will need to go beyond Hume. The politics of judgment point to the need to connect moral sentiment theory to liberal and democratically engaged forms of public deliberation.

Judgment, Deliberation, and Democratic Politics

Hume himself was no advocate of active democratic deliberation, of course. The notion of an engaged citizenry was associated in his mind with political turbulence, including the excesses of the English civil war and the instability of ancient republics.[39] Although he was an advocate of enlightenment – he hoped that his new moral science would dispel superstition and humanize moral and political life – the last thing he wanted was more people passionately involved in debates about public affairs. He feared religious and partisan enthusiasm in politics and believed that the violent passions they engendered should be subdued. To be fair, constitutional liberal democracy was still in its infancy, and Hume could not predict the transformations it would bring. In the centuries since he wrote, the development of liberal-democratic political institutions has mitigated the dangers of extremism and instability. By tempering the power of the democratic sovereign through mechanisms such as the rule of law, the separation of powers, and individual rights, liberal democracy has constructed a safer arena for the kind of active deliberation that so worried Hume. This activism may be precisely what his theory of evaluative judgment most needs.

After all, we can imagine the sentiments of others much better if they are able to tell us about them. The access to public deliberation that individual rights protect for members of minority groups facilitates such communication and supports regular contestation and debate, which extend the reach of the imagination and influence the contents of our judgments accordingly.[40] Hume himself maintains that judgments in "human affairs, and the Duties of common life" benefited immeasurably from "conversation" with others. Philosophy, he complains, "went to Wrack" by its "moaping recluse method of study." What else could be expected, he asks, from men who "never consulted Experience in any of their Reasonings, or who never search'd for that Experience, where alone it is to be found, in common Life and Conversation?"[41] Conversation – much like history, literature, and art – allows us to "correct" our "false tastes" and erroneous judgments by bringing the sentiments of others and the facts of human experience to bear on our own sympathetic imagination. Yet for Hume the art of conversation is, or should be, well insulated from politics.

We should not, however, be bound by the limits of his vision in this regard. The incentive structure that follows from equal rights to political participation supports the extension of sympathetic imagination, both in citizens themselves and in their elected representatives and other officials. A liberal-democratic political system in effect forces us to extend the generalized perspective of judgment, to consider the sentiments of those who have the power to obstruct our purposes or vote us out of office. Such a system can therefore make Humean-style judgment more fully impartial than Hume's own account allows. The right political context can also mitigate the tendency of Hume's model to reify the status quo. The latter constitutes another common complaint about Humean judgment: namely, that Hume gives us a merely conventionalist account of judgment, one that is not amenable to social criticism or reform. But where public institutions are structured so as to permit different voices to raise issues of concern to them and to bring novel perspectives and interests into the public eye, the social fabric of moral sentiment may actually make Humean-style judgment and deliberation quite responsive to reform – more responsive than a model that postulates a withdrawn solitary judge reasoning in abstraction from the sentiments of others. Given the right political context, deliberation in this form carries the potential to sustain the critical perspectives and motivating sentiments that generate social change and political reform. It is perhaps worth emphasizing that the relevant context will include both liberal and democratic components. The separation of powers, rule of law, and individual rights that figure so importantly here are largely liberal mechanisms rather than democratic ones. Yet the cultivation of a suitably extensive faculty of moral sentiment will require more in the way of social equality and contestatory public discourse than liberal rights on their own can provide.

Conclusion

Some will worry that by recognizing the ways in which sentiment-based responses figure in judgment and deliberation we may inadvertently unleash the ugliest and most dangerous parts of human nature. Sympathy communicates sentiments of aversion as well as approbation, after all. And when people act on their aversions in politics, things can get ugly very fast. This valid concern has a long and distinguished lineage in the history of Western political philosophy. Hume was sensitive to the dangers of certain passions in politics, and we should be too. Liberal-democratic political institutions, individual rights, and the rule of law all set limits on what we can do to one another, and they may force us to show consideration for the sentiments of other persons even when we contemplate such persons with aversion. These factors are crucial both to a decent society and to sound judgment and deliberation.

A Humean approach need not deny the value of liberal-democratic protections against the influence of untutored passion. Indeed, such protections can be justified from the perspective of Humean judgment and are required for its fullest flourishing. What the Humean approach denies is the possibility of deliberating in a way that fully abstracts from passions and the horizons of concern they constitute. It also denies the viability of a sanitized theory of moral sentiment, along the lines defended by one recent commentator, that welcomes "positive emotions" such as benevolence and fellow-feeling but seeks to exclude such "negative emotions" as shame and disgust.[42] Our aversions, when they result from a properly structured moral perspective, tell us as much about how we should act as our feelings of approbation do. The fact that people sometimes will feel (and try to act on) aversions that do not result from impartial judgment is not a reason to turn away from the sentiment-based model of judgment – because no sentiment-*free* form of judgment is available to us. In this sense, no real choice exists between the sentiment-based model and the rationalist one, because we cannot deliberate about practical ends without affect. So to argue, with Hume, for a sentiment-based model of judgment and deliberation is not to recommend bringing more passions into politics or to encourage people to be more emotional and less reasoned in their judgments. It is rather to defend a clearer understanding of what is already happening (and what cannot help but happen) when we deliberate well about what to do in politics. But to bring to fruition the great promise of Hume's teaching in this regard we will need to learn from democratic theory as well. The theory of moral sentiment needs a political theory – a theory of social equality, liberal rights, and contestatory public deliberation – to make it whole.

In the end, perhaps the most valuable aspect of Hume's approach to judgment is the challenge it poses, which is to think more carefully about the relationship between the affective and cognitive components of judgment, and about the place of moral sentiment in political deliberation. Hume reminds us that while we can achieve a measure of impartiality in our judgments (and we should strive for this), we cannot rid our judgments of passions, emotions, and desires. Our affective concerns justify as well as motivate our actions, and they figure centrally in our judgments about what justice means and what it requires of us. To abandon them would undercut our capacity for sound and impartial judgment, which would be a blow to democratic citizenship. For democratic citizens are not simply bound by the laws but are also bound to think critically about the laws. By illuminating the faculties of mind and heart involved in this critical reflection, Hume helps us to sustain democratic citizenship and to properly orient ourselves, as citizens, to the laws and institutions that structure our common life.

Pity, Pride, and Prejudice: Rousseau on the Passions

Ingrid Makus

Jean-Jacques Rousseau uniquely combines modern liberal assumptions about the individualistic and competitive nature of human beings with classical notions that the human potential for virtue is situated in the nexus of reason and emotion. Rousseau's insights are useful in exploring the underlying psychological dimensions of contemporary liberal democratic politics. In particular, he illuminates the often puzzling and contradictory behaviour of individuals in modern liberal regimes.[1] In his *First and Second Discourses* Rousseau makes an elaborate plea for the necessity of looking into the heart of man (and perhaps more importantly, but with more difficulty, the heart of woman)[2] for knowledge about the human condition. He provides a speculative account, addressed to our hearts and minds, of the fundamental human and animal passions in the original state of nature, and traces their evolution through to advanced stages of civil society.[3] To the extent that his narratives continue to speak to us moderns (or postmoderns), they provide a rich source for a continuing dialogue on the complex and contradictory place of the passions in contemporary political life.[4]

Any full discussion of the place of the passions or emotions in political life requires a consideration of how they translate into political action. One might feel anger at injustice, pity at the suffering of another, love for one's neighbour, or fear for one's life in a conflict. And, as the articles in this collection propose, the articulation and experience of such emotions has a rational dimension: they are intricately tied to the exercise of our reason, our deliberative faculties, and our moral judgments. But how do these emotional assessments move us to act politically – to rectify injustice, alleviate suffering, or kill in war? How do our reasoned passions generate political action or inaction, whether good or bad?

In this chapter I want to explore some possible answers to such questions by drawing on aspects of Rousseau's account of the fundamental human passions, in particular his attempt to formulate a conception of pity as a basis for human interaction. My intention is not to provide a conclusive or comprehensive interpretation of Rousseau on the passions in general or even pity specifically. Rather, I offer a reading of relatively familiar passages in the *Discourses* that encourages further examination of the complex and multifold account of pity embedded there.[5] As part of this endeavour, I propose that there is evidence in the *Discourses* of two forms of pity, which I call "active pity" and "passive pity." These are my terms, not Rousseau's, but they capture an important nuance and distinction in the way he writes about pity. Furthermore, I suggest that what activates the former has to do with two other concepts we can formulate by drawing on Rousseau's account of human and animal behaviour: pride, resting on Rousseau's depiction of *amour-propre,* and prejudice, a term that refers literally to the tendency to "pre-judge" something and likely get it wrong. The concept of prejudice can apply to Rousseau's description of a form of wrong reasoning (those forms of reasoning that impede action). The interrelation of pity, pride, and prejudice forms a conceptual frame that can aid our understanding of what propels us to act or to refrain from action, to do good or do harm.

Pity In Nature

In his preface to the *Discourse on the Origin and Foundations of Inequality among Men,* where Rousseau elucidates what he tells us are the "simplest operations of the human soul," he sets out two "principles anterior to reason" that animate human beings in their original condition. The one (*amour de soi*) "interests us ardently in our well-being and our self-preservation," and the other (*pitié*) "inspires in us a natural repugnance to see any sensitive being perish or suffer, principally our fellow-men."[6] The combination of these two principles, Rousseau says, establishes a foundation for the rules human beings are both willing to submit to and capable of following. As long as one does not "resist this inner compulsion of commiseration," one will not "harm another man or even another sensitive being" (96). The legitimate exception is where the need for self-preservation overrides the impulse not to do harm. Clearly a repugnance to see another suffer or perish and an inner commiseration with another's suffering form an important basis for our relations to other beings (both human and animal). They ground an obligation not to harm another sentient being in situations where our own preservation is not threatened.

That pity is a disposition universally shared by humans and even some animals is stated in a key passage from the *Second Discourse* where Rousseau takes Hobbes to task for failing to recognize the tempering influence of pity. Even the cynical Bernard Mandeville, Rousseau notes, acknowledges the compassionate and sensitive element in human nature. The image that Rousseau presents here (drawing on Mandeville's account in *The Fable of the Bees*) to illustrate the force of natural pity (*pitié*) is striking. A man, imprisoned, sees "a wild beast tearing a child from his mother's breast, breaking his weak limbs in its murderous teeth, and ripping apart with its claws the palpitating entrails of this child." Rousseau tells us that the man "takes no personal interest" in this event. Presumably he has no particular attachment to the child or its mother. Moreover, he has nothing to lose or to gain by the child's life or death; he does not perceive the fate of the child or its mother to be connected to his own well-being. Yet the man feels "horrible agitation" at the sight of the suffering child and the "fainting mother." More important, he feels enormous "anguish" that, being imprisoned, he is unable to come to their aid (131).

As Rousseau describes this fable from Mandeville, there is a strong sense of pity as an active passion that generates much more than simple passive resistance to doing harm. This form of pity propels positive action to prevent harm to another suffering being to whom one is neither necessarily attached nor connected by mutual interest. This natural sentiment "carries us without reflection to the aid of those whom we see suffer" (133). If he were not physically restrained, the man in Mandeville's fable would have intervened upon observing the agony of mother and child. This intervention, we can imagine, might have caused harm to the man, as the wild beast would have been likely to turn on him as he attempted to stop the slaughter. In this case, the strength of pity would override, not merely temper, the imperative of self-preservation: pity would lead the man to aid another, even at the expense of his own well-being.

The merit of adopting pity as a foundation for relations among humans, Rousseau notes, is that pity is antecedent to reason in the form of reflection or contemplation. In the original state of nature, humans are not philosophical beings. Yet they can be propelled by pity not only to refrain from harming another but in some instances to actively prevent harm to another being, even at the cost of their own preservation. This is not to say that the sentiment of pity is unrelated to the use of any sort of faculty of reasoning or intelligence. It rests on, even requires, a kind of reasoning that consists in perceiving and measuring the physical relations among things. The ability to exercise this form of reasoning, according to Rousseau, is shared by humans and animals. Examining what Rousseau says about how humans and animals differ is therefore essential to understanding his accounts of pity.

In the preface to the *Second Discourse*, Rousseau addresses the "ancient dispute about the participation of animals in natural law" by proposing that animals share with humans a sensitivity to suffering and pain. As such, animals too partake in natural law, in the sense that humans have a duty not to harm animals in the same circumstances and on the same grounds as they have a duty not to harm other humans. Unlike humans, however, animals do not have enough intellect and freedom to recognize, submit to, and carry out the natural law themselves. Therefore they have no duty to refrain from harming other animals or humans (96).

In another passage in the *Second Discourse*, Rousseau maintains that the consciousness of being a free agent distinguishes humans from animals more clearly than do differences in the use of intellect. Like humans, animals have understanding; they use reasoning in the form of perceiving, calculating, and measuring the physical distances among things. They have ideas that are formed through putting together what they perceive through their senses. An animal "even combines its ideas up to a certain point, and in this regard man differs from a beast only in degree" (114). But animals lack free will: they follow their instincts, which may entail calculation and measurement and reasoning. Humans, however, are free to choose to acquiesce to their instincts or to resist them. Most importantly, humans are conscious of their ability to do so. Because humans can choose, they can choose to do the wrong thing or the right thing; humans are thus moral agents, while animals are not.

Pride and Injury

More often than not, Rousseau laments, history shows humans choosing wrongly. The capacity to choose defines the notion of perfectibility, which Rousseau introduces as the factor that most clearly distinguishes humans from animals. Perfectibility, combined with motivating circumstances such as natural disasters or events, accounts for humans moving out of an original state of nature and developing an increasingly more complex form of social and political structure under the rubric of "civil society," as opposed to animals, who remain in their original condition. Much of Rousseau's *First and Second Discourses* is an attempt to demonstrate to us the human suffering, inequality, and injustice that has resulted from developing the current form of civil society.

Why do humans choose actions that harm others and themselves? Two important factors according to Rousseau are pride, or vanity, and prejudice, or the tendency to make false judgments that are based on opinion rather than on measurement. The two are interrelated, as pride often induces one to deceive oneself and others about the actual relations among things.

Rousseau often contrasts the naturalness of self-love with the artificiality of vanity: "I say that in our primitive state, in the true state of nature, vanity does not exist" (222). This is not to say that he depicts vanity as something that human beings could simply do without or could have failed to develop either as individuals or as a species. Indeed, the seeds of vanity are sown in the original state of nature. Human beings in that condition do have the capacity to make comparisons. And vanity rests on comparisons, albeit comparisons in which humans measure themselves against one another. The central dynamic of vanity is that it "inclines each individual to have a greater esteem for himself than for anyone else" (222). It requires reciprocity, moreover: others must confirm that one is first in their estimation as well.

Thereby it becomes tied to the opinions of others. Vanity is thus in turn tied to a recognition of the will of another, necessarily a human will.

In an original condition, where humans and animals live in close proximity and where interactions among them, both violent and peaceful, are inevitable, humans learn to measure themselves against animals. Humans calculate relative strength, skill, and distance, and use their faculty of intelligence coupled with free will to choose to fight or flee. Humans may recognize that some wild animals could cause them physical pain. But they do not recognize them as causing injury or offence, which depend on an intention to harm. Lacking free will, or the ability to choose to go against their instincts, animals cannot exhibit such an intention. They may attack out of extreme hunger, or on the basis of a calculation that their preservation is threatened, but they do not attack simply because they choose to do harm.

Most remarkable about Rousseau's account of an original condition is the suggestion that, in such a state, humans interact with one another as they would with animals. That is, they do not yet recognize other human beings as willing agents. Any violent encounter, whether human or animal, is perceived as natural necessity. Such encounters may cause pain, but not injury or offence. This is possible because pride is not yet activated. Humans in the original state are self-regarding: they do not recognize other humans as sources of comparison or estimation or esteem or will. The desire to harm another is therefore also absent. In a lengthy note to the *Second Discourse*, Rousseau describes such a state, where each individual

> could have neither hate nor desire revenge, passions that can arise only from the opinion that some offense has been received and as it is scorn or intention to hurt and the harm that constitutes the offense, men who know neither how to evaluate themselves nor compare themselves can do each other a great deal of mutual violence when they derive some advantage from it, without ever offending one another. In a word, every man, seeing his fellow-men hardly otherwise than he would see animals of another species, can carry off the prey of the weaker or relinquish his own to the stronger, without considering these plunderings as anything but natural events, without the slightest emotion of insolence or spite, and with no other passion than the sadness or joy of a good or bad outcome. (222)

Pride or vanity is activated at the point where humans compare and rank themselves against other human individuals, simultaneously recognizing them as willing agents capable of choosing. Vanity inspires "in all men the harm they do to one another" (222), and greatly enlarges the potential for human suffering. In a state resembling the original condition, humans may suffer as a result of natural necessity: physical pain due to combat, or hunger and cold due to deprivation. But they do not experience the suffering that comes from injury, that is, harm directed at them intentionally by another human will.

Rousseau's distinction between these kinds of suffering provides an important insight into the psychology of human experience that remains relevant in a contemporary context. For example, if I fall down the stairs and break my leg, I suffer the physical pain of the damaged limb. But if someone deliberately pushes me down the stairs, I suffer not only the physical pain but also the injury that comes with recognizing that another human being intends to harm me. If I am pushed accidentally, I might feel annoyance as well as physical pain, but I would not feel injury. If my dog pushes me down the stairs, I might feel anger at the dog. But I would attribute his action to unruliness, hunger, miscalculation, or a reflexive lashing out at me if I have kicked him. Because he is an animal, I cannot attribute to him the will to do me harm. Similarly, if I am pushed down the stairs by a gust of wind, I would attribute it to "natural necessity" and suffer solely the physical pain of a broken leg. Only a recognition of the will of another human being who intends to harm me can elicit the kind of intense suffering that is distinctive of feeling injury.

Suffering caused by human will, in Rousseau's terms, damages our pride or vanity. And damage to our pride, or the estimation others have of us, is ultimately more injurious than the experience of physical pain and deprivation. We can comprehend why those Wall Street executives who lost their stocks during the Depression might have suffered more, even to the extent of committing suicide, than those numerous jobless individuals who travelled hungry in boxcars to look for work. We understand that torture consists not simply in levying physical discomfort on a sentient being; it consists precisely in conveying the message that one is wilfully harming them by treating them as if they did not count in one's estimation at all.

The Paradoxes of Pity

When we consider how pity in its active form might generate action to alleviate human and animal suffering, some interesting questions and paradoxes emerge that indicate that the imperative of human behaviour that Rousseau ascribes to an original condition continues to resonate with us, perhaps more unconsciously. Human behaviour in contemporary liberal democracies suggests we are less inclined to come to the aid of one who suffers from human injury than one who suffers from physical pain due to natural necessity. Donations to victims enduring the effects of natural disasters such as earthquakes, hurricanes, and floods are much more forthcoming than donations to individuals enduring suffering caused by more clearly discernible acts of human will, such as war. Indeed, no matter how close or distant the victims are – the neighbour whose house has burned down, inhabitants of a nearby city who have lost everything in a flood, or citizens of a nation across the continent far away who have been devastated by an earthquake – suffering caused by natural necessity seems to elicit an outpouring of activity aimed at alleviating it. In contrast, aid to victims of political injustice, such as oppressive regimes or even genocidal slaughter, is difficult to elicit. Paradoxically, however, we recognize that their suffering, caused by human will, is much greater than that experienced by victims of natural necessity. Is there something in Rousseau's description of pity that might give us a clue to why one might come to the aid of some who suffer, but not others?

I have proposed there is evidence in Rousseau's account of two forms of pity. Passive pity is a feeling of commiseration that lends itself to refraining from harmful action, in particular from harming other sentient beings. This is the kind that humans share with animals. In animals it manifests itself, for example, in the reluctance of horses to trample on animals beneath them. In humans it provides the guideline for the imperative to do no harm, or as Rousseau says, "Do what is good for yourself with the least possible harm to others" (133). Active pity is associated with positive action to alleviate the suffering of another sentient being, as shown in the Mandeville parable of the man watching the child torn apart by a wild animal. Active pity contains the elements of choice and will, which makes it distinctive to humans. In the original condition, active pity is more predominant than it is in more advanced or complex states of human interaction. Interestingly, human suffering that results from natural necessity is also more predominant in the original condition than it is in more advanced states of human interaction. As suffering that results from the imposition of human will becomes more possible, I suggest that active pity becomes less common.

For Rousseau, the emergence of vanity or pride is thus coupled with the diminishing of active pity. Rousseau maintains that the development of pride is concomitant with the development of reason in the form of reflection: "Reason engenders vanity and reflection fortifies it; reason turns man back upon himself, it separates him from all that bothers and afflicts him" (132). The active pity that is present in the original condition entails a form of reasoning based on perceiving, measuring, and calculating the actual relations among things. This is what allows humans to judge their relative strength and skill against another. In any encounter, the capacity to judge physical distances between aggressor and prey, for example, is integral to the decision to fight or flee, or in the case of active pity to come to the aid of a suffering being. It may be that humans in the original condition have the advantage of not being subject to prejudice (wrong reasoning) and pride (the desire to be esteemed in the opinion of others). Therefore they are not as prone to the resulting distortions in judgment and not as easily deceived about the actual relations among things.

Philosophical reflection in particular, according to Rousseau, often works against active pity. Why? In part because the philosopher in civil society, animated by pride and prejudice, is less capable of perceiving and measuring the relations or distances between entities, whether objects or individuals. Rousseau evokes a vivid image of the philosopher: "Philosophy isolates him; because of it he says in secret, at the sight of a suffering man: Perish if you will, I am safe. No longer can anything except dangers to the entire society trouble the tranquil sleep of the philosopher and tear him from his bed. His fellow-man can be murdered with impunity right under his window; he has only to put his hands over his ears and argue with himself a bit to prevent nature, which revolts within him, from identifying him with the man who is being assassinated" (132). This picture of the philosopher in an upstairs room, while down below his fellow-man is suffering injury from another, compels us to think about the question of distance (and provides an interesting mirror of the scene from the Mandeville fable). The philosopher in this situation detaches or removes himself from the encounter, establishing and perceiving an artificially great distance between himself and an other. He might easily reach out to offer help, perhaps simply by opening the window and threatening to call the police, without harming himself. Or he could come to the aid of the attacked man at the risk of some detriment to his own well-being.

Similarly, the tyrant detaches himself completely from the suffering of another for which he is in fact responsible. Conversely, he is also prone to artificially collapsing entirely the distance between himself and another. The tyrant Alexander engages in misperception by aligning himself so closely with the actor who is feigning suffering on stage that he moans and cries in the audience (131). Pity, in either its active or passive form, may entail commiseration, or feeling, or identifying with the suffering of another. But active pity, paradoxically, may require that one *not* collapse completely the distance between the oneself and the one who suffers to the extent that one cannot distinguish who, in fact, is suffering. We would not feel compelled to aid another suffering being if we mistook their suffering for our own. Such a mistake signals a distortion of the actual relations among things. It is an example of prejudice that distorts measurement and works against active pity.

The capacity to experience what is common to us, Tracy Strong argues, is precisely the quality identified by Rousseau that is increasingly missing from modern life. To experience the "natural" in one another requires that each see the other as a separate entity. Commiseration or sharing with another works only when there is an acknowledgment of separation and proper distance. And this dynamic is manifest above all in pity. Strong writes: "To know what I have in common with someone else, I must be able to stand outside myself. Pity is the archetypical activity that makes the commonly human and the humanly common available. Nor can one experience the common (or the human alone). Pity involves seeing someone else and seeing that one is like that other being. There is a theatrical presupposition to pity: It requires the witnessing of an action. It requires that I have differentiated myself from another whom I recognize as like myself."[7] Interestingly, Strong's interpretation of what Rousseau is saying about human interaction contains a back-and-forth movement between designating pity as something that entails an "activity" or "sets us in motion" and describing pity as "relatively ineffective in the state of nature": "nothing, however, follows from it."[8] Strong's assessment reflects the conceptual distinction I make between active and passive pity, suggesting that it can clarify what Rousseau is saying about pity even in its most elemental form and make sense of the extent to which it can generate action.

Another seeming paradox in Rousseau's account of pity – whether it can be extended only to particular individuals who are in close proximity or whether it can be extended to all of humanity – can also be ameliorated by considering the conceptual relationship among pity, pride, and prejudice and the conditions that generate active pity. Because prejudice entails an improper measurement of the relative distance among things and humans, it works against active pity. A proper measurement of actual relative distances can entail, in some instances, reaching out a great distance to a great number, and in other instances, reaching out to only one or a few who are nearby. Clifford Orwin's discussion of the complexities of pity or compassion in Rousseau is relevant here. Orwin maintains that reason makes a vital contribution to compassion in two ways. First, reason through imagination generates the social virtues of friendship, benevolence, and generosity, which can take root in advanced civil society. Second, the most powerful presentation of compassion by Rousseau is linked to the "most reasonable of men" – those "great cosmopolitan souls" whose clarity of vision enables them to extend a form of compassion (benevolence) to all.[9] There are only a few of these individuals, who seem to have godlike, or at least supra-human, qualities. Does this mean that pity in its ultimate form (transformed from compassion into benevolence) can be extended only by the few to all of humanity in a state of advanced civil society? Or is it the case that, following Tracy Strong, the ultimate form pity takes for Rousseau is something that is experienced by ordinary humans as what is common to them all, and most present or accessible to them in the original human condition?

Conclusion

If we return to the conceptual apparatus of pity, pride, and prejudice, as I have outlined them above, some of this can be sorted out. Active pity, I suggest, entails reasoning that is based on perceiving and measuring the actual relations among things – a capacity that exists in both the state of nature and civil society, in both savage and sophisticated humanity. It is curtailed by prejudice or improper measurement, which can similarly occur in either the state of nature or advanced civil society. What changes in civil society is that human suffering takes on its most vicious form: suffering that derives from injury imposed by another human will.

The importance of proper perception and measurement may be relevant to understanding why individuals in contemporary liberal regimes tend to mobilize so quickly when it comes to alleviating the suffering of not only victims of natural disasters but also mistreated animals and children. Neither animals nor children can be associated with the exercise of a free, fully developed human will and, concomitantly, the intention to harm. It may be that we choose to eschew active pity where human will to harm is involved because we sense it complicates, distorts, and makes unclear the actual relations among things, whether the entities are individuals, interest groups, or sovereign states. We may perceive, for example, that we are being deceived by revolutionary armies when asked to give aid to those suffering injustice in a civil war. We donate money and goods to victims of a hurricane because the problem is clear, the solution simple, and the connection between action and outcome straightforward. Our donations go to food, water, and shelter, and modern transportation makes it possible to provide these across great distances. As soon as human will is involved, however, measuring the connection between action and outcome becomes more difficult. Paradoxically, then, the greater the human suffering, the less we are inclined to act to alleviate it.

According to Ruth Grant, Rousseau's *Discourses* show us not simply an image of human beings in an imagined or hypothetical state to which they cannot return,[10] but an image of ourselves as beings perpetually situated between the potential for corruption and the potential for ethical regeneration. The key to the latter, Grant argues, is the ideal of integrity, interpreted as entailing both purity and wholeness.[11] Integrity as wholeness is compatible with the ideal of authenticity – a particularly contemporary concern that has its roots in Rousseau. And *amour-propre* (pride), whereby one lives in and becomes dependent on the opinion of others and experiences dividedness rather than wholeness, is the main factor in undermining such authenticity. Rousseau's essential contribution to our understanding of contemporary ethical behaviour, Grant persuasively argues, is that the fundamental source of corruption is not power, but "the desire for preeminence, a desire that can be found in almost everyone."[12] Grant ends her book with an insight that captures an important dimension of what might be at work in active pity that is not derailed by pride or prejudice. Rousseau's analysis illuminates the problem of resistance and collaboration, Grant maintains, by offering us the image of a person of integrity: "People of this sort may be found anywhere, but they are more likely to be found among simple people who have not obscured the voice of conscience with a fog of sophistication, philosophic speculation, and the false moral ideal of balanced moderation. A Rousseauian political science would predict, for example, that the French peasants would be more likely to hide persecuted Jews in their homes, while the Parisians would rationalize collaboration with the Nazis."[13]

Feelings in the Political Philosophy of J.S. Mill

Marlene K. Sokolon

What kind of theoretical foundation does John Stuart Mill provide for understanding the role of feelings or emotions in social and ethical decision making?[1] This may seem like an unorthodox question, because J.S. Mill, his father, James Mill, and Jeremy Bentham are the principal founders of utilitarianism. This ethical philosophy, in general, rejects a reliance on emotions in the evaluation of right and wrong; instead, utilitarianism stresses a situation-based, rational calculus that determines the "greatest good for the greatest number." One common critique of utilitarian ethics is this confidence in rational calculus and tendency to treat human beings as "reasoning machines." This criticism, however, oversimplifies the depth of and disagreement within classical utilitarian thought. J.S. Mill uses the term "reasoning machine" to criticize Bentham's version as an oversimplification of human decision making.[2] In contrast, J.S. Mill argues that emotions play a more prominent role in ethical decision making and in the pursuit of knowledge and truth. Mill emphasizes that truth, for example, requires not only logical understanding of suppositions but also a deep emotional commitment. He suggests that an education devoid of emotional training undermines the capacity for human sympathy. Without sympathy or the capacity to recognize and feel the emotions of others, he believes utilitarian philosophy is unable to incline narrow self-interest toward the interest of others, the greatest good, or even the principles of human progress.

Mill relies more on the importance of feelings in his political philosophy than do earlier versions of utilitarianism; however, this chapter argues that he fails to provide a sufficient theoretical foundation concerning the role of feelings in sociopolitical and ethical decision making. Mill's theoretical approach to feelings offers a limited view of their sociopolitical and ethical relevance. Mill stresses, for example, that feelings have only artificial connections to actions. Untutored by reason, feelings are capable only of reinforcing unconsidered and culturally determined prejudices concerning ethical behaviour. More often than not, unconsidered and prejudiced feelings of right and wrong simply reinforce the majority's standards of acceptable behaviour, which stifles liberty, individuality, and human progress. Furthermore, Mill categorizes feelings in a polarized manner: he identifies "good" feelings with self-constraint and "bad" feelings with self-conceit. Only the good feelings have a role in encouraging noble pursuits or providing a commitment to truth. Most significantly, he maintains that emotions make no independent contributions to ethical decision making without the guidance of higher culture, education, and rationality.

Nevertheless, Mill's theoretical perspective is relevant for contemporary theory concerning emotions for two important reasons. First, Mill's version of utilitarian ethical philosophy remains influential in contemporary ethical debates, and Mill is still considered a philosophic authority.[3] Second, although contemporary utilitarian thought has been influenced by other philosophers since Mill's writings, this chapter highlights the potential for utilitarian thought to under-represent the contribution of emotions to sociopolitical and ethical decision making.[4] It is beyond the scope of this analysis to account for the evolution and diversity of contemporary ethical thought; however, highlighting the limitations of Mill's utilitarian philosophy offers important insights and questions for exploring the role of emotions in contemporary utilitarian thought.

In order to explore the role of feelings in Mill's political philosophy, the argument is divided into three sections. First, I discuss Mill's approach to feelings, including the differences between his and Bentham's views, the influence of tradition, and the importance of feelings to his theory of truth, happiness, and ethics. Second, I explore the insights of Mill's understanding of feelings, including his argument that feelings have only artificial associations, the relationship between intellect and feelings, and emotional polarity. Third, I examine Mill's perspective as it relates to current theories of emotions, highlighting the ways in which Mill's approach to feelings may actually work to undermine the very political goals, such as an egalitarian and just society, shared by Mill and modern followers.

Mill's General View of Feelings

Since Mill reports that his own perspective regarding feelings is, at least partially, a response to theoretical deficiencies in earlier formulations of utilitarianism, it is essential to explore the context in which Mill developed that perspective. To be fair to Bentham and James Mill, feelings are a necessary aspect of their determination of ethical judgments. At its core, Bentham's ethics is founded on his principle of utility: right actions have the overall tendency to promote the greatest happiness for the greatest number. Bentham identified happiness with pleasure (and those things which he understands as synonymous to pleasure, such as benefit, advantage, good, or happiness) and the absence of pain. His theory, as the calculation of the "net sum" of pleasures and pains, pays considerable attention to human emotions and other forms of affect that are connected with pleasure and pain. A common criticism of Bentham's theory – and the aspect that Mill found personally debilitating, as we shall see – is that Bentham did not postulate qualitative differences among pleasures and pains. The net sum calculation is a purely quantitative distinction that includes variations in intensity, duration, certainty, propinquity, and tendency to produce other pleasures. Thus, the pleasure of helping others is held in no higher regard than pleasures associated with sex or food. Note that this view is distinct from ancient or medieval understandings of emotions and associated pleasures; Ferry's analysis in Chapter 4 of this volume, for example, reveals that Aquinas' view of emotions posits a difference in both degree and kind. In contrast, Bentham made distinctions only in degree of affect. Furthermore, as there is no discernment between pleasures and other affective states, the goals inspired by feelings are indistinguishable.[5] In other words, Bentham's theory does not provide a foundation from which to argue that utilitarian goals are more pleasurable or ethical than any other goal or experience.

Mill provides a critique of this nondiscrimination of pleasure and feelings based on his personal experience. In his *Autobiography*, Mill suggests that his inability to discern and qualify pleasure was a main reason for the nervous breakdown and state of depression he experienced in his mid-twenties. In the autumn of 1826, Mill felt a "dull state of nerves" due to the realization that he would not feel joy or happiness even if all the objects of his life were accomplished. Mill had been brought up solely under his father's tutelage, with an education that emphasized the development of rational and analytic habits. His depression, Mill believed, was due to his "habit of analysis [that] strengthen[ed] associations between causes and effects, means and ends, but tend[ed] altogether to weaken those which are ... a matter of feeling." In another passage, he emphasizes this point by saying that the habit of analysis had a tendency to wear away or "perpetually worm at the root" of feelings. Mill understood his personal crisis as a response to a deficiency in his attachment to the truth of his goals; he felt no pleasure in achieving any of his goals, including the creation of a just and utilitarian society. Most importantly, he recognized that his education lacked a means by which he could develop or cultivate discrete pleasures or preferences for utilitarian goals. Mill found a therapy for his depression through poetry. This poetic education, especially Wordsworth's poetry, cultivated and encouraged "sympathetic and imaginative pleasures, which could be shared by all human beings." Because of his breakdown and subsequent realization of the importance of feelings, the "cultivation of the feelings became one of the cardinal points in [Mill's] ethical and philosophical creed."[6]

Given Mill's personal reflections on the value of feelings in the development of his philosophical view, it is not surprising to find that they are important in his ethical and political philosophy.[7] For example, he understands that social behaviour is not guided solely by reason but also by the tenets of custom that form social and antisocial affections. Certain social affections have developed from the obvious interests of society, but others, even those mistaken for the moral sentiments, have little to do with the interests of society. The influence of feeling can be seen in Mill's argument for freedom of speech: without the attachment of feeling, truth lacks vitality. Feelings are also essential in Mill's application of the principle of utility and in his theories of individuality and human progress.

Feelings as an Aspect of Custom and Tradition

In the introduction to *On Liberty*, Mill addresses the inherent danger in democracies to tend toward the tyranny of the majority in political deci-sion making. The tendency of the majority to force their opinions on others underlies Mill's concept of the harm principle, which asserts that the only circumstance in which "power can be rightfully exercised over any member of a civilized community, against his will, is to prevent harm to others."[8] Over any actions or opinions that primarily concern the rationally mature agent, he or she is sovereign. Mill's justification for this principle, which allows each individual to be his own guardian and to possess the liberty to govern his own opinions and actions, is the progress of human nature. At one point in human progress, Mill explains, the aim of political philosophy and action was to establish institutional checks and limitations on governmental power; however, at the point when democracy is established, the rulers become identified with the will of the majority of the people. For Mill such a majority consists in either numerical strength or the most active part of the citizenry. At this point, constitutional checks may hold the rulers accountable, but, according to Mill, society itself can become tyrannical by executing its own mandates, which can penetrate "much more deeply into the details of life, and enslav[e] the soul itself."[9]

From Mill's perspective, social tyranny is the greatest threat to freedom and human progress. This danger remains, despite constitutional and political checks, because there exists "a feeling in each person's mind that everyone should be required to act as he, and those with whom he sympathizes, would like them to act."[10] In addition, Mill stresses that opinions on the regulation of human conduct are not always supported by reason, but only by the belief that the agent's feelings on whatever subject, including how others ought to behave, are a sufficient criterion for sanction. Hence, human beings judge others' behaviour by self-reinforcing standards, in which the proper behav-iour is that which is liked by the agent and improper behaviour that which is disliked. When the collectivity of individuals all likes the same behaviour, they impose their own ideas and practices as rules of conduct on all others, leading to social tyranny.

The underlying purpose of the harm principle for Mill is to prevent this unreflective desire for conformity from becoming socially tyrannical. Human feeling limits punitive authority over conduct (based on our own conduct) and the desire to enforce our preferences on all others. Mill argues that political protections against tyranny are insufficient, because in this case coercion derives from social and not political standards. Although Mill recognizes the potential danger of social formation of emotional response, his underlying approach is similar to the classical view highlighted by Kingston (Chapter 5) and Abizadeh (Chapter 3) in this volume. Mill's emphasis on the social contribution to collectivized feelings is similar, for example, to Aristotle's view of the contribution of *nomos* to a collective norm of emotional responses.[11]

Mill also describes the source of our self-enforcing, egocentric preferences and behavioural norms. They are not, he argues, based on universal or rational principles, but on the tenets of custom. The desire for conformity, which manifests itself through an enforcement of preferences, arises from the "magical influence of custom."[12] Although all societies have to place practical limits on individual independence and social control, the rules in no two countries or ages are alike. But the community of any given age and country acts as if its rules are universally agreed-upon and obvious to the rest of mankind. Consequently the only universal or natural aspect to morality is the feeling that the rules are self-evident and self-justifying. The force of custom is so strong that it is continually mistaken as "natural," and people are accustomed to believe that "their feeling on subjects of this nature is better than reasons and render reasons unnecessary." Therefore majority consensus alone cannot determine the boundary between individual liberty and social conduct. This consensus is nothing more than a collectivity of non-rational, self-enforcing feelings that everyone ought to behave according to the majority's standards. Mill's harm principle is necessary because it establishes a limit that is based not solely on custom but on a rational standard of societal inference.

Feelings and Truth

Thus far, this chapter has explored Mill's concerns regarding the influence of unconsidered culture and feelings on ethical standards; importantly, however, feelings are also an essential aspect of his argument for freedom of speech and commitment to truth. Admittedly, Mill understands that feelings can work against truth. As with the self-enforcing beliefs of custom, the common human assumption of infallibility and our general indifference to the actual truth result in self-enforcing opinions concerning truth and falsity. The assumption of infallibility and correctness of opinion relies on uncontested feelings of superstition and prejudice. In other words, human beings generally assume their opinions are true and dislike having this assumption challenged. At the same time, the belief in the "infallibility" of opinion is also acknowledged to be insincere since, in fact, "everyone well knows himself to be fallible."[13] Realistically, Mill argues, opinions fall into three categories: an opinion can be true, it can be false, or it can contain a mixture of truth and falsity. Freedom of speech proves necessary for all three categories. When the opinion is partially or entirely false, Mill argues that freedom of speech allows each individual to replace his or her false opinions with the truth of each subject matter.

Yet more importantly, Mill argues specifically that freedom of speech is necessary even when an opinion is true. In this case, without the active challenge from opposing positions and lively engagement in discussion, truth becomes nothing more than received opinion or simply "dead dogma." For Mill, truth that is assumed or taught, independent of argument, is simply an irrational prejudice; the only truth that ought to be held so by a rational being is an opinion derived from the cultivation of intellect and judgment. Furthermore, Mill stresses that truth is meaningful only when (1) it can be defended with arguments that are rationally persuasive and (2) the whole force of the struggle to adjudicate competing positions leading to the true view has been felt by the subject. Lively apprehension of the truth is not found in rational argument, but in truth that has "penetrated the feelings" or has been realized in "the imagination, the feelings, or the understanding." Truth, therefore, cannot be received, but is found in rational argumentation and in the feeling of its rational ground.

As with the necessity of limiting conformity with regard to action, Mill bases his argument for freedom of thought and discussion in lively emotive affiliation to true principles.[14] Significantly, in the case of human opinion and pursuit of truth, our feelings can have either negative or positive effects. On the one hand, feelings potentially reinforce prejudice and dogma, while on the other hand, feelings challenge irrational discrimination and are necessary for an attachment to those truths of rational persuasion. Hence, a rational apprehension of truth also requires an emotional association with the truth of rational propositions.

Feelings and Happiness

Beyond their importance in attaching human beings to rational truth, feelings are also involved in Mill's analysis concerning individuality and the pursuit of individual happiness. According to Mill, human happiness lies in the freedom to pursue "our own good in our own way" as long as we do not harm others.[15] Liberty is necessary to protect the choice of action as much as of thoughts and opinions. The good each person pursues ought to be based on individual character and not on a simple imitation of unconsidered traditions and customs, which provide a narrow and often unsuitable experience to individuals. Since custom does not provide the conditions that foster human faculties of perception, judgment, and discriminative feelings, when it is the sole guide of individual choice it provides simply "dead" experience. Genuine choice is made only when the individual goes beyond and challenges the narrow experience of tradition. As Mill would put it, the comparative worth of a human being comes from the genuine choice of her own plan of life.

In addition, since human beings have diverse tastes, what one person enjoys or what helps her cultivate her higher feelings is often a distracting burden or a hindrance to another. As a consequence, without diversity in the mode of human experience, human beings can neither obtain their fair share of happiness nor develop their mental, moral, or aesthetic potential. The fount of individuality is found, thus, in experiencing a diversity of pleasures and pains. Through diverse experience each person can choose those pleasures that suit his or her own character. Although Mill admits that not everyone is necessarily capable of pursuing the higher pleasures, liberty provides the conditions that enable the pursuit of pleasures not supported by custom, including all higher pleasures of the intellect and ethical ends. Mill also suggests that such higher pleasures would be preferred to lower pleasures by most individuals. Although such views of the distinctions between higher and lower pleasures may seem elitist, Mill's theory protects only actions that do not harm another; all human beings, regardless of what they find pleasurable, should be able "to carry these [pleasurable actions] out in their lives without hindrance, either physical or moral, from their fellow men, so long as it is at their own risk and peril."[16] Importantly, for Mill, individual happiness, as well as the means by which happiness is pursued, is not solely rational or logical. Mill argues that happiness requires the recognition and cultivation of one's unique feelings of pleasure with all one's facilities of judgment and emotion.

Feelings in Ethics

Mill's understanding of individuality, as connected to the diversity of pleasures and pains, also highlights the role of feelings in his utilitarian ethics. Simply put, the foundation of morality is the utility or greatest happiness principle.[17] This principle postulates that actions are right if they tend, in proportion, to promote happiness; wrong actions are those that tend, in proportion, to produce unhappiness. Mill defines happiness as "pleasure and absence of pain" and unhappiness as "pain and the privation of pleasure." Even on this basic level, utilitarianism posits a role for human affect, as it is affect that "feels" pleasure and pain. Mill also understands feelings as the key element that allows utilitarianism to surmount the individualistic hedonism of seeking only one's own pleasure, because human beings have the capacity for sympathy and affection for our fellow creatures.[18] Like Adam Smith, Mill does not understand sympathy as an emotion; however, unlike Smith's focus on sympathy as an evaluation of appropriateness, Mill's view concerning sympathy is more akin to David Hume's.[19] For Mill, sympathy is a faculty or capacity that is affected by observing another's emotions or feelings to such an extent that the agent takes on, or feels, another's pleasure and pain. In other words, the agent feels his own pleasure at another's pleasure and his own pain at another's pain. This view of sympathy helps to account for how human beings can identify with and motivate actions beyond immediate self-interested pleasure. Thus the faculty of sympathy makes it possible to maximize pleasure that leads to the greatest happiness for all. The capacity for sympathy and emotions such as affection and love allows utilitarian ethics to move beyond calculations of actions with purely self-interested or egoistic presuppositions.

Sympathy is also essential to Mill's understanding of how human beings develop abstract notions of justice. Mill argues that the two key ingredients underlying the concept of justice are the desire to punish those who have done harm and the knowledge that harm has been done.[20] The desire to punish is the outgrowth of two natural instincts: the impulse of self-defence and sympathy. For Mill, it is not social sanctions, but the subject's own impulse or instinct for self-defence that motivates cessation and retaliation against harms that affect her. This human impulse is natural, since even animals defend themselves against aggressors who hurt them or their young. In human beings, the capacity for sympathy allows human beings to extend this natural desire for individual self-defence to a desire to retaliate against the harms done to others. Finally, human intelligence allows human beings to apprehend a community of interest not only between individuals, but also between an individual and the highest principles of her society. Since the restriction of individual liberty (except to protect self and others from harm) is one of the greatest threats to societal progress, Mill stresses that a just society requires the development of sympathy for the protection not only of others but of the progress of society. Thus ethical and judicial rules that forbid mankind to harm others, including wrongful interference with freedoms, can be supported as a natural outgrowth of human sympathy.

In addition, Mill argues that feelings offer more than an abstract theoretical commitment to ethical rules: they provide the intensity or energy that underlies and motivates ethical action. First, the energy of emotion can inspire moral feelings that are so strong as to become self-sanctioning. For Mill, a true moral feeling would be based on self-sanctioning behaviour without relying on incentives of reward and punishment.[21] Second, as Mill stresses, "desires and impulses are as much a part of a perfect human being as beliefs and restraints."[22] Although Mill admits the potential for desires to motivate vicious action, even extremely strong desires or feelings are not necessarily dangerous. Mill argues that "strong desire is simply another name for energy"; therefore desires that are stronger, more diverse, and properly cultivated "are capable, possibly of more evil, but certainly of more good." In fact, the greatest danger lies in passively following tradition without the passion and energy of pursuing individuality, noble pleasures, and ethical action. Passivity of feelings denotes a deficiency of personal impulses, which in turn cultivates indolent and submissive characters. According to Mill, people act badly not because their desires are strong, but because their consciences are weak.

As a final point, the development of a strong conscience and commitment to avoid harming others requires a systematic cultivation and education of feelings. It is only through the proper education that feelings become associated with ethical actions; for Mill, there are no natural associations between certain feelings and particular actions, objects, individuals, or ideas.[23] In other words, there are no natural moral emotions; feelings are based on arbitrary associations with ethical objects. Mill believes that no one naturally feels pleasure in fulfilling her duties or pursuing the greatest good for the greatest number. Doing one's duty can only be felt as pleasurable if one is taught to feel pleasure in doing so or in "protecting societal progress."

At this juncture, Mill's criticism of his own education can be understood. His education excelled in rational analysis but failed to cultivate emotional feelings or develop a sufficient sympathy for others. Although Mill possessed a highly rational comprehension of ethical rules, he lacked both "energy" and any feeling of pleasure associated with his humanitarian goals. He suggests that his late education in poetry cultivated a strong pleasure in the love of natural scenery, and also, through sympathy with the poet's emotions, his ability to feel another's pleasure and pain. In this sense, Mill would agree with philosophers, such as Aristotle, who understand ethics as dependent upon the education or habituation of emotions. Furthermore, like Martha Nussbaum's argument for a therapeutic education, Mill would disagree that such an education could be primarily rational or philosophical.[24] It is poetry, or an aesthetic education, that Mill recognizes as essential to promoting a capacity for sympathy and creating the proper association of pleasure with the tenets of utilitarian philosophy. Thus a special emotional education is required to associate pleasure with proper, ethical goals. Left unconsidered, feelings or emotions would attach to the prejudices of custom or, as in Mill's case, be underdeveloped and debilitating.

Insights of Mill's Approach to Emotions

Despite Mill's break from his disproportionately analytical education and the relatively prominent role given to feelings in his theories of truth, liberty, individuality, and ethics, his philosophy remains committed to three interdependent assumptions regarding the role of affect in human decision making. First, as mentioned above, he argues that the connection of feelings to objects is entirely based on the cultivation of arbitrary or artificial associations. Second, he assumes that intellect and feelings are entirely separate realms of the human mind.[25] Third, he believes that feelings consist of a negative-positive polarity based on pleasurable or painful associations. Mill breaks with Bentham's theory by suggesting a qualitative hierarchy to pleasures: in one sense this means that "good" and pleasurable feelings are higher than "bad" or painful feelings. In consequence, Mill's thought opens up the possibility of educating the artificial emotional associations to connect all ethical behaviour with good feelings and all immoral behaviour with bad feelings, and his theory suggests that bad feelings can be altogether condemned. Therefore, despite the importance of deep feelings, reason remains predominant in determining moral ends and ensuring feelings are educated with the proper artificial associations. In the final estimation, Mill's call for a poetic education may do little to counteract the dependency on reason and limited role for feelings in his ethical theory.

Emotional Associations

Mill remains committed, in his understanding of the role of feelings in ethical and political theory, to the idea that feelings have no natural connection with objects, situations, ideas, or circumstances. As Mill stresses in his *Autobiography*, no objects or goals in the external world are naturally pleasurable or painful; our emotional associations with them always contain something artificial and causal. He stresses that his education lacked attention to the development of a strong or deep association between his pleasure and "creation of utilitarian society." The correct education would create associations that "become so intense and inveterate as to be practically indissoluble."[26] But because analysis tends to wear away artificial associations, these intense associations must be established before an education in rational analysis. Thus, a vibrant poetic education, especially developing associations of pleasure to emotions connected with human sympathy, should be a precursor to analytic education.

Mill's position on artificial emotional associations has several consequences for his theory of ethics. Mill stresses that affect is a part of ethical decisions: the energy from strong feelings, for example, motivates people to act on their desire to punish offenders. Nevertheless, in general, neither reason nor blind culture associates the emotions with "good" or "bad" ethical objects. Unlike Hume, who suggests that objects possess certain qualities that naturally produce particular feelings (as Krause discusses in Chapter 6 of this volume), Mill argues that emotional attachments are solely the products of our experience and education. In *Utilitarianism*, for example, Mill criticizes philosophers who argue that there is a natural moral sense or faculty that informs us of right and wrong.[27] We may, he agrees, have a natural inclination to punish those who harm or injure us, but turning that inclination towards defending another or feeling pleasure at doing one's duty is a product of our experience, not nature. In his view, "moral feelings are not innate, but acquired," in much the same way as speech or agriculture is acquired, by education and experience. Thus, only through purposeful cultivation do human beings come to feel pleasure in the happiness of others and in their own moral actions.

Mill stresses that since we are social beings, the desire to be in unity with others provides a strong incentive to develop these moral feelings. In and of themselves, however, moral feelings are not natural; in fact, feelings are capable of being cultivated in almost any direction "by sufficient use of the external sanctions and of the force of early impressions." It is possible, therefore, to control completely the development of these feelings and their associations with pleasure and pain by external manipulation. The right sort of education would encourage the association of pleasure with ideas or actions that would benefit humanity, but education could instead create individuals who feel pleasure, for example, in another's pain. The association of feelings with moral objects is, in modern language, entirely malleable to experience.

Intellect and Feelings

The idea of artificial emotional attachments has an important consequence in Mill's perspective concerning the relationship between feelings and the intellect. Mill recognizes the human mind as more than a calculative faculty; he criticizes Bentham's utilitarianism for ignoring the complexity of human motivations and positing too narrow a conception of human beings as "reasoning machines." Yet Mill understands feelings and the intellect to be discrete or distinctive. In his argument for freedom of speech, for example, Mill states that suppressing dissenting opinions is dangerous because it lulls both the mind and the heart. He also suggests that commitment to the truth requires that it live in both the feelings and understanding. His language reveals that this experience of truth is really on two separate levels. First, for rational beings, there is an intellectual apprehension of the truth by means of "knowledge of the grounds of the opinion" such that one could defend it against objections. Without this intellectual understanding or "knowing the truth," one possesses only superstition. Second, there is a decline in the living power of opinion when the truth remains unchallenged and no longer penetrates the feelings. Mill believes human beings often are taught ideas that are not fully realized until personal experience has brought them home. Truth requires both an intellectual understanding and an emotional commitment to the correct judgment. Thus, Mill argues that comprehension of truth requires two distinctive aspects – "clear apprehension and deep feeling of truth."[28]

Beyond arguing that affect and reason are discrete aspects of the mind, Mill also argues that each requires a different kind of education. And reason must direct the proper education of affective associations. For example, we know from Mill's *Autobiography* that he blamed his breakdown on a lack of an education that developed sympathy for others' emotions.[29] As Mill experienced it in his own life, an analytical education can undermine all but the most intensely experienced emotional associations. Yet it is important to recognize that these associations, even if intense, remain artificial. The poetic education, like tradition or custom, can only make those associations seem natural.

Although Mill does not develop a precise psychology, his general picture of the relationship between reason and emotion is that of a dualistic mind. First, affect and reason remain separate aspects of the psyche that require separate and distinctive – poetic and analytic – forms of education. Second, without attention to the proper, discrete education of each aspect, Mill understands the rational and emotional aspects of the mind to work in opposition to the other. Without rational analysis, for example, emotional associations are reinforced and learned through the "magical influence of custom." Custom associates feelings with rules of conduct based on prejudice and superstition. Supported by the assumption of infallibility, the feelings associated with superstition can work against liberty and, for Mill, ultimately against truth and human progress. Human rationality then challenges and dispels the prejudice of uncontested and conformist feelings associated solely with cultural rules of conduct. In this instance Mill's view of emotions is similar to Hume's and to what Bradshaw suggests in Chapter 9 of this volume: i.e., giving priority to political and educational reform rather than relying on the emotions as key to reforming political consciousness. Unrestrained rationality, conversely, also presents a danger to truth and progress when intellectual understanding and analysis are unsupported by strong associations of deep feeling for the truth. An intellectual education can undermine the feelings required for ethical action, such as affection and benevolence.

Mill thinks that the proper education – first in aesthetics and then in analysis – can cultivate a psychological state in which intellect and affect support the same goals. Importantly, this educational system is rationally directed (even if the curriculum is also aesthetic) and requires a prior political commitment to certain ethical goals. Even more important, his position on education and cultivation of affect and reason underlines a dualistic psychological portrait; each aspect of the psyche is relevant to ethical action and progress but each aspect is naturally distinct and disconnected from the other.

Emotional Polarity

A second consequence of Mill's position concerning artificial associations is the assumption of a negative-positive polarity to feelings, based on whether they are experienced as pleasurable or painful. Not unexpectedly for a utilitarian, pleasurable feelings are considered good or positive, and painful feelings are bad or negative. In Bentham's understanding of this polarity, pleasure and pain come in degrees and can be measured in comparison to each other on a single scale. Bentham's utility calculus includes an assessment of short-term pain versus longer-term pleasure, but he does not distinguish between higher and lower pleasures. Mill, however, posits a qualitative distinction between different types of pleasures and pains. His famous example in *Utilitarianism* is that there are intrinsically superior kinds of pleasures and those who pursue such higher pleasures are more happy than those who pursue lower pleasures. The higher pleasures, for Mill, are connected with the cultivation of a noble character. Again, not coincidentally, such a character would feel pleasure in the goals of utilitarian philosophy, such as pursuing the greatest amount of happiness for all. Thus, Mill is able to pronounce: "It is better to be Socrates dissatisfied than a fool satisfied."[30]

Mill's insistence on qualitative differences among pleasures allows him to categorize feelings along a negative and positive scale indicating whether the emotion is properly an object of admiration or of contempt.[31] Admirable feelings are those that encourage the individual toward the ideal perfection of human nature, such as pleasure in self-constraint, amicability, and pleasures of the intellect. Contemptible feelings include self-destructive pleasures, such as rashness and self-conceit, and antisocial pleasures such as malice, envy, irascibility, love of domineering others, greed, and pride. In *On Liberty*, Mill argues that the only legitimate social and government interference is the harm principle; individuals who pursue self-destructive pleasures may be avoided or pitied, but it is unjustifiable to interfere with these pleasures or any purely self-regarding actions influenced by them. Nevertheless, in this same work he also argues that not only the actions inspired by certain antisocial feelings but the antisocial feelings themselves are fit objects of moral retribution and punishment. In other words, there are positive feelings, undesirable (but permissible) feelings, and feelings that are strictly negative and within the purview of social control and punishment. In Mill's approach, an ethical society that accepts the harm principle can justifiably condemn certain feelings.

Contemporary Implications of Mill's Approach to Feelings

Mill's theoretical insights into feelings, especially as regarding principles of liberty and ethics, are comparable to contemporary approaches to emotions.[32] Mill's theory is reflected in contemporary approaches that assume: (1) that emotional associations are entirely plastic and determined by experience; (2) that reason and emotions are discrete psychological states; and (3) that there is a negative-positive emotional polarity and that certain negative emotions can properly be disallowed. Certain contemporary approaches reflect Mill's argument for extricating emotions deemed unacceptable from political and ethical decision making.

The implications of Mill's theory emerge from the interaction of the three insights outlined above. To summarize the first point, Mill understands feelings to have purely artificial connections to objects; no natural or necessary connections exist between feelings and ideas, people, or objects, including moral objects. Through proper emotional development, certain feelings can function like a "moral sentiment," but Mill stresses that there is no natural moral sentiment. Furthermore, the human capacity for nobler or affectionate feelings is "a tender plant, easily killed."[33] This artificiality also means that, in essence, emotional responses are entirely malleable and, in modern terms, culturally constructed.

Also significant is that in Mill's view reason and feelings are discrete, even requiring entirely unique educational experiences. Since feelings have no natural connections to ethical objects, we use our rational judgment to determine ethical objects and educate feelings toward the proper objects. Thus, reason tends to the "tender plant" of the emotional capacities, which on their own form merely customary attachments or, as in Mill's own situation, form no real attachments at all. Mill understands rationally determined proper attachments to be a pleasure felt in the nobler pursuits of the intellect, self-control, and in sympathizing with others. He stresses that, like self-destructive actions, purely self-destructive feelings may be the objects of pity, but never of resentment or anger. Nonetheless, the rationally determined emotional associations can be taught to abhor not only antisocial actions but also antisocial feelings, such as envy, love of domination, or pride.

Mill's theory potentially obscures the purpose of emotions in sociopolitical and ethical decision making. Mill's assumption of an emotional polarity of "good" and "bad" emotions is being challenged on several fronts. As Robert Solomon argues, a theory of emotional polarity is both simplistic and detrimental to serious research on emotions.[34] Solomon maintains that emotions are not connected in any meaningful way to pleasures and pains; for example, love can be pleasurable, but most of us have also experienced it as painful. Fear, which is typically regarded as a negative, painful emotion, is also necessary for self-protection in dangerous situations. From this perspective emotions are neither positive nor negative, and thus no emotion exclusively contributes to positive or negative sociopolitical actions. Mill's account of emotional polarity clouds the complexity of emotional response and the relationship between emotions and reason. Affect is connected to more than simply pleasures and pains; it includes a response to external stimulus and circumstances. And contemporary research finds that social decision making is an interaction requiring both rational and emotional contributions.[35] A seemingly bad or painful emotion thus may be essential in a complex decision-making process.

Other current approaches also challenge Mill's assumption that emotions have no natural or innate associations with external objects, including sociopolitical and ethical objects. Ronald de Sousa and others, for example, argue that emotions are natural evolutionary adaptations that facilitate survival by providing suitable reactions to external stimuli.[36] This approach also suggests that a wide range of emotions, from desire for revenge to indignation, benevolence, and pity, are natural aspects of moral decision making. This perspective does not deny variability in human morality, nor does it propose a strict predetermined connection between emotions and abstract universal judgments or ethical rules. Emotions are interactions between innate inclinations and social experiences that result in a degree of (but not absolute) malleability of responses. Benevolence, for example, can vary in degree and object of attachment, but it is a natural attachment to others that exists before any aesthetic or poetic education. This view understands emotional associations as plastic but not artificial: the natural emotional association can become destabilized only with extreme manipulation, and such manipulation generally results in serious psychological dysfunction. Seen in this light, Mill's breakdown was not due to a lack of aesthetic education but to an education that tried to suppress and eliminate natural emotional associations.

In this view, emotions are a natural and crucial part of the decision-making process that facilitate socially beneficial or ethical behaviour. The associations between feelings and moral objects are neither entirely malleable nor completely under the influence of experience or reason. Although the degree and specificity of emotions vary across cultures, emotions are part of the natural human repertoire for facilitating survival and co-operation in our social environment. The connection between emotions and objects is influenced by education or culture, but emotions contain an innate affiliation for certain kinds of objects, including moral objects. Thus, cultural, political, or educational attempts to suppress or control completely these natural associations will have debilitating psychological and social results.

Mill's assumption that there are essentially no natural emotional associations and that they are completely malleable has implications for analyzing the role of emotions in ethical and sociopolitical decision making. Mill's assumptions provide support for arguments, such as that by Martha Nussbaum, which suggest that there are appropriate and inappropriate emotions in political and legal decision making.[37] Specifically, Nussbaum argues that disgust – not just excessive disgust or inappropriately directed disgust – is always unsuitable in political and legal decision making. Disgust is unsuitable because it expresses a non-egalitarian sentiment towards the individuals who are its object and therefore undervalues the dignity of human beings. She suggests that a more appropriate moral emotion would be indignation at the harm of others. Her approach suggests that legal and social policy should incorporate certain emotions as part of ethical decision making and avoid or negate the role of other emotions deemed undesirable. The "negative" emotions are assumed to have no necessary connection to ethical decision making or to socially beneficial political behaviour.

In challenge to this position is the perspective that all emotions contain some natural ties with external objects or individuals. This challenge also rejects the assumption that emotions have a positive-negative polarity; instead, emotions are natural adaptations that facilitate social and co-operative behaviour. In this approach, no emotion can be rejected a priori in decision making. By way of illustration, Christina Tarnopolsky's analysis of shame in Chapter 2 of this volume reveals that shame, which is typically dismissed as a negative emotion, can be respectful and essential to democratic political deliberation. Another example of this position can be found in Dan Kahan's argument for incorporating disgust in legal decision making. Even though Kahan and Nussbaum support similar political goals, Kahan argues that disgust is a natural emotion associated with ethical decision making and as such is a necessary aspect in developing policy.[38] Disgust is not intrinsically negative, but can potentially be directed at either inappropriate or appropriate ends. Disgust can inspire antisocial behaviour, which undermines a just society; but equally, disgust (for example, at unjust treatment of cultural or social groups) can inspire ethical action and a just society.

Finally, the danger of Mill's approach lies in the assumption that emotions, including those typically categorized as negative, such as shame, envy, and disgust, are not essential for sociopolitical decision making. For one thing, the perspective that emotions are negative undermines the role of emotion and inflates the role of reason in ethical decision making. Such a perspective may have debilitating individual and social effects, such as those experienced by Mill himself. Second, this restrictive view of emotions may undermine the goals of producing a more egalitarian society or reducing cruelty towards those who act outside cultural norms. If ethical decision making is not entirely rational, and emotions have some innate associations with particular sociopolitical actors and behaviours, then disregarding certain emotions, like disgust or hate, may provide opponents of equal treatment with the upper hand.[39] Without including disgust, envy, or hate in decision making concerning morality, rational arguments may lack what Mill calls "energy" in the commitment to ethical and political goals. In contrast, those who instead utilize disgust as an aspect of decision making employ a more dynamic position even with less rational or preferable goals. In the end, Mill does not reconcile his argument for emotional energy with his refusal of bad feelings such as anger, hate, envy, or spite. Thus, Mill's approach does not provide sufficient theoretical understanding of the complexity of emotions in ethical decision making and, in consequence, may potentially undermine the very goals he desired – the creation and stability of a just society.

Conclusion

In contrast to previous versions of utilitarian philosophy, Mill argues that feelings have an essential role in ethical decision making and action. First, he supports a position in which feelings are essential to a commitment to truth and philosophic principles. An ethical position, therefore, requires not just a rational, analytic argument but a deep feeling of commitment to the truth of the proposition. Second, Mill postulates a distinction among pleasures and argues that liberty of action and thought is necessary to allow for the pursuit of ideas and ways of life that challenge culturally accepted orthodoxy. Despite this broader understanding of the role of feelings, Mill's argument suggests such a strong degree of emotional artificiality that it undermines the potential innate relationship of feelings to individuals and circumstances. Most significantly, Mill's analysis supports the idea that certain feelings, such as envy, disgust, and hate, are always negative and justifiably censured. Such emotions, however, may lead to behaviour that has positive social or individual outcomes in certain contexts. Furthermore, a perspective that neglects the potential of all emotions to facilitate both positive and negative social behaviour fails to encompass the complex role of emotions in ethical decision making. Ultimately, such a diminished perspective does not incorporate all the potential "deep feelings" of truth and morality. At the heart of this issue, Mill's analysis highlights the necessity for a comprehensive account of the ways in which emotions contribute to ethical decision making and solidify our commitment to both ethical principles and the welfare of others in the community.

Emotions, Reasons, and Judgments

Leah Bradshaw

The relationship between passions and reason is one of the central concerns of political philosophy. In the classical accounts of Plato and Aristotle, the passions are situated in the middle of the tripartite structure of the human soul, between appetites and reason, and they function as the engine that keeps the whole soul in motion. In Plato's *Phaedrus*, Socrates gives us the powerful metaphor of the charioteer and the steeds, reason and destination guiding the energy of the passions. We all have appetites, for food and sex, but we have varying degrees of commitment to these appetites. The satiation of hunger is a long way from the obsessions of the gourmand; the satisfaction of sexual needs differs from the raging *eros* of an Alcibiades. We have the capacity for reason, but we are capable of employing that reason for all manner of lunatic projects, including the building of fantastical cities in our minds, and perhaps passionate commitment to realizing them, even if their fruition results in murderous politics. The passionate core of the human being is in some way the most interesting and puzzling part of our makeup. As Len Ferry writes in Chapter 4 of this volume, centred on the ideas of Aquinas, the passions are intricately bound up with the will: while we all experience passions welling up in the soul, we know also that we are capable to some degree of deciding whether or not to act on them, which is where the will makes its entrance.

The Greeks, as far as I know, had no term for the will, but they certainly understood that the disjunction between passion and deliberation causes a lot of trouble for people. For Aristotle, perhaps the most common human ethical problem is "incontinence": knowing that one ought not to act on a passion, but doing it anyway. He points out, "Those who make the best decisions do not seem to be those with the best beliefs; on the contrary, some seem to have better beliefs, but to make the wrong decisions because of vice."[1] Human beings are conflicted creatures with inclinations that easily contradict each other. For Aristotle, what mitigates this conflict, and can elevate us to a more virtuous state of being, is the capacity for deliberation.

Deliberation is the kind of reason that is tied to the emotions, and to the active life. Aristotle is well aware that there are other kinds of reasoning, tied to contemplation of things that are eternally true, or to scientific modes of investigation, and even to production and craft, but "no one deliberates about what cannot be otherwise or about what cannot be achieved by his action" (NE 1140b). When Aristotle discusses the meaning of intelligence, he says that "it seems proper to an intelligent person to be able to deliberate finely about what is good and beneficial for himself, not about some restricted area – e.g., about what promotes health or strength – but about what promotes living well in general" (NE 1140a25). Deliberation is thus a nonspecialized kind of reasoning, the imaginative capacity that human beings have to forge an ethical life for themselves. The sort of intelligence that deliberation reaches for is "a state grasping the truth, involving reason, concerned with action about what is good or bad for a human being" (NE 1140b5).

The Aristotelian formulation of deliberation, and of its peculiar kind of character-forming intelligence, has been sidelined in modern ethics, probably because of its somewhat slippery status. If we want to live an active life that expresses human virtues, Aristotle seems to suggest that we shall have to accept the fuzziness of categories. Intelligence, virtue, character, and feeling are yoked together in a compound, and not easily separated without doing an injustice to our understanding. I begin this paper with Aristotle because I am interested in exploring his "compounded" understanding of what it is to live a full human life, with the right sort of ordering among appetites, emotions, and reasons. I shall use the term "deliberation" to mean what Aristotle thought it meant: the kind of reasoning that is appropriate for choosing a path of action. After laying out a schematic for how Aristotle understands the relations among emotions, reasons, and judgments for action, I will try to show how two principal currents in modern philosophy – Kantian rationality and Richard Rorty's emotivist/sentimental theory – spin off into a kind of excess in one direction or another, thus breaking the tension (and the truth) of Aristotle's compounded understanding. Toward the end of the paper I return to Aristotle and to one of his most ardent supporters in modern thought, Martha Nussbaum, to try to show how Aristotle can still illuminate ethical questions for us.

Originally, in the West, it was thought that a virtuous life requires some education of the passions in accordance with a reasoned view of purpose. This is certainly true of Aristotle, whose virtue ethics require that passions be disciplined by deliberation in the right way. *Phronēsis*, Aristotle's highest practical virtue, is a combination of intellectual understanding and correct feeling. Aristotle concedes that "feelings actually seem to arise from the body; and in many ways virtue of character seems to be proper to feeling" (NE 1178a15). Undoubtedly for Aristotle, feelings and passions are central to the practice of virtue. A good person is compassionate about the right things, gets angry only at appropriate times, loves things and people that are worth loving, and so on. Yet these feelings are not isolated and do not function in a vacuum. Although separate from the faculty of reason, they are profoundly affected by it: "Intelligence is yoked together with virtue of character, and so is this virtue with intelligence. For the origins of intelligence express the virtues of character; and correctness of character expresses intelligence. And since these virtues are also connected to feeling, they are concerned with the compound" (NE 1178a20). A life of practical virtue is for Aristotle both moral and intelligent, and virtue or excellence is a compound of all the parts of the soul, properly aligned so that we feel the right things in appropriate circumstances. Central to Aristotle's views on ethics is the conviction that desires can be educated. For this reason ethics is closely aligned with politics and the function of law.

Aristotle remarks that nature (what we are given in terms of intelligence), habit (what we are given by familial and political habituation), and teaching (deliberate instruction) all figure in the compound of an ethical human being. It is not easy to sort out and weigh these forces. Arguments and teaching do not influence everyone equally, and "someone whose life follows his feelings would not even listen to an argument turning him away, or comprehend it if he did listen" (NE 1179b25). Those who are raised in conditions of freedom and licence (advanced democracies, perhaps) find it hard to see the need to restrain their passions, because the young especially tend to resist temperance and restraint. In the best-case scenario, a person will order himself, and will "attend to reason because his life aims at what is fine," but in the case of most people intemperate passions must be constrained by law and punishment: "Law has the power that compels; and law is a reason that proceeds from a sort of intelligence and understanding" (NE 1180a20). Political communities and laws are absolutely crucial for Aristotle in the education of the passions, because while we can understand how the passions ought to be directed, the confusing truth about the human condition is that the ill-governed passions seem to struggle for dominance. They have to be beaten back by reason, by law, and sometimes by force.

Throughout the *Nicomachean Ethics*, we read that almost all human foibles are caused by wayward passions. Aristotle regards emotion as a pouring forth of the spirited part of the soul, without guidance from deliberative judgment. For example, in his discussion of bravery (a virtue that Aristotle deems highly important for the defence of political communities), he notes that some count emotion as bravery, "for those who act out of emotion also seem to be brave – as beasts seem to be when they attack those who have wounded them – because brave people are also full of emotion." But truly brave people "act because of what is fine and their emotion cooperates with them" (NE 1116b25). People who fight "because of their feelings" have something similar to bravery, but they display real courage only once decision and goal have been added to the emotional outburst (NE 1117a5). This seems to make sense. A man who routinely drinks too much in bars and gets into fights is not equivalent to a disciplined soldier who risks his life in the line of duty. Each is capable of passionate response, but we make a moral distinction between the two. The difference according to Aristotle is that the brave person will not do something "shameful," and this of course requires an assessment of *what* is shameful, whether that is defined by the state, i.e., political custom, or whether it is measured by an internal standard of virtue (NE 1116b20).

Clearly, however, Aristotle thinks some kinds of people are *constitutionally* unfit for virtue, and these include women. In fact, the principal reason that Aristotle believes women fit for political (equal) rule in the household, but unfit for political rule in the public realm, seems to be that he thinks women incapable of governing their emotions. Women, he says in the *Politics*, have the capacity for deliberation but lack the authority to carry it out. In the *Rhetoric*, Aristotle remarks disparagingly that the refusal to bear hardship with dignity is shameful because it shows "effeminacy," a lack of resolve and fortitude.[2] He expects that we will condemn those men who do not withstand pains or pleasures unless their weakness is owing to some innate tendency or disease. Aristotle's examples of blameless weakness are the "hereditary effeminacy of the royal family of Scythia and the inferior endurance of the female sex as compared with the male" (NE 1150b). We shall see that contemporary philosophers pick up on this thread in Aristotle (and indeed throughout the Western tradition of thought); in trying to defend the emotions as the seat of judgment, they align themselves with an avowedly feminist position against what is identified as a male-centred tradition.

Modern Western political philosophy, insofar as it has been grounded on principles of right, broke radically with the "compounded" Aristotelian understanding of ethics and its inclusion of right-ordered emotions as intrinsic to virtue. Perhaps the greatest exponent of the new rights-based morality is Immanuel Kant. Kant famously separates duties from desires, and argues that acting ethically requires that we conform to universal laws that can be known by pure reason and are untainted by desire. Being moral, for Kant, means not that we renounce the pursuit of happiness (which is impossible), but that we must "*abstract* from such considerations as soon as the imperative of duty supervenes." A moral actor "must indeed make every possible conscious effort to ensure that no *motive* derived from the desire for happiness imperceptibly infiltrates his conceptions of duty."[3] Kant's ethics are much less ambitious than Aristotle's because they do not aim for the fusion of appetites, passions, and reasons. For Kant, it is not important that we want to do the right thing; it's only important that we do it: "The motive provided by the idea of the highest possible earthly good, attainable only through his collaboration, is therefore not that of his own intended happiness, but only of the idea as an end in itself and of obedience to it as a duty."[4] In a way,

Kant's resolution to the problem of the passions is to factor them out as far as possible though the steely voice of reason, coupled with the strong authority of the state. Kant cares not whether you sin in your heart; he cares only that you keep it to yourself.

Kant's ethics are inseparable from his politics, just like Aristotle's, but Kant's politics are vastly different, grounded in the modern principle of right. If duty is severed from desires as Kant believes, and if the rules governing our duties can be known by reason alone, then we need an object of duty that is divorced from the passions, and for Kant that object is the concept of right. A decent political community for Aristotle is one that fuses nature, habit, education, and law in order to bring about the greatest possible harmony among the three aspects of the soul. For Kant, a decent political community is one that recognizes as far as possible the autonomy and freedom of individuals. The end of the state, "which is indeed the highest formal condition (*conditio sine qua non*) of all other external duties, is the *right* of men *under coercive public laws* by which each can be given what is due to him and secured from any attack by others ... *Right* is the restriction of each's individual freedom so that it harmonizes with the freedom of everyone else (insofar as this is possible within the terms of a general law). And *public right* is the distinctive quality of the *external laws* which make this constant harmony possible."[5] Famously, Kant declared that it was possible to create a just state, under just laws, governing a race of "devils." In the Kantian world, politics no longer concerns the cultivation of moral character, or the education of the emotions and passions; it properly concerns framing the laws that guarantee the greatest amount of individual autonomy. Kant does see progress toward a more rational human community, but envisages this progress as almost inadvertent. Violence, Kant predicts, will decrease in the modern world, and there will be more charity, less quarrel, more "reliability in keeping one's word," and so on. But these steps toward cosmopolitan humanity will be taken "partly from a love of honour, and partly from a lively awareness of where one's advantage lies."[6] In short, better political communities will arise from the combination of rational commitment to right and the unintentional consequences of the pursuit of self-interest. The place of the passions as the "engine" of the soul disappears.

Kant leaned toward disembodied reason as the staff that would bear the burden of modern ethics, and the aridity of Kantian political philosophy may be responsible for the reaction against him and his intellectual progeny. As Arash Abizadeh pronounces at the beginning of Chapter 3 in this collection, "Moral philosophers have become increasingly impressed with the Aristotelian insight that good practical reasoning systematically relies on the emotions." The swing away from Kantian detachment may have a lot to do with the failure of humanity, especially Western liberal democratic humanity, in the political catastrophes of the twentieth century. The principles of right, and their correlative duties, did not prevent people from inflicting some of the most insidious political crimes in history against their fellow human beings. Many people have asked how it was possible for the German citizens to turn on their fellow (Jewish) citizens, people with the same rights as they, living under the same laws. The devils apparently did and do make a difference to the justice of states. It seems in retrospect only reasonable that philosophers and political thinkers would return to a consideration of the emotions and passions to try to understand how different sorts of characters respond variously to a common situation.

The turn away from Kantian duty included a radical move in the opposite direction, toward a full embrace of emotions as the *true* locale of good judgment. An extreme example of this position is found in the work of Richard Rorty. Rorty rejects the universalist ethics of Kant, and he also breaks from the kind of compounded embrace of reason and emotion found in Aristotle. He calls himself a pragmatist, and though he defends a liberal democratic view of justice, he sees this as a consequence of beliefs, desires, and emotions that do not require any referent outside themselves (such as an appeal to an idea of right, or even an Aristotelian understanding of a supreme good).[7] Rorty believes that it is ethically sufficient that one is loyal to one's own traditions and culture, without superimposing on that culture any broader or transcending notions of truth or meaning. He chronicles modern developments in thought to make his case, noting that anthropologists have "blurred the distinction between innate rationality and the products of acculturation," that philosophers like Martin Heidegger have helped us to see that human beings are historically grounded all the way through, and that psychoanalysis has "blurred the distinctions between morality and prudence." The result has been to destroy the picture of the self that held ascendancy through the Western tradition from Greek metaphysics, through Christian theology, to Enlightenment rationalism.[8]

In an article on human rights, Rorty argues that there have been enormous advances in the last century, which he measures by increased wealth, literacy, and leisure for more people, plus the deracination of authoritarian political structures and the expansion of individual choice. He writes, "Moral progress is made by changing the extension of the term 'we,' enlarging the range of people taken to be moral agents and subjects – raising the possibility that the situation of the helots, or the blacks, or the workers, or the women, is not natural, but a suitable topic to discuss with them. It is made by enlarging the range of imaginable conversational partners, the range of people with whom one can imagine discussing the question 'is your trust in us, the possessors of power, justified?'"[9] These markers of progress are not all that different from Kant's, but Rorty's justification for them is not Kantian at all. Rorty rejects the moral postulation of the autonomous individual, and the Kantian abstraction of freedom, as a "hyper-rational" construct. Citing Kant and Friedrich

Nietzsche as the chief exponents of the rational, free individual, Rorty rejects their kind of "self-conscious self-sufficiency." He also rejects more temperate and worldly accounts of rational consensus, such as Jürgen Habermas' theories of intersubjectivity. He describes Habermas' philosophy as the "sort of philosophy that will keep what is still usable in Enlightenment rationalism while jettisoning both metaphysical attempts to ground this rationalism in the nature of the subject and ironist attempts to subvert it."[10]

Implicit in the Enlightenment notions of individual will and moral legislation, Rorty says, is the desire for a pure reason that is divorced from the passions and appetites that move us. Characterizing Kantian reason in gender terms, Rorty claims that it exhibits repulsion for anything "sticky, slimy, wet, sentimental and womanish."[11] Drawing on John Dewey, Rorty aligns himself explicitly with feminism. "We pragmatists," he remarks, "see universalism and realism as committed to the idea of a reality-tracking faculty called 'reason' and an unchanging moral reality to be tracked, and thus unable to make sense of the claim that a new voice is needed. So we commend ourselves to feminists on the ground that we can fit that claim into our view of moral progress with relative ease."[12] To the extent that there has been moral progress in the modern world, Rorty believes this has little to do with the advancement of abstract notions of right, and much more to do with a sentimental education, which he explicitly associates with a characteristically feminine viewpoint.

We are moved to care for others, not because of any abstract idea about the inherent dignity of all persons (Kant), or because of any theoretical meditations on justice, but because we hear the stories of others and feel an affinity with their suffering. Rorty claims that to broaden the scope of justice, we need above all to be more attentive to the stories of others: "Sentimental stories only work on people who can relax long enough to listen."[13] We will be drawn to the plight of the raped woman in Bosnia, for example, if we can imagine what it would be like to be her grieving mother or sister. Similar stories, says Rorty, repeated over the centuries, have induced the safe and the powerful to cherish the powerless. In another example, from an exchange with the anthropologist Clifford Geertz on ethnocentrism, Rorty points to the inclusion of Native Americans in the "democratic conversation." In his view, the move from exclusion to inclusion was brought about by the media, who had in turn been prodded by intellectuals, specifically anthropologists who made partners of the Indians: "If the anthropologists had not sympathized with, learned from, even sometimes loved, the Indians, Indians would have remained invisible to the agents of social justice."[14] Rorty concludes, "To rely on the suggestions of sentiment rather than on the commands of reason is to think of powerful people gradually ceasing to oppress others, or to countenance the oppression of others, out of mere niceness rather than out of the obedience to the moral law."[15]

"Sentiment" is a murky word, often disparaged by rigorous thinkers as a mawkish identification with the superficial, but Rorty appears to use this term as an umbrella for good emotions. Note that while Rorty claims to be attentive to the cultural and particular rootedness of traditions and ways of living and thinking, he nonetheless embraces the *universal* goals of expansion of individual choice, increased levels of affluence, and so on. Thus although Rorty rejects the universalist assumptions of reason, he accepts in some fashion the universalist experiences of emotion. For Rorty, reason is an artifice, constructed by the powerful for the advancement of their own superiority and power, but the authentic and universal core of humanity is gut-response emotion. If liberated from the constraints of power and poverty, emotions will tend toward compassionate identification with others and recognition of their fundamental equality and freedom. This is a huge assumption. Robert Solomon, in Chapter 10 of this collection, offers good grounds for questioning it. He argues that there is such a thing as a "political" approach to the emotions. This approach "takes as its framework for describing emotions neither the mind nor the body, but the social structure in all of its elaborate ethical and interpersonal complexity, a view that is interestingly similar in Aristotelian and Confucian ethics." While Solomon echoes Rorty that "'emotional' and 'sentimental' are employed as put-downs, in a long standing (and still not extinct) dismissal of women and 'effeminate' men from positions of responsibility," he is cautious about attributing any universal character to the emotions. Whether anything can properly be called "human emotion" (in the sense of being natural, or universal) "is something to be found out, something to be investigated, whether or not a final theory of 'human nature' will ever be available. The question will always be open: do we understand?"

Solomon brings the whole issue of the emotions back to the problem of understanding, which suggests that we cannot escape the issue of intelligence, or reason. Solomon's principal point of course is that pure emotions do not exist. They are tainted by habituation, power dynamics, culture, gender, and the very structure of the human psyche, which has the capacity not just to feel but also to understand (or misunderstand). The freer sharing of emotion does not necessarily unleash "natural compassion." The rejection of excessively abstract Enlightenment notions of right, in favour of the emotive expressivism of sentiment, does not solve the problem of ethics. Next I want to address this issue in two specific ways, first by taking another look at the expanded progressive inclusion of previously marginalized people, and second by drawing on Hannah Arendt to consider how sentiment on a grand, politically charged scale may be politically destructive.

The Bounds of Pity

Richard Rorty, as noted, rejects abstract reason, and in particular the formulation of universal rights, as a basis for advancing social justice, and instead appeals to our capacity to be open to the sentimental stories of others. Taking instruction from Aristotle (and Solomon), I have serious reservations about this optimism. If Aristotle is correct that emotions are always compounded with appetites and deliberation, then emotional responses to the plights of others are very much informed by our singular dispositions, our habituation, and our education. In the *Nicomachean Ethics*, where Aristotle catalogues the moral virtues, we find detailed descriptions of how they can go wrong in many ways. Generosity, for instance, is an identifiable virtue, but it cannot be understood independent of the situation in which it is exercised: who is doing the giving, why is she doing it, and what are the consequences? A profligate person is not virtuous, because she probably needs gratitude from others; a miserly person is mean-spirited.

Emotional responses in themselves do not warrant our praise or blame. Emotions elicit pleasure or pain (sensations rooted in the body, in the appetitive part of the soul), and they include anger, fear, confidence, envy, hate, love, joy, longing, jealousy, and pity (NE 1106a20). But we assess emotional responses based on their object. I might be terrified by something, for example, but I can react to that terror in only one of two ways: with courage or with cowardice. I may be racked by love, but as Socrates says in the *Republic*, love lives like a tyrant in the souls of the mad. There is nothing praise- or blameworthy about my fear or my love, only about how I decide to act on them. People can conquer fears, and we admire that because there is deliberation and will involved. Aristotle says clearly, "We are neither called good nor called bad in so far as we are simply capable of feelings" (NE 1106a5). Even if we feel pity for someone, there is nothing virtuous about *feeling* bad about their situation. For compassion to have any substance politically, it has to be converted to virtue, which is measured by reasoned actions. Virtues are not feelings but "decisions of some kind" (NE 1106a5). When Aristotle praises aspects of character like courage, temperance, kindness, and so on, he is making a judgment about a wilfully chosen course of action. The person we praise is one who has a sound character, who knows how to act under given circumstances, and who can give reasons to defend his or her actions. Practised toward others, virtue, a condition of character, becomes justice: "Virtue is the same as justice, but what it is to be virtue is not the same as what it is to be justice. Rather insofar as virtue is related to another, it is justice, and insofar as it is a certain sort of state unconditionally, it is virtue" (NE 1130a10).

Aristotle is particularly interesting on pity, the closest thing in his corpus to what we might call compassion. Aristotle defines pity as "a feeling of pain caused by the sight of some evil, destructive or painful, which befalls one who does not deserve it, and which we might expect to befall ourselves or some friend of ours, and moreover to befall us soon" (*Rhetoric* 1385b10-15). A key element of pity is thus sympathy, the identification that someone is suffering something that might afflict me. This seems to fit well with Rorty's evocation of compassion for the woman in Bosnia. I am likely to feel compassion for a victim if I can imagine that she is my mother or sister, or that this terrible thing can happen to me. Aristotle adds, however, that we are more likely to extend pity to those who are like us in "character, age, disposition, social standing or birth" (*Rhetoric* 1386a25). This is the case because pity as a virtue is closely allied with the emotion of fear, and we are more likely to pity those whose misfortunes are the things we fear.[16] For example, if I am a middle-aged executive in an economic downturn, my pity may extend far more easily to a fellow executive who has been downsized from his corporate lifestyle than to the plight of Native Canadians on a polluted reserve in the far north. Pity, for Aristotle, is tied to a strong sense of self-interest.[17] Aristotle's reading of pity may lead us to question Rorty's assumption that my sense of compassion can extend to the victim in Bosnia, whom I might regard as far removed from the circumstances of my life and the range of misfortunes that might befall me. The most glaring example of this gulf right now may be that between North Americans and Africans afflicted by AIDS.

There is another insight from Aristotle worth noting regarding pity: it applies only to the great moderate middling ranks of society. Pity is felt neither by the ruined, who "suppose that no further evil can befall them, since the worst has befallen them already," nor by the "insolent" who imagine themselves so privileged that they are immune from ordinary sufferings. When people think that they possess all the goods in life — such as wealth, good fortune, good friends, good health – they tend to think it impossible that evil should befall them. (*Rhetoric* 1385b20-30) We cannot expect that the chronically poor, diseased, ill-fed, and persecuted will feel compassion for the downsized executive. Neither can we expect that the prosperous individual with an interesting and productive life will necessarily feel compassion for the marginalized. Aristotle's message is that those who are on the margins of the great middle, the very rich and the very poor, are outside the bounds of pity.

Pity, Empathy, and Indignation

The emotion of pity is vaguely contemptuous. It lacks respect and genuine empathy for the other, and may contain an element of smug satisfaction. In feeling pity for another, I am feeling fear that the other's misfortune could befall me, as well as relief that it has not. The emotion of pity rests on a fundamental selfishness in the one who exhibits it. Empathy, in contrast, presupposes equality between people, and empathy can lead to a kind of political solidarity that pity can never achieve. Hannah Arendt made this point in her study of revolutions, noting that pity for the downtrodden and the romanticization of their plight was a major factor in the mood of France before the Revolution. Compassion, Arendt says, belongs in the sphere of intimacy, where the heart aches for another. Its correlative sentiment, pity, "is not stricken in the flesh, and keeps its sentimental distance," and for this reason it can be employed as a political tool to reach out beyond intimacy to the plight of the afflicted in general. Pity, Arendt warns, can be "enjoyed" and used to glorify the suffering of others. Arendt suspects that whenever pity is invoked in politics as a catalyst for emancipation of the oppressed, the sentimental praise of suffering is a pretext for the lust for power. This is why, in her understanding, the French Revolution ended so badly: "Pity, taken as the spring of virtue, has proved to possess a greater capacity for cruelty than cruelty itself. *'Par pitie, par amour pour humanité, soyez inhumains!'* – these words, taken almost at random from a petition of one of the sections of the Parisian Commune to the National Convention, are neither accidental nor extreme: they are the authentic language of pity."[18]

Pity can never be truly inclusive of others in an impartial way because it cannot move from its sentimental *pathos* to a broader sense of political responsibility. "Pity, in contrast to solidarity," Arendt writes, "does not look upon both fortune and misfortune, the strong and the weak, with an equal eye; without the presence of misfortune, pity could not exist, and therefore it has just as much vested interest in the existence of the unhappy as thirst for power has a vested interest in the existence of the weak."[19] This seems to me an extremely important insight. Aristotle writes in the *Rhetoric* that the emotion *directly* opposed to pity is indignation (1386a5): "Pain at unmerited good fortune is, in one sense opposite to pain at unmerited bad fortune, and is due to the same moral qualities. Both feelings are associated with good moral character; it is our duty both to feel sympathy and pity for unmerited distress, and to feel indignation at unmerited prosperity; for whatever is undeserved is unjust, and that is why we ascribe indignation even to the gods" (1386a10). But indignation, unlike pity, is tied to an assessment of justice, not just to one's own fears. Pity is rooted in the emotions, while indignation is a compound of emotion and judgment. Aristotle distinguishes between pity and indignation because the latter appeals beyond self-interest. Aristotle writes that we feel indignation "if we are really good and honest people; our judgment is then sound, and we loathe any kind of injustice" (*Rhetoric* 1387b5). Pity is extended only to those who are less fortunate, while indignation broadens the scope by actually assessing what is truly just and unjust. It requires going beyond self-regard and thinking about others in a comprehensive way.

I suggest that indignation, not compassion or pity, is the chief catalyst for political reform. The victims of injustice do not want to be pitied; they want to be treated as the equals they are. Though Hannah Arendt talks about rage rather than indignation, she seems to make a point similar to Aristotle's:

Rage is by no means an automatic reaction to misery and suffering as such; no one reacts with rage to an incurable disease or to an earthquake, or for that matter, to social conditions that seem to be unchangeable. Only where there is reason to suspect that conditions could be changed and are not does rage arise. Only when our sense of justice is offended do we react with rage, and this reaction by no means necessarily reflects personal injury, as is demonstrated by the whole history of revolution, where invariably members of the upper class touched off and then led the rebellions of the oppressed and downtrodden.[20]

Looking at the history of the civil rights movement in the United States, Arendt attacks the response to the demands of black Americans "fashionable among white liberals." When they cry, "we are all guilty," "Black Power has proved only too happy to take advantage of this 'confession' to instigate an irrational 'black rage.' Where all are guilty, no one is; confessions of collective guilt are the best possible safeguards against the discovery of culprits, and the very magnitude of the crime the best excuse for doing nothing."[21] The message is, I think, that compassion and pity bestowed by the privileged and powerful on the beleaguered and marginalized is hypocritical. As Aristotle tells us, pity is neither to be commended nor condemned, because it is an emotion, not a virtue, and ultimately is always an extension of self-interest. Those who are the objects of compassion and pity may respond with indignation, by pronouncing, "No, you do not know my predicament, no, I am not just like you; I want justice and recognition, not sentiment," but to become indignant is to assert oneself, to demand justice, and this requires agency, or at least the possibility of it. Starkly, but truthfully, Aristotle declares that "servile, worthless, unambitious persons are not inclined to indignation, since there is nothing they can believe themselves to deserve" (*Rhetoric* 1387b15).

While Rorty advocates opening up the conversation to the marginalized and including them in the circle of compassion, Aristotle and Arendt provoke us to think about the complexity of sharing stories and experiences. If, as Aristotle says, emotional responses are tied up with appetites, reasons, habits, culture, and education, there may be enormous gulfs between different kinds of people that cannot be bridged by compassionate identification (though perhaps they can be bridged by other means). This may explain how white people can live alongside black people who are desperately poor, even enslaved, and though witnessing their sorrows and afflictions not feel moved to identify with them in any way that leads to greater inclusion or justice. It may explain how men can live with and among women and regard them, for most of history and still in parts of the world today, as not fully human and not entitled to any privileges of ownership or independence.

A convincing argument can be made that most effective movements in the modern world toward greater inclusion of the marginalized have arisen from the indignant demands of the excluded, and not from the emotive sympathies of the privileged and the powerful. Women were included in the conversation of liberal democracy when they demanded to be. Black

Americans needed a civil rights movement to gain political recognition. The single act of Rosa Parks refusing to move to the back of the bus has become a great symbol of emancipation for good reason: Rosa Parks *demanded* that she be recognized as equal by the white people on the bus. Apart from the fact that these demands are made on the grounds of justice, it seems important to consider that they aroused *passionate* responses. Arendt's thoughts on revolution make us think about the difference in intensity between pity and rage. Pity is an emotion, but it does not seem right to categorize it as a passion. Pity is an emotional state that can be evoked in a variety of circumstances and in many ill-defined ways. Hannah Arendt says that "sentiments, as distinguished from passion and principle are boundless,"[22] and pity, like any sentiment, is boundless if it is not constrained by some principle of action. Rage is a passion directed at something specific, at some discernible injustice, and it disrupts and provokes action of some sort. There is something hypocritical and inadequate about relying on pity and compassion as the basis for achieving justice. For Arendt, pity is a "perversion" of true feeling, which can have a consequence in politics comparable to that of detachment: "Absence of emotions neither causes nor promotes rationality. 'Detachment and equanimity' in view of 'unbearable tragedy' can indeed be terrifying, namely, when they are not the result of control but an evident manifestation of incomprehension. In order to respond reasonably one must first of all be 'moved,' and the opposite of emotional is not 'rational,' whatever that may mean, but either the inability to be moved, usually a pathological phenomenon, or sentimentality, which is a perversion of feeling."[23]

Perhaps it is the case that to have rightly ordered *passions*, and not merely sentiments, one needs a properly ordered soul, and this brings us back to the place of reason in alliance with the emotions. When Aristotle makes a distinction between pity and indignation, he describes indignation as the nobler emotion because it responds to a comprehensive notion of justice. We pity someone who is worse off than we are if we can imagine ourselves suffering their plight, but we become indignant at injustice, whether it is unmerited good fortune or unmerited bad fortune, to others. Indignation contains within in it an element of impartiality that goes beyond self-interest. Also, pity does not necessarily lead to any kind of action, whereas indignation usually does. Could it be that real *passions* – the ability to be truly moved – are irrevocably tied to a grasp of justice, that is, that passions (as opposed to sentiments) always have a deliberative element?

Passions and Justice

Martha Nussbaum has considered the relationship between passions and justice at length in her writings. Nussbaum is a careful reader of Aristotle, and admires much about Aristotle's compounded understanding of virtue as a melding of reasons and passions. Looking at the importance of anger (or indignation), Nussbaum affirms Aristotle's view that anger is an important element in ethics because there are things that are worthy of our indignation: "In the case of the deepest commitments, not to take some action seems to show a lack of 'perception,' and if one has those practical perceptions, then one seems bound to be angry. Anger, in these cases, is a recognition of the truth." But emotions have to be educated, as we know from Aristotle, so that the passions are directed at the correct objects: "So educated, [the passions] are not just essential as forces motivating to virtuous action, they are also recognitions of truth and value. And as such, they are not just instruments of virtue, they are constituent parts of virtuous agency; virtue, as Aristotle says again and again, is a 'mean disposition' (disposition to pursue the appropriate) 'with regard to both passions and actions.'"[24]

The education of the emotions is not just a matter of directing emotions by reason, but is a project embedded in the social and political context of a human existence, as we noted earlier in this chapter, and as is fleshed out in Robert Solomon's chapter. Emotions can be guided and modified by reason because human beings are capable of thinking through the implications of what they do, but Aristotle makes a clear distinction between the formation of character and the philosophical pursuit of ethics. Echoing this distinction, Nussbaum writes that a person is the

> child of her parents: their love or care, or the absence of it, shape her. She is the child of material circumstances of need or plenty; she is healthy or ill, hungry or full: and this, once again, shapes her – shapes not only her health, but shapes her hopes, expectations and fears, her capability for reasoning. She is the child of her city and its institutions: and these institutions shape her capacity for shame and self-esteem, for stinginess or generosity, for greediness or moderation. This shaping reaches deep into the soul, profoundly affecting, even with philosophy, what it can become.[25]

Here, finally, we come to a central conundrum of ethics and politics. What are the ordering relationships among reasons, passions, habituation, and judgment? Philosophers like Kant tried to solve this problem by separating duty from desire, and recommending political institutions that would abide rigorously by the principles of right. This resolution neglects the importance of cultivating character, and the role that emotions have in people's ethical commitments. Philosophers like Richard Rorty have reacted against this abstract view of human beings by trying to locate ethics in universal emotions, specifically those of compassion and pity; but this approach fails because without a broader sense of justice, and what we are fitted for, these emotions decline into mere sentiment and characteristically exhibit an inability to reach beyond self-interest. In Nussbaum's understanding, ethics is a complex mix of habituation, right reasons, and properly ordered passions, which is much like Aristotle's view. She rails against Aristotle's excessive emphasis on habituation, though, because of the limitations this puts on the free capacity of people to reform themselves. She calls for therapeutic ethics that can not only analyze the way in which human beings behave, but can heal them so that they can become better, more free, more resolute in their choices. Therefore she moves from Aristotle to the Epicureans and the Stoics, in whom she sees a greater "recognition that existing desires, intuitions, and preferences are socially formed and far from totally reliable."[26] Nussbaum remains confident that educating the emotions is possible through the employment of reason, but not only or even primarily the reason of philosophers. "As a general rule," she claims, "Stoic therapy holds that you cannot get a pupil to be critical of a more abstract or general belief, except through the medium of the concrete."[27]

Without assessing whether Nussbaum's allegiance to the Stoics is sound (something I am not competent to assess), I find that her attention to the concrete, and her optimism about the possibilities of individuals purposefully educating their desires, is appealing and convincing. We are political and social creatures, but we are not so *all the way through*. Our emotional responses are undoubtedly shaped by the context in which we live, but to the extent that we are encouraged to see alternatives, surely change is possible. Robert Solomon makes the point, as we have noted, that emotions are politically charged and shaped by intentions and calculations of consequences. For example, he says in Chapter 10, "A young female soon learns to win favours by being submissive, which involves feeling submissive, and so she learns to feel submissive." I wonder if this interpretation is wholly accurate. It seems to me far more likely that the girl in this scenario is conflicted. She may feel submissive, and at the same time unworthy and shamed, and her conflicted feelings may result in depression, or in a resistant mode of becoming manipulative and deceptive in order to assert herself.[28] It may be hard to alter this behaviour in a culture where young girls are systematically habituated into submission, but it is not impossible.

Solomon's example brings us back to something we have touched upon, but not yet explored systematically, which is the consideration of gender. As far back as the Greeks, unharnessed emotions have been associated with females. Women were disparaged, and barred from citizenship, probably because of the belief that women are incapable of restricting their emotions through deliberation. Feminine emotion is amorphous, unfocused, and sentimental, lacking the proper objects of moral consideration. Let us return to Aristotle's long discussions in the *Nicomachean Ethics* and the *Rhetoric* about the relationship between anger and courage. Courage is understood as principally a male virtue because it requires acting contrary to a deep-seated fear. For Aristotle, the greatest exhibition of virtue is the passionate and correct response to a bodily state such as fear. Aristotle admires bravado even when it is misplaced, and he forgives an impetuous character more than he does a deliberative but weak one: "Among incontinent people, those who abandon themselves [to desire, i.e., the impetuous] are better than those [i.e., the weak] who have reason but do not abide by it" (NE 1151a). Females, in his view, do not characteristically exhibit courage, but endurance. They suffer pains and fears well, but they do not act to conquer them. The elevation of pity and compassion in some quarters in modern philosophy may be seen as the feminization of philosophy, because it lacks the hard edge of judgment and action that we apply to acts of courage.

To hold, as Martha Nussbaum does, that emotions are educable is to make judgments about what sorts of emotional responses are appropriate in what circumstances, and also to adhere in some way to the classical notion that *passionate* commitment in the name of worthy goals is superior to the passive endurance of suffering. Masculine self-assertion is preferable to feminine passivity. Justifiable rage at injustice is better than pity for the afflicted. Focused indignation at another's unmerited position is more admirable than diffuse compassion. Good emotions are *decisive ones* that lead to action and autonomy and self-assertion. No matter what the culture, or the context, Nussbaum affirms these goals. In a schematic that Nussbaum lays out as a guide to ethical conduct (which she calls "Aristotelian essentialism"), she identifies the "capability of choosing itself" as among the most fundamental elements of human essence.[29]

Women in particular should beware of sentiment-based theories, because throughout the tradition of Western thought, they are the ones most frequently associated with the "soft," diffuse, and passive emotions of compassion and pity. For Nussbaum, a free person, whether male or female, reveres the world, its mystery, and its wonder, and "she reveres the capacity of persons to choose and fashion a life." The free person sees a "beautiful, rich and difficult world, in which a community of persons regard one another as free and equal but also as finite and needy – and therefore strive to arrange their relations on terms of justice and liberty." It is always a radical claim, Nussbaum says, "to make the demand to be seen as human rather than as someone's lord or someone's subject. I believe it is best for women to embrace this vision and make this demand."[30]

The forceful passions that make demands have historically been ascribed to men, not women, to the privileged and free, not the oppressed and the unfree. Perhaps one needs more than sentiment, compassion, pity, and niceness to make one's way in the world. Perhaps one needs to have the more forceful passions and virtues – indignation, anger, bravery, courage – to be a free agent, and perhaps too the potential of experiencing these more forceful passions and virtues is necessarily attached to deliberation about just ends, and, more significantly, to the capacity to carry out actions. The capacity to feel, and act upon, forceful passions is not sex based by some rigid definition of nature, but has been identified as such by history and convention. Maybe to *feel* certain passions, one needs the confidence and the opportunity to think about the real possibility of changing things, and of gaining some independence of will and judgment. This perspective places a priority on political and educational reform as the agent of emotional opportunity, and is really the opposite of relying on emotions or sentiments to expand political consciousness.

The Politics of Emotion
Robert C. Solomon

What is an emotion? William James asked that question in the title of one of his most famous psychological essays in 1884. James offered several different answers to that question, even in that same essay, but the one every student of emotions knows is summarized in his heavily italicized statement, *"our feeling of [bodily changes] as they occur IS the emotion."*[1] Ever since (and long before, of course), the idea that the core of emotion is some sort of physiological arousal has governed a good deal of psychological and, until recently, philosophical theorizing about emotion. An emotion, in short, is a physiological disturbance, caused by some untoward or disturbing perception (thought or memory), which is *felt* in some more or less distinctive way. Thus the focus on emotion is aimed at the individual organism, its physiology and feelings. Today, of course, the neurophysiology of emotion is attracting a good deal of attention, but the basic model of emotion as arousal remains the same.

What is an emotion? That same question was also asked, rather casually, by Aristotle, some twenty-three hundred years before James. Aristotle mentioned feelings, physical agitation, and arousal only in passing when he defined anger, as a paradigm of emotion, as "a distressed desire for conspicuous vengeance in return for a conspicuous and unjustifiable contempt/slight of one's person or friends."[2] What should strike us first and foremost about this characterization is that it seems to have much more to say about ethics, politics, and social relationships than it does about anything that most psychologists would recognize as emotions. The key terms – "vengeance," "contempt," "person or friends," as well as the repeated "conspicuous" – suggest that the nature of anger is essentially entangled in questions of perceived status, questions of offence and appropriate retaliation, and interpersonal relationships. Indeed, Aristotle goes on to insist that only fools don't get angry, and that while overly angry people may be "unbearable," the absence of anger (aimed at the right offences) is a vice rather than a virtue. It is a "contempt/slight" that causes the anger (perhaps an instance of "scorn, spite, or insolence"), but because of this, it is right, even obligatory, to be angry (on the right occasion, for the right reasons, to the appropriate degree). Because they have a great deal to do with relationships between people living together in society, anger, and other emotions, are political in nature.

Between the two of them, James and Aristotle establish a certain dialectic in emotion research. On the one hand, an emotion is a relatively primitive mental state or process, some combination of physiology and feeling. Like most "mental" phenomena, an emotion is a feature of the individual organism, something "inner" or – if "inner experience" is to be eschewed as too unscientific (James himself often denied "the existence of consciousness") – then something literally inside the skull, that is, in the brain. In psychology, because of methodological suspicion of private experience and because the science of neurology is still in development, the study of emotions is tentatively reduced to or focused on the superficialities of behaviour – expressions on the face, short-term behavioural sequences, or the not always credible self-reports of nineteen-year-old psychology students. On the other hand, there is what I have called the political approach to emotions. It takes as the framework for describing emotions neither the mind nor the body but the social situation, in all of its elaborate ethical and interpersonal complexity.

Beyond the Cartesian Tradition

Part of what I find so appealing about the political approach to emotions is the way it bypasses what is now generally called the Cartesian tradition in mind-body research. That tradition, well summarized in recent debates between Dan Dennett, John Searle, David Chalmers, and many others, focuses on the "question of consciousness" – obviously a central concern for James as well – and slips back and forth, in tellingly technical language, between (more or less) commonsense dualism and reductive materialism.[3] Aristotle, of course, was burdened with no such concerns, enjoying the twin benefits of his innocence of both Cartesian dualism (or any such notion as consciousness) and the reductive obsessions of modern science. The emotions, in particular, play an awkward – some would say unintelligible – role in the Cartesian picture, as an unwieldy causal complex of physiological processes, on the one hand, and personal experiences (or "feelings"), on the other. Descartes, who was as sophisticated as anyone in the physiology of his day, spent considerable time (in his *Passions of the Soul*) worrying about how the "animal spirits" in the blood effect the appropriate changes in the soul.[4]

On the mental side of the causal relation, however, Descartes' language changes abruptly. Hatred, for example, "ultimately arises from the perception of an object's potential harmfulness and involves a desire to avoid it."[5] Though he may have been fascinated by physiology, Descartes (like Aristotle) was ultimately interested in a value-oriented, wisdom-minded analysis of emotion: how emotions fit into and define a good life. Nevertheless, the

tradition that bears his Latinate name has tended to give scant attention to the political dimension of emotion and excessive attention to the emotions as feelings or affects. There is some awestruck and occasionally apocalyptic admiration for the possibilities of neurological research, but Cartesian dualism has pretty much delimited emotions as a phenomenon defined on the one side by a neurology that is still very speculative and on the other side by a set of experiences – variously described as rich and meaningful or as primitive and inchoate – that each person allegedly has as his or her own private domain.

My own work, which is usually labelled (not by me) a "cognitive" account of emotions, has tended to remain within the same Cartesian tradition.[6] You may take this as a confession. My largely phenomenological approach emphasizes the role of judgment in emotions, following (among others) Aristotle, the ancient Stoics, and (more recently) Jean-Paul Sartre. To be sure, I often emphasized the interpersonal and ethical nature of those judgments – as in judgments of affinity, intimacy, and responsibility – but insofar as I have continued to treat emotions as personal experiences, I found that I tend to neglect several important dimensions of emotion. I have come to especially appreciate this in my interdisciplinary work with social scientists and psychobiologists since the 1990s. Neurology and the connection between brain processes and emotion are still beyond my ken, but I paid inadequate attention to more readily accessible aspects of emotion, such as the role of facial expressions and cultural "display rules" in emotion, despite their prominence in psychology and anthropology, respectively. Indeed, to this day, philosophers in general seem not to have discovered the significance of the face in emotion theory, despite the fact that this has all but ruled the work of the psychologists across the hall for more than twenty years. The reason, of course, is Cartesianism. The face is but superficial body. It is, at best, *expression*. But that, supposedly, tells us very little about that *of which* it is an expression, namely, the emotion. And the emotion, on the Cartesian account, is necessarily something "inner," not in the face or the expression but in the private experience of the subject.

Here we might return to James, who had his own confusion about where to identify the emotion. Like David Hume before him, James nominally identified the emotion itself as a sensation (or a set of sensations, an "impression"), which he distinguished from the causes and the expressions of emotion. As a physician, James was naturally struck by the importance of the bodily responses, and he was keenly aware of the complex relations between an emotion and its bodily expressions, so much so that he famously urged that the latter caused the former (although he sometimes conflated the behavioural with the physiological) and suggested, anticipating today's Hallmark greeting cards, that putting on a happy face will result in feeling happy as well. Nevertheless, the official Jamesian doctrine, which resembled

the doctrines of so many philosophers before him, was that the emotion IS the feeling, the distinctive set of sensations. An adequate integration of the "felt" and the physical aspects of emotion continued to evade him.

The Cartesian view of emotions has taken many different forms. Many philosophers and psychologists have thought that the definitive feature of those sensations that make up emotions was the fact that they are either pleasurable or painful. Hume, for instance, distinguished love and hate, pride and humility, in this way. Benedict de Spinoza sometimes made similar suggestions, and Spinoza's best twentieth-century incarnation, in the person of Dutch psychologist Nico Frijda, has argued the same.[7] Others, notably the Stoics and later Spinoza, suggested that the emotions were not so much feelings as judgments or thoughts about the world and oneself. I locate myself in this tradition. Frijda, leaning toward behavioural (but not behaviourist) analysis, insisted that they were proto-actions, intentions, action tendencies. Outright behaviourists suggested, with varying degrees of implausibility, that emotions were *nothing but* behaviour and dispositions to behave in certain ways, thus remaining Cartesians while simply denying "the ghost in the machine." More often than not, however, they hung onto some vestige of the mental – for instance, Gilbert Ryle's infamous "twinges and itches" and Ludwig Wittgenstein's "wheel that plays no part in the mechanism."[8] Others suggested that emotions were complexes of beliefs and desires – the rather simple-minded model of "folk psychology" that now reigns supreme in some cognitive science circles. But what all of these views have in common is their shared acceptance (or, in the case of behaviourism, defiant rejection) of an emotion as an "inner" psychological state. The differences between these views are significant, of course, and I have spent much of my career defending one of them over the others. But I now see the challenge in a very different way, one that provides a Hegelian *aufhebung* to the "emotions are judgments" view and relocates it in non-Cartesian space.

One of the philosophers who best pursued a non-dualistic alternative to the understanding of emotion was James' pragmatist colleague, John Dewey. He insisted on a holistic, all-embracing view of emotion. Others are Martin Heidegger, whose obscurity on other matters did not seem to cloud his view of "moods" (*Stimmung*, but which, in his treatment, clearly includes many emotions), and Sartre, who despite his seemingly Cartesian ontology defended a view of emotions (and consciousness in general) as thoroughly political.[9] Similar views can be found scattered through the history of philosophy and psychology (before those fields were so unfortunately wrenched apart by university administrators and mutually jealous colleagues). But the prototype of the political approach still seems to me to be Aristotle. What all of *these* views have in common is a perspective on emotions as primarily situated in human relationships and inextricable from ethics.[10] The problem, as I now see it, is to retain the personal and experiential (or phenomenological) grasp of emotions

while situating the emotions in a larger social context, treating them not only as the result of, but also as constituted in, relations with other people.[11]

The Purpose(s) of Emotions

One of the more exciting theses about emotion to (re)emerge in the twentieth century is the insistence that emotions are purposive. They have what Jean-Paul Sartre called *"finalité."*[12] That is to say, they are not only functional and occasionally advantageous, and they are not just the fortuitous residue of fickle evolution; emotions are *in themselves* strategic and political. To put it differently and somewhat controversially, emotions do not just happen to us, as the whole language of "passion" and "being struck by" would suggest. They are, with some contentious stretching of the term, activities that we "do," stratagems that work for us, both individually and collectively. Or, to put it yet another way, the emotions can be said to be rational (or irrational) despite the fact that "rationality" is often restricted to those contexts involving articulate thought and calculation. (Vengeance born of anger is exemplary here.) But rationality is often used in an instrumental way as well, to refer to the choice of means employed to reach some end. Insofar as emotions are purposive, they have ends. It is not just a matter of their occurring (and how to get rid of or enjoy them). There are also questions about what will *satisfy* them. As strategies, emotions seek their own satisfaction: in anger, through vengeance, in hatred, through vanquishing, in love, through "possessing." This is not to say that all emotions can be satisfied or have conditions of satisfaction. (Grief, for example, is an emotion with no such conditions, except *per impossible*, the resurrection of the lost loved one.) Nevertheless, even such emotions may have a purpose or purposes – for example, to mend a suddenly broken life, not only for the individual but for the group together.

No doubt much of this can be explained via both biological and cultural evolution, but that is not the critical point. Of course, one can readily surmise that the energizing supplied by anger or fear prepares an organism for extraordinary bursts of aggression or retreat, as the case may be. Such an account of emotions requires nothing whatever by way of self-awareness or voluntariness. In evolutionary theory, an individual or a species need not figure out its adaptive advantages; it simply lucks into them. It turns out that frogs and butterflies that resemble poisonous members of their classes have a competitive advantage, because they are eaten less often. It turns out that certain male birds with more tail plumage are more likely to attract a mate and thus have a reproductive advantage. So, too, it will turn out that creatures with a certain temperament, who react emotionally and express certain emotions in appropriate situations, may have a competitive or reproductive advantage. A dog that growls and attacks may be better suited to survive in certain environments. Dogs that run, hide, or cuddle may have competitive or reproductive advantages in other environments. (Dog breeders thus supplement nature with marketing considerations.) I take it that none of this, as such, is particularly controversial.

But most of what passes for evolutionary explanations of emotion in both psychology and philosophy these days is no more enlightening than Molière's famous explanation of the powers of a sleeping potion. To show that something serves a purpose or a function says no more and no less about the evolutionary process than the crudest creationist or contingency theories. Evolution is the new magic wand, which with a wave changes something inexplicable into something only seemingly explained. As Nietzsche famously noted, we always prefer bad explanations to no explanation at all.

But evolutionary theory is only background to what I am arguing here. Emotions, according to the evolutionary hypothesis, turn out to be strategic or functional because they happen to contribute to "fitness," with all of the ambiguities and objections that term has inspired in the past century or so. A person (or creature) who has an emotion, according to the evolutionary line, does not have it because he, or she, or the creature has a purpose (or because anyone, including "nature," has a purpose) but because that emotion has proved to be useful and alternative strategies have proved to be fatal. In such cases, the emotional responses themselves may be (what used to be called) instinctual, or, in current computer-based jargon, hardwired. An overly simple example (because it isn't really an emotion) is the startle reaction. Much more complicated are various forms of maternal affection and protectiveness, territorial jealousy, and fear at the sight of certain shapes or in the presence of certain smells. But what I am arguing is that however biologically based our emotions may be, whether hardwired or not – indeed, whether voluntary or not – our understanding of emotion gains a great deal when we shift from thinking about emotions and emotional responses as mere products and think of them instead as strategies: strategies for dealing with others, and strategies for dealing with ourselves.

The idea that emotions are purposive and functional can be found in ancient and medieval philosophy, and some of the world's great philosophers and religions have endorsed love and compassion in particular as divine strategies. But the thesis emerges with particular power not only in evolutionary accounts of emotion and their development but also, more controversially, in the anti-Jamesian theories of William James' contemporary and fellow pragmatist John Dewey and, more recently and more radically, in the writings of the French existentialist Jean-Paul Sartre. Sartre famously tells us that emotions are "magical transformations of the world," by which he means that emotions are intentional and strategic ways of coping with difficult situations.[13] We choose them, and we choose them for a purpose.

This Sartrian view of the strategic nature of emotions will, no doubt, strain the credulity of most contemporary emotion theorists, although similar if more modest evolutionary-functionalist theses have been argued by many psychological investigators. Perhaps I could blunt some doubts by noting that nothing in this voluntaristic thesis requires emotional strategies to be recognized, articulated, or even articulatable as such. In other words, they do not have to be conscious, in the usual sense of that term, and the "choices" we make need not be explicit, deliberative choices. Nevertheless, an emotion may be a strategy, a way of coping, and, in particular, a way of coping with other people. Especially when that way of coping involves power, I believe that we are justified in calling it politics, the politics of emotion. But this ambitious phrase admits of quite a few very different interpretations.

The Deweyian-Sartrian view takes on a good deal more ontological baggage than the traditional Cartesian model of emotions. Essential to this view is the idea that emotions are intentional, which means that they are directed towards objects (real or imaginary) in the world. They therefore involve concepts and cognition, including recognition. Of course, they also involve neurology and physiology, and intentional states may therefore have an instinctual or hardwired biological basis. (William James certainly suggests that this is so.) But what this notion of intentionality tends to do is to break down the Cartesian barrier between experience and the world, between the "inner" and the "outer." Of course, the objects of emotion are not always real: they may be merely imagined, or remembered, or, in extreme cases, hallucinated. In this case we might continue to talk about the whole process remaining "inside" the subject. But in the more usual case, in which Harry loves Sally, in which Fred hates spinach, in which Woody is jealous of Alan, the intentionality of emotion is clearly directed at something real and in the world. There is an enormous philosophical literature about how to deal with these issues, whether the case of the nonexistent object is to be given priority or rather treated as some sort of odd exception. But these intrigues need not slow us down here. The point is that an emotion is not merely a feeling, as, say, pain is a feeling. It is also an outlook, an attitude, a reaching out to the world.

As such a reaching out, it has aims and values (not just "appraisals," as some of the prominent psychological literature would suggest; appraisal is much too observational to be strategic). We perceive things, people, and events – and have emotions directed toward them – that embody our attitudes of approval and disapproval, desires and repulsion, and goals of much more intricate sorts. Whatever else they may be, emotions are intimately and not merely contingently tied to behaviour. (This is why they were, for so many years, coupled as a poor cousin to "motivation" in psychology textbooks. No one knew where else to put them.) Strict behaviourists, of course, would simply say that an emotion IS the behaviour, but here the conceptual tie is too tight, even with the usual qualifications.[14] Others (Nico Frijda, for instance) would more judiciously insist only that an emotion is a set of action tendencies.[15] But it is in the conceptual connection to behaviour – which is to say, clumsily, that the emotion and its expression are one thing and not two – that the politics of emotion becomes particularly prominent.

If emotion were simply an impersonal judgment, or a strictly inner appraisal, like a spectator sitting passively hundreds of yards from the field of play, the idea of emotional strategies and politics would make, at most, minimal sense. But emotions are tied to action, whether the cool and protracted strategies of revenge that sometimes flow from anger or the spontaneous and momentary expression of delight or surprise on someone's face. The controlled, unexpressed, hidden emotion therefore requires special explanation, not the connection between emotions and their expression. When an employee gets angry with her boss, or when a mature, respectful child gets angry with a teacher or a parent, it is not the absence of expression that is notable but the restraint, the distortion of expression, which is almost always evident to those who know what to look for. There are also many emotions for which their expressions are of no significance, not because the expressions are controlled but because they occur in a situation in which there is no one to notice or be affected by them: we often have emotions when we are alone. Accordingly it is important to note that there is an internal politics of emotions, so long as we do not take this in a Cartesian way. A subject may adopt an emotional strategy quite independently of any bit of behaviour, display, or expression of emotion, and in the absence of any other person or creature who might be influenced, affected, or even amused. Nevertheless, the emotion – not just its expression – takes place in a public space, not a mysterious Cartesian one. The emotion is "in the world," not in the mind, the psyche, or the soul.

The Politics of Emotion

The politics of emotion might be divided into four different realms, each of which I will discuss briefly. There is first of all a general thesis about the ontology – or better, the conceptual geography – of emotions: what they are, where they are to be located, and the terms in which they should be discussed. Second is the most obvious sense in which emotions are political, that is, they are about power, persuasion, manipulation, intimidation. Anger is the most familiar example here, but love, jealousy, shame, resentment, envy, sadness, and even despair deserve recognition as well. Third, there is what we might call the internal politics of emotion, the ways in which we position and (one might even say) manipulate ourselves in relation to the world, quite apart from the effects of our emotions or expressions on other people. In fact, when I first started seeing the importance of emotional strategies, given my (unacknowledged) Cartesian stance, it was such internal politics that initially intrigued me.[16] Again, getting angry is a paradigm example. One gets angry to "save face," not only in other people's eyes (the overtly public politics of anger) but in one's own eyes as well. Finally, the politics of emotion extend to the "meta" realm of emotion: labelling, recognition, reportage, description, and theorizing about emotion. This aspect of emotional politics is not easily separated or, sometimes, even distinguished from the other realms of politics in emotion and emotional expression.

The Ontology of Emotion

Ontology refers us to the basic nature of things, their place in the universe, and how they relate to other things. The ontology of psychology and psychological phenomena has long been trapped in the Cartesian picture, which, crudely, means that mental states, processes, or acts had to be treated either as odd manifestations or misleading descriptions of material states, processes, and behaviour (John Watson and B.F. Skinner in psychology, Gilbert Ryle in philosophy) or as extremely odd non-material entities, what Ryle famously mocked as "the ghost in the machine." But Descartes himself was keenly aware that the emotions, in particular, straddled this ontological abyss, composed, he said, of both kinds of "substances" (material and immaterial), agitations of the animal spirits (material) on the one hand defined by beliefs and desires (immaterial thoughts) on the other. Behaviourism, whatever its obvious absurdities, had the good sense to reject this impossible dichotomy and point out, with various levels of sophistication, that almost everything we know and just about everything we want to say about emotion depends on behaviour (including verbal behaviour, notably first-person reports). What was left over, of course, was that nagging first-person case, the subjective "feel" of emotions, but a variety of deft and sometimes daft strokes whittled away at the prominence of this residue.

Without denying subjectivity, it could nevertheless be plausibly maintained that much of what philosophers had formerly described as "inner" could just as plausibly be redescribed as "outer"—for example, in the expressions of the face, in tendencies to particular actions or action types (aggression, possession, caring for, withdrawing), and in the verbal descriptions and evaluations that were employed to express the emotion. Sadness, for example, can be understood only minimally in terms of the twinges and sense of deflation that characterize the distinctive feeling of sadness. The bulk of this basic emotion can be better understood through an analysis of appraisals and evaluations of loss. So, too, the difference between embarrassment and shame can be understood not so much in terms of any particular differences in feeling or sensation (are there any?) but rather in terms of the differences in attribution of these emotions in decidedly distinctive contexts.[17] Describing an emotion as shame implies an accusation of blame, whereas describing an emotion as embarrassment implies no such accusation. Thus, in the wake of Wittgenstein, Ryle, and their psychological counterparts, the mysterious mental elements came to play a minimal role in the discussion of emotion.

Talk of evaluations and judgments can be neutral with regard to the Cartesian dichotomy. To be sure, a judgment may be made *by* a particular person, the subject, but nothing much follows about the subjectivity (in the crucial sense of first-person privacy) of judging. A judgment or an evaluation is *about the world*, and is made or can be articulated in a public language in terms of (more or less) shared concepts and standards. Even if a person keeps a judgment to herself, that judgment is, nevertheless, about the world and analyzable in perfectly public terms. So, too, these judgments or evaluations can themselves be judged to be judicious, faulty, biased, or foolish. Thus, the conceptual geography of emotion suggests that the realm of emotion is neither the mind nor the world but both together: the world as experienced, the world as phenomenon.

Phenomenology, adequately described, is the natural medium for emotion description. Any description of the body, the brain, the circumstances, or the behaviour is bound to be incomplete or missing the point (the point of view, that is). Any description of merely inner sensation is bound to be pathetic. One can misdescribe the phenomenology as the peculiarity of the first-person case and raise the puzzle of how we recognize our own emotions and what they feel like, as opposed to how we recognize and understand other people's emotions. But the question of where emotions are to be located – in the material or the strange immaterial world – no longer serves any purpose. Emotions are, in every important sense, "out there," in the world. Or rather, there is no "out there" because there is no contrasting "in there," unless, perhaps, one wishes to speak rather peculiarly about processes "in" the brain. This is not what is commonly called materialism, which disappears along with the odd view – held only by philosophers, neurologists and some social scientists – that emotions are "all in the brain." Nor is it in any way to deny the "existence of consciousness," whatever that phrase is supposed to mean. The point is that emotions are vital experiences had by conscious social creatures (even if the very limited role of the social in their lives is a constant awareness of predators and the occasional awareness of an available mate). Emotions involve any number of interrelated aspects of such creatures' sensibilities, social relationships, self-awareness, shared and individual outlooks on the world, physiology, and various expressions in speech and behaviour. Such complex creatures should not be split up into a simplistic and arbitrary ontology of bodies and minds.

Emotions, Power, and Persuasion
On this view, the most obvious sense in which emotions are political is that we use them to move other people, or other creatures. Our dogs respond rather quickly to a shout or a scowl, even if it is disciplinary and feigned rather than genuine emotion. This, of course, raises a crucial point about the politics of emotion: the convincing expression of emotion, rather than what one might call the emotion itself, is doing the work. But, in our account of the conceptual geography of emotions, I tried to cast some doubt on the

distinction between emotion and expression and argue – as William James did – that a convincing display of emotion either presupposes or tends to create the very emotion being displayed. Could one gain the same ends by pretending, by acting *as if* one has the emotion in question without, in fact, having it at all? In theory, perhaps, but I think the practical answer is that few of us are such accomplished actors that we could bring off such a performance, so that actually having the emotion seems necessary. If this is so, then it seems to follow that one has the emotion precisely in order to bring about the desired results. Regardless (and certainly the range of cases is far richer than James' simple formula would suggest), emotions are clearly not just self-contained or usually so, but are more or less continuous with their expression. This means that the lines dividing authenticity, self-deception, and bad faith get enormously complicated here, but I want to remark, rather baldly, on just one piece of this intricately human puzzle: to have an emotion for a purpose does not entail "not really having" the emotion. That thesis, of course, would undermine everything else I've said here. Nico Frijda puts the thesis correctly, I think, when he suggests that the kind, intensity, and manifestation of emotions are determined not only by significant eliciting events, but also to an important degree by the anticipated desirable effects they exert upon others.[18] Emotions, in other words, are strategies, and there is little reason to doubt that our emotional expressions evolved, in part, because of their effectiveness in communicating our emotions to others.

Sometimes, our emotions and emotional displays express the need to evoke solicitude. Expressions of submissiveness, shrieks of terror, a baby's cries of distress, are all directed (which is not to say consciously or intentionally) to getting the attention and directing the actions of others. Because they work so well, they can also be learned, cultivated, practised, and thus employed in an intentional (which is not to say feigned) way. A young female soon learns to win favours by being submissive, which involves feeling submissive, and so she learns to feel submissive. A clever young monkey learns to scatter the troop, at least once, and get the food for himself, by overreacting to a sign of merely modest danger. Babies, children, and even adults learn to cry to win over the sympathies of others, and, again, they are not "faking it" but rather just being particularly alert about finding things to cry about. (A young woman on *Seinfeld* bursts into genuine tears when her hotdog slips out of its bun, but later shows no sign of sadness at all when her grandmother dies. She may be despicable, but she is not a fraud.)

Many emotions are about power, persuasion, manipulation, and intimidation. We use anger, for example, not only to pump up the energy and boldness needed for a confrontation but to intimidate the opposition as well. One of the more unpleasant members of my academic department had the habit of highlighting every meeting in which there was a controversial issue by standing up (he was very tall), leaning menacingly over the conference table, and shouting quite threateningly at whomever was opposing his position. Since most of the controversial issues discussed were also quite trivial, the opposition virtually always gave in, and he had his way. What was telling was that these cheap victories rarely had any correlation to the merits of the case, and, more telling still, there was no reason whatever to suppose that his angry displays would ever lead to actual violence. (In fact, the fellow was a coward who would most probably have backed away from any real fight.) But, for most of us, our fear and foreboding of anger is so visceral that the mere display of anger leads us to act *as if* there is a real threat of harm behind it, even when we know there isn't.

So, too, of the seductive emotions. How many of us have been taken in by appeals that, we even knew at the time, were insincere, misleading, or disasters-in-waiting? Advertising and salesmanship depend on such vulnerabilities. Our responses to emotions, as well as the emotions and the expressions themselves, are inbred, habituated, cultivated, and, possibly, sometimes, hardwired. It is no surprise, then, that emotions have this obvious political element, that their existence is not a neutral social or psychological fact but a political force, moving us and influencing our actions in any number of ways.

When we begin to discuss the many aspects of the display and expression of emotion, the power of such strategies should be obvious. Paul Ekman and Carroll Izard have maintained for years that the facial expressions they have classified have an evolutionary basis, and they take this to mean not only that they happened to appear in evolutionary history but that they in fact served some social, and therefore reproductive, advantage. What is true in the evolutionary story must surely be true in the more ordinary social story. Bad-tempered people tend to get their way by being intimidating. (They could possibly get their way by just pretending to be angry, but, their thespian talents aside, actually getting angry would seem to give them a double advantage, for reasons suggested above.) To what extent this is true of other emotions will involve emotion-by-emotion analysis. A case can surely be made for love, generally considered. Shame and guilt would suggest an advantage for the group, but perhaps not directly for the individual. Grief and sadness invite speculation. (There is certainly manipulative grief, and tears by way of a plea.) Pity and gratitude would be fascinating cases to explore. (Nietzsche has done so polemically, and at some length.)[19] But all such analyses would be looking for the ways in which expression and display constitute a strategic advantage over other people (whether intentional or not).

The Internal Politics of Emotion
The internal politics of emotion are the ways in which we position and (one might even say) manipulate ourselves in relation to the world, quite apart

from the effects of our emotions or expressions on other people. When Frijda writes that emotion politics is "displaying or even experiencing a given emotion because of its desired effects," there is an important ambiguity in the word "experiencing."[20] What we experience certainly influences or even determines our attitudes and our behaviour, which in turn influence, move, or coerce other people. But we can sometimes see a truncated version of the process in which the effects are unexpressed or unrecognized, in which they are even intended to remain so. Anger is a hostile emotion that adopts a familiar stance in the world, if only in one's own perspective. But that perspective has a purpose, whether or not it has expression or results in action – even if the subject goes off alone and avoids all possible detection or prompting to action. Anger is a judgmental stance, one that resembles the courtroom scenario succinctly captured by Lewis Carroll in *Alice in Wonderland* (in the Mouse's tale): "'I'll be judge, I'll be jury,' Said cunning old Fury."[21] The strategic advantage, I think, should be obvious. Emerging from a situation in which one has been hurt, offended, or humiliated, one positions oneself as nevertheless superior, even as righteous. This is a powerful psychological position. It is emotional politics at its most profound and subtle, whether or not effective in the world.

A similar example is developed at length by Nietzsche in his *Genealogy of Morals*, where he suggests that resentment, by its very nature, is an emotion that evades direct expression and confrontation but prefers to alter the world as perceived to suit its own particular vulnerabilities and weaknesses.[22] Thus one might talk about these internal politics as the strategic rearrangement of one's own attitudes. This internal politics of emotion fits in very well with what I have often referred to as the judgmental role of emotion, following certain Stoics, who argued a similar thesis two thousand years ago. The question for the Stoics was not how our emotional behaviour affected the world (negatively or negligibly, most of them argued) but rather how our emotional judgments affected our own outlook on the world and, consequently, our chances for happiness. A somewhat more public version of the same idea has been nicely characterized by Ronald de Sousa, whose *Rationality of Emotion* introduced the notion of "paradigm scenarios" in which one learns not only the appropriateness of certain emotions and emotional behaviours but also their power and significance.[23] What one learns, presumably, is not only the effect of one's emotional responses on others (and their approval or disapproval and responses in return) but the way an emotion makes one feel, where the feeling in question is by no means to be confused with the sensations caused by the concurrent physiology or that inchoate sense of "affect" so often alluded to by authors who lack the facility to pin the felt emotion down.[24] One could (and de Sousa encourages this) provide an evolutionary background story for such scenarios. But for my purposes here, it is important to insist that these scenarios are not and need not be, as such, public or physically situated. No doubt they originally always are public and physically situated. But once one has internalized the paradigm of an emotion, one can, as it were, play it back privately, rehearse and instantiate a strategy as if it were public, and, in so doing, achieve a sort of competitive advantage, even if only in one's own eyes.

The Politics of Emotion Language and Theory

Thus far, I have been talking about the politics of emotion strictly in terms of the strategies of and in emotion. But they are only part of the story. We do not just have emotions, we know that we have them. We label them, talk about them, devise theories about them, and, not incidentally, make a good living from those theories. Here is a second level of competitive advantage, if you will, not in the emotions, but in the "meta-level" in which talk about the emotions comes into play. I suggest that, because we so easily tend to think of language as something over and above the emotions, a facility or faculty quite separate from the "having" of an emotion, we do not tend to take emotion-talk as part of the same set of phenomena. But the truth is, our language, our concepts, and our conceptions of emotions pervade, define, and are intimately linked with the emotions themselves. (This is not for a moment to deny that animals and preverbal infants have emotions. It is only to deny that adult humans, who do have such a language, are capable of clearly separating their emotions from their talk and thinking about them.)

There are several dimensions of this "meta" reflection on emotions. The simplest has to do with the nature of emotions' names, that is, what we call them, or what psychologists refer to as "labelling." Whether a person labels her hostile feelings "hatred," "anger," or "resentment," for example, makes quite a difference in how she will express, evaluate, think about, and talk about her emotion. More complicated is the way we talk about and sometimes mythologize emotions. Love in America is an apt illustration. It is a highly mythologized, one might say "hypercognated," emotion, so much so that cynics have often suggested that "love" is *only* a word, a confusion of fantasies, not a genuine emotion.[25] Finally, and most sophisticated of all, is the way we, as philosophers and psychologists, conceptualize and theorize about emotions. The target of my arguments for almost twenty-five years now has been the still strong tendency to "primitivize" emotions, by way of denying, I suggest, our responsibility for them. To say that we choose our emotions is, I admit, something of a stretch. But as a self-fulfilling prophecy, as a way of taking control and becoming increasingly aware of the emotional choices we do make, I believe it is an invaluable piece of existentialist wisdom. The primary alternative, thinking of emotions as physiological disruptions and psychic forces beyond our control, is also a self-fulfilling prophecy, an invitation to think of ourselves as victims and make excuses for our own behaviour. Thus the politics of emotions becomes part and parcel of the politics of personal responsibility and the self-cultivation of the virtues.

Does it matter whether we call an emotion "anger" or "childishness" or "*riri*" or "ire" – or even "fury" or "outrage" or "moral indignation"? (What are the differences here?) Jean Briggs has famously told us that in Utku the naming of (what we call) anger "childishness" serves to demean the emotion even as it is identified.[26] Similarly, Robert Levi has shown us how "*riri*" in Tahitian demonizes the emotion even before it is described. "Ire" (directly from the Latin) has a nobility about it that "anger" lacks.[27] So, too, "fury" suggests violence, "outrage" indicates violation, and "moral indignation" suggests righteousness. (Mere "irritation" or being "pissed off" is dismissive, by contrast.) "Rage," I would suggest, refers to something much more (or much less) than anger, a totalizing neurological response that is, comparatively, out of control and involuntary. There is more in a name, dear Juliet, than that which arbitrarily names that which smells so sweet. And when a person supplies a name to his or her own emotion (as Schachter and Singer have shown), it is the emotion itself, and not merely its name, that alters.[28]

The politics of emotion language is by no means limited to the naming of emotion. Consider, for example, the general dismissal of emotion in such terms as "sentimentality" and, simply, "getting emotional." Once upon a time, the word "sentimentality" suggested the superior sensibility of aristocrats. No more. Today, it tends to refer to bad art, cheap morals, and a distinctive defect of character. "Emotional" and "sentimental" are employed as put-downs – for example, in a long-standing (and still not extinct) dismissal of women and "effeminate" men from positions of responsibility.[29]

Finally, there is the politics of our theories, including the now controversial depiction of what are misleadingly called "folk psychological" theories. A good deal of common sense theory (and the language of emotions) implies what I have called the "hydraulic theory," the dismissive view that emotions are nothing but physiological pressure, as drawn, for example, by Freud in his "boiler system" model of the "psychic apparatus," in the early decades of his career. My objection here is not only theoretical but existential or ethical. The politics of the hydraulic model (and a good deal of folk psychology) is a politics of irresponsibility: our emotions are an "it," not part of the "I." So, too, those ancient theories that make out love and anger to be a breed of madness, rather than strategies. Here is where Sartre comes charging in with his existential theory: the emotions do not "take us over" or "sweep us away"; they are strategies and we *choose* them. Personal responsibility is an important piece of the emotions story, and any theory that does not face up to this is itself political – or politically irresponsible.

The Startle Response and the Primitivization of Emotion

Finally, I want to discuss one of the most straightforward examples of what I call the primitivization of the emotions in the recent philosophical literature:

Jenefer Robinson's defence of the startle response as a paradigm of emotion.[30] Robinson rightly suggests that this example provides a striking contrast to the "judgmental view" of emotions as cognitive, defended by many philosophers but (she says, incorrectly) not by many psychologists. Being startled is, one might say, a pure and primitive emotion, without the cause or accompaniment of belief, thought, or judgment and certainly not constituted by them. Being startled is an immediate and involuntary physiological response. Robinson suggests that philosophers pay more attention to the psychological research on emotion and, in particular, physiologically hardwired emotional responses. Indeed, she is right that philosophers (with some obvious exceptions) have paid too little attention to the sometimes fascinating work going on in psychology and, especially, neurology (though it must be said that the neglect has mostly been mutual). But the startle response is, I want to argue, much too primitive to count as an emotion – even given the messiness and open-endedness of that category – and certainly too primitive and unpromising to serve as a paradigm of emotion or a "basic" emotion.[31]

The range of emotions, if one were to (mistakenly) conceive them along the line of a single dimension, extends from almost straightforward physiological reactions (disgust, elation) to extremely sophisticated, fully cognitive responses (indignation, humiliation, certain forms of romantic love and devotion). But even disgust presupposes some (disgusting) perception, and although elation need not be accompanied by an articulated thought or belief to the effect that "all is well," the attribution of elation would be difficult to defend without some such evaluative judgment. Similarly, even the most extreme judgmentalist will agree that indignation, humiliation, love, and devotion involve some possibly intense, probably involuntary, neurologically based response, although the causal story in such cases promises to be both bidirectional and extremely complex. I will ignore the longer-duration emotions, such as lasting love, enduring anger, envy, and resentment, and lifelong guilt or shame in my response to Robinson, although it seems to me to be an enormous if long-standing mistake to ignore these emotions, or to think of them as merely dispositions or derivative of more episodic responses. Indeed, I would argue that the more durable emotions, "the passions," ought to serve as our paradigm, in part because it is so obviously they, and not the sudden movements of the moment, that carry political weight and significance.

The idea that some version of surprise is a basic emotion isn't new, of course. Descartes lists wonder ("a sudden surprise of the soul") as one of six "primitive passions," but the convoluted description that follows makes it clear that being startled is not what he has in mind: "which causes it to apply itself to consider with attention the objects which seem to it rare and extraordinary. It is thus primarily caused by the impression we have in the brain which represents the object as rare."[32] One could helpfully distinguish here between surprise, astonishment, shock – as in "I was shocked to find X," not physiological shock – being stunned, and being startled (and, perhaps, being merely unprepared). The difference between shock and startle and the difference between shock and its pathological namesake (a collapse of circulatory function) are particularly revealing. Startle is, as Robinson argues, an autonomic reflex; even one-celled organisms arguably display it, for example, when poked. Shock is a sudden emotional disturbance, but it is not only caused by some sudden event; it also has that event (or some complex surrounding that event) as its object. Shock therefore presents itself as a candidate for emotionhood.

The relationship between emotional shock and the sudden pathological malfunction of circulation is worth noting. Of course, one can lead to the other: the shock of being arrested for a serious crime or seeing the body of one's mangled loved one dangling from a fence will probably cause physiological shock as well. Physiological shock, like some other medical conditions, can be caused by physical trauma (e.g., extensive loss of blood) as well as by psychological trauma (e.g., extremely intense emotion). Jean-Paul Sartre probably overstates the case when he suggests that a young woman who is shocked by her companions' comments faints as a strategic response, but some relationship between emotion and the "magical transformation" of the body is not unfamiliar in medical circles.[33] This relationship between emotion and physiology pervades the study of emotions. For example, extreme anger can give way to rage, a physiological reaction. (Neurological experiments with cats has demonstrated that this response can be triggered by stimulating a specific part of the brain.) So, too, extreme fear gives way to panic, arguably another "primitive" physiological response defined by limited cognition or judgment. I have been arguing that there is no clear dividing line between psychology and physiology in emotion, but the attribution of emotion as opposed to mere reflex would seem to be precisely the presence of some cognition – some directedness towards an object – as opposed to the physiological response alone, as in the startle reaction.[34]

It is worth noting that at least one of the psychologists to whom Robinson appeals most often in her argument, Paul Ekman, has himself given up the view that the startle response counts as an emotion. He has instead moved to surprise as a basic emotion, where this is understood not merely as "being startled" but as "being surprised by."[35] The startle response as such is impossible to stimulate or inhibit. Indeed it is only in the most generous sense a response at all; rather, it is a reflex. This distinction is particularly significant because Ekman's theory of emotion leans very heavily on a particular kind of hardwired physiological response, namely, facial expressions. Of course, what is particularly interesting here is that such expressions can be either voluntary or involuntary. For an expression to be hardwired, in other words, does not mean it is therefore fully determined by physiology. (One might note that even Robert Zajonc, the harshest critic of cognitive theories in psychology, speaks unflinchingly of "motor systems" as "representational" and as "encoded." And Joseph LeDoux, to whose neurological views Robinson appeals, insists on the significance of interactions between the subcortical parts of the brain essential to emotion and the neocortex and hippocampus, suggesting that cognition is not irrelevant even in the most primitive emotion.)[36]

Why not include startle, as Robinson argues, at the extreme primitive end of the emotion spectrum? One could, of course, question whether the spectrum model makes much sense for what is in fact an extremely complex and by no means obviously related set of psychological phenomena. (Erotic love certainly involves an enormous number of autonomic [enduring] physiological responses. It also involves historically and cultural bound concepts of considerable complexity.) One could also challenge the notion of an emotion as a response. So, too, Robinson: "According to my model, my response is a bodily response which makes this event salient to me and registers it as significant to my goals and values."[37] But doesn't the event have to be perceived as salient in order to provoke any such bodily response? My primary concern, however, is not how we circumscribe or carve up the territory we too casually identify as "the emotions," but the purpose at which such primitivizing moves aim. (This is a particularly tantalizing question in Robinson's case, for she has written some sensible and sensitive essays on the role of emotion in the arts.) I suspect that the primitivizing move more often than not precedes a debunking, the suggestion that emotions as such are too conceptually uninteresting for philosophers to talk about.

Let me offer a brief example of such debunking, "An Assessment of Emotion" by Jerome Shaffer. Shaffer begins his assessment with a most unflattering example of "undergoing an emotion": "I am driving around a curve and see a log across the road. I take it that bodily harm is likely and I don't want that. I turn pale, my heart beats faster, I feel my stomach tighten. I slam on the brakes." Not surprisingly, Shaffer uses this and similar examples of emotion to conclude that emotions are not very pleasant or valuable experiences and, accordingly, are "neither necessary nor in general desirable for the main concerns of life."[38] A log in the road is not merely a matter of being startled; indeed, I suspect that it falls into the category of an unwelcome surprise. But should we characterize (much less define) surprise by turning pale, a faster heartbeat, a tightened stomach? Consider the very different analysis that would accompany taking as our lead example, say, experiencing a powerful sense that justice has not been done, or the possibly decades-long experience of being passionately in love. (Shaffer's analysis of love as an emotion in the same essay reduces love to "butterflies in the stomach" and other such "waves, currents, surges or suffusions," concluding that love, too, is an emotion of little value. This is hardly the passion that moved Tristan and Isolde.) Furthermore, we can readily agree that coming across a log in the road is an undesirable experience without concluding that the surprise itself is an undesirable experience. Indeed, in safer surroundings, millions of people stand in line in order to pay to have the wits satisfyingly shocked out of them not only by misplaced logs but by killer sharks, madmen, monsters, and chainsaw murderers.

Emotions are still on the defence in philosophy (and they have come into prominence in psychology only since the 1990s). For that reason, one might well agree with Robinson that emotions have a primitive component and, in a few cases, are extremely primitive themselves, but still insist on focusing on just those emotions that are comparatively sophisticated. Such emotions have the sorts of conceptual components that are the familiar subject matter of philosophical analysis: an interest in symbolic logic or scientific curiosity, being awestruck by the beauty of a golden eagle, being warily suspicious of an insurance salesman, being embarrassed about wedding publicity, falling in love, having a keen sense of justice, becoming indignant or jealous, joyful or even depressed. One need not deny physiology to engage in philosophy, but neither should we allow the facts of physiology to eclipse significant philosophical investigations.

Conclusion

One further form of politics in the study of emotion ought to be mentioned, and that is the academic politics of departments and professional prestige. We redefine emotions to suit our methods. Philosophers, not surprisingly, tend to view emotions through the frame of conceptual analysis, as the phenomenology of experience, as cognitive science. Neurologists tend to view emotions as first of all neurological. Behavioural psychologists naturally tend to view emotion by way of expression, and so on. There is nothing wrong with this tendency in itself, but we all too easily let our politics obstruct joint efforts and mutual understanding. Philosophers are particularly skilled at dismissing as conceptual confusion or nonsense the most devoted efforts of the social scientists, without applying the principle of charity to seek out what they might be saying that philosophers have systematically ignored or overlooked. In return, predictably, the social scientists lampoon "armchair philosophers" without bothering to see what serious suggestions might be sitting there.

So to end, I want to return to John Dewey's thoughtful commentary on William James, in which he insists on a holistic, all-embracing view of emotion. Emotions have a multiplicity of dimensions and aspects and, consequently, a multiplicity of lines of investigation. But let's not be like those legendary blind Persians, each dogmatic about their own particular part of the elephant. If we are aware of the politics that pervade and surround not only emotion but also our treatments of emotion, we can work together to answer some of the hardest questions, namely how these different approaches fit together. There may be no single objective standpoint. Indeed, there may be no objective standpoint at all. The ultimate truth about human emotion may be that we never get outside ourselves, and so political interests and power relationships will always permeate both emotion and the study of emotions. But the fact that emotions are political may be precisely why they remain of such enduring interest, not as a test case for Cartesian dualism but as an eminently practical matter regarding our getting along in the world.

Notes

Introduction: The Emotions and the History of Political Thought

1 "Passion" is often used colloquially in English to signify strong or violent emotions. But passion is also frequently used synonymously with emotion rather than being treated as a species of the larger genus. We use the terms interchangeably. Much the same could be said for the term "feeling" (see, for example, Chapter 8 in this volume), but in this introduction we distinguish between passions and emotions on the one hand and feelings on the other in order to reserve for the latter the technical sense of the physiological component of an emotion or passion. Robert C. Roberts asserts that "feelings are very close to the paradigm cases of adult human emotions and can provide the beginnings of a model for understanding the emotions." See *Emotions: An Essay in Aid of Moral Psychology* (Cambridge: Cambridge University Press, 2003), 68. But Roberts limits his observations to what he calls "feelings of construed condition," which he differentiates from feelings of sickness inasmuch as the former depend less on sensory awareness of one's body than do the latter.

2 Some recent works in political theory that seek to explore these themes include Cheryl Hall, *The Trouble with Passion: Political Theory beyond the Reign of Reason* (New York: Routledge, 2005); Barbara Koziak, *Retrieving Political Emotion: Thumos, Aristotle and Gender* (University Park: Pennsylvania State University Press, 2000); George E. Marcus, *The Sentimental Citizen: Emotion in Democratic Politics* (University Park: Pennsylvania State University Press, 2002); W.R. Newell, *Ruling Passion: The Erotics of Statecraft in Platonic Political Philosophy* (Lanham, MD: Rowman and Littlefield, 2000); C. Pateman, "The Disorder of Women: Women, Love and the Sense of Justice," in *The Disorder of Women: Democracy, Feminism and Political Theory*, 17-32 (Palo Alto, CA: Stanford University Press, 1989); Michael Walzer, *Politics and Passion: Towards a More Egalitarian Liberalism* (New Haven, CT: Yale University Press, 2004); and Marlene K. Sokolon, *Political Emotions: Aristotle and the Symphony of Reason and Emotion* (DeKalb: Northern Illinois University Press, 2006).

3 "For pure practical reason the passions are cancerous sores": Immanuel Kant, *Anthropology from a Pragmatic Point of View* (The Hague: Martinus Nijhoff, 1974), s. 81, p. 133. The term invoked in the original German is "Krebsschäden."

4 On Chrysippus and the Stoics in general, see Cicero, *Cicero on the Emotions: Tusculan Disputations 3 and 4*, trans. Margaret Graver (Chicago: University of Chicago Press, 2002). See William James' classic statement of his position in the 1884 essay, "What Is an Emotion?" in *What is an Emotion? Classic Readings in Philosophical Psychology*, ed. Cheshire Calhoun and Robert C. Solomon (New York: Oxford University Press, 1984), 128-29: "Our natural way of thinking about these standard emotions is that the mental perception of some fact excites the mental affection called the emotion, and that this latter state of mind gives rise to the bodily expression. My thesis on the contrary is that *the bodily changes follow directly the* PERCEPTION *of the exciting fact, and that our feeling of the same changes as they occur* IS *the emotion.* Common sense says, we lose our fortune, are sorry and weep; we meet a bear, are frightened and run; we are insulted by a rival, are angry and strike. The hypothesis here to be defended says that this order of sequence is incorrect, that the one mental state is not immediately induced by the other, that the bodily manifestations must first be interposed between, and that the more rational statement is that we feel sorry because we cry, angry because we strike, afraid because we tremble, and

not that we cry, strike, or tremble, because we are sorry, angry, or fearful, as the case may be. Without the bodily states following on the perception, the latter would be purely cognitive in form, pale, colourless, destitute of emotional warmth. We might then see the bear, and judge it best to run, receive the insult and deem it right to strike, but we could not actually feel afraid or angry," emphasis in original.

5 As we hope that the preceding discussion has indicated, the "newness" of this work is questionable. Many of the philosophers in the Western tradition have held something like a cognitive account of the emotions. As Michael Stocker pointedly remarks: "A current historical fiction about the emotions is that only recently have philosophers succeeded in understanding them as cognitive, desiderative, and evaluative, and not simply as somatic feelings. But it is difficult to think of any important philosopher from Socrates to James, unlike some writers in this century, who did not enjoy that success." "Emotional Thoughts," *American Philosophical Quarterly* 24, 1 (1987): 59.

6 Making this point has itself become commonplace in the literature. See, for example, Kristjan Kristjansson's opening sentence in a recent paper on problems with cognitive theories: "Since the 1970s *cognitivism* has been the reigning research paradigm in philosophical and psychological explorations of the emotions." "Some Remaining Problems in Cognitive Theories of Emotion," *International Philosophical Quarterly* 41, 4 (2001): 393. We make no effort to date precisely the shift in conceptualizations of the emotions to which we refer here, but point to Gilbert Ryle's *The Concept of Mind* (New York: Barnes and Noble, 1949) as an early precursor. While it did not offer a cognitive theory of emotion, it cleared a path by rejecting other theories. Within about fifteen years of Ryle's book, more overtly cognitive approaches were in circulation: see Anthony Kenny, *Action, Emotion and Will* (London: Routledge and Kegan Paul, 1963); Errol Bedford, "Emotions," *Proceedings of the Aristotelian Society* 57 (1956-57): 281-304; and George Pitcher, "Emotion," *Mind* 74, 295 (1965): 326-46. Since the seventies the sheer volume of work has become daunting. Here is an abbreviated list of some of this material, arranged chronologically: Bernard Williams, "Morality and the Emotions," in *Problems of the Self*, 207-29 (New York: Cambridge University Press, 1973); Gabriele Taylor, "Justifying the Emotions," *Mind* 84 (1975): 390-402; Robert C. Solomon, *The Passions* (New York: Doubleday, 1976; rev. ed., Indianapolis, IN: Hackett, 1993); Irving Thalberg, *Perception, Emotion and Action* (Oxford: Basil Blackwell, 1977); Amélie Rorty, ed., *Explaining Emotions* (Berkeley: University of California Press, 1980); Michael Stocker, "Psychic Feelings: Their Importance and Irreducibility," *Australian Journal of Philosophy* 61 (1983): 5-26; Ronald de Sousa, *The Rationality of Emotion* (Cambridge, MA: MIT Press, 1987); Robert Roberts, "What an Emotion Is: A Sketch," *Philosophical Review* 97, 2 (1988): 183-209; Patricia Greenspan, *Emotions and Reasons: An Inquiry into Emotional Justification* (London: Routledge, 1988); Simon Blackburn, *Ruling Passions* (Oxford: Clarendon Press, 1998); Peter Goldie, *The Emotions* (Oxford: Clarendon Press, 2000); Aaron Ben-Ze'ev, *The Subtlety of Emotions* (Cambridge, MA: MIT Press, 2000); Ronald de Sousa, "Moral Emotions," *Ethical Theory and Moral Practice* 4 (2001): 109-26; Martha C. Nussbaum, *Upheavals of Thought: The Intelligence of Emotions* (Cambridge: Cambridge University Press, 2001); Peter Goldie, "Emotions, Feelings, and Intentionality," *Phenomenology and the Cognitive Sciences* 1 (2002): 235-54; Robert Roberts, *Emotions: An Essay in Aid of Moral Psychology* (New York: Cambridge University Press, 2003); Robert C. Solomon, *Not Passion's Slave: Emotions and Choice* (New York: Oxford University Press, 2003); Aaron Ben-Ze'ev, "Emotions Are Not Mere Judgments," *Philosophy and Phenomenological Research* 68, 2 (2004): 450-57; Robert C. Solomon, *Thinking about Feeling: Contemporary Philosophers on Emotions* (New York: Oxford University Press, 2004).

7 Too often, cognitive theorists of emotion are tempted to treat "cognitive" as synonymous with "mental" and to then slide casually into the habit of treating some level of cognitive activity as also proving that a higher level of rational activity is involved. The complexity of the mental activity involved in an emotion became a wedge dividing the Stoics over whether or not animals could experience emotions.

8 Robert Nozick, *The Examined Life: Philosophical Meditations* (New York: Simon and Schuster, 1989), 87, emphasis in original.

9 Ronald de Sousa argues that even characterizing the emotions as arational will not exclude them from entering into questions of the good life: "The claim that emotions are arational – that they are beyond the pale of rational assessment – is sometimes confused with the very different claim that they are *irrational*. Strictly speaking, the two claims are incompatible, since the ascription of *arationality* amounts to the claim that emotions can be neither rational nor irrational. But there is a complication that excuses the confusion: If emotions are arational, questions must still arise about the proper place of such arational factors in a well-ordered human life. And it may then appear either rational or irrational to give arational elements pride of place in a rational life plan (or, for that matter, in a

principled refusal to live life according to any plan)." "Emotion," in *The Encyclopedia of Ethics*, ed. L.C. Becker and C.B. Becker, vol. 1 (New York: Garland Publishing, 1992), 302, emphasis in original.

10 Nozick, *Examined Life*, 93. Michael Stocker has independently reached a similar judgment about the emotions and the moral life: "In conclusion, then, emotions are essential to value and are themselves valued and valuable. They are forms of lived, engaged, human value. In addition, emotional knowledge – knowledge and understanding of emotions and the knowledge shown in emotions – is important, often vital, for knowledge and understanding of value, because much of this knowledge is emotional knowledge." "How Emotions Reveal Value and Help Cure the Schizophrenia of Modern Ethical Theories," in *How Should One Live? Essays on the Virtues*, ed. Roger Crisp (New York: Oxford University Press, 1996), 190.

11 This is an example inspired by a passage in Nozick's text. See *Examined Life*, 88. Nozick takes up pride as his example, and we have done likewise. In fleshing it out and in examining the issues surrounding it we do not profess any fidelity to Nozick's concerns, though we do hope to capture some of his insights.

12 Thomas Hobbes, *Leviathan*, ed. J.C.A. Gaskin (Oxford: Oxford University Press, 1996), 41.

13 René Descartes, *The Passions of the Soul*, trans. Stephen H. Voss (Indianapolis, IN: Hackett Publishing, 1989), 107.

14 Goldie, *Emotions*.

15 Kenny, *Action, Emotion and Will*.

16 Benedict de Spinoza, *Ethics*, Preceded by *On the Improvement of the Understanding*, ed. James Gutmann (New York: Hafner Press, 1949), 180.

17 Charles Taylor, "Self-Interpreting Animals," in *Human Agency and Language* (New York: Cambridge University Press, 1985), 55.

18 Nozick, *Examined Life*, 88.

19 Spinoza, *Ethics*, 228.

20 David Hume, *A Treatise of Human Nature*, ed. L.A. Selby-Bigge (Oxford: Clarendon Press, 1968), vol. 2, part 1, chap. 7. On the idea of pride and its relation to liberal and democratic theory, see also Paul J. Weithman, "Thomistic Pride and Liberal Voice," *The Thomist* 60 (1996): 241-74.

21 Nozick, *Examined Life*, 89.

22 Jean-Paul Sartre, *Existentialism and Human Emotions* (Secaucus, NJ: Carol Publishing Group, 1997), 23.

23 John Rawls, *A Theory of Justice* (Cambridge, MA: Harvard University Press, 1971). This is even more evident in his *Political Liberalism* (New York: Columbia University Press, 1993), especially 82-85. On this issue also see Susan Moller Okin, "Reason and Feeling in Thinking about Justice," *Ethics* 113, 2 (1999): 229-59; and Hall, *Trouble with Passion*, chap. 3.

24 Cass Sunstein, *Laws of Fear* (Cambridge: Cambridge University Press, 2005).

25 See Paul Kahn, *Putting Liberalism in Its Place* (Princeton, NJ: Princeton University Press, 2005), 120-23.

26 This vast amount of commentary includes Jean Elshtain, *Public Man, Private Woman: Women in Social and Political Thought* (Princeton, NJ: Princeton University Press, 1981); Susan Moller Okin, *Justice, Gender and the Family* (New York: Basic Books, 1989); and Genevieve Lloyd, *The Man of Reason: "Male" and "Female" in Western Philosophy* (Minneapolis: University of Minnesota Press, 1984).

27 Madeleine Bunting, "Consumer Capitalism Is Making Us Ill – We Need a Therapy State," *Guardian*, 5 December 2005, 25; and Madeleine Bunting, "Can You Be Taught How to Feel?" *Guardian*, 28 November 2005, s. G2, 3.

28 On this point, see Chapter 6 in this volume.

29 Judith Shklar, *Ordinary Vices* (Cambridge, MA: Belknap Press, 1984); Judith Shklar, "The Liberalism of Fear," in *Liberalism and the Moral Life*, ed. Nancy Rosenblum, 21-38 (Cambridge, MA: Harvard University Press, 1989); Alexis de Tocqueville, *Democracy in America*, trans. Harvey C. Mansfield and Delba Winthrop, vols. 1 and 2 (Chicago: University of Chicago Press, 2000).

30 For recent debates on the nature of republicanism, see, for example, Philip Petit, *Republicanism* (Oxford: Oxford University Press, 1997); Maurizio Viroli, *For Love of Country* (Oxford: Oxford University Press, 1997); and Jean-Fabien Spitz, *Le Moment Républicain en France* (Paris: Gallimard, 2005).

31 This approach, often called "constructionism," is associated with Rom Harré and Claire Armon-Jones. See, for example, Rom Harré, ed., *The Social Construction of Emotions* (Oxford: Basil Blackwell, 1986); and Claire Armon-Jones, "The Thesis of Constructionism," in *Philosophy and the Emotions*, ed. Stephen Leighton, 181-203 (Peterborough, ON: Broadview Press, 2003.

32 Michael Walzer, "Passion and Politics," *Philosophy and Social Criticism* 28 (2002), 617-33.

33 See, for example, Marcus, *Sentimental Citizen*.

Chapter 1: Explaining Emotions

Many people contributed to the writing of this chapter. Ernest Loevinsohn and Adam Morton helped shape an early draft. Jonathan Bennett and Georges Rey showed me how to eliminate some unnecessarily baroque elaborations. Mark Johnston and Graeme Marshall gave me some distinctions when I needed them most.

1 The contrast between voluntary actions and involuntary passions is generally too sharply drawn. For an account of the degrees in the voluntary control and redirection of the emotions, see Iris Murdoch, "The Idea of Perfection," in *The Sovereignty of Good*, 1-149 (London: Routledge and Kegan Paul, 1970).

2 Russell Dancy and Nancy Cartwright suggested an emotion need not be irrational or inappropriate to be anomalous: it may simply be out of character. Identifying an emotion as anomalous can, but need not, presuppose a normative judgment. Michael Stocker convinced me that even apparently appropriate and rational responses can be baffling: the question "Why did he do *that?*" always has a purchase.

3 A person's emotion is irrational if correcting the belief presupposed by the emotion fails to change it correspondingly, or if the person uncharacteristically resists considerations that would normally lead him to correct the belief. But an emotion can be irrational even if the presupposed belief is true, because the true belief presupposed by an emotion need not be its cause, even when the person does genuinely hold it. That is, the emotion may be caused by beliefs or attitudes that bear no relation to the belief that would rationalize it, quite independently of whether the person does in fact also hold the rationalizing belief. The rationality or irrationality of an emotion is a function of the relation between its causes and the beliefs that are taken to justify it. But irrational emotions can sometimes be perfectly appropriate to the situation in which they occur; and an emotion can be inappropriate when there is no irrationality (if, for instance, it is too strong or too weak, and out of balance with other emotions that are appropriate). Judgments of both rationality and appropriateness involve conceptions of normality that have normative force. Disagreements about the classification of an emotion often disguise disagreements about what is wholesome or right.

4 Compare W.V. Quine, *Word and Object* (Cambridge, MA: MIT Press, 1960), 57-61; Donald Davidson, "Belief and the Basis of Meaning," *Synthese* 27, 3-4 (1974): 309-23. For some modifications of the principle of causal reconstruction, see Richard E. Grandy, "Reference, Meaning and Belief," *Journal of Philosophy* 70, 14 (1973): 439-52; and Colin McGinn, "Charity, Interpretation, and Belief," *Journal of Philosophy* 74, 9 (1977): 521-35.

5 Compare William P. Alston, "Feelings," *Philosophical Review* 78, 1 (1969): 3-34; and William P. Alston, "Emotion and Feeling," in *Encyclopedia of Philosophy*, ed. Paul Edwards (New York: Macmillan, 1967), 479-86. See also R.E. Lazarus, "Emotions and Adaptation: Conceptual and Empirical Relations," *Nebraska Symposium on Motivation*, ed. W.J. Arnold, 175-266 (Lincoln: Nebraska University Press, 1968); P.T. Young, *Motivation and Emotions* (New York: Wiley, 1961); and Magda Arnold and J.A. Gasson, "Feelings and Emotions as Dynamic Factors in Personality Integration," in *The Nature of Emotion*, ed. Magda Arnold, 203-21 (New York: Penguin, 1968). This anthology and Arnold's *Emotion and Personality* (New York: Columbia University Press, 1960) contain an excellent selection of papers, surveying contemporary psychological theories of the emotions.

6 But compare Michael Tanner, "Sentimentality," *Proceedings of the Aristotelian Society* 77 (1977): 127-47, which describes a range of objectless (and sometimes pointless) emotions.

7 J. de Rivera, *A Structural Theory of the Emotions* (New York: International Universities Press, 1977).

8 For discussions of genetic and physiological determinants of emotions, see Charles Darwin, *The Expression of the Emotions in Man and Animals* (New York: Appleton, 1896); and D. Hamburg, "Emotions in the Perspective of Human Evolution," in *Expression of the Emotions in Man*, ed. Peter Knapp, 300-17 (New York: International Press, 1963). See also Paul Ekman, "Darwin and Cross-Cultural Studies of Facial Expression," in his *Darwin and Facial Expression: A Century of Research in Review* (New York: Academic Press, 1973); Paul Ekman, Wallace V. Friesen, and Phoebe Ellsworth, *Emotion in the Human Face* (New York: Pergamon Press, 1972); Paul Ekman, *Unmasking the Face* (Englewood Cliffs, NJ: Prentice-Hall, 1975); Silvan A. Tomkins, *Affect, Imagery and Consciousness*, 2 vols. (New York: Springer, 1962-63); and C.E. Izard, *The Face of Emotion* (New York: Appleton-Century-Crofts, 1971). For discussions of cultural and social factors, see John Middleton, ed., *From Child to Adult: Studies in the Anthropology of Education* (New York: Natural History Press, 1970). The essays by Margaret Mead, Meyer Fortes, and Dorothy Eggan are especially useful for an account of the socialization of the emotions. See also Hildred Geertz, "The Vocabulary of the Emotions," *Psychiatry* 22 (1959): 225-37; and

Jean Briggs, *Never in Anger* (Cambridge, MA: Harvard University Press, 1970). For a controversy about the priority of social structure and "basic" human sentiments, see Rodney Needham, *Structure and Sentiment* (Chicago: University of Chicago Press, 1962); and George Homans, *Sentiments and Activities* (New York: Free Press, 1962). For a general discussion of the genetic and the social determinants of emotions, see James Averill, "The Sociocultural, Biological, and Psychological Determinants of Emotion," in *Explaining Emotions*, ed. A.O. Rorty, 37-72 (Berkeley: University of California Press, 1980).

9 This terminology is meant to be neutral between competing analyses of causality and of the logic of dispositional terms. I shall speak of dispositions and habits interchangeably; but I want to examine the relation between the cause of a disposition and its triggering conditions, and to note the possibility that the component elements of a disposition may be quite heterogeneous. I would hope that the account of dispositions – as it finally emerges from the specialists concentrating on that issue – will show us why and how some dispositions have a magnetizing momentum of their own: the more they are acted upon, the more likely one is, and the easier it becomes to fall into that way of responding.

10 For an excellent account of how traits dispose a person to have characteristic *sorts* of beliefs and desires, see N. Hirschberg, "A Correct Treatment of Traits," unpublished manuscript.

11 Compare G.E.M. Anscombe, "On the Grammar of 'Enjoy,'" *Journal of Philosophy* 64, 19 (1967): 607-14; Anthony Kenny, *Action, Emotion and Will* (New York: Humanities, 1963), chaps. 1-3; D.F. Pears, "The Causes and Objects of Some Feelings and Psychological Reactions," *Ratio* 4, 2 (1962): 91-111; George Pitcher, "Emotion," *Mind* 74, 295 (1965): 326-46; and Irving Thalberg, "Constituents and Causes of Emotion and Action," *Philosophical Quarterly* 23, 90 (1973): 1-14.

12 Compare Gilbert H. Harman, "Knowledge, Reasons, and Causes," *Journal of Philosophy* 67, 21 (1970): 841-55. Harman's solution to the Gettier problem provides an analogue to my account of the conservation of the emotions. But as Bas C. van Fraasen has shown in "The Pragmatics of Explanation," *American Philosophical Quarterly* 14, 2 (1977): 143-50, the phrase "inference to the best explanation" is incomplete: apparently competing claims are sometimes compatible because different questions are at issue. For instance, sometimes we want to know why a person has that emotion (is resentful rather than hurt) and sometimes we want to know why her emotion is directed to that object (angry with her son rather than her boss).

13 Compare Keith S. Donellan, "Reference and Definite Descriptions," *Philosophical Review* 75, 3 (1966): 281-304, and Saul Kripke, "Naming and Necessity," in *Semantics of Natural Language*, ed. D. Davidson and G. Harman (Boston: Reidel, 1972), especially 269-72, 301-3.

14 Compare H. Hartmann, "Ego Psychology and the Problem of Adaptation," trans. David Rapaport, *Journal of the American Psychoanalytic Association*, series 1 (New York: International University Press, 1958); and H. Hartmann, E. Kris, and R. Loewenstein, *Papers on Psychoanalytic Psychology* (New York: International Universities Press, 1964).

15 One might worry that this involves the sort of circularity that is supposed to trouble claims that the reasons that sometimes cause actions also identify them. But Donald Davidson, among others, has made headway in answering these objections by distinguishing action-types and action-events. These solutions can be transposed to emotion contexts. Compare Davidson, "Actions, Reasons, and Causes," *Journal of Philosophy* 60, 23 (1963): 685-700; and G.E.M. Anscombe, *Intention* (Ithaca, NY: Cornell University Press, 1958), 11, 45-46. A different solution is proposed by Alvin Goldman, *A Theory of Human Action* (Englewood Cliffs, NJ: Prentice-Hall, 1970).

16 Compare Jean-Jacques Rousseau, "Fragments pour *Émile*," in *Oeuvres complètes de Jean-Jacques Rousseau*, ed. Bernard Gagnebin and Marcel Raymond, vol. 4 (Paris: Gallimard, 1969): "Nos passions sont des instruments spirituels dont la nature arme nôtre coeur pour la defense de nôtre personne et de tout ce qui est necessaire à nôtre bien-être. Plus donc nous avons besoin de choses étrangères, plus d'obstacles peuvent nous nuire, plus aussi nos passions sont nombreuses et exaltées; elles se mesurent naturellement sur les besoins de nôtre coeur."

17 Steven Stich, "Beliefs and Subdoxastic States," unpublished manuscript, Rutgers University, 16. Stich gives excellent arguments for the necessity of postulating intentional states that are not beliefs. Though he is primarily concerned with perception, the argument can be generalized.

18 Compare Robert C. Solomon, "The Logic of Emotion," *Nous* 11, 1 (1977): 41-49. For an excellent discussion of ambivalence, see Patricia Greenspan, "A Case of Mixed Feelings: Ambivalence and the 'Logic' of Emotion," in Rorty, *Explaining Emotions*, chap. 9, 223-50.

19 As part of his general program of mapping the facial configurations characteristic of particular emotions, Paul Ekman has begun to specify the configuration of facial muscles associated with various

forms of deception. See Paul Ekman, Wallace V. Friesen, and Klaus R. Scherer, "Body Movement and Voice Pitch in Deceptive Interaction," *Semiotica* 16 (1976): 23-27.

20 It is common in such circumstances to deny the attribution, saying of an adrenally charged person, "Oh, he isn't angry; it's just glands." Sometimes, at any rate, we shy away from attributing an emotion because the person's condition hasn't got the right sort of causal history.

21 Compare Stanley Schachter and Jerome Singer, "Cognitive, Social and Physiological Determinants of Emotional States," *Psychological Review* 69, 5 (1962): 379-99. Following Walter B. Cannon, they argue that, because the same visceral changes occur both in a variety of emotional states and in nonemotional states, our perception of these changes cannot identify distinctive emotions. They also hold that "cognitions arising from the immediate situation as interpreted by past experience provide the framework within which one understands and labels feelings" (380). The cognition therefore determines whether the state of psychological arousal will be labelled "anger," "exuberance," or "fear." Their experiments led them to conclude that "emotional states may be considered a function of a state of physiological arousal and a cognition appropriate to that arousal" (398). But, "given a state of physiological arousal, for which an individual has no immediate explanation, he will label that state and describe his feelings in terms of the cognitions available to him" (398). The subject's reports of his emotions, and sometimes his behaviour, can be manipulated by exposing him to modelling behaviour or by misinforming him about the drugs administered to him. These classical experiments have been subjected to a variety of criticism, ranging from criticisms of experimental design to criticisms that the data do not warrant the conclusions. In any case, Singer and Schachter do not discuss whether the psychological factors they introduce can be re-described in physical terms.

22 See William James, *The Principles of Psychology*, vol. 2 (New York: Holt, 1893), 499: "The bodily changes follow directly the perception of the exciting fact, and ... our feeling of the same changes as they occur *is* the emotion." It is difficult to establish whether or to what extent James can be called a physicalist. On the one hand, he seems to hold that particular perceptions can be distinguished from one another by their felt qualities. On the other, he does not reduce the content of propositional attitudes to extensionally described brain states.

23 Compare the controversy in John O'Connor, ed., *Modern Materialism: Readings on Mind-Body Identity* (New York: Harcourt, Brace, and World, 1969).

24 Compare Paul MacLean, "Sensory and Perceptive Factors in the Emotional Functions of the Triune Brain" and "The Triune Brain, Emotion and Scientific Bias," both in *The Neurosciences: Second Study Program,* ed. F.O. Schmitt, 336-49 (New York: Rockefeller University Press, 1970). See also P. Black, ed., *Physiological Correlates of Emotion* (New York: Academic Press, 1970).

25 Compare Clifford Geertz, "Deep Play: Notes on the Balinese Cockfight," in his *The Interpretation of Cultures* (New York: Basic Books, 1973), esp. 448-53.

26 Adam Morton, "Framing the Psychological," unpublished manuscript, provides an illuminating account of how we attribute and explain psychological states in ordinary contexts.

27 Compare Graeme Marshall, "Overdetermination and the Emotions," in Rorty, *Explaining Emotions,* 197-222.

28 Compare Robert C. Solomon, "Emotions and Choice," in Rorty, *Explaining Emotions,* 251-81; and Jean-Paul Sartre, "Bad Faith," in *Being and Nothingness* (New York: Philosophical Library, 1956). Of course it might also be useful to think of choices and voluntary judgments as the expressions of certain sorts of habits, and so as also evincing the problems of conservation. Sartre constructs an ontological explanation for the conservation of habits of choice: consciousness' evasion of its own nonbeing. More naturalistic explanations are given by Melanie Klein, "On the Development of Mental Functioning," in *Envy and Gratitude* (New York: Delta, 1975), 236-46; and by John Dewey, *Human Nature and Conduct* (New York: Modern Library, 1930), part 3, 172-210.

29 The distinction that Harry Frankfurt has made between first-order desires and their second-order evaluations can be applied to the emotions. See "Freedom of the Will and the Concept of a Person," *Journal of Philosophy* 68, 5 (1971): 5-20. There is, however, much more latitude in second-order emotions than in second-order attitudes toward desires. A person can enjoy being afraid, be angry at being afraid, regret being afraid, fear being afraid, etc.

30 I am grateful to Sara Ruddick for this point, and to Jerome Neu for his discussion of it in "Jealous Thoughts," in Rorty, *Explaining Emotions,* 425-64.

31 See, for example, Rom Harré, ed., *The Social Construction of the Emotions* (Oxford: Basil Blackwell, 1986) and William Ruddick, "Hope and Deception," *Bioethics* 13, 3-4 (1999): 343-57.

Chapter 2: Plato on Shame and Frank Speech in Democratic Athens

1 All citations of the Platonic text refer to the Stephanus pages. All English quotations of the *Gorgias* are from the translation by James H. Nichols Jr. (Ithaca, NY: Cornell University Press, 1998).

2 See E.R. Dodds, *Gorgias* (Oxford: Oxford University Press, 1959), 30-34; and Charles Kahn, *Plato and the Socratic Dialogue: The Philosophical Use of a Literary Form* (Cambridge: Cambridge University Press, 1996), 51-55. As Dodds puts it, "Apart from some short passages in the *Laws*, nowhere else in the dialogues has Plato told us *directly* what he thought of the institutions and achievements of his native city" (32), emphasis in original.

3 Dodds, *Gorgias,* 31; Kahn, *Plato and the Socratic Dialogue,* 52. Both Dodds and Kahn attribute this notion of a Platonic "Apology" to Friedrich Schleiermacher in the introduction to his translation of the dialogue.

4 As J. Peter Euben, John R. Wallach, and Josiah Ober point out, "Debates over reform of the British Parliament and the French Revolution found conservatives criticizing the politics of their own day in terms of the excesses of democratic Athens and ... *The Federalist Papers* did likewise to justify their redefinition of republicanism and the need for a distant federal government." "Introduction," in *Athenian Political Thought and the Reconstruction of American Democracy,* ed. J. Peter Euben, John R. Wallach, and Josiah Ober (Ithaca, NY: Cornell University Press, 1994), 10. See also Frank M. Turner, *The Classical Heritage in Victorian Britain* (New Haven, CT: Yale University Press, 1981), chaps. 1 and 5; and Alexander Hamilton, John Jay, and James Madison, *The Federalist (The Gideon Edition),* ed. George W. Carey and James McClellan (Indianapolis, IN: Liberty Fund Press, 2001), papers no. 8-10, 14, 55, 63. Plato's views on the "noble lie" in the *Republic* are often equated with Leo Strauss' interpretation of Plato's views on the "noble lie" or with the views of certain followers of Strauss; even critics of these modern interpretations make this equation. See, for example, Earl Shorris, "Ignoble Liars: Leo Strauss, George Bush, and the Philosophy of Mass Deception," *Harper's Magazine,* June 2004, 68.

5 Euben, Wallach, and Ober, *Athenian Political Thought,* 11.

6 See ibid., 9-13. According to Euben, Wallach, and Ober, "Part of this renaissance can be traced to the discovery of new sources of evidence, notably the mass of inscriptions that have come to light in the American excavations of the Athenian agora, part of it to the reassessment of well-known sources of evidence (comedy, tragedy and the corpus of political and legal speeches by classical Athenian orators) in light of new analytic paradigms" (9).

7 For an alternative argument that the distinction between negative and positive emotions is simplistic, see Robert C. Solomon, *Not Passion's Slave: Emotions and Choice* (New York: Oxford University Press, 2003), chap. 10.

8 Douglas Cairns, *Aidos: The Psychology and Ethics of Honour and Shame in Ancient Greek Literature* (Oxford: Clarendon Press, 1993), 2-3, 455. As Cairns points out, "In the 'I feel shame before' usage the status of the other is irrelevant, and, although one 'takes them seriously' because they may criticize, one does not in any way recognize any special status of theirs. In the case of the 'I respect' usage, however, one does precisely that; the feeling of *aidōs,* entailing concentration on the self and one's own status, is prompted by and focuses on consideration of the status of another, a person of special status in one's own eyes" (3).

9 For purposes of this chapter, I focus only on the differences between Gorgianic "flattering" shame and Socratic "respectful" shame, and not on the differences between Socratic and Platonic respectful shame. For this latter distinction, see Christina Tarnopolsky, "Prudes, Perverts and Tyrants: Plato and the Contemporary Politics of Shame and Civility," *Political Theory* 32, 4 (2004): 468-94.

10 My treatment of the relationship between shame and *parrhēsia* in Socratic and Platonic philosophy differs from the one presented by Arlene Saxonhouse in *Free Speech and Democracy in Ancient Athens* (Cambridge: Cambridge University Press, 2006). I do not agree that "shame and free speech [*parrhēsia*] represent opposing points in the political order that play off one another in the construction of a stable democratic polity" (8). Her interpretation associates shame with a kind of covering, and *parrhēsia* or shamelessness with a kind of uncovering or exposure. This interpretation, however, relies on the kind of opposition between shame and shamelessness that (as I have argued in "Prudes, Perverts and Tyrants") fails to do justice to the complexities of the emotion of shame. Also, Saxonhouse alternately presents Socrates as a shameless *parrhēsiastēs* (116, 117, 212) and as someone who refashions shame so that it no longer relies on the gaze of an other (113, 211). I argue, however, that Socratic respectful shame (like all forms of shame) still relies on the gaze of or comportment towards an other, but that the stance taken towards this other is very different from that involved in the flattering shame of Polus, Callicles, and Gorgias.

11 Michel Foucault, *Fearless Speech*, ed. Joseph Pearson (Los Angeles: Semiotext(e), 2001), 13.
12 As Bernard Williams argues, one of the features of the Greeks' way of understanding the ethical emotions is that action always stands "between the inner world of disposition, feeling, and decision and an outer world of harm and wrong. *What I have done points* in one direction towards what has happened to others, in another direction to what I am." *Shame and Necessity* (Berkeley: University of California Press, 1993), 92. Robert Solomon argues that this may well be the key to understanding the nature of the emotions more generally: "Virtually every emotion consists of both objective and subjective intentions, intentions to change the world and transformation of one's (view of) his world." *Not Passion's Slave*, 37. This is precisely why Solomon employs a phenomenological analysis of emotions that rejects the ontological dualism between self and the world and that instead tries to capture emotional experience as a kind of "seeing as," i.e., as simultaneously passive and perspectival, yet also constructive and enabling. For a fuller elaboration of this theme see Solomon, Chapter 10 in this volume.
13 In democratic Athens, law courts were essentially political gatherings where the litigant had to make his case in front of a mass audience (e.g., five hundred heard the accusation against Socrates), all of whom were ready to shout him down if they didn't like what they heard. For the similarities between law courts and political gatherings, see Josiah Ober, *Mass and Elite in Democratic Athens: Rhetoric, Ideology and the Power of the People* (Princeton, NJ: Princeton University Press, 1989), 144-48; Josiah Ober, *The Athenian Revolution: Essays on Ancient Greek Democracy and Political Theory* (Princeton, NJ: Princeton University Press, 1996), 24; Laura McClure, *Spoken Like a Woman: Speech and Gender in Athenian Drama* (Princeton, NJ: Princeton University Press, 1999), 10, 14; and James H. Nichols, Jr., "Introduction," in Plato, *Gorgias*, 33n22.
14 The word used for shame throughout the *Gorgias* is *aischunē*, not *aidōs*, which has the primary connotation of dishonour or disgrace. But by Plato's time *aischunē* also included the connotation of respect before another human being and was used interchangeably with *aidōs*. See Cairns, *Aidōs*, 372n84, 455. For the argument that Aristotle's notion of *aischunē* also entailed notions of respect for the other, see David Konstan, "Shame in Ancient Greece," *Social Research* 70, 4 (2003): 1046.
15 For the argument that shame depends upon a love of applause and honour rather than a love of truth, see Allan Bloom, "Interpretive Essay," in *The Republic of Plato*, trans. Allan Bloom, 2nd ed. (New York: Basic Books, 1968), 336.
16 For a careful and extensive analysis of the different meanings of *aidōs* in Euripides' *Hippolytus*, see Williams, *Shame and Necessity*, 95-97; and Douglas Cairns, *Aidōs*, 314-42.
17 For a fuller treatment of *aidōs/aischunē* in this play, see Cairns, *Aidōs*, 270-72; and S. Goldhill, *Reading Greek Tragedy* (Cambridge: Cambridge University Press, 1986), 162-65.
18 See Antiphon frag. B 44 A Diels-Kranz; Democritus frag. B 181 DK; and Cairns, *Aidōs*, 360-70.
19 For a critique of Kant's views of shame from an ancient Greek perspective, see Williams, *Shame and Necessity*, 75-102.
20 For recent scholarship that focuses on the connection between specific aspects of Athenian democratic culture and Plato's depiction of philosophy, see Arlene Saxonhouse, "Plato and the Problematical Gentleness of Democracy," in *Athenian Democracy: Modern Mythmakers and Ancient Theorists* (Notre Dame, IN: University of Notre Dame Press, 1996), 87-114; Arlene Saxonhouse, "Democracy, Equality and *Eidē*: A Radical View from Book 8 of Plato's *Republic*," *American Political Science Review* 92, 2 (1998): 273-84; J. Peter Euben, "Democracy and Political Theory: A Reading of Plato's *Gorgias*," in Euben, Wallach, and Ober, *Athenian Political Thought*, 208-14; J. Peter Euben, *Corrupting Youth: Political Education, Democratic Culture and Political Theory* (Princeton, NJ: Princeton University Press, 1997), chaps. 8 and 9; John Wallach, "Plato's Socratic Problem, and Ours," *History of Political Thought* 18 (1997): 377-91; Sara Monoson, *Plato's Democratic Entanglements* (Princeton, NJ: Princeton University Press, 2000); and Foucault, *Fearless Speech*, 20-24, 77-107. I borrow the phrases "democratic imaginary" and "normative imagery" from Monoson, *Plato's Democratic Entanglements*, 9.
21 Euben, *Corrupting Youth*, 91-108. Similarly, Arlene Saxonhouse argues that the gentleness and variety so characteristic of Athenian democracy are also integral to Plato's own practice of philosophy. "Problematical Gentleness," 87-114; and "Democracy, Equality and *Eidē*," 273-84.
22 Monoson, *Plato's Democratic Entanglements*, chap. 6; Foucault, *Fearless Speech*, 23-24. Monoson's work on *parrhēsia* is indebted to the lectures originally delivered by Foucault in 1983 at the University of California at Berkeley that were published as *Fearless Speech* in 2001.
23 Plato *Laches*, 178a, 179c, 189a; *Gorgias*, 487a, 487b, 487d, 491e, 492d, 521a; *Republic*, 450c, 473c, 557a-b; *Laws*, 806c, 806d, 835c. For a fuller explanation of these passages as examples of *parrhēsia*, see

Monoson, *Plato's Democratic Entanglements*, 155-70. For another description of *parrhēsia* in the *Laches, Laws,* and *Apology,* see Foucault, *Fearless Speech,* 91-107.

24 Monoson, *Plato's Democratic Entanglements,* 13.

25 For a fuller treatment of the *Republic* passages, see ibid., 172-77; for a fuller treatment of the *Gorgias* passages, see Euben, "Democracy and Political Theory," 208-14.

26 In a related comment, Nathan Tarcov has pointed out that "what are often quoted as Plato's harshest criticisms of democracy actually occur in [his] account of the degeneration of democracy into tyranny rather than in the preceding description of democracy as such." "The Meanings of Democracy," in *Democracy, Education and Schools,* ed. Roger Soder (San Francisco: Jossey-Bass, 1996), 7.

27 Monoson, *Plato's Democratic Entanglements,* 176; Euben, "Democracy and Political Theory," 211.

28 Charles Kahn, "Drama and Dialectic in Plato's *Gorgias*," *Oxford Studies in Ancient Philosophy* 1 (1983): 95-96.

29 At 521a9, Callicles tells Socrates that he should engage in flattery and gratify the Athenians in order to avoid having his goods confiscated or being put to death. As Foucault points out, danger and risk were integral to the democratic ideal of *parrhesia,* especially when the individual was speaking to the majority of other citizens. The critic was always in a position of inferiority with respect to his audience. *Fearless Speech,* 17-18.

30 H.G. Liddell and R. Scott, *An Intermediate Greek-English Lexicon* (Oxford: Clarendon Press, 2000), 611.

31 Monoson, *Plato's Democratic Entanglements,* 52.

32 Ibid., 54-55. According to Foucault, *parrhēsia* evolved from the democratic practice of frank speaking between citizens both in the agora and in the assembly, in the fourth century BC, into the practice of advisors or counsellors speaking frankly to their king with the later rise of the Hellenic monarchies. *Fearless Speech,* 22, 86.

33 Ober, *Mass and Elite,* 296; Monoson, *Plato's Democratic Entanglements,* 56.

34 Monoson, *Plato's Democratic Entanglements,* 57; Ober, *Mass and Elite,* 296.

35 Quoted in Monoson, *Plato's Democratic Entanglements,* 59; see also McClure, *Spoken Like a Woman,* 11-15.

36 Ober, *Mass and Elite,* 189; McClure, *Spoken Like a Woman,* 10-11.

37 Monoson, *Plato's Democratic Entanglements,* 60; Ober, *Mass and Elite,* 296; Foucault, *Fearless Speech,* 14.

38 Monoson, *Plato's Democratic Entanglements,* 60; Foucault, *Fearless Speech,* 15-16.

39 Foucault, *Fearless Speech,* 17.

40 Ibid., 12.

41 Monoson, *Plato's Democratic Entanglements,* 62. As Michel Foucault points out, *parrhēsia* itself eventually took on this pejorative sense of chattering or reckless and outspoken ignorance, and it became identified with the excesses of Athenian democratic institutions. *Fearless Speech,* 13, 77-84.

42 Monoson, *Plato's Democratic Entanglements,* 61.

43 Ibid.; Foucault, *Fearless Speech,* 18.

44 See Liddell and Scott, *Greek-English Lexicon,* 248.

45 Williams, *Shame and Necessity,* 90.

46 See also ibid., 81; Cairns, *Aidōs,* 18.

47 See also Williams, *Shame and Necessity,* 82-83.

48 This description of shame reflects what has come to be known as the "two components" view of emotions. See Stanley Schachter and Jerome Singer, "Cognitive Social and Physiological Determinants of Emotional States," *Psychological Review* 69, 5 (1962): 379-99; Cheshire Calhoun and Robert C. Solomon, eds., *What Is an Emotion? Classical Readings in Philosophical Psychology* (New York: Oxford University Press, 1984), 4. However, as Amélie Oksenberg Rorty points out, the degree to which various emotions include these elements varies considerably. See "Introduction," in *Explaining Emotions,* ed. A.O. Rorty (Berkeley: University of California Press, 1980), 1-3.

49 See, for example, blushes by Thrasymachus (*Republic,* I, 350d), Charmides (*Charmides,* 158c), Clinias (*Euthydemus,* 275d), Dionysodorus (*Euthydemus,* 297a), Hippothales (*Lysis,* 204b), Lysis (*Lysis,* 213d), and Hippocrates (*Protagoras,* 312a).

50 Cairns, *Aidōs,* 7; Paul Redding, *The Logic of Affect* (Ithaca, NY: Cornell University Press, 1999), 8.

51 For the view that emotions involve evaluations, appraisals, and judgments, see Robert C. Solomon, "Emotions and Choice," in Rorty, *Explaining Emotions,* 258-9, 274-6; Cairns, *Aidōs,* 5; Martha C. Nussbaum, *Upheavals of Thought: The Intelligence of Emotions* (Cambridge: Cambridge University Press, 2001); Martha C. Nussbaum, *Hiding from Humanity: Disgust, Shame and the Law* (Princeton:

Princeton University Press, 2004); and Jon Elster, *Alchemies of the Mind: Rationality and the Emotions* (Cambridge: Cambridge University Press, 1999).

52 Cairns, *Aidōs*, 10-12. See also Calhoun and Solomon, *What Is an Emotion?* 24; Rorty, "Introduction," in *Explaining Emotions*, 2; and Michael Stocker, "Intellectual Desire, Emotion, and Action," in Rorty, *Explaining Emotions*, 323-38.

53 I borrow this example and explanation from Elster, *Alchemies of the Mind*, 244.

54 As Jon Elster puts it, "I might acutely desire never to experience shame but also desire to have a disposition to feel shame – in fact, the latter desire presupposes the former" (ibid.).

55 Cairns, *Aidōs*, 11; Calhoun and Solomon, *What Is an Emotion?* 24.

56 Cairns, *Aidōs*, 11.

57 Here I agree with the first part of Arlene Saxonhouse's treatment of Hippocrates' blush in the *Symposium*, i.e., that it is "the human response to the gaze of another", but I disagree that the blush is also simultaneously the desire to "be unseen, to hide." See *Free Speech and Democracy*, 183. For me, the desire to hide or cover the self is characteristic of one possible reaction to the moment of recognition within the occurrent experience of shame, but the occurrent experience of shame itself (manifested by a blush) is not equivalent to this hiding/covering reaction or desire. Although my treatment of shame is consistent with some of the insights articulated by both Saxonhouse, in *Free Speech and Democracy*, and Martha Nussbaum, in *Hiding from Humanity*, I think that their treatments of shame suffer from the fact that they never clearly and consistently distinguish between the occurrent experience of shame, which involves a kind of uncovering of the truth about oneself or the world, and the reaction or second-order disposition of shame, which involves a reaction to this experience that may be one of covering the self, but may also involve transforming the self or world or contesting the other that first causes the feeling of shame. For a fuller elaboration of these points, see Tarnopolsky, "Prudes, Perverts and Tyrants," 487. Jon Elster's treatment of shame seems much closer to my own in that he distinguishes between the "cognitive antecedent" of shame that involves the awareness of an other and the "action tendencies" of shame, which primarily involve hiding. But his account is not clear about how hiding could be the primary action tendency of shame if, as he states (in *Alchemies of the Mind*, 145, 154), shame is also the most painful and thus important emotion for making us conform to social norms. This suggests to me that the "action consequence" of transforming the self must be equally prevalent.

58 Cairns, *Aidōs*, 3.

59 Erwin Straus, "Shame as a Historiological Problem," *Phenomenological Psychology* 25 (1979): 223.

60 The association of medicine and pain would have resonated much more with Socrates' Athenian contemporaries because their medical procedures involved such procedures as cutting and drawing blood without, of course, the benefits of modern painkillers.

61 For this distinction, see Straus, "Shame as a Historiological Problem," 223.

62 See Jeffrey Green, "The Shame of Being a Philosopher," *Political Theory* 33, 2 (2005): 266-72; and Christina Tarnopolsky, "Response to Green," *Political Theory* 33, 2 (2005): 273-79. Saxonhouse's treatment of Socrates is equivocal on precisely this point.

63 I follow Oona Eisenstadt in thinking that because of this kind of shame, Socrates might well have felt ashamed of not being able to educate more of his fellow Athenians during his lifetime so that they would have been able to recognize his elenctic activities as just and therefore acquit him at his trial. For a fuller elaboration of this point, see Eisenstadt, "Shame in the *Apology*," in *Politics, Philosophy, Writing: Plato's Art of Caring for Souls*, ed. Zdravko Planinc (Columbia: University of Missouri Press, 2001), 40-59. See also Raymond Geuss' helpful distinction between the shamelessness of Diogenes and the shame of Socrates in *Public Goods, Private Goods* (Princeton, NJ: Princeton University Press, 2001), 30-31.

64 This translation is taken from "Plato's Apology of Socrates" in *Four Texts on Socrates*, trans. Thomas G. West and Grace Starry West (Ithaca, NY: Cornell University Press, 1984), 80.

65 For an alternative example of the transmutation of envy into indignation, see Elster, *Alchemies of the Mind*, 99.

66 Foucault, *Fearless Speech*, 77-87.

67 For a fuller treatment of this theme in the *Republic*, see Christina Tarnopolsky, "Power's Passionate Pathologies," paper presented at the annual meeting of the American Political Science Association, Washington, DC, 2 September 2006.

68 Nussbaum, *Hiding from Humanity*, 200. Although I agree with Nussbaum on this specific point, I disagree with her overall argument in this book that emotions like shame and disgust usually (though not always) involve a denial of our humanity and a problematic desire for omnipotence. For me this

problematic desire is not the primary and inevitable remnant of our experience of infantile omnipotence (as it is for Nussbaum, Sigmund Freud, and Donald Winnicott) but rather the result of certain contingent personal or political upbringings and institutions that involve a breakdown of the mutual interplay or true intersubjectivity between the self and the other that characterizes respectful shame. For a criticism of Freud's view of infantile omnipotence as the first bond or primary relationship for individual development, see Jessica Benjamin, *Psychoanalysis, Feminism, and the Problem of Domination* (New York: Pantheon Books, 1988).

69 As Peter Euben puts it, "Socrates' attempt to exorcise the glamour of tyranny and thus break the unholy alliance between the would-be tyrant and the many who surreptitiously envy him, even at their own moral and political expense, makes the philosopher an ally of democracy." "Democracy and Political Theory", 208.

Chapter 3: The Passions of the Wise

I wish to thank Danielle Allen, Seyla Benhabib, Peter Berkowitz, Jill Frank, Karina Galperín, Patchen Markell, Pratap Mehta, Heidi Northwood, Chad Noyes, Jennifer Pitts, Nancy Schwartz, Dominic Scott, and Richard Tuck, as well as participants at the Harvard Political Theory Research Workshop (spring 1999), the 43d Annual Congress of the Canadian Philosophical Association in Sherbrooke, Quebec (June 1999), and the Wesleyan Ethical and Political Theory Workshop (spring 2001) for their comments on a previous draft of this chapter.

1 Aristotle *On Rhetoric* 1.13.1373b2-7, 1.13.1374a18-28, 1.10.1368b7-9; compare with *The Politics* 3.16.1287b5-9. The translations of Aristotle's *The Politics* (hereafter *Politics*) and *On Rhetoric* (hereafter *Rhetoric*) I cite, sometimes with slight modifications, are *On Rhetoric: A Theory of Civic Discourse*, trans. George A. Kennedy (New York: Oxford University Press, 1991); and *The Politics*, trans. Carnes Lord (Chicago: University of Chicago Press, 1984).

2 That ethics is in an important sense uncodifiable has been much discussed in Aristotle scholarship. See, for example, John McDowell, "Virtue and Reason," *Monist* 62, 3 (1979): 331-50; Norman O. Dahl, *Practical Reason, Aristotle, and Weakness of the Will* (Minneapolis: University of Minnesota Press, 1984), 79; Nancy Sherman, *The Fabric of Character: Aristotle's Theory of Virtue* (Oxford: Clarendon Press, 1989), 16-18; and Eugene Garver, *Aristotle's Rhetoric: An Art of Character* (Chicago: University of Chicago Press, 1994). Daniel T. Devereux makes the interesting statement that "in the case of practical knowledge ... it is the universals that are indeterminate and imprecise while the judgments about particular acts in particular circumstances are precise and determinate. If there is a discrepancy between the particular judgment of the practically wise person and a universal rule which applies to the situation, the defect is on the side of the universal; it is the particular judgment that is authoritative." "Particular and Universal in Aristotle's Conception of Practical Knowledge," *Review of Metaphysics* 39, 3 (1986): 497-98.

3 Aristotle *Nicomachean Ethics* 1.3.1094b12-26. The translation of the *Nicomachean Ethics* (hereafter "NE") I cite, sometimes with slight modification, is that of Terence Irwin (Indianapolis, IN: Hackett, 1985).

4 *Rhetoric* 1.13.1374a28-b1.

5 Concerning goods that are good *haplōs*, Aristotle believes that though "human beings pray for these and pursue them, they are wrong; the right thing is to pray that what is good *haplōs* will also be good for us, but to choose [only] what is good for us" (NE 5.1.1129b4-7). Aristotle makes a parallel distinction in the *Politics*, where he distinguishes a regime that is best *haplōs* from regimes that are best for most cities and those that are best given the circumstances (4.1.1288b22-28). Compare Garver, *Aristotle's Rhetoric*, 57.

6 NE 5.10.1137b12-30; *Rhetoric* 1.13.1374a26-28.

7 NE 5.10.1137b12-30, emphasis added.

8 The context of the discussion is Aristotle's attempt to identify "two species of just and unjust actions (some against written, others unwritten laws)." He proceeds to refer to "two species of unwritten law. These are, on the one hand, what involves an abundance of virtue and vice ... and on the other hand things omitted by the specific and written law. Fairness [*epieikes*], for example, seems to be just; but fairness is justice that goes beyond the written law" (*Rhetoric* 1.13.1374a18). So fairness falls under the second species of unwritten laws.

9 *Politics* 3.15.1286a19-22.

10 *Politics* 3.16.1287a29-33.

11 *Politics* 3.16.1287b22-23.

12 Aristotle identifies three species of rhetoric (*Rhetoric* 1.2.1357a36-b29). The first is deliberative rhetoric

(*sumbouleutikon*), whose *telos* is the advantageous or expedient (*sumpheron*) and the harmful, and which concerns exhortation or dissuasion about future action. This is the kind of rhetoric used in the political councils that deliberate about the common matters of the *polis,* seeking the advantageous (compare *Politics* 4.14.1298a-b). (Collective political deliberation has a broad and a narrow sense in Aristotle. "Deliberation" in the broad sense designates both political deliberation proper [in the councils] and judicial deliberation. In the narrow sense it distinguishes political deliberation proper from judicial deliberation [compare *Politics* 7.9.1329a3-5]. The locution "deliberative rhetoric" employs the term in the restricted sense.) The second is judicial rhetoric (*dikanikon*), whose *telos* is the just and unjust, and which concerns accusation or defence regarding a past action. This kind of rhetoric takes place in the courts, where deliberation seeks a judgment that renders justice (compare *Politics* 7.8.1328b13-15). The third species of rhetoric is epideictic. Its *telos* is the noble and shameful, and it involves praising or blaming someone or something presently. I am concerned only with the first two species, because these are the ones appropriate to the "deliberative" element of the *polis* – the councils and the courts.

13 *Rhetoric* 1.2.1355b25-26. Kennedy notes on pp. 36-37 of his translation that (in each case) *peri hekaston* "refers to the fact that rhetoric deals with specific circumstances (particular individuals and their actions)."

14 Garver, *Aristotle's Rhetoric,* chap. 1.

15 See ibid., 29-33. "Unless achieving the external end were desirable, no one would ever develop an art. Arts do not lose their given ends when they develop their own autonomous ends in addition" (28).

16 *Rhetoric* 1.2.1356a1-20.

17 Similarly, Aristotle uses the word *politeia* both to designate "regime" in the broad sense of any regime, including monarchy and aristocracy, and to designate the specific regime translated as "polity" or "constitutional government."

18 *Rhetoric* 1.2.1356b4-7. The meaning of the Greek word *sullogismos* is not quite the same as what we normally mean in English by "syllogism," with its two premises and conclusion, so I have left it transliterated from the original. On this point, see M.F. Burnyeat, "Enthymeme: Aristotle on the Rationality of Rhetoric," in *Essays on Aristotle's* Rhetoric, ed. A.O. Rorty (Berkeley: University of California Press, 1996), 100. Earlier he notes that "a sullogismos as Aristotle defines it is at least the following: a valid deductive argument in which the premises (note the plural) provide a logically sufficient justification for a conclusion distinct from them" (95).

19 *Rhetoric* 2.24.1400b37, 1.1.1355a4-7.

20 Burnyeat, "Enthymeme," 94.

21 *Rhetoric* 2.1.1377b20-28, 2.1.1378a6-9.

22 *Rhetoric* 2.1.1378a19-21.

23 That Aristotle takes the proper emotional responses to be constitutive of *ēthos* is, I think, beyond question: "No good person would be distressed when parricides and bloodthirsty murderers meet punishment; for it is right to rejoice in such cases, as in the case of those who deservedly fare well; for both are just things and cause a fair-minded person to rejoice ... All these feelings come from the same moral character, and opposite feelings from the opposite" (*Rhetoric* 2.9.1386b26-32). And elsewhere: "Let us go through the kinds of character, considering what they are like in terms of emotions and habits and age of life and fortune [*tuchē*]" (*Rhetoric* 2.12.1388b31-32). For discussion, see L.A. Kosman, "Being Properly Affected: Virtues and Feelings in Aristotle's Ethics," in Rorty, *Essays on Aristotle's* Rhetoric, 103-16.

24 *Rhetoric* 1.1.1354a16-18.

25 Jacques Brunschwig, "Aristotle's Rhetoric As a 'Counterpart' to Dialectic," in Rorty, *Essays on Aristotle's* Rhetoric, 45-46.

26 *Rhetoric* 1.1.1354a15-16. For further discussion of this issue, and in particular the relation of Chapter 1 to the rest of the work, see Kennedy's comments in Aristotle, *On Rhetoric,* 27-28; Robert Wardy, "Mighty Is the Truth and It Shall Prevail?" in Rorty, *Essays on Aristotle's* Rhetoric, 62-63; Troels Engberg-Pedersen, "Is There an Ethical Dimension to Aristotelian Rhetoric?" in Rorty, *Essays on Aristotle's Rhetoric,* 131; and Glenn W. Most, "The Uses of Endoxa: Philosophy and Rhetoric in the *Rhetoric,*" in *Aristotle's* Rhetoric: *Philosophical Essays,* ed. David J. Furley and A. Nehamas (Princeton, NJ: Princeton University Press, 1994), 167-90. As will become clear, my view is different from Jürgen Sprute's attempt to resolve the apparent discrepancy. He suggests that the emotion-free rhetoric of Chapter 1 is an "ideal rhetoric" described in order to "determine what is essential to rhetoric in general." Sprute seems to suppose that

appeals to emotion and atechnical appeals are one and the same, and concludes that Aristotle's proscription of atechnical appeals is also directed against the emotions. For example, he says that for Aristotle the laws ought "to forbid speaking outside the subject and hence using means of persuasion like arousing emotions," and so concludes that "arousing emotions and representing character, are not directly concerned with the subject but have only a supplementary function in persuading." "Aristotle and the Legitimacy of Rhetoric," in Furley and Nehamas, *Aristotle's* Rhetoric, 119, 122. But arousing emotions is not always atechnical, and *ēthos* and *pathos* are constitutive *pisteis* of rhetoric.

27 Martha C. Nussbaum, *The Therapy of Desire: Theory and Practice in Hellenistic Ethics* (Princeton, NJ: Princeton University Press, 1994), 81-88; Sherman, *Fabric of Character*, 45; John M. Cooper, "Some Remarks on Aristotle's Moral Psychology," *Southern Journal of Philosophy* 27, supplement (1988): 34-35; Stephen R. Leighton, "Aristotle and the Emotions," in Rorty, *Essays on Aristotle's* Rhetoric, 210, 217; Wardy, "Mighty Is the Truth," 63.

28 Compare Wardy: "The famous first words of the treatise [*On Rhetoric*], 'rhetoric is the counterpart of dialectic' (1354a1), flatly rejects Socrates' uncompromising thesis that philosophical arguments are categorically distinct from rhetorical pleas." "Mighty Is the Truth," 58.

29 *Politics* 7.1.1323a14-1324a13.

30 *Rhetoric* 1.1.1355a29-31.

31 As Kennedy notes, in Aristotle, *On Rhetoric*, 34n27.

32 *NE* 1.2.1094a28.

33 I am tempted to say that collective decisions must have a propensity to coincide with what the phronetic person would decide. But this formulation faces two objections. First, it is not clear that every phronetic person would come up with the same decision, according to Aristotle. (On this question, see Amélie Oksenberg Rorty, "Structuring Rhetoric," in *Essays on Aristotle's* Rhetoric, 14.) Second, and more significantly, this way of putting things might imply, contrary to Aristotle's intentions, that discussion makes no difference to the outcomes of practical reason. To avoid this objection, I say instead that ethical rhetoric is "consistent with *phronēsis*" in the sense that it issues forth in decisions whose wisdom or rightness phronetic persons can recognize.

34 *Rhetoric* 1.1.1355a14-17, 20-23, 36-38. On Aristotle's optimism, see Wardy, "Mighty Is the Truth," 59-60.

35 Phronetic deliberation requires the right conclusion, by the correct process, at the right time, for the correct end (*NE* 6.9.1142b21-34): "For it is not merely a state consistent with correct reason, but the state involving correct reason, that is virtue. And it is *phronēsis* that is correct reason ... we cannot be fully good without *phronēsis*, or phronetic without virtue of *ēthos*." *NE* 7.1.1145a26-32.

36 See Christopher Lyle Johnstone, "An Aristotelian Trilogy: Ethics, Rhetoric, Politics, and the Search for Moral Truth," *Philosophy and Rhetoric* 13, 1 (1980): 1-24, for a similar claim that there is a structural similarity for Aristotle between practical deliberation and rhetoric, stemming from viewing practical deliberation as a sort of internal dialogue: "The activity of the practical intellect is essentially rhetorical in nature" (11). Lois S. Self makes the explicit link between *phronēsis* and rhetoric, suggesting an integral theoretical connection "which derives from the nature of the art [of rhetoric] itself; more specifically, that the ideal practitioner of Aristotle's Rhetoric employs the skills and qualities of Aristotle's model of human virtue, the Phronimos or 'man of practical wisdom.'" "Rhetoric and Phronesis: The Aristotelian Ideal," *Philosophy and Rhetoric* 12, 2 (1979): 131.

37 *NE* 2.9.1109b21-23. He also states: "practical reason is of the last thing [*tou eschatou*], which is an object not of science [*epistēmē*] but of perception" (*NE* 6.8.1142a27-8). In *NE* 6.11.1143b2 6, he identifies perception of the ethically relevant features of a practical situation with practical *nous*: "In demonstrations, *nous* is about the unchanging terms that are first, whereas with respect to what is done in action, it is about the last term ... the end to be aimed at ... We must, then, have perception [*aisthēsis*] of these particulars, and this perception is *nous*."

38 John M. Cooper provides a version of this position. He argues that, according to Aristotle, deliberation does not issue forth in particular individual actions; rather deliberation ends with the determination of only a type of action, and then perception takes over and renders a particular action. Thus the particulars about which we deliberate with respect to action refer to judgment regarding specific types of action and not to individual actions themselves. See *Reason and Human Good in Aristotle* (Cambridge, MA: Harvard University Press, 1975), 23, 39-41. For criticism, see Fred D. Miller, "Aristotle on Rationality in Action," *Review of Metaphysics* 37, 3 (1984): 499-520, and Devereux, "Particular and Universal."

39 *NE* 6.8.1142a22, 28.

40 Nancy Sherman says that "character is expressed in what one sees as much as what one does. Knowing how to discern the particulars, Aristotle stresses, is a mark of virtue" (*Fabric of Character*, 4). She explains, "Preliminary to deciding how to act, one must acknowledge that the situation requires action ... Perception is thus informed by the virtues ... much of the work of virtue will rest in knowing how to construe the case, how to describe and classify what is before one" (29). For a similar view, see Gisela Striker, "Emotions in Context: Aristotle's Treatment of the Passions in the *Rhetoric* and His Moral Psychology," in Rorty, *Essays on Aristotle's* Rhetoric, 297-98.

41 Sherman, *Fabric of Character*, 29.

42 *Rhetoric* 2.1.1377b20-28, 1378a6-9.

43 On subjects of deliberation, see *Rhetoric* 1.4.1359b18-1360a38; on legal customs, see *Rhetoric* 1.8.1365b22-1366a23; and on the *ēthos* and emotional makeup of the audience, see *Rhetoric* 2.1.1378a19-24. Besides the discussion of the subject matters of deliberation (in the restricted sense of deliberative as opposed to judicial rhetoric) and forms of regime that Aristotle undertakes in Book 1 of *On Rhetoric*, Book 2 contains ten chapters on the *pathos* of the audience, and five subsequent chapters discussing the particular characters of the young, the old, the middle-aged, the well-born, the wealthy, and the powerful. In Book 1, Aristotle also states that "since pisteis not only come from logical demonstration but from speech that reveals character (for we believe the speaker through his being a certain kind of person, and this is the case if he seems to be good or well disposed to us or both), we should be acquainted with the kinds of character distinctive of each form of constitution; for the character distinctive of each is necessarily most persuasive to each" (*Rhetoric* 1.8.1366a8-13). Kennedy notes that this passage indicates that a speaker should "at least show an understanding of the political views of the community" (Aristotle, *On Rhetoric*, 77n159).

44 Recall that Aristotle explicitly says that the trust must arise from the (*ēthos* of the speaker demonstrated in the) speech itself and not from some antecedent information about the *ēthos* of the speaker (*Rhetoric* 1.2.1356a8-10).

45 Engberg-Pedersen ("Is There an Ethical Dimension?" 124-27) suggests that Aristotle thought that the institutional context of rhetoric (in Athens) skewed rhetorical deliberation toward factual, ethical, or political truth. While Engberg-Pedersen's general argument seems much too strong to me, the valid core of his position can be accounted for by the argument which I have just advanced, that the structure of rhetoric provides incentives for perception of relevant particulars.

46 For example, the fact that the citizens of a certain *polis* have well-established feelings of goodwill and friendship for citizens of another *polis* may well be an ethically relevant reason to conduct foreign policy in one way rather than another.

47 Compare Wardy, "Mighty Is the Truth," 63: "Explicating the second, emotive means of persuasion, he says that 'the orator persuades through his hearers, when they are led into pathos by his logos; for when pained or loving we do not render judgment similarly to when in joy or hating' (1356a14-16). The possibility is thus left open that the proper use of rhetorical skill will indeed speak to our emotions, but only when the *pathē* so formed enhance our receptivity to truthful logos, rather than setting our feelings at odds with our reasoning."

48 Johnstone has pointed to the structural similarity between practical deliberation and rhetoric for Aristotle: "If we can reasonably visualize deliberation as a sort of internal dialogue, then the practically wise person, when he or she deliberates, functions as both rhetor and auditor. The 'right rule' or 'rational principle' of practical wisdom is none other than the faculty for apprehending or observing valid justifications for actions." "An Aristotelian Trilogy," 12. He cites Isocrates to illustrate this tendency of the Greeks to view even monological deliberation in terms of an internal dialogue. Barbara Warnick, however, has taken exception to such an interpretation of Aristotle, which assimilates "rhetoric to internal reasoning and dialogue." "Judgment, Probability, and Aristotle's Rhetoric," *Quarterly Journal of Speech* 9 (1989): 301. Two points need to be made in this connection. First, Warnick objects to drawing a parallel between monological deliberation and rhetoric in part because she takes herself to be arguing against a position that betrays the "urge to elevate the logical element of rhetoric and to devalue its emotive dimensions ... to emphasize logos and deprecate pathos and ethos" (299). But I am taking precisely that position she opposes – rather than mitigating the role of the emotions (in rhetoric), my argument aims to highlight their role (in deliberation). The second part of Warnick's concern is that the "need (1) to incorporate audience convictions and values, (2) to simplify argument structures for the comprehension of the multitude, and (3) to direct one's claims toward decisions affecting the state and the polis are all neglected when Aristotelian rhetoric is applied to forums and situations that Aristotle

himself did not consider in the *Rhetoric*" (301). Warnick's point is well taken – rhetoric is obviously not the same as monological deliberation on all counts – but the two still have important structural similarities.

49 NE 6.7.1141b15-18, 6.8.1142a15.

50 *Politics* 3.15.1286a21-22.

51 Heidi Northwood has suggested that passages such as *Politics* 3.15.1286a32-35 (in which Aristotle says, "The judgement of a single person is necessarily corrupted when he is dominated by anger or some other passion of this sort") indicate that it is not because of but in spite of the passions that men are able to apply laws to particular cases (commentary presented at the 43rd Annual Congress of the Canadian Philosophical Association, Sherbrooke, QC, June 1999). But these passages indicate only that the passions can lead deliberation astray – if, for example, they dominate or overwhelm cognitive processes in an adverse manner. To suggest that Aristotle saw the emotions as playing a constructive, constitutive, and necessary role in practical reasoning is not to make the obviously false assertion that Aristotle was blind to the negative and even debilitating cognitive effects the emotions might have on practical reasoning.

52 One sort of Thomist response, which I do not canvass here, would be to seek ethical grounding not just in reason but in nature or natural justice, drawing on NE 5.7.1134b19-27. But this would require us to take Aristotle as saying that the emotions intuit natural right.

53 For a survey of the literature on deliberative democracy, see James Bohman, "Survey Article: The Coming of Age of Deliberative Democracy," *Journal of Political Philosophy* 6, 4 (1998): 400-25.

54 *Rhetoric* 1.2.1356a8-10.

55 Garver, *Aristotle's Rhetoric*, 176-77.

56 Ibid., 196.

57 *Politics* 4.4.1292a21-24, 5.11.1314a2-3.

58 *Politics* 5.5.1305a13-14.

59 *Politics* 3.15.1286a10-13, 21-22.

60 *Politics* 3.15.1286a32-36, a38-b2, emphasis added.

61 *Politics* 3.4.1277b26.

62 NE 6.10.1143a10.

63 Stephen Halliwell, "The Challenge of Rhetoric to Political and Ethical Theory in Aristotle," in Rorty, *Essays on Aristotle's Rhetoric*, 178-79. On *sunesis*, see *Politics* 4.4.1291a28; on the need for *phronēsis*, see *Politics* 7.9.1329a2-9.

64 More generally, see the discussion of institutions in Kenneth Baynes, "Liberal Neutrality, Pluralism, and Deliberative Politics," *Praxis International* 12, 1 (1992): 50-69.

65 Miriam Galston, "Taking Aristotle Seriously: Republican-Oriented Legal Theory and the Moral Foundation of Deliberative Democracy," *California Law Review* 82, 2 (1994): 329-99.

Chapter 4: Troubling Business

Many thanks to the copy editor, Sarah Wight, whose thoroughness forced me to address several weaknesses in this chapter.

1 The condition of freezing in the presence of a frightening event, person, or thing is characterized in the evolutionary psychology of contemporary neuroscience in specifically nonmoral, or involuntary, terms. Joseph LeDoux writes: "Although lab rats come from breeding colonies that have been isolated from cats for many, many generations, any one of them, upon seeing a cat for the first time, will 'freeze' dead in its tracks. This is Mother Nature at work, since the rat (and his immediate ancestors) never had the opportunity to learn from personal experience that cats are dangerous ... Freezing is not a choice but an automatic response, a preprogrammed way of dealing with danger." *Synaptic Self: How Our Brains Become Who We Are* (New York: Penguin, 2002), 6. The notion that the passions are hardwired features of the animal psyche, common to human and nonhuman animal alike, is not new to contemporary neuroscience, of course. In the "Sixth Meditation" Descartes makes much the same type of claim about sadness: "Why does a certain sadness of the mind follow from some unknown sensation of pain, and a certain happiness from a sensation of pleasure? ... I clearly had no explanation except that I was taught this by nature. There is no other connection ... between the sensation of something that causes pain and the thought of sadness that results from it." *Descartes' Meditations and Other Metaphysical Writings*, trans. Desmond Clarke (New York: Penguin, 1998), 60. In a letter to Princess Elizabeth dated May 1646 he writes: "The machine of our body is made in such a way that one single thought of joy, of love or of

something similar is enough to send the animal spirits through the nerves into all the muscles that are required to cause the various movements of the blood, which I claimed accompany the passions" (165). For more on the passions in Descartes, see Chapter 5.

2 This example is drawn from Aristotle's *Nicomachean Ethics*: "Those who go to excess in raising laughs seem to be vulgar buffoons ... Those who would never say anything themselves to raise a laugh, and even object when other people do it, seem to be boorish and stiff. Those who joke in appropriate ways are called witty, or, in other words, agile-witted. For these sorts of jokes seem to be movements of someone's character, and characters are judged, as bodies are, by their movements." Translated by Terence Irwin (Indianapolis, IN: Hackett, 1999), 4.8.1128a5-12.

3 Aristotle, *On Rhetoric: A Theory of Civic Discourse*, trans. George A. Kennedy (New York: Oxford University Press, 1991), 2.1 1378a8.

4 I am referring to his acknowledged "running [of] the ultimate risk" in refusing to bring "his children and many of his friends and family into court to arouse as much pity as he could." Plato, "Apology," in *The Trial and Death of Socrates*, trans. G.M.A. Grube, rev. John Cooper (Indianapolis, IN: Hackett, 2000), 34c-d.

5 René Descartes, *Discourse on Method and Related Writings*, trans. Desmond Clarke (New York: Penguin, 1999), 20. Descartes confesses his indebtedness for this maxim to what must be the Stoics, though without mentioning any specific figure by name: "I believe that this was principally the secret of those philosophers who were able, in earlier times, to withdraw from fortune's dominion, to despise suffering and poverty and to rival their gods in happiness. For by constant reflection on the limits set for them by nature, they convinced themselves that there was nothing so completely in their power, apart from their own thoughts, that this alone was enough to prevent them from having any affection for other things; and their absolute control over their thoughts gave them reason to think that they were richer, more powerful, freer and happier than others who, however favoured by nature and fortune they might be, never have such control over everything they wish because they lack this philosophy" (21).

6 Immanuel Kant, *Critique of Pure Practical Reason*, in *The Philosophy of Kant: Immanuel Kant's Moral and Political Writings*, trans. Carl J. Friedrich (New York: Modern Library, 1949), 218. Kant explicitly separates the freedom characteristic of morality, expressed in the formality of the universal, categorical imperative, from the empirical content of our subjective desires (218-20). Moral freedom is character- ized specifically by the fact that the individual agent gives her or himself the law, whereas our desires are determined by the same laws of causality that determine all mere phenomena of nature: "Moral law is actually a law of the causality of free agents, and is therefore [a law] of the possibility of a supersen- sible system of nature, just as the metaphysical law of events in the world of sense is a law of causality of the sensible system of nature" (240). The very idea of obligation requires that the inclinations characteristic of the finite nature of human beings be excluded from the practical laws that govern human beings as rational rather than as finite animals (227). Kant rejects an ethics rooted in a conception of the good insofar as it would require a connection between moral law and desire (252). What is most appealing in Kant's thought, its aspirational character, is also most disappointing inasmuch as it marginalizes the human for the superhuman: "The second view ['the moral law within me'] raises my value infinitely, as an *intelligence*, through my personality; for in this personality the moral law reveals a life independent of animality and even of the entire world of sense" (262, emphasis in original).

7 Kant, *Religion within the Limits of Reason Alone*, in *Philosophy of Kant*, 394. Passages such as this are tricky. Kant goes on to say that the harmonizing of such inclinations belongs to the faculty of "prudence," which for him is of very limited relevance to the calculation of moral value. In *The Critique of Pure Practical Reason* he contends that "morality and self-love" are "sharply and clearly defined": "The maxim of self-love (prudence) only *advises*, the law of morality commands. There is a great difference between what we are advised to do and what we are *obliged* to do" (229, emphasis in original). And in *The Critique of Judgment*, he denies to the "general instruction for attaining happiness, nor yet the restraining of the passions or the affections for this purpose" any part in "practical philosophy" because these are "nothing more than rules of skill which are only practical in a technical sense, as a skill is directed to producing an effect possible according to natural causes and effects" (267). It is difficult to accept, therefore, recent attempts, such as that of Nancy Sherman, to rescue Kant's moral philosophy from charges of excluding the emotions by suggesting that for Kant the emotions "are a central feature of the best in human moral perfection." *Making a Necessity of Virtue: Aristotle and Kant on Virtue* (New York: Cambridge University Press, 1996), 361. Even more difficult to accept is her contention that it

belongs to philosophy to map out the ways of achieving such harmony, since Kant clearly relegates this task to prudence.

8 Cheryl Hall, "'Passion and Constraint': The Marginalization of Passion in Liberal Political Theory," *Philosophy and Social Criticism* 28, 6 (2002): 743, emphasis in original.

9 Michael Stocker, "How Emotions Reveal Value and Help Cure the Schizophrenia of Modern Ethical Theories," in *How Should One Live? Essays on the Virtues*, ed. Roger Crisp (New York: Oxford University Press, 1996), 173-90.

10 The positions of these figures are briefly catalogued in Beth Dixon's "Animal Emotion," *Ethics and the Environment* 6, 2 (2001): 24-25.

11 Ibid., 28. It is unclear why it must be either one or the other because one could argue, as Martha Nussbaum does, that many of our evaluations are themselves socially constructed. See *Upheavals of Thought: The Intelligence of Emotions* (New York: Cambridge University Press, 2001), 139-73.

12 Following the Stoics in this regard, Cicero is forthright in refusing emotions to animals: "For the mind's sicknesses and emotions do not come about except through some spurning of reason. Thus they occur only in humans: animals do not have emotions, though they do have similar behavior." *Cicero on the Emotions: Tusculan Disputations 3 and 4*, trans. Margaret Graver (Chicago: University of Chicago Press, 2002), 4.31.

13 Plato, *Laws*, trans. A.E. Taylor, in *The Collected Dialogues of Plato*, ed. Edith Hamilton and Huntington Cairns (Princeton, NJ: Princeton University Press, 1961); Plato, *Republic*, trans. G.M.A. Grube, rev. C.D.C Reeve (Indianapolis, IN: Hackett, 1992).

14 Dixon is anxious to unsettle "the distinction between emotionality and rationality," but she thinks that doing so makes it difficult to claim that "animals, literally, have emotions" ("Animal Emotion," 23). Dixon puts Plato to different and seemingly contradictory uses. On the one hand, she cites him as a historical antecedent for characterizing the emotions as "irrational and bodily," a characterization that she herself wishes to deny. On the other hand, she enlists Plato as one who denies to animals the capabilities required for experiencing emotion: "For Plato and Descartes, the attribution of emotion to animals is one way of marking off animals from humans as qualitatively distinct in their mental capacities. Animals lack an essential property of humanness which is either described as a rational soul or an intellectual faculty of the mind" (23). As evidence of the former Plato, Dixon cites two texts in the *Republic*, both of which refer to the poet's practice of arousing specific emotions that are unbecoming the guardian class (604a-b and 605b). I do not mean to suggest that there is no evidence that Plato claims the emotions are irrational, only that these texts are rather poor examples for such a claim. Regardless of Plato's actual position, these seemingly contrary uses to which Dixon puts his work in her text hardly assist the reader in unpacking Plato.

15 Dixon, "Animal Emotion," 29n6.

16 Aristotle, *History of Animals*, in Richard McKean, ed., *The Basic Works of Aristotle*, trans. D'Arcy Wentworth Thompson (New York: Random House, 1941), 610a6-8.

17 Dixon argues, "Following Aristotle, suppose we characterize anger as essentially involving the judgment that one has been wronged ... Suppose a lion has blood boiling around the heart and chases a hyena away from its food in a menacing way. Then the psychological state in the lion resembles the psychological state we call anger in humans. Is it anger? We might be tempted to say so initially. But suppose the very property that fails to be present in the psychology of the lion is something correspond-ing to the judgment of wrongdoing. Then the psychological state of the lion is not anger" (27-28).

18 Aristotle does hold that a sharp and final distinction can be drawn between human and nonhuman animals, because only the former fully have "intellect." He proposes, however, that the higher animals are possessed of at least similar powers to humans, and he insists on maintaining a downward connection between human and nonhuman animals as well – that is, humans get their animality from the same powers as do nonhuman animals: "Other animals than man have the power of locomotion, but in none but him is there intellect ... For it is not the whole soul that constitutes the animal nature, but only some part or parts of it," specifically the power of motion. See *Parts of Animals*, in McKeon, *The Basic Works of Aristotle*, 641b6-10.

19 Dixon, "Animal Emotion," 25.

20 Ibid. Dixon uses this assertion in a hypothetical argument: "Suppose a lion has blood boiling around the heart and chases a hyena away from its food in a menacing way. Then the psychological state in the lion resembles the psychological state we call anger in humans. Is it anger? We might be tempted to say so initially. But suppose the very property that fails to be present in the psychology of the lion is something

corresponding to the judgment of wrongdoing. Then the psychological state of the lion is not anger, on the assumption that judgments are an essential ingredient in the analysis of anger in humans" (28). It is worth noting, without going too far afield, that talk of "psychological states" in relation to the emotions might itself be misleading in the Aristotelian context. The passions are themselves ways of being affected or moved and often enough lead to further activity (whether of flight or pursuit).

21 Stephen Loughlin, "Similarities and Differences between Human and Animal Emotion in Aquinas's Thought," *Thomist* 65 (2001): 45n2.

22 St. Thomas Aquinas, *Summa Theologica,* trans. Fathers of the English Dominican Province (Allen, TX: Christian Classics, 1948), I 80, 1. Hereafter cited in the text as ST, with appropriate part, section, and article numbers indicated.

23 Two early but excellent textbook discussions of this material are Etienne Gilson, *Moral Values and the Moral Life*, trans. Leo Richard Ward (Hamden, CT: Shoe String Press, 1961), 91-133; and James E. Royce, *Man and His Nature: A Philosophical Psychology* (Toronto: McGraw-Hill, 1961), 155-224. More recent work includes Robert Pasnau, *Thomas Aquinas on Human Nature* (New York: Cambridge University Press, 2002); Peter King, "Aquinas on the Passions," in *Thomas Aquinas: Contemporary Philosophical Perspectives*, ed. Brian Davies (New York: Oxford University Press, 2002), 353-84; and Elisabeth Uffenheimer-Lippens, "Rationalized Passion and Passionate Rationality: Thomas Aquinas on the Relation between Reason and the Passions," *Review of Metaphysics* 56, 3 (March 2003): 525-58.

24 Since I have already given reasons for believing that strong cognitivist accounts like that offered by Nussbaum fail to capture the *feel* of the emotions, I am not avoiding the question of the unsatisfactory nature of mentalist accounts. Besides, despite the present ascendancy of cognitive-like accounts even in experimental psychology, research establishing strong physiological links between material properties of the body and the experience of the emotions is still being done. And some of this research, while calling for the integration of "research on emotion and cognition," may establish the bodily component of emotion: "The amygdala receives inputs from the cortical sensory processing regions of each sensory modality and projects back to these as well." Jospeh LeDoux, "Emotion Circuits in the Brain," *Annual Review of Neuroscience* 23 (2000): 174-75.

25 Thomas Aquinas, *Summa Theologica*, I-II 40, 1.

26 Loughlin takes Aquinas' remarks on hope as indicative of a problem in the theory of emotion as it is normally understood: "From Aquinas's definitions and descriptions of the irascible emotions it is clear that they all require some degree of rationality in their arousal, operation, and completion ... These and other characteristics, essential to the irascible emotions, belong only to beings possessing reason." "Similarities and Differences," 47. He resolves the issue by contending that with nonhuman animals the apprehension is not really something undertaken by the animal but something that the animal participates in through the Wisdom of God, who gives such apprehensions to the animal as instinctively structured behaviour. For both human and nonhuman animals the movements of the sensitive appetite are "immediate and necessary" when presented with their proper object (48). But human emotions lack the "total determinism" that marks out the nonhuman animal's experience, insofar as the actions urged by and the cognitions summoning the emotions are under our control (49). If animals experience hope they do so somewhat vicariously, because "the judgment required for the emotion of hope has, in a sense, already been made according to the mind of the Creator of the animal's nature, as the instinctual behaviors of the animal represent the judgments of God in the determination of its nature" (53). Human and nonhuman animal emotions do not differ with respect to the movements of the sensitive appetite but with respect to "the cognitive precedents to emotion, and the subsequent actions urged by them" (59). Aquinas seems to open the way for such a reading in the article under discussion: "The movement of the natural appetite results from the apprehension of the separate Intellect, Who is the Author of nature; as does also the sensitive appetite of dumb animals, who act from a certain natural instinct" (ST I-II 40, 3). The problem is that the static nature of this interpretation limits the capacities of animals too narrowly. It is fair enough to say, as Loughlin does, that the sheep can judge the wolf to be a threat, and so an object of fear, because its power of so judging is instinctively set up to do so (61), but what about the sheep that learns to fear a certain farm boy who perpetrates acts of cruelty? Has this too has been programmed? What of a large roadway? John Deely argues that Aquinas' thesis with respect to animal behaviour is far more complex: "The distinction between *instinct* strictly so-called, i.e., between a species dominated by a pattern of behavior which is 'species-predictable' or 'ubiquitous in its distribution' among *all* members of a species *without exception*,' and *intelligence*, i.e., species the behavior of which does not seem to be dominated by a gene-determined pattern as much as it is

governed by a 'principle of nonrational estimations which bear the mark of individual experience and which are ceaselessly transformed by the acquisitions of experience.'" John Deely, "Animal Intelligence and Concept Formation," *Thomist* 35 (1971): 62, emphasis in original.

27 William Lyons, *Emotion* (Cambridge: Cambridge University Press, 1980).

28 John Deely, *What Distinguishes Human Understanding* (South Bend, IN: St. Augustine's Press, 2002), 34. He identifies a twofold determination in that sensation depends upon both "the individual constitution of the organism knowing and the material constitution of the environmental aspects of which the organism becomes aware."

29 John of St. Thomas (one of the last, and perhaps the most important, of the Latin commentators on the work of Aquinas) makes clear that perceptions *are* decidedly cognitive, as are sensations, though not yet at the same level as human understanding, in his *Naturalis Philosophiae Quarta Pars: De Ente Mobili Animato* (1635): "We suppose that there are iconic specifications, or ideas, at work in perception, just as there is cognition there. For if perceptions are higher in the knowing process than are sensations, they also require higher forms of specification, or at least ones ordered in a higher way, in order to bring forth a higher level of awareness. But specifiers of a more perfect and elevated type are seen to be necessary particularly when the objects represented are of a more abstract character [i.e., more removed from the here-and-now immediacy of sensation], as is the case with such perceptible but unsensed characteristics as hatred, unfriendliness, offspring, parents, and so forth. For these formalities are not represented in the external senses, and yet they are known in perception; therefore there exists some principle representative of them, which must not be so material and imperfect as to obtain at the level of the sensed objects as such, at which level the cognitions of external sense are constrained. Therefore it must be a form of specification more perfect than a specification of external sense, which represents only sensed [as contrasted to perceived] things" (quoted in ibid., 39-40n3).

30 Ibid., 32, emphasis in original.

31 Ibid., 42. See also the quotation at 58n7.

32 I am, of course, speaking of the abstract account of the operation of the sensible form on the appropriate sensible organ, not of what different species of animal might be capable of experiencing in their interaction with the physical environment.

33 Thomas Aquinas, *Commentary on the Nicomachean Ethics*, trans. C.I. Litzinger (Notre Dame, IN: Dumb Ox Books, 1993), 1215. Hereafter cited in text as "CNE."

34 Thomas Aquinas, *Commentary on Aristotle's De Anima*, trans. Kenelm Foster and Silvester Humphries (Notre Dame, IN: Dumb Ox Books, 1994). Hereafter cited in text as "CDA." The number refers to the sequentially numbered sections of the commentary rather than the book and lecture numbers. References to Aristotle's text are to the translation that accompanies the *Commentary* in this edition, and they are cited using standard citation practices for Aristotle's texts.

35 We must be careful not to exaggerate differences at the level of sensitive apprehension. For human animals, of course, each of the internal sense powers are coloured by the intellect, as is true even of the external senses. The point remains that both human and nonhuman animals have, i.e., Aquinas' theory of emotion, sensitive apprehensive or cognitive powers (memory, imagination, and the *vis estimativa* or *vis cogitativa*) that account for the cognitive component of an emotion. Besides, Aquinas not only distinguishes between degrees of perfection from human to nonhuman animal but identifies degrees of perfection in such faculties between higher and lower level nonhuman animals:

(a) all animals have imagination in some sense of the term; but the lower animals have it indeterminately ... And if ants and bees seem to differ in this respect from the rest of the lower animals, through their apparent exercise of a great deal of intelligence, the truth is, nevertheless, that ants and bees behave so cleverly not because they are aware of definite images distinct from exterior sensation, but by a natural instinct. (CDA 644)

b) [imperfect animals] do not move with a definite end in view, as if intending to arrive at any particular spot, as do the animals that move from one place to another and that form an inward image of things at a distance, and so desire these things and move towards them. The imperfect animals form images only of objects actually present to their exterior sense – not of things at a distance ... They have a confused imagination and desire. (CDD 839)

36 Aquinas highlights the same powers of the soul in the passage quoted from the *Summa*, where he also

points out that the principal source of error among the early philosophers was their attempt to locate the source of life in the body: "Now life is shown principally by two actions, knowledge and movement. The philosophers of old, not being able to rise above their imagination, supposed that the principle of these actions was something corporeal: for they asserted that only bodies were real things; and that what is not corporeal is nothing: hence they maintained that the soul is something corporeal" (ST I 75, 1).

37 Aquinas takes Aristotle to have emphatically rejected the Platonic idea of separate souls existing in the same subject: "Plato held that there were several souls in one body, distinct even as to organs, to which souls he referred the different vital actions, saying that the nutritive power is in the liver, the concupiscible in the heart, and the power of knowledge in the brain. Which opinion is rejected by Aristotle, with regard to those parts of the soul which use corporeal organs; for this reason, that in those animals which continue to live when they have been divided, in each part are observed the operations of the soul, as sense and appetite. Now this would not be the case if the various principles of the soul's operations were essentially different, and distributed in the various parts of the body. But with regard to the intellectual part, he seems to leave it in doubt whether it be *only logically* distinct from the other parts of the soul, *or only locally*. See ST I 76, 3.

38 The hierarchical order of animate beings is determined by the addition of powers: "Aristotle likens the nature of things to numbers; which increase by tiny degrees, one by one. Thus among living things there are some, i.e., plants, which have only the vegetative capacity, – which, indeed, they must have because no living being could maintain an existence in matter without the vegetative activities. Next are the animals, with sensitivity as well as vegetative life; and sensitivity implies a third power, appetition, which itself divides into three: into desire, in the stricter sense, which springs from the concupiscible appetite; anger, corresponding to the irascible appetite – both of these being in the sensitive part and following sense-knowledge; and finally, will, which is the intellectual appetite and follows intellectual apprehension." CDA 288.

39 On intentionality in Aquinas' theory, see Mark P. Drost, "Intentionality in Aquinas's Theory of Emotions," *International Philosophical Quarterly* 13, 4 (December 1991): 449-60.

40 At this point a difficulty with respect to vocabulary becomes all but inescapable. Aquinas explicitly denies that the emotions are cognitive. They depend on cognitions, whether those cognitions take the form of nonhuman perception or human perception and/or intellect. But the passions themselves are, properly speaking, passive potentialities of the appetitive power. The terminological difficulty stems from the fact that some modern defenders of emotion claim little more than this, whereas Nussbaum attributes a high level of rationality explicitly to the emotions. For the most part, I will reserve the term "rationality" for Nussbaum's strong thesis, rather than "cognition." In effect, even though emotions do not belong to cognition, without cognition there would be no emotion for Aquinas. It is therefore not wholly inappropriate to refer to his and Aristotle's theory as cognitive, without implying that emotions *are*, as Nussbaum would have it, judgments of the human intellect.

41 "Since ... the intellectual soul contains virtually what belongs to the sensitive soul, and something more, reason can consider separately what belongs to the power of the sensitive soul, as something imperfect and material. And because it observes that this is something common to man and to other animals, it forms thence the notion of the *genus*; while that wherein the intellectual soul exceeds the sensitive soul, it takes as formal and perfecting; thence it gathers the difference of man." ST I 76 3*ad*4.

42 For an example of such a theorist, see Chapter 10 in this volume.

43 Thomas Aquinas, *Summa contra Gentiles, Book Three: Providence,* part 2, trans. Vernon J. Bourke (Notre Dame, IN: University of Notre Dame Press, 1975), 87.

44 In *Commentary on the Nicomachean Ethics*, Aquinas notes that the voluntary is defined by the absence of the two features that Aristotle considers capable of rendering an act involuntary, violence and ignorance: "The voluntary seems to be: that which the agent himself originates (thus violence is excluded) in such a way that the agent knows the individual circumstances that concur with the action. Thus ignorance as the cause of the involuntary is excluded" (425).

45 Robert C. Solomon, "Emotions and Choice," in *What Is an Emotion?* ed. Cheshire Calhoun and Robert C. Solomon (New York: Oxford University Press, 1984), 309, 317 316.

46 Aquinas, *Disputed Question on the Virtues in General,* trans. Ralph McInerny (South Bend, IN: St. Augustine's Press, 1999), article 4.

47 Aquinas makes the very same point in the *De Anima* commentary: "Note too that, as desire and cognition are both found in the sensitive part, the same division appears in the intellectual part also. Hence love, hatred, delight and so forth can be understood either as sensitive, and in this sense they

are accompanied by a bodily movement; or as exclusively intellectual and volitional, without any accompanying sensuous desire; and understood in this sense they are not movements, for they involve no accompanying bodily change" (162).

48 Recently Martha C. Nussbaum has argued *from* the attribution to "god or gods" of emotions *to* the denial of a need for a bodily component in accounts of the emotions. She writes, "If we should adopt an account that makes a particular physiological process a necessary condition for an emotion of a given type, its consequence would be that all of these thinkers [those who attribute emotions to "god or gods"] are talking nonsense when they make these ascriptions. We may or may not believe that their accounts are correct, but it is a heavy price to pay to adopt from the start a view that entails that they are suffering from a profound conceptual confusion" (*Upheavals of Thought/The Intelligence of the Emotions* [New York: Cambridge University Press, 2001], 59-60). Here we see the dilemma faced by current cognitive and noncognitive theories of the emotions: we appear to be saddled with a choice between *either* an account that eschews the bodily component *or* an account that eschews the ascription of emotions to an immaterial (that is, bodiless) substance. Yet the disjunctive choice of the dilemma is, on Aquinas' account, both unnecessary and untrue. Nussbaum mistakes the predication of emotion terms, at least for a thinker like Aquinas, who does attribute emotions to God, as univocal rather than analogous. Aquinas does not attribute emotions properly so called to God *because*, like noncognitive theorists, he accepts that the emotions necessarily involve a bodily component; but he is willing to extend, analogously, the application of emotion terms to God *because* he is unwilling to deny the similarities in effects of emotion-like experiences that occur at the level of rational appetite.

Chapter 5: The Political Relevance of the Emotions from Descartes to Smith

Many thanks to Duncan Ivison and an anonymous reviewer for their helpful comments on earlier versions of this chapter.

1 In order to focus immediately on what I take to be most important in this historical shift, I will use the terms "emotions" and "passions" interchangeably here, despite the arguments that the distinction has great significance. See, for example, Thomas Dixon, *From Passions to Emotions: The Creation of a Secular Psychological Category* (Cambridge: Cambridge University Press, 2003). In addition, for reasons of space I have skirted the important discussion of how to reconceptualize the relation between reason and passion.

2 Cheryl Hall, "'Passion and Constraint': The Marginalization of Passion in Liberal Political Theory," *Philosophy and Social Criticism* 28, 6 (2002): 727-48.

3 This discussion draws in part on Cheryl Hall's analysis in *The Trouble with Passion: Political Theory beyond the Reign of Reason* (New York: Routledge, 2005), chap. 1.

4 George E. Marcus, *The Sentimental Citizen: Emotion in Democratic Politics* (University Park: Pennsylvania State University Press, 2002).

5 See, for example, Alexander Hamilton, John Jay, and James Madison, *The Federalist (The Gideon Edition)*, ed. George W. Carey and James McClellan (Indianapolis, IN: Liberty Fund Press, 2001) and John Rawls, *A Theory of Justice* (Cambridge, MA: Harvard University Press, 1971).

6 Judith Shklar, *Ordinary Vices* (Cambridge, MA: Belknap Press, 1984); Judith Shklar, "The Liberalism of Fear," in *Liberalism and the Moral Life*, ed. Nancy Rosenblum, 21-38 (Cambridge, MA: Harvard University Press, 1989); John Rawls, *A Theory of Justice* (Cambridge, MA: Harvard University Press, 1971).

7 Many defend the merits of liberalism precisely because of its attempts to sideline and devalue the passions. See, for example, Stephen Holmes, *Passions and Constraint* (Chicago: University of Chicago Press, 1995). Still, as Michael Walzer recognizes, one cannot readily conceive of a politics without passions and indeed, first and foremost, passions as a necessary basis for strong liberal commitments. See *Politics and Passion: Towards a More Egalitarian Liberalism* (New Haven, CT: Yale University Press, 2004).

8 Philip Fisher argues for a greater appreciation of the vehement passions (like fear, anger, grief, and shame) as a means by which individuals can connect with their own selves and with others in a more meaningful way. *The Vehement Passions* (Princeton, NJ: Princeton University Press, 2002).

9 I am thinking of the efforts of Christina Tarnopolsky to resuscitate a conception of respectful shame, and Luce Irigaray recognizing the importance of love for a true appreciation of difference as essential to democratic citizenship. See Tarnopolsky, "Prudes, Perverts and Tyrants: Plato and the Contemporary Politics of Shame and Civility," *Political Theory* 32, 4 (2004): 468-94; Tarnopolsky, "Plato on Shame and

Frank Speech in Democratic Athens," Chapter 2 in this volume; and Irigaray, *The Way of Love* (New York: Continuum, 2002). See also Hall, *Trouble with Passion,* which seeks to retrieve an understanding of political passion grounded in Platonic *eros.*

10 "Passionate intensity has its legitimate place in the social world, not only when we are getting money but also when we are choosing allies and engaging opponents. This extension of rational legitimacy to the political passions seems to me a useful revision of liberal theory, which has been too preoccupied in recent years with the construction of dispassionate deliberative procedures. It opens the way for better accounts of social connection and conflict and for more explicit and self-conscious answers to the unavoidable political question: Which side are you on?

"I think that the old dichotomy invites an even more radical denial. It's not that reason and passion can't be conceptually distinguished ... They are, however, always entangled in practice – and this entanglement itself requires a conceptual account ... This is how things actually are: there are 'good' and 'bad' combinations of reason and passion, which we distinguish rationally and passionately." Walzer, *Politics and Passion,* 126.

See also Michael Walzer, "Passion and Politics," *Philosophy and Social Criticism* 28 (2002), 617-33; and Martha C. Nussbaum, *Hiding from Humanity: Disgust, Shame and the Law* (Princeton, NJ: Princeton University Press, 2004). These attempts to reframe our understanding of liberalism should not be confused with anti-foundationalism, particularly that of Richard Rorty (see his *Contingency, Irony and Solidarity* [Cambridge: Cambridge University Press, 1989], especially Chapter 9). Rather, they should be understood as attempts to incorporate a fuller and more realistic ontology into contemporary political theory.

11 See, for example, Barbara Koziak, *Retrieving Political Emotion: Thumos, Aristotle and Gender* (University Park: Pennsylvania State University Press, 2000).

12 In this sense this essay goes much further than many contemporary accounts within social and cultural theories of emotion, for I suggest that not only can social and political causes work to explain a possible spectrum of emotional responses, such as suggested by Amélie O. Rorty in "Explaining Emotions" (Chapter 1 in this volume), but that in certain instances particular types of emotional disposition can be associated with particular political arrangements.

13 I do not wish to suggest that the realm of the public should be limited to those areas where there is common feeling or consensus among citizens. Certainly politics has room for differing emotions among citizens towards objects of community importance and relevance. My point relates to the idea that on some matters citizens can share an emotional response that is a valuable contribution to political life. The eradication of this idea was a key step leading to the dismissal of the idea that the emotions could have any positive role in political life. I thank an anonymous reviewer for bringing this issue to my attention.

14 Albert Hirschman, *The Passions and the Interests* (Princeton, NJ: Princeton University Press, 1977).

15 "The discourse ... is so simple and so brief that it will reveal that my purpose has not been to explain the Passions as an Orator, or even as a moral Philosopher, but only as a Physicist." René Descartes, *The Passions of the Soul,* trans. Stephen H. Voss (Indianapolis, IN: Hackett, 1989), art. 1, 17.

16 As Descartes states in a letter to Elizabeth on 28 June 1643, "Je remarque une grande différence entre ces trois sortes de notions, en ce que l'âme ne se conçoit que par l'entendement pur; le corps, c'est-à-dire l'extension, les figures et le mouvement, se peuvent aussi connaître par l'entendement seul, mais beaucoup mieux par l'entendement aidé de l'imagination; en enfin, les choses qui appartiennent à l'union de l'âme et le corps, ne se connaissent qu'obscurément par l'entendement seul, ni même par l'entendement aidé de l'imagination; mais elles se connaissent très clairement par les sens. D'où vient que ceux qui ne philosophent jamais, et qui ne se servent que de leurs sens, ne doutent point que l'âme ne meuve le corps, et que le corps n'agisse sur l'âme; mais ils considèrent l'un et l'autre comme une seule chose, c'est-à-dire, ils conçoivent leur union; car concevoir l'union qui est entre deux choses, c'est les concevoir comme une seule." René Descartes, *Correspondance avec Elisabeth et autres lettres* (Paris: Flammarion, 1989), 73-74. So while we might say that for Descartes the soul and body have different properties considered in themselves, an element of common sense dictates to him that in functional terms they are not to be considered as separate. Therefore Descartes cannot be said to subscribe to a doctrine of a strict separation of soul and body. Still, he does not ascribe to the soul any vegetative or appetitive functions (as do Plato and Aristotle, for example).

17 "I also take into consideration that we notice no subject that acts more immediately upon our soul than the body it is joined to, and that consequently we ought to think that what is a Passion in the former is

commonly an Action in the latter. So there is no better path for arriving at an understanding of our Passions than to examine the difference between the soul and the body, in order to understand to which of the two each of the functions within us should be attributed." Descartes, *Passions of the Soul*, art. 2, p. 19. See also art. 47, pp. 44-46. Stephen Gaukroger argues that in more immediate terms Descartes was led to write his treatise by the growing confusion in attempts to amalgamate elements of the scholastic and Stoic traditions in a theory of the passions. "Descartes' Theory of the Passions," in *Descartes*, ed. John Cottingham (Oxford: Oxford University Press, 1998), 211-24.

Indeed, according to Thomas Dixon, the shift from the ancient idea that we can be deemed responsible for at least a portion of our own emotional life to the modern idea that our emotions are of one general sort and open to "management" but not to control, given their origin in physiological causes and their generalized irrational nature, marks an important impoverishment of our understanding of the life of the soul. However, Dixon traces this shift to the early nineteenth century in Anglo-American thought and does not does not explore its roots in earlier Continental philosophy. See *From Passions to Emotions*.

18 Descartes, *Passions of the Soul*, art. 39, p. 40. See also art. 36, p. 39.

19 Susan James, "Explaining the Passions: Passions, Desires and the Explanation of Action," in *The Soft Underbelly of Reason: The Passions in the Seventeenth Century*, ed. Stephen Gaukroger (London: Routledge, 1998), 21.

20 Desmond M. Clarke, *Descartes's Theory of Mind* (Oxford: Oxford University Press, 2003), 117.

21 Ibid., especially Chapter 4.

22 As Clarke succinctly states in the closing lines of his work: "Cartesian dualism ... is not a theory of human beings but a provisional acknowledgement of failure, an index of the work that remains to be done before a viable theory of the human mind becomes available." Ibid., 258.

23 "The same thing can be observed in beasts, for even though they have no reason and perhaps no thought either, all the movements of the spirits and the gland that excite the passions in us still exist in them, and serve in them to maintain and strengthen, not the passions as in us, but the nerve and muscle movements that usually accompany them." Descartes, *Passions of the Soul*, art. 50, p. 48. Also, "this use of the passions is the most natural one they can have, and ... animals that lack reason all direct their lives entirely by bodily movements like those which usually follow them in us, to which they incite our souls to consent" (art. 138, p. 93).

24 "Il me semble que la différence qui est entre les plus grandes âmes et celles qui sont basses et vulgaires, consiste, principalement, en ce que les âmes vulgaires se laissent aller à leurs passions, et ne sont heureuses ou malheureuses, que selon que les choses qui leur surviennent sont agréables ou déplaisantes; au lieu que les autres ont des raisonnements si forts et si puissants que, bien qu'elles aient aussi des passions, et même souvent de plus violentes que celles du commun, leur raison demeure néanmoins toujours la maîtresse, et fait que les afflictions même leur servent, et contribuent à la parfaite félicité dont elles jouissent dès cette vie." Descartes, *Correspondance avec Elisabeth*, 96.

25 James, "Explaining the Passions," 30.

26 See Leonard Ferry, "Troubling Business: The Emotions in Aquinas' Political Psychology," Chapter 4 in this volume.

27 This divergence from the classical idea of rational affection is perhaps best illustrated by the closing statement of Descartes' work: "Wisdom is useful here above all: it teaches us to render ourselves such masters of [the passions], and to manage them with such ingenuity, that the evils they cause can be easily borne, and we even derive Joy from them all." *Passions of the Soul*, art. 212, p. 135.

28 See John M. Cooper, "Plato's Theory of Motivation," in *Plato II*, ed. Gail Fine (Oxford: Oxford University Press, 1999), 189-90; and Charles Kahn, "Plato's Theory of Desire," *Review of Metaphysics* 1 (1987), 77-103. For purposes of brevity, I focus here on Plato's discussion of the soul as put forward in the *Republic*. Although Plato's understanding of the elements of the soul did evolve, the general principle that I am developing here, namely that what was most important for the ancients was a sense of the soul in context, is operative throughout Plato's writings.

29 Plato, *Republic*, trans. G.M.A. Grube, rev. C.D.C. Reeve (Indianapolis, IN: Hackett, 1992), 485d.

30 This is somewhat akin to the more recent criticism of Humean and Humean-inspired understandings of the emotions as found in the work of Robert C. Solomon, who writes, "An emotion, as a system of judgments, is not merely a set of beliefs about the world but rather an active way of structuring our experience, a way of experiencing something." "Nothing to Be Proud of," in *Not Passion's Slave: Emotions and Choice* (Oxford: Oxford University Press, 2003), 55. For a discussion of the intentionality of the passions and emotions, see Robert C. Solomon, "Emotions' Mysterious Objects," in *Not Passion's Slave*, 57-75.

31 Pierre-François Moreau, "Les Passions: Continuités et tournants," in *Les Passions antiques et mediévales*, ed. Bernard Besnier, Pierre-François Moreau, and Laurence Renault (Paris: Presses Universitaires de France, 2003), 1-12. This idea is also expressed by Daniel M. Gross in "Early Modern Emotion and the Economy of Scarcity," *Philosophy and Rhetoric*, 34, 4 (2001): 308-21. As he states, "For Aristotle ... anger is a deeply social passion provoked by perceived slights unjustified, and it presupposes a public stage where social status is always subject to performative infelicities" (309).

32 Alexandre Koyré, *Introduction à la lecture de Platon* (Paris: Gallimard, 1962), 7.

33 See Bernard Williams, "The Analogy of City and Soul in Plato's *Republic*," in Fine, *Plato II*, 255-64; and Julia Annas, *An Introduction to Plato's Republic* (Oxford: Oxford University Press, 1981).

34 G.R.F. Ferrari, *City and Soul in Plato's Republic* (Chicago: University of Chicago Press, 2005).

35 Christopher Bobonich, *Plato's Utopia Recast* (Oxford: Oxford University Press, 2002), chap. 1.

36 This dimension is stressed by Jonathan Lear, *Open Minded: Working Out the Logic of the Soul* (Cambridge, MA: Harvard University Press, 1998).

37 Aristotle, *On Rhetoric: A Theory of Civic Discourse*, trans. George A. Kennedy (New York: Oxford University Press, 1991), 1.8, 77.

38 See Pierre Ansart, *Les Cliniciens des passions politiques* (Paris: Seuil, 1997).

39 Thomas Hobbes, *Leviathan*, ed. J.C.A. Gaskin (Oxford: Oxford University Press, 1996).

40 As Locke famously comments: "To ask how you may be guarded from harm, or injury, on that side where the strongest hand is to do it, is presently the voice of faction and rebellion: as if when men quitting the state of nature entered into society, they agreed that all of them but one, should be under the restraint of laws, but that he should still retain all the liberty of the state of nature, increased with power, and made licentious by impunity. This is to think, that men are so foolish, that they take care to avoid what mischiefs may be done them by pole-cats, or foxes; but are content, nay, think it safety, to be devoured by lions." John Locke, *Second Treatise of Government* (Indianapolis, IN: Hackett, 1980), s. 93, 50. One modern commentator has sought to resuscitate Hobbes' understanding of the manipulation of fear as the basis for a more sophisticated analytical weaponry to make the citizenry more aware of the means by which political and economic elites seek to shape their emotional lives for the end of greater political control. See Corey Robin, *Fear: The History of a Political Idea* (Oxford: Oxford University Press, 2004).

41 Earl of Shaftesbury, "A Letter Concerning Enthusiasm to My Lord ***," in *Characteristics of Men, Manners, Opinions, Times*, ed. Lawrence E. Klein (Cambridge: Cambridge University Press, 1999), 7.

42 Ibid.

43 Earl of Shaftesbury, "An Inquiry Concerning Virtue or Merit," in *Characteristics of Men*, 192.

44 Ibid., 199-200.

45 "Thus in a civil state or public we see that a virtuous administration and an equal and just distribution of rewards and punishments is of the highest service, not only by restraining the vicious and forcing them to act usefully to society, but by making virtue to be apparently the interest of everyone, so as to remove all prejudices against it, create a fair reception for it and lead men into that path which afterwards they cannot easily quit. For thus a people raised from barbarity or despotic rule, civilized by laws, and made virtuous by the long course of a lawful and just administration, if they chance to fall suddenly under any misgovernment of unjust and arbitrary power, they will on this account be the rather animated to exert a stronger virtue in opposition to such violence and corruption." Ibid., 186.

46 Adam Smith, *The Theory of Moral Sentiments* (Indianapolis, IN: Liberty Fund, 1982), Part I, Section i, Chapters 3 and 4, 16-19. All further references to this text will be cited as TMS, followed by part, section, and chapter numbers.

47 TMS, I, i, 4.

48 This ties in with Fonna Forman-Barzilai's idea that Smith was first and foremost engaged in a descriptive (rather than normative) exercise in his *Theory of Moral Sentiments*. See Forman-Barzilai, "Sympathy in Space(s): Adam Smith on Proximity," *Political Theory* 33, 2 (2005): 191.

49 TMS, I, i, 4.

50 Susan James, *Passion and Action* (Oxford: Clarendon Press, 1997).

51 TMS, I, i, 4.

52 Glenn R. Morrow, "The Significance of the Doctrine of Sympathy in Hume and Adam Smith," *Philosophical Review* 32, 1 (1923): 60-78.

53 Another defence of Smithian sympathy, as a foundation for his idea of the impartial spectator, is offered by Nicholas Phillipson: "What is curious and distinctive about Smith's theory is that he does not think

that we simply put ourselves in another man's shoes in order to see whether, were we him, we would approve of what he was doing. That would have introduced an element of egotism into the theory which he was particularly anxious to avoid. In his account we exercise our imaginative curiosity quite hard in order to achieve what we judge to be a genuinely critical detachment in our understanding of another man's behaviour. Thus, to take a particularly graphic Smithian example, a man does not ask what he would suffer if he were a woman in labour; he tries to imagine what it would be like to be a woman in labour. Only after we have undergone this demanding imaginative and critical exercise and acquired what we feel is a satisfactory degree of detachment, do we decide whether or not to bring the encounter to a close by offering our sympathetic approval of the other man's behaviour." "Adam Smith as Civic Moralist," in *Wealth and Virtue*, ed. I. Hont and M. Ignatieff (Cambridge: Cambridge University Press, 1983), 183.

54 TMS, V, vii, 2.

55 Morrow, "Doctrine of Sympathy," 72-73.

56 TMS, V, vii, 2. Emma Rothschild, *Economic Sentiments: Adam Smith, Condorcet and the Enlightenment* (Cambridge, MA: Harvard University Press, 2001). Thanks to Amélie Rorty for alerting me to this text. These limits on custom found in Smith can be compared with those detailed by Hume, as argued by Sharon Krause in Chapter 6 in this volume.

57 As D.D. Raphael and A.L. Macfie assert, "It is nature that teaches us to put family, friends and nation first, while also providing us with the judgements of the impartial spectator to check any excessive attachment." "Introduction," in Smith, *Theory of Moral Sentiments*, 10. In this sense, the impartial spectator can be seen as a constant regulative presence for these otherwise natural inclinations.

58 Ibid.; and Martha C. Nussbaum, "Mutilated and Deformed: Adam Smith on the Material Basis of Human Dignity," a talk presented at the 32nd International Hume Conference, University of Toronto, July 2005. This disengagement is reinforced by Smith's call for the reader to be wary of the fury of "the mob," TMS, I, ii, 3, and in his description of the "social passions" in Chapter 4, such as "generosity, humanity, kindness, compassion, mutual friendship and esteem," focusing on examples from the intimate lives of friends and the family. These "social passions," though regarded with some approval by Smith, can often evoke pity when they are considered to be excessive: "There is a helplessness in the character of extreme humanity which more than any thing interests our pity." These descriptions render political mobilization on the basis of "unsocial passions" as naturally abhorrent to us, and mobilization on the basis of "social passions" as improbable, TMS, I, ii, 3.

59 Forman-Barzilai, "Sympathy in Space(s)," 204.

60 TMS, IV, i, 11.

Chapter 6: Passion, Power, and Impartiality in Hume

1 For discussion, see Duncan Forbes, *Hume's Philosophical Politics* (Cambridge: Cambridge University Press, 1975), esp. 32-58; J.L. Mackie, *Hume's Moral Theory* (London: Routledge, 1980), esp. 14-30; David Fate Norton, "Hume, Human Nature, and the Foundations of Morality," in *The Cambridge Companion to Hume*, ed. D.F. Norton (Cambridge: Cambridge University Press, 1999), 150-58; and Knud Haakonssen, *Natural Law and Moral Philosophy: From Grotius to the Scottish Enlightenment* (Cambridge: Cambridge University Press, 1996).

2 David Hume, *An Enquiry Concerning the Principles of Morals* (LaSalle, IL: Open Court, 1966), 4; and see *A Treatise of Human Nature*, ed. L.A. Selby-Bigge (Oxford: Clarendon Press, 1968), 458. Hereafter references to the *Enquiry* will appear parenthetically in the text with the page number preceded by the letter "E"; references to the *Treatise* will be preceded in the text by the letter "T."

3 Immanuel Kant, *Grounding for the Metaphysics of Morals*, trans. James W. Ellington (Indianapolis, IN: Hackett, 1981), 46 [442], 59 [460]; and see A.J. Ayer, *Hume: A Very Short Introduction* (Oxford: Oxford University Press, 1980), 104. This interpretation is contested by others such as Larry Arnhart, "The New Darwinian Naturalism in Political Theory," *American Political Science Review* 89, 2 (1995): 389; Annette Baier, *A Progress of Sentiments: Reflections on Hume's Treatise* (Cambridge, MA: Harvard University Press, 1999), 180; Donald Herzog, *Without Foundations: Justification in Political Theory* (Ithaca, NY: Cornell University Press, 1985), 165; Terrence Penelhum, *David Hume: An Introduction to his Philosophical System* (West Lafayette, PA: Purdue University Press, 1992), 137; Barry Stroud, *Hume* (London: Routledge, 2000), 182; and Jacqueline Taylor, "Hume and the Reality of Value," in *Feminist Interpretations of David Hume*, ed. Anne Jaap Jacobsen (University Park: Pennsylvania State University Press, 2000), 114-15.

4 Páll S. Árdal, *Passion and Value in Hume's Treatise* (Edinburgh: Edinburgh University Press, 1966), 45.

5 Hume is somewhat ambiguous in this example as to whether the object of our value and esteem is the man's riches or the rich man himself. He sometimes seems to mean the former, saying that sympathy gives us "an esteem for power and riches, and a contempt for meanness and poverty" (T 362). Elsewhere, however, he suggests that the person of the rich man is the object of approbation, as sympathy with his pleasures and those of his expected beneficiaries generate esteem and respect for the man himself. He invokes the latter logic to explain the culture of deference surrounding the rich that was characteristic of eighteenth-century European societies, including his own (T 616). Our society, by contrast, values wealth but not necessarily the wealthy (or at least our esteem for the rich is far more ambivalent than what Hume describes). Comparison and self-interest also enter into the equation in ways that alter the effects of sympathetic communication. Even in Hume's time, an equally common response to perceiving the pleasures of the wealthy must have been envy and resentment. So the sentiments that inform our judgments of the wealthy are more complex than Hume's example of the rich man suggests, although this complexity is in principle fully compatible with the general method of judgment Hume describes. The example does point to one of the dangers of Humean judgment, however, which is that sympathy may be hindered by social inequalities, resulting in distorted judgments. This issue is addressed below.

6 Jacqueline Taylor, "Hume on Luck and Moral Inclusion," panel paper presented at the annual meeting of the American Political Science Association, Philadelphia, PA, August-September 2003.

7 Ibid.; Jacqueline Taylor, "Justice and the Foundations of Social Morality in Hume's Treatise," *Hume Studies* 24, 1 (1998): 5-30; and see Sabina Lovibond, *Realism and Imagination in Ethics* (Minneapolis: University of Minnesota Press, 1983), 134-35.

8 Aryeh Botwinick, *Ethics, Politics, and Epistemology: A Study in the Unity of Hume's Thought* (Lanham, MD: University Press of America, 1980), 51, 59.

9 Sympathy is natural enough, Hume says, that it is "conspicuous in children, who implicitly embrace every opinion propos'd to them," and "also in men of the greatest judgment and understanding, who find it very difficult to follow their own reason or inclination, in opposition to that of their friends and daily companions" (T 316).

10 The standard of usefulness has an especially important role, which explains why Hume is often considered to be a utilitarian or proto-utilitarian thinker. See Ayer, *Hume*, 99-100; Jonathan Harrison, *Hume's Theory of Justice* (Oxford: Clarendon Press, 1981), viii; and Forbes, *Hume's Philosophical Politics*, 109. Yet the useful does not stand alone in moral judgment, according to Hume, but is "intermix'd in our judgments of morals" with what is immediately agreeable (T 590). For discussion of the non-utilitarian aspects of Hume's theory, see Baier, *Progress of Sentiments*, 199, 203; John B. Stewart, "The Public Interest vs. Old Rights," *Hume Studies* 21, 2 (1995): 171; and Sharon R. Krause, "Hume and the (False) Luster of Justice," *Political Theory* 32, 5 (2004), 634-38.

11 Iris Marion Young, "Asymmetrical Reciprocity: On Moral Respect, Wonder, and Enlarged Thought," in *Judgment, Imagination, and Politics: Themes from Kant and Arendt,* ed. Ronald Beiner and Jennifer Nedelsky (Lanham, MD: Rowman and Littlefield, 2001), 209.

12 M. Jamie Ferriera, "Hume and Imagination: Sympathy and the Other," *International Philosophical Quarterly* 34, 1 (1994): 47.

13 This assertion may seem to generate a problem of infinite regress. The standard suggested by human nature, to be discussed presently, sets some limits in this regard. Still, there is no avoiding the fact that any one moral judgment invokes values that rest on other judgments. Or rather, the only way to avoid this feature of moral judgment is to posit a source of moral authority that is wholly independent of the human concerns and purposes that generate values and motivate action. This putative solution raises more problems (both motivational and normative) than it resolves, however, and consequently the Humean approach rejects it.

14 David Hume, "Of the Standard of Taste," in *Essays: Moral, Political, and Literary* (Indianapolis, IN: Liberty Fund, 1987), 239, 240-41, 242.

15 Ibid., 246.

16 David Hume, "Of Commerce," in *Essays*, 265.

17 David Hume, "Of the Populousness of Ancient Nations," in *Essays*, 383. See also Norman Kemp Smith, *The Philosophy of David Hume* (London: Macmillan, 1964), 45. Numerous cultures have instituted slavery, which suggests that there may be something natural in the urge to dominate others, or to have somebody else do one's dirty work. Still, one cannot act on this desire, however common it may be,

without causing harm to others. Nobody wants to be enslaved, after all; many common desires are thwarted and legitimate human purposes rendered impossible by this status. And while acting on the desire to dominate imposes direct harm on others, the desire not to be enslaved imposes no such consequences. Human nature as a standard in Hume does not include everything that comes "naturally" to human beings, or everything they can be seen to desire. It privileges common human concerns the satisfaction of which does not entail the systematic imposition of suffering.

18 Hume says, along these lines, that "justice, humanity, magnanimity, prudence, [and] veracity" are applauded "in all nations and ages" because they respond to fundamental human concerns. "Of the Standard of Taste," 228. See also John W. Danford, *David Hume and the Problem of Reason* (New Haven, CT: Yale University Press, 1990), 104.

19 See Paul Russell, *Freedom and Moral Sentiment: Hume's Way of Naturalizing Responsibility* (New York: Oxford University Press, 1995), 68; and Norton, "Hume, Human Nature," 148.

20 Richard H. Dees, "Hume and the Contexts of Politics," *Journal of the History of Philosophy* 30, 2 (1992): 231.

21 David Hume, "A Dialogue," in *David Hume: Enquiries Concerning Human Understanding and Concerning the Principles of Morals*, ed. P.H. Nidditch (Oxford: Clarendon Press, 1998), 335.

22 Along these lines, Hume refers in the *Enquiry* to the "necessary and infallible consequences of the general principles of human nature, as discovered in common life and practice" (E 66).

23 The role of human nature in establishing evaluative standards speaks to the fact that Hume does connect "is" and "ought," contrary to some common interpretations of his comments at *Treatise* 3.1.1 (469-70). As Baier says, Hume has been wrongly "saddled by some commentators with 'Hume's law,' which says ... that no sound inference or reasonable transition from *is* to *ought* can be made." *Progress of Sentiments*, 176-77. This is not what Hume meant to convey in the relevant passage. The point of the passage, as Stroud (*Hume*, 187) puts it, is rather that "because of the special character of moral judgments," transitions from "is" to "ought" cannot be perceived by reason alone. This reading squares with what Hume says in the paragraph immediately preceding: "Take any action allow'd to be vicious ... You never can find it [vice], till you turn your reflexion into your own breast, and find a sentiment of disapprobation, which arises in you, towards this action. *Here is a matter of fact; but 'tis the object of feeling, not of reason.* It lies in yourself, not in the object. So that when you pronounce any action or character to be vicious, you mean nothing, but that from the constitution of your nature you have a feeling or sentiment of blame from the contemplation of it" (T 469, emphasis added). For further discussion of this passage and the common misreadings of it, see A.C. MacIntyre, "Hume on 'Is' and 'Ought,'" in *Hume*, ed. V.C. Chappell (Notre Dame, IN: University of Notre Dame Press, 1968), 242-64; John Rawls, *Lectures on the History of Moral Philosophy* (Cambridge, MA: Harvard University Press, 2000), 83-84; and Elizabeth Radcliffe, "Kantian Tunes on a Humean Instrument: Why Hume Is Not Really a Skeptic about Practical Reasoning," in *Hume: Moral and Political Philosophy*, ed. Rachel Cohon (Aldershot, UK: Ashgate/Dartmouth, 2001), 68.

24 For discussion of the affective dimensions of judgment in Aristotle, see Arash Abizadeh, "The Passions of the Wise," Chapter 3 in this volume.

25 See Christine Korsgaard, *The Sources of Normativity* (Cambridge: Cambridge University Press, 1996), 56-67.

26 Ibid., 63.

27 Ibid., 65-66.

28 Baier, *Progress of Sentiments*, 151-52; Jacqueline Taylor, "Humean Ethics and the Politics of Sentiment," *Topoi* 21 (2002): 176-77.

29 Stuart Hampshire, *Innocence and Experience* (Cambridge, MA: Harvard University Press, 1989), 18; cited in Taylor, "Humean Ethics," 176. See also Rawls, *History of Moral Philosophy*, 36, 50; and Jean Hampton, "Does Hume Have an Instrumental Conception of Practical Reason?" *Hume Studies* 21, 1 (1995): 57-74.

30 At any rate, Hume did not work this out in his philosophical works. His *History of England* (Indianapolis, IN: Liberty Fund, 1983) contains examples of what he had in mind, however. Some interpreters have even argued that the *History* offers the best view into Hume's concept of political judgment and his political theory more generally. See Danford, *David Hume*, 77, 88; Herzog, *Without Foundations*, 200; Donald Livingston, "On Hume's Conservatism," *Hume Studies* 21, 2 (1995): 158; and Andrew Sabl, "When Bad Things Happen from Good People (and Vice Versa): Hume's Political Ethics of Revolution," *Polity* 35, 1 (2002): 73, 79.

31 Practical deliberation for Hume can be either moral or prudential. If moral, deliberation is guided by moral sentiment; if prudential, it is guided by interest, or by desires and concerns not tutored by the generalized perspective or measured against the claims of human nature. In what follows, my main concern is with moral deliberation.

32 This example brings out another difference between desires and concerns. To have a desire, at least in common parlance, is to *feel* desire. Our concerns, by contrast, contribute to the constitution of our characters and to our general dispositions in ways that are not always consciously felt, even though they always carry motivational force. Hence we can sometimes find ourselves acting in ways that mystify us until, through reflection, we come to identify the unconscious concerns behind our action.

33 Bernard Williams, "Internal and External Reasons," in *Moral Luck* (Cambridge: Cambridge University Press, 1981), 104.

34 David Hume, "The Sceptic," in *Essays*, 170. See Richard H. Dees, "Hume on the Characters of Virtue," *Journal of the History of Philosophy* 35, 1 (1997): 60.

35 Hume, "Sceptic," 171.

36 Dees, "Hume on the Characters of Virtue," 63, emphasis in original.

37 That is to say, this is an aspiration we can endorse from within the moral standpoint. This consideration supplements Hume's prudential justification for why we should adopt the generalized perspective in the first place. We need morality because we are by nature socially interdependent: we depend on others to meet basic needs and satisfy fundamental purposes. The only way to achieve the needed social co-ordination is for people to interact reliably on the basis of common rules and shared standards, and the best way to arrive at these rules and standards is by means of a generalized perspective in conjunction with an empirical understanding of human nature.

38 Alexis de Tocqueville, *Democracy in America*, trans. Harvey C. Mansfield and Delba Winthrop (Chicago: University of Chicago Press, 2000), vol. 2, 535-39.

39 On political turbulence in general, see David Hume, "Of the Idea of a Perfect Commonwealth," in *Essays*, 523, 528; and Hume, "Of Public Credit," in *Essays*, 355. On the civil war, see Hume, "Of the Coalition of Parties," in *Essays*, 500. On ancient politics, see Hume, "Of the Populousness of Ancient Nations," 416.

40 On this point, see Taylor, "Humean Ethics," 184.

41 Hume, "Of Essay-Writing," in *Essays*, 534-34.

42 Martha C. Nussbaum, *Hiding from Humanity: Disgust, Shame and the Law* (Princeton, NJ: Princeton University Press, 2004), 13-15. In contrast to Nussbaum's account, Christina Tarnopolsky makes a strong case for the potentially valuable role of shame in democracy. See "Plato on Shame and Frank Speech in Democratic Athens," Chapter 2 in this volume.

Chapter 7: Pity, Pride, and Prejudice

1 By suggesting that Rousseau's account of human behaviour is useful for understanding contemporary interactions, I am siding with the interpretation that his depictions of the original condition, or the state(s) of nature, and the movements leading to an advanced form of civil society provide a complex but relatively consistent narrative of human psychology as played out in liberal democracies. For example, Charles Taylor argues that contemporary conflicts over identity politics can be best understood in light of Rousseau's insight into the contradictory impulses of *amour-propre*. See Taylor, *Multiculturalism and the Politics of Recognition* (Princeton, NJ: Princeton University Press, 1992); and Taylor, *The Malaise of Modernity* (Concord, ON: Anansi Press, 1991).

2 The question of how Rousseau depicts the similarities and differences between men and women is challenging. Although I am not engaging this question fully here, elsewhere I argue that Rousseau associates "woman" with deception and concealment; she is more difficult to "see into" yet knowledge of her is more important, because civil society rests on the possibility of women being (rather than merely appearing) virtuous. See Ingrid Makus, "The Politics of 'Masculine Openness' and 'Feminine Concealment' in Rousseau," in *Feminist Interpretations of Rousseau*, ed. Lynda Lange (University Park: Pennsylvania State University Press, 2002), 187-211.

3 Jean-Jacques Rousseau, *The First and Second Discourses*, ed. and trans. Roger D. Masters and Judith R. Masters (New York: St. Martin's Press, 1964). For a detailed assessment of Rousseau's description of humans emerging from a primal state and developing into an advanced civil society in relation to scientific theories of human evolution such as Darwin's, see Roger D. Masters, "Rousseau and the Rediscovery of Human Nature," in *The Legacy of Rousseau*, ed. Clifford Orwin and Nathan Tarcov (Chicago: University of Chicago Press, 1997), 110-40.

4 Interpretations of Rousseau's account of the passions note that he elevates the role of the passions in human conduct, seemingly at the cost of reason. Most commentators agree that reason and passion remain linked for Rousseau in complex ways, however. For example, see Peter Emberley, "Rousseau and the Management of the Passions," *Interpretation*, May 1985, 151-76, who maintains that Rousseau abandons the classical ideal of a self-governed soul in which reason rules the passions, replacing it with a notion of the individual whose passions are regulated and educated by an external lawgiver and tutor. See also Cheryl Hall, *The Trouble with Passion: Political Theory beyond the Reign of Reason* (New York: Routledge, 2005), who argues that Rousseau provides a rational and passionate justification for the importance of the educated passions in securing public engagement.

5 Commentary on Rousseau that emphasizes the importance of pity to his thought tends to elide the multiple ways that this concept is formulated in the *Discourses* themselves, focusing instead on how pity is reformulated in sections of *Émile*. The implication is that what needs to be sorted out is how pity moves from being prominent in the state of nature to being relatively weak in civil society and, if so, how it can form a basis for virtue in civil society or underpin a social contract that is embedded in the general will. For example, Cheryl Hall questions how and why pity, along with the other passions, seems to "disappear" in Rousseau's most political work, *The Social Contract*. Hall, *Trouble with Passion*, 81.

6 Jean-Jacques Rousseau, *Second Discourse*, in *The First and Second Discourses*, 95. Subsequent citations in the text are to pages in this edition.

7 Tracy Strong, *Jean-Jacques Rousseau: The Politics of the Ordinary* (Thousand Oaks, CA: Sage Publications, 1994), 42.

8 Ibid. Often these contradictory ways of describing pity occur on the same page, and even within the same passage.

9 Clifford Orwin, "Rousseau and the Discovery of Political Compassion," in *The Legacy of Rousseau*, ed. Clifford Orwin and Nathan Tarcov (Chicago: University of Chicago Press, 1997), 300-1.

10 The difficulty in interpreting the function of Rousseau's account of the state of nature, or original condition, as developed in the *Discourses*, and ascertaining its relevance to Rousseau's prescriptions for political community in *The Social Contract*, as well as to assessments of contemporary political life, is well-documented. Peter Emberley expresses the problem succinctly: "How can the original state of nature or the original endowment to man provide a standard for evaluating contemporary life if man is an historical animal and his earlier stages are irrecoverable?" "Rousseau and the Management of the Passions," 162. Cheryl Hall attempts to address the problem by proposing that Rousseau's original condition is a hypothetical state, an "imaginary history of humanity." *Trouble with Passion*, 74, 81-82. How is it useful to us then? Hall maintains that its appeal is precisely a rhetorical one, addressed to our passions and imaginations. The paradox in Hall's assessment is that it requires admitting that Rousseau's account of human nature in the *Discourses* is relevant to us moderns, since we continue to be responsive to and subject to such appeals (71-92).

11 Ruth W. Grant, *Hypocrisy and Integrity: Machiavelli, Rousseau, and the Ethics of Politics* (Chicago: University of Chicago Press, 1997). For a parallel discussion of the self divided between "private" and "public," see Margaret Ogrodnick, *Instinct and Intimacy: Political Philosophy and Autobiography in Rousseau* (Toronto: University of Toronto Press, 1999), chap. 6.

12 Grant, *Hypocrisy and Integrity*, 154.

13 Ibid., 170.

Chapter 8: Feelings in the Political Philosophy of J.S. Mill

1 As discussed by Rorty and Solomon (Chapters 1 and 10 in this volume), precise definitions for the affective states Mill describes remain a matter of dispute among modern psychologists, neuroscientists, and philosophers. There exists no consensus on what to label "feeling," "emotion," or "affect." One resolution is to use "feeling" to describe a perception of internal physiological changes, such as those associated with hot, cold, and hunger. In contrast, "emotion" describes more deliberate and conscious evaluations or intentional states concerning external events, such as anger, fear, love, and hate. "Affect" tends to be an overarching term to describe all nonrational states. Mill's analysis typically refers to "feeling" whenever describing physiological perceptions as well as conscious or deliberate, but not logical or rational, evaluations or commitments. To remain faithful to Mill's discussion, I use the term "feeling" synonymously with "emotion" in reference to states such as anger, fear, pity, and so forth. For further discussion on modern attempts to define emotion, see John T. Cacioppo and Wendy L.

Gardner, "Emotion," *Annual Review of Psychology* 50 (1999): 1-12; Paul Ekman and Richard J. Davidson, "How Are Emotions Distinguished from Moods, Temperaments, and Other Related Affective Constructs?" in *The Nature of Emotions: Fundamental Questions*, ed. Paul Ekman and Richard J. Davidson (Oxford: Oxford University Press, 1994), 44-96; and Paul E. Griffiths, *What Emotions Really Are* (Chicago: University of Chicago Press, 1997).

2 John Stuart Mill, *Autobiography* (New York: P.F. Collier and Son, 1909), 66. In his essay "Bentham," Mill directly criticizes Bentham's utilitarianism for its paucity of discussion of human nature, especially in understanding emotions beyond purely selfish passions. In particular, Mill argues that Bentham ignores such essential aspects of human nature as desire of approval from others, a sense of honour and personal dignity, the passion of the artist, the love of power over others, and love of ease. In *Mill on Bentham and Coleridge* (New York: Harper Torchbooks, 1950), 66-70.

3 Elizabeth Rapaport, "Introduction," in John Stuart Mill, *On Liberty* (Indianapolis, IN: Hackett, 1978), viii. An example of Mill as a continuing authority can be seen in Martha C. Nussbaum, *Hiding from Humanity: Disgust, Shame and the Law* (Princeton, NJ: Princeton University Press, 2004).

4 The continuing influence of utilitarianism on contemporary ethical debates can be illustrated by the case of biotechnology, in which utilitarianism is a key ethical perspective. See, for example, Richard Sherlock and John D. Morrey, eds., *Ethical Issues in Biotechnology* (Lanham, MD: Rowman and Littlefield, 2002), 16-29; and Thomas A. Mappes and David Degrazia, eds. *Biomedical Ethics*, 5th ed. (Boston: McGraw-Hill, 2001), 4-2, 7.

5 Jeremy Bentham, *The Principles of Morals and Legislation* (New York: Macmillan, 1948). For a discussion of Bentham's perspective, see Martha C. Nussbaum, "Mill between Aristotle and Bentham," *Daedalus* 133, 2 (2004): 60-68; and George Loewenstein, "Emotions in Economic Theory and Economic Behavior," *American Economic Review* 90, 2 (2000): 426-32.

6 Mill, *Autobiography*, 89, 91, 97, 95.

7 For Mill, emotions were also essential in the promotion of a scientific approach to ethology or character development. Although this idea was not well developed, in his system of logic Mill argued that rigorous thinking ought to be applied to a true science of morality. Such a science of character would demand a systematic, biological, and emotionally oriented psychology. See David E. Leary, "Fate and Influence of John Stuart Mill's Proposed Science of Ethology," *Journal of the History of Ideas* 43, 1 (1982): 153-62.

8 Mill, *On Liberty*, 9.

9 Ibid., 4.

10 Ibid., 5.

11 For discussion of Aristotle's understanding of the influence of culture on emotional variation, see Marlene K. Sokolon, *Political Emotions: Aristotle and the Symphony of Reason and Emotion* (Dekalb: Northern Illinois University Press, 2006).

12 Mill, *On Liberty*, 5.

13 Ibid., 17, 50, 33-39.

14 Frederick Rosen maintains that, in the argument of *On Liberty*, Mill himself follows this pattern. The text is not simply a rational argument addressing the intellect alone but is "intended to appeal to deep feelings and strong emotions" in order to convince people of the truth of the argument. Specifically, Rosen is arguing against an interpretation that the Anglo-American tradition lacks an appeal to emotions, feelings, and sensory responses in its ethical arguments. "J.S. Mill on Socrates, Pericles and the Fragility of Truth," *Journal of Legal History* 25, 2 (2004): 181, 192.

15 Mill, *On Liberty*, 55-57, 65.

16 Ibid., 53.

17 John Stuart Mill, *Utilitarianism* (Amherst, NY: Prometheus Books, 1987), 16, 40-41.

18 L.A. Paul, "The Worm at the Root of the Passions: Poetry and Sympathy in Mill's Utilitarianism," *Utilitas* 10, 1 (1998): 86-87.

19 See Kingston (Chapter 5 in this volume) and Krause (Chapter 6).

20 Mill, *Utilitarianism*, 68-69, 78, 74.

21 Mill makes this comment on true moral feelings in a letter dated 28 May 1859 to Dr. W.G. Ward, quoted in D.G. Brown, "Mill on Liberty and Morality," *Philosophic Review* 81, 2 (1972): 156.

22 Mill, *On Liberty*, 56-57.

23 Mill, *Autobiography*, 93-98. See also Paul, "Worm at the Root," 84.

24 Martha C. Nussbaum, *The Therapy of Desire: Theory and Practice in Hellenistic Ethics* (Princeton, NJ:

Princeton University Press, 1994). For more discussion on Nussbaum's understanding of emotional education, see Bradshaw, Chapter 9 in this volume.

25 For more discussion on these first two assumptions, see Paul, "Worm at the Root," 84.

26 Mill, *Autobiography*, 91.

27 Mill, *Utilitarianism*, 17, 44-45.

28 Mill, *On Liberty*, 39, 34, 41, 44.

29 Mill, *Autobiography*, 90-92.

30 Mill, *Utilitarianism*, 18-20.

31 Mill, *On Liberty*, 76-77.

32 For a good summary of contemporary approaches to the study of emotions, see Griffiths, *What Emotions Really Are*, 1-20, 50-55, 77-99. See also Robert C. Solomon, *Not Passion's Slave: Emotions and Choice* (Oxford: Oxford University Press, 2003). For a good example of contemporary adoption of the polarity assumption, see Loewenstein, "Emotions in Economic Theory," 426.

33 Mill, *Utilitarianism*, 20.

34 See Chapter 10 in this volume; and Solomon, *Not Passion's Slave*, 177.

35 Antonio R. Damasio, *Descartes' Error* (New York: Harper Collins, 1994); Joseph LeDoux, *The Emotional Brain* (New York: Simon and Schuster, 1996).

36 Ronald de Sousa, *The Rationality of Emotion* (Cambridge, MA: MIT Press, 1987). For other approaches from this perspective, see Larry Arnhart, *Darwinian Natural Right* (Albany: State University of New York Press, 1998); Dylan Evans, *Emotions* (Oxford: Oxford University Press, 2001); and Jonathan Turner, *On the Origins of Human Emotions* (Palo Alto, CA: Stanford University Press, 2000).

37 Martha C. Nussbaum, *Hiding from Humanity: Philosophical Meditations* (New York: Simon and Schuster, 1989).

38 Dan M. Kahan, "The Progressive Appropriation of Disgust," in *Passions of Law*, ed. Susan Bandes (New York: New York University Press, 1999). For a similar approach, see William Miller, *The Anatomy of Disgust* (Cambridge, MA: Harvard University Press, 1997).

39 For an example of hate as another emotion thought to be necessarily problematic in contemporary approaches to political decision making, see Rush W. Dozier, Jr., *Why We Hate* (Chicago: Contemporary Books, 2002).

Chapter 9: Emotions, Reasons, and Judgments

I would like to thank Edward Andrew, Ronald Beiner, Jon Jacobs, and Connie Missimer, all of whom provided helpful criticism on earlier conference paper drafts of this chapter.

1 Aristotle, *Nicomachean Ethics*, trans. Terence Irwin (Indianapolis, IN: Hackett, 1999), 1112a. Hereafter cited parenthetically in the text as "NE".

2 Aristotle, *The Politics*, trans. Carnes Lord (Chicago: University of Chicago Press, 1984), 1260a; Aristotle, *The Rhetoric*, in *The Rhetoric and Poetics of Aristotle*, trans. Rhys Roberts, ed. Friedrich Solmsen (New York: Modern Library, 1954), 1384a.

3 Immanuel Kant, "On the Relationship of Theory to Practice in Morality in General," in *Kant's Political Writings*, trans. H.B. Nisbet, ed. H.S. Reiss (Cambridge: Cambridge University Press, 1970), 64, emphasis in original.

4 Ibid., 65n.

5 Ibid., 73, emphasis in original.

6 Immanuel Kant, "The Contest of Faculties," in *Kant's Political Writings*, 188.

7 Richard Rorty, "Postmodern Bourgeois Liberalism," in *Philosophical Papers*, vol. 1: *Objectivity, Relativism and Truth* (Cambridge: Cambridge University Press, 1991), 199.

8 Richard Rorty, "The Priority of Democracy to Philosophy," in *Objectivity, Relativism and Truth*, 176.

9 Richard Rorty, "Why Can't a Man Be More Like a Woman," and Other Questions in Moral Philosophy," *London Review of Books*, 24 February 1994, 3-4.

10 Richard Rorty, "Feminism and Pragmatism," in *Philosophical Papers*, vol. 4, *Truth and Progress* (Cambridge: Cambridge University Press, 1998), 181-82.

11 Richard Rorty, "Human Rights, Rationality and Sentimentality," in *On Human Rights: Oxford Amnesty Lectures*, ed. Steven Smith and Susan Hurley (New York: Basic Books, 1993), 131.

12 Rorty, "Feminism and Pragmatism," in *Truth and Progress*, 208.

13 Rorty, "Human Rights," in *On Human Rights*, 128.

14 Richard Rorty, "On Ethnocentrism," in *Objectivity, Relativism and Truth*, 206.

15 Rorty, "Human Rights," in *Truth and Progress*, 181-82.
16 John Rawls arguably built his theory of justice on this foundation. Rawls' liberal-democratic justice relies on our capacity to put ourselves in the "original position" of not knowing what our outcome would have been in the lottery of birth. We are to imagine that we do not know the extent of our wealth, the state of our health, the limits of our talents, etc. From that position, we are led to support the kind of social and political infrastructure that would assist us were we to land in the worst-off position. Rawls cautions, however, that this formula works only given the starting assumptions of a liberal democratic constitutional state in which individuals enjoy the same basic rights and freedoms, and in which there is a great deal of mobility for individuals on the economic and social scale. In other words, Rawls' justice works only where the "great middle" dominates. It would not work, he concedes, for states that are class structured, or states in which there are severe differences in status (such as the caste system in India, or medieval feudal aristocracy). *A Theory of Justice* (Cambridge, MA: Harvard University Press, 1971).
17 Of course, philosophers since Aristotle, especially the Romantics, have elevated pity to the status of a fundamental human virtue. Rousseau, for example, identifies pity and compassion as the most natural sentiments known to man. Interestingly, though, he associates pity with self-love. In the *Second Discourse on the Origin of Inequality*, in *The Social Contract and Discourses*, trans. G.D.H. Cole (London: Dent, Everyman's Library, 1973), 67, Rousseau says candidly that one is likely to extend pity to another sentient creature only when one can see the other's suffering as potentially one's own: "Were it true that pity is no more a feeling which puts us in the place of the sufferer, a feeling obscure yet lively in a savage, developed yet feeble in civilized man; the truth would have no consequence than to confirm my argument. Compassion must, in fact, be stronger, the more the animal beholding any kind of duties identifies himself with the animal that suffers" (68). This is not far off Aristotle's view of pity: that it is intimately connected to fear for one's own welfare. Pity is an extension of self-interest, or in Rousseau's terms, an extension of *amour de soi*.
18 Hannah Arendt, *On Revolution* (New York: Penguin, 1963), 89.
19 Ibid.
20 Hannah Arendt, "On Violence," in *Crises of the Republic* (New York: Harcourt Brace Jovanovich, 1969), 162.
21 Ibid.
22 Arendt, *On Revolution*, 89.
23 Arendt, *On Violence*, 161.
24 Martha C. Nussbaum, *The Therapy of Desire: Theory and Practice in Hellenistic Ethics* (Princeton, NJ: Princeton University Press, 1994), 96.
25 Ibid., 99-100.
26 Ibid., 488.
27 Ibid., 338.
28 To be fair to Solomon, he does not see emotions as "pure" feelings, and he makes the case that not only are emotions framed by particular political contexts, but that there is an element of free choice: "It would be nonsense to insist that, regarding our emotional lives, we are the 'captains of our fate,' but nevertheless we are the oarsmen and that is enough to hold that we are responsible for our emotions." Robert Solomon, "Is There a 'Cognitive Theory' of the Emotions?" in *Philosophy and the Emotions*, ed. Anthony Hatzimoysis (Cambridge: Cambridge University Press, 2003), 18. I think the situation of the submissive young woman is probably more complex than he asserts. There may be no such thing as "feeling submissive" without feeling resistance to that state. Among the wealth of literature on the complexity of female emotions and responses in patterns of submission, Jessica Benjamin's analysis of the "bonds of love" is particularly insightful. Examining male-female patterns of domination and submission in light of Georg Hegel's master-slave dialectic, Benjamin makes a case that feelings of submission are always overlaid with modes of resistance: "The longing for recognition lies beneath the sensationalism of power and powerlessness ... the unrecognizable forms often taken by our desire are the result of a complicated but ultimately understandable process – a process which explains how our deepest desires for freedom and communion become implicated in control and submission. From such desires the bonds of love are forged." *The Bonds of Love* (New York: Pantheon Books, 1988), 84.
29 Martha C. Nussbaum, "Human Functioning and Social Justice: In Defense of Aristotelian Essentialism," *Political Theory* 20, 2 (1992): 208.
30 Martha C. Nussbaum, *Sex and Social Justice* (Oxford: Oxford University Press, 1999), 80.

Chapter 10: The Politics of Emotion

1 William James, "What Is an Emotion?" was first published in *Mind* in 1884. It is reprinted in *What Is an Emotion? Classic Readings in Philosophical Psychology*, ed. Cheshire Calhoun and Robert C. Solomon (New York: Oxford University Press, 1984). See also Phoebe Ellsworth on James' theory, "William James and Emotion," *Psychological Review* 101, 2 (1994): 222-29; and Jack Barbalet, "William James' Theory of Emotion," *Journal for the Theory of Social Behavior* 29, 3 (1999): 251-66.

2 Jon Solomon, "Translations of Aristotle's *Rhetoric*," 1378-80, in Calhoun and Solomon, *What Is an Emotion?* 44-48. Aristotle's *Rhetoric* is translated in full by George A. Kennedy (New York: Oxford University Press, 1991).

3 Daniel C. Dennett, *Consciousness Explained* (Boston: Little, Brown, 1991); John Searle, *The Rediscovery of the Mind* (Cambridge MA: MIT Press, 1992); David Chalmers, *The Conscious Mind: In Search of a Fundamental Theory* (New York: Oxford University Press, 1996); and John Searle, "Consciousness and the Philosophers," review of *The Conscious Mind* by David Chalmers, *New York Review of Books*, 6 March 1997. See also a compendium of articles over the past century, William Lyons, *The Philosophy of Mind* (London: Penguin, 1996), and my review of it in *Philosophy East and West* 46, 3 (1996): 389-99.

4 René Descartes, *The Passions of the Soul*, trans. Stephen H. Voss (Indianapolis, IN: Hackett, 1989). In fact, one might say (without absurdity) that Descartes was no Cartesian. See, notably, Gordon Baker and Katherine Morris, *Descartes* (Oxford: Oxford University Press, 1996).

5 Descartes, *Passions of the Soul*, art. 25.

6 Specifically, Robert Solomon, *The Passions* (New York: Doubleday-Anchor, 1976; rev. ed., Indianapolis, IN: Hackett, 1993); and more recently, "On Emotions as Judgments," *American Philosophical Quarterly* 25, 2 (1988): 183-91.

7 Nico Frijda, *The Emotions* (Cambridge: Cambridge University Press, 1987).

8 Gilbert Ryle, *The Concept of Mind* (New York: Barnes and Noble, 1950), especially Chapter 4; Ludwig Wittgenstein, *Philosophical Investigations* (Oxford: Blackwell, 2002).

9 This is less true of Sartre's early monograph, *The Emotions*, trans. B. Frechtman (New York: Citadel, 1948), where he characterizes emotions as "magical transformations of the world," a subjective form of "escape behavior," but is the case throughout his monumental *Being and Nothingness*, trans. H. Barnes (New York: Philosophical Library, 1956).

10 A bit of perversity needs to be noted here. Continental philosophers since Friedrich Nietzsche, notably Heidegger and, following him, Sartre and Emmanuel Levinas, insist on denying that they are doing "ethics." This is nonsense, a misleading way of indicating their disapproval of what Sartre disdainfully calls "bourgeois ethics," and they clearly have a Kantian model in mind. Levinas, in particular, takes the "priority of the ethical to ontology" as the hallmark of his philosophy.

11 The difference here bears on my disagreements with "social construction theory" (e.g., Rom Harré, James Averill). Part of the disagreement focuses on the existence of some natural or rudimentary emotion-responses that precede socialization, although of course such responses are greatly modified and embellished by society. But, more to the point here, it is not so much that the emotions are constructed *by* society as that emotions define and are defined by the relationships and the societies in which they play an essential role. Love, for example, is not just a "feeling," nor is it biology (or as Freud put it, "lust plus the ordeal of civility"). It is, to be sure, both of these, as well as socially constructed. But the relationship is not something entirely distinct from the mutual emotions (which include, of course, much more than love), nor can the emotions be readily distinguished from the relationship. There are many cases, of course, of unrequited love, and, needless to say, it makes perfectly good sense to speak of one person's feeling for another. But the love, to put it crudely, is *in the relationship*; it is not, as some famous poets have tended to suggest, two parallel but wholly distinct sets of inner vibrations in happy harmony.

12 Sartre, *Emotions*, 41.

13 Ibid., 90-91.

14 Ryle (in *Concept of Mind*), for example, fudges the issue with the idea of "multi-track dispositions," making clear that the number of such hypothetical tracks might be, for any given emotion, indefinitely large.

15 Frijda, *Emotions*, 195.

16 Robert C. Solomon, "Emotions and Choice," *Review of Metaphysics*, 27, 105 (1973); repr. in Cheshire and Calhoun, *What Is an Emotion?* 20-42.

17 Errol Bedford, "Emotions," *Proceedings of the Aristotelian Society* 57 (1956-57): 281-304; repr. in *Essays in*

Philosophical Psychology, ed. D. Gustafson, 77-98 (New York: Doubleday-Anchor, 1963).

18 Frijda, *Emotions,* chap. 6.

19 Friedrich Nietzsche, *Daybreak,* trans. R.J. Hollingdale (Cambridge: Cambridge University Press, 1982).

20 Nico Frijda, "Emotion, Politics: Manipulation of Emotion in Social Interaction," in *Proceedings of the 8th Conference of the International Society for Research on Emotions* (Storrs, CT: ISRE Publications, 1994), 39-42.

21 Lewis Carroll, *Alice's Adventures in Wonderland* (New York: Random House, 1946), 31.

22 Friedrich Nietzsche, *Genealogy of Morals,* trans. Walter Kaufmann and R.J. Hollingdale (New York: Vintage, 1989).

23 Ronald de Sousa, *The Rationality of Emotion* (Cambridge, MA: MIT Press, 1987), 181-84.

24 Among the more sophisticated such attempts, see Robert Kraut, "Love," in *Emotion,* ed. G. Myers and K.D. Irani (New York: Haven Press, 1993); and Michael Stocker, "The Schizophrenia of Modern Ethical Theories," *Journal of Philosophy* 73 (1976): 453-66.

25 Such cynics include François de la Rochefoucauld, Albert Camus, and W.C. Fields.

26 Jean Briggs, *Never in Anger* (Cambridge, MA: Harvard University Press, 1970). See Robert C. Solomon, "Getting Angry: The Jamesian Paradigm in Anthropology," in *Culture Theory,* ed. A. Levine and R. Schweder (Cambridge: Cambridge University Press, 1984).

27 Robert Levi, *The Tahitians* (Chicago: University of Chicago Press, 1973).

28 Stanley Schachter and Jerome Singer, "Cognitive, Social and Physiological Determinants of Emotional States," *Psychological Review* 69, 5 (1962): 379-99.

29 See Robert C. Solomon, "In Defense of Sentimentality," *Philosophy and Literature* 14 (1990): 304-23.

30 Jenefer Robinson, "Startle," *Journal of Philosophy* 92, 2 (1995): 53-74.

31 See Robert C. Solomon, "Back to Basics: On the Very Idea of 'Basic Emotions,'" in *Not Passion's Slave* (New York: Oxford University Press, 2003), 115-42.

32 Descartes, *The Passions of the Soul,* art. 69.

33 Sartre, *Emotions,* 90-91.

34 This distinction between response and reflex played a critical role in the discussion of emotion at least as far back as James and Dewey, and it is the crux of the debate in psychology today. See, for example, Paul E. Griffiths, *What Emotions Really Are* (Chicago: University of Chicago Press, 1997).

35 Paul Ekman, Wallace V. Friesen, and Ronald C. Simons, "Is the Startle Reaction an Emotion?" *Journal of Personality and Social Psychology* 49, 5 (1984): 1416-26.

36 Robert Zajonc; Joseph LeDoux, *The Emotional Brain: The Mysterious Underpinnings of Emotional Life* (New York: Simon and Schuster, 1996).

37 Robinson, "Startle," 18-19.

38 Jerome Shaffer, "An Assessment of Emotion," in Myers and Irani, *Emotion,* 202-3, 220.

Bibliography

Alston, William P. "Emotion and Feeling." In *Encyclopedia of Philosophy*, ed. Paul Edwards. New York: Macmillan, 1967.
—. "Feelings." *Philosophical Review* 78, 1 (1969): 3-34.
Annas, Julia. *An Introduction to Plato's Republic*. Oxford: Oxford University Press, 1981.
Ansart, Pierre. *Les Cliniciens des passions politiques*. Paris: Seuil, 1997.
Anscombe, G.E.M. "On the Grammar of 'Enjoy.'" *Journal of Philosophy* 64, 19 (1967): 607-14.
—. *Intention*. Ithaca, NY: Cornell University Press, 1958.
Aquinas, Thomas. *Commentary on Aristotle's* De Anima. Translated by Kenelm Foster and Silvester Humphries. Notre Dame, IN: Dumb Ox Books, 1994.
—. *Commentary on the Nicomachean Ethics*. Translated by C.I. Litzinger, OP. Notre Dame, IN: Dumb Ox Books, 1993.
—. *Disputed Question on Virtue*. Translated by Ralph McInerny. South Bend, IN: St. Augustine's Press, 1999.
—. *Summa contra Gentiles*, Book Three, *Providence*. Part 2. Translated by Vernon J. Bourke. Notre Dame, IN: University of Notre Dame Press, 1975.
—. *Summa Theologica*. Translated by Fathers of the English Dominican Province. Allen, TX: Christian Classics, 1948.
Árdal, Páll S. *Passion and Value in Hume's Treatise*. Edinburgh: Edinburgh University Press, 1966.
Arendt, Hannah. *On Revolution*. New York: Penguin, 1963.
—. "On Violence." In *Crises of the Republic*, 103-98. New York: Harcourt Brace Jovanovich, 1968.
Aristotle. *The Basic Works of Aristotle*. Translated by D'Arcy Wentworth Thompson, edited by Richard McKeon. New York: Random House, 1941.
—. *History of Animals*. In *The Basic Works of Aristotle*, 631-40.
—. *Nicomachean Ethics*. Translated by Terence Irwin. Indianapolis, IN: Hackett, 1999.
—. *On Rhetoric: A Theory of Civic Discourse*. Translated by George A. Kennedy. New York: Oxford University Press, 1991.
—. *Parts of Animals*. In *The Basic Works of Aristotle*, 641-61.
—. *The Politics*. Translated by Carnes Lord. Chicago: University of Chicago Press, 1984.
—. *The Rhetoric and Poetics of Aristotle*. Translated by Rys Roberts, edited by Friedrich Solmsen. New York: Modern Library, 1954.
Armon-Jones, Claire. "The Thesis of Constructionism." In *Philosophy and the Emotions*, ed. Stephen Leighton, 181-203. Peterborough, ON: Broadview Press, 2003.
Arnhart, Larry. *Darwinian Natural Right*. Albany: State University of New York Press, 1998.
—. "The New Darwinian Naturalism in Political Theory." *American Political Science Review* 89, 2 (1995), 389-400.
Arnold, Magda. *Emotion and Personality*. New York: Columbia University Press, 1960.
Arnold, Magda, and J.A. Gasson. "Feelings and Emotions as Dynamic Factors in Personality Integration." In *The Nature of Emotion*, ed. Magda Arnold, 203-21. New York: Penguin, 1968.
Averill, James. "The Sociocultural, Biological, and Psychological Determinants of Emotion." In Rorty, *Explaining Emotions*, 37-72.

Ayer, A.J. *Hume: A Very Short Introduction*. Oxford: Oxford University Press, 1980.

Baier, Annette. *A Progress of Sentiments: Reflections on Hume's Treatise*. Cambridge, MA: Harvard University Press, 1999.

Baker, Gordon, and Katherine Morris. *Descartes*. Oxford: Oxford University Press, 1996.

Barbalet, Jack. "William James' Theory of Emotion." *Journal for the Theory of Social Behavior* 29, 3 (1999): 251-66.

Baynes, Kenneth. "Liberal Neutrality, Pluralism, and Deliberative Politics." *Praxis International* 12, 1 (1992): 50-69.

Bedford, Errol. "Emotions." *Proceedings of the Aristotelian Society* (1956-57): 281-304. Reprinted in *Essays on Philosophical Psychology*, ed. D. Gustafson, 77-98. New York: Doubleday-Anchor, 1963.

Benjamin, Jessica. *The Bonds of Love*. New York: Pantheon Books, 1988.

—. *Psychoanalysis, Feminism, and the Problem of Domination*. New York: Pantheon Books, 1988.

Bentham, Jeremy. *The Principles of Morals and Legislation*. New York: Macmillan, 1948.

Ben-Ze'ev, Aaron. "Emotions Are Not Mere Judgments." *Philosophy and Phenomenological Research* 68, 2 (2004): 450-57.

—. *The Subtlety of Emotions*. Cambridge, MA: MIT Press, 2000.

Black, P., ed. *Physiological Correlates of Emotion*. New York: Academic Press, 1970.

Blackburn, Simon. *Ruling Passions*. Oxford: Clarendon Press, 1998.

Bloom, Allan. "Interpretive Essay." In Plato, *The Republic of Plato*, 307-436.

Bobonich, Christopher. *Plato's Utopia Recast*. Oxford: Oxford University Press, 2002.

Bohman, James. "Survey Article: The Coming of Age of Deliberative Democracy." *Journal of Political Philosophy* 6, 4 (1998): 400-25.

Botwinick, Aryeh. *Ethics, Politics, and Epistemology: A Study in the Unity of Hume's Thought*. Lanham, MD: University Press of America, 1980.

Briggs, Jean. *Never in Anger*. Cambridge, MA: Harvard University Press, 1970.

Brown, D.G. "Mill on Liberty and Morality." *Philosophic Review* 81, 2 (1972): 133-58.

Brunschwig, Jacques. "Aristotle's Rhetoric as a 'Counterpart' to Dialectic." In Rorty, *Essays on Aristotle's Rhetoric*, 34-55.

Bunting, Madeleine. "Can You Be Taught How to Feel?" *Guardian*, 28 November 2005, G2, 3.

—. "Consumer Capitalism Is Making Us Ill – We Need a Therapy State." *Guardian*, 5 December 2005, 25.

Burnyeat, M.F. "Enthymeme: Aristotle on the Rationality of Rhetoric." In Rorty, *Essays on Aristotle's Rhetoric*, 88-115.

Cacioppo, John T., and Wendy L. Gardner. "Emotion." *Annual Review of Psychology* 50 (1999): 1-12.

Cairns, Douglas. *Aidōs: The Psychology and Ethics of Honour and Shame in Ancient Greek Literature*. Oxford: Clarendon Press, 1993.

Calhoun, Cheshire, and Robert C. Solomon, eds. *What Is an Emotion? Classical Readings in Philosophical Psychology*. New York: Oxford University Press, 1984.

Carroll, Lewis. *Alice's Adventures in Wonderland*. New York: Random House, 1946.

Chalmers, David. *The Conscious Mind: In Search of a Fundamental Theory*. New York: Oxford University Press, 1996.

Cicero. *Cicero on the Emotions: Tusculan Disputations 3 and 4*. Translated by Margaret Graver. Chicago: University of Chicago Press, 2002.

Clarke, Desmond M. *Descartes's Theory of Mind*. Oxford: Oxford University Press, 2003.

Cooper, John M. "Plato's Theory of Motivation." In *Plato II*, ed. Gail Fine, 186-206. Oxford: Oxford University Press, 1999.

—. *Reason and Human Good in Aristotle*. Cambridge, MA: Harvard University Press, 1975.

—. "Some Remarks on Aristotle's Moral Psychology." *Southern Journal of Philosophy* 27, supplement (1988): 25-42.

Dahl, Norman O. *Practical Reason, Aristotle, and Weakness of the Will*. Minneapolis: University of Minnesota Press, 1984.

Damasio, Antonio R. *Descartes' Error*. New York: Harper Collins, 1994.

Danford, John W. *David Hume and the Problem of Reason*. New Haven, CT: Yale University Press, 1990.

Darwin, Charles. *The Expression of the Emotions in Man and Animals*. New York: Appleton, 1896.

Davidson, Donald. "Actions, Reasons, and Causes." *Journal of Philosophy* 60, 23 (1963): 685-700.

—. "Belief and the Basis of Meaning." *Synthese* 27, 3-4 (1974): 309-23.

de Rivera, J. *A Structural Theory of the Emotions*. New York: International Universities Press, 1977.

de Sousa, Ronald. "Emotion." In *The Encyclopedia of Ethics*, ed. L.C. Becker and C.B. Becker, vol. 1, 302-4. New York: Garland Publishing, 1992.

—. "Moral Emotions." *Ethical Theory and Moral Practice* 4 (2001): 109-26.

—. *The Rationality of Emotion*. Cambridge, MA: MIT Press, 1987.

Deely, John. "Animal Intelligence and Concept Formation." *Thomist* 35 (1971), 43-93.

—. *What Distinguishes Human Understanding*. South Bend, IN: St. Augustine's Press, 2002.

Dees, Richard H. "Hume and the Contexts of Politics." *Journal of the History of Philosophy* 30, 2 (1992), 219-42.

—. "Hume on the Characters of Virtue." *Journal of the History of Philosophy* 35, 1 (1997), 45-64.

Dennett, Daniel C. *Consciousness Explained*. Boston: Little, Brown, 1991.

Descartes, René. *Correspondance avec Elisabeth et autres lettres*. Paris: Flammarion, 1989.

. *Discourse on Method and Related Writings*. Translated by Desmond Clarke. New York: Penguin, 1999.

—. *The Passions of the Soul*. Translated by Stephen H. Voss. Indianapolis, IN: Hackett, 1989.

—. "Sixth Meditation." In *Descartes Meditations and Other Metaphysical Writings*, trans. Desmond Clarke, 57-70. New York: Penguin, 1998.

Devereux, Daniel T. "Particular and Universal in Aristotle's Conception of Practical Knowledge." *Review of Metaphysics* 39, 3 (1986): 483-504.

Dewey, John. *Human Nature and Conduct*. New York: Modern Library, 1930.

Dixon, Beth. "Animal Emotion." *Ethics and the Environment* 6, 2 (2001): 22-30.

Dixon, Thomas. *From Passions to Emotions: The Creation of a Secular Psychological Category*. Cambridge: Cambridge University Press, 2003.

Dodds, E.R. *Gorgias*. Oxford: Oxford University Press, 1959.

Donellan, Keith S. "Reference and Definite Descriptions." *Philosophical Review* 75, 3 (1966): 281-304.

Dozier, Rush W., Jr. *Why We Hate*. Chicago: Contemporary Books, 2002.

Drost, Mark P. "Intentionality in Aquinas's Theory of Emotions." *International Philosophical Quarterly* 13, 4 (1991): 449-60.

Eisenstadt, Oona. "Shame in the *Apology*." In *Politics, Philosophy, Writing: Plato's Art of Caring for Souls*, ed. Zdravko Planinc, 42-59. Columbia: University of Missouri Press, 2001.

Ekman, Paul. *Approaches to Emotion*. Hillsdale, NJ: Erlbaum, 1984.

—. "Darwin and Cross-Cultural Studies of Facial Expression." In *Darwin and Facial Expression: A Century of Research in Review*, 169-222. New York: Academic Press, 1973.

—. *Unmasking the Face*. Englewood Cliffs, NJ: Prentice-Hall, 1975.

Ekman, Paul, and Richard J. Davidson. "How Are Emotions Distinguished from Moods, Temperaments, and Other Related Affective Constructs?" In *The Nature of Emotions: Fundamental Questions*, ed. Paul Ekman and Richard J. Davidson, 49-96. Oxford: Oxford University Press, 1994.

Ekman, Paul, Wallace V. Friesen, and Phoebe Ellsworth. *Emotion in the Human Face*. New York: Pergamon Press, 1972.

Ekman, Paul, Wallace V. Friesen, and Klaus R. Scherer. "Body Movement and Voice Pitch in Deceptive Interaction." *Semiotica* 16 (1976): 23-27.

Ekman, Paul, Wallace V. Friesen, and Ronald C. Simons. "Is the Startle Reaction an Emotion?" *Journal of Personality and Social Psychology* 49, 5 (1984): 1416-26.

Ellsworth, Phoebe. "William James and Emotion." *Psychological Review* 101, 2 (1994): 222-29.

Elshtain, Jean. *Public Man, Private Woman: Women in Social and Political Thought*. Princeton, NJ: Princeton University Press, 1981.

Elster, Jon. *Alchemies of the Mind: Rationality and the Emotions*. Cambridge: Cambridge University Press, 1999.

Emberley, Peter. "Rousseau and the Management of the Passions." *Interpretation*, May 1985, 151-76.

Engberg-Pedersen, Troels. "Is There an Ethical Dimension to Aristotelian Rhetoric?" In Rorty, *Essays on Aristotle's* Rhetoric, 161-41.

Euben, J. Peter. *Corrupting Youth: Political Education, Democratic Culture and Political Theory*. Princeton, NJ: Princeton University Press, 1997.

—. "Democracy and Political Theory: A Reading of Plato's *Gorgias*." In *Athenian Political Thought and the Reconstruction of American Democracy*, ed. J. Peter Euben, John R. Wallach, and Josiah Ober, 198-226. Ithaca, NY: Cornell University Press, 1994.

Euben, J. Peter, John R. Wallach, and Josiah Ober. "Introduction." In *Athenian Political Thought and the Reconstruction of American Democracy*, ed. J. Peter Euben, John R. Wallach, and Josiah Ober, 1-26. Ithaca, NY: Cornell University Press, 1994.

Evans, Dylan. *Emotions*. Oxford: Oxford University Press, 2001.

Ferrari, G.R.F. *City and Soul in Plato's Republic*. Chicago: University of Chicago Press, 2005.

Ferriera, M. Jamie. "Hume and Imagination: Sympathy and the Other." *International Philosophical Quarterly* 34, 1 (1994): 39-59.

Fisher, Philip. *The Vehement Passions*. Princeton, NJ: Princeton University Press, 2002.

Forbes, Duncan. *Hume's Philosophical Politics*. Cambridge: Cambridge University Press, 1975.

Forman-Barzilai, Fonna. "Sympathy in Space(s): Adam Smith on Proximity." *Political Theory* 33, 2 (2005): 189-217.

Foucault, Michel. *Fearless Speech*. Edited by Joseph Pearson. Los Angeles: Semiotext(e), 2001.

Frankfurt, Harry. "Freedom of the Will and the Concept of a Person." *Journal of Philosophy* 68, 5 (1971): 5-20.

Frijda, Nico. *The Emotions*. Cambridge: Cambridge University Press, 1987.

—. "Emotion, Politics: The Manipulation of Emotion in Social Interaction." In *Proceedings of the 8th Conference of the International Society for Research on Emotions*. Storrs, CT: ISRE Publications, 1994.

Galston, Miriam. "Taking Aristotle Seriously: Republican-Oriented Legal Theory and the Moral Foundation of Deliberative Democracy." *California Law Review* 82, 2 (1994): 329-99.

Garver, Eugene. *Aristotle's Rhetoric: An Art of Character*. Chicago: University of Chicago Press, 1994.

Gaukroger, Stephen. "Descartes' Theory of the Passions." In *Descartes*, ed. John Cottingham, 211-24. Oxford: Oxford University Press, 1998.

—, ed. *The Soft Underbelly of Reason: The Passions in the Seventeenth Century*. London: Routledge, 1998.

Geertz, Clifford. "Deep Play: Notes on the Balinese Cockfight." In *The Interpretation of Cultures*, 412-53. New York: Basic Books, 1973.

Geertz, Hildred. "The Vocabulary of the Emotions." *Psychiatry* 22 (1959): 225-37.

Geuss, Raymond. *Public Goods, Private Goods*. Princeton, NJ: Princeton University Press, 2001.

Gilson, Etienne. *Moral Values and the Moral Life*. Translated by Leo Richard Ward. Hamden, CT: Shoe String Press, 1961.

Goldhill, S. *Reading Greek Tragedy*. Cambridge: Cambridge University Press, 1986.

Goldie, Peter. *The Emotions*. Oxford: Clarendon Press, 2000.

—. "Emotions, Feelings, and Intentionality." *Phenomenology and the Cognitive Sciences* 1 (2002): 235-54.

Goldman, Alvin. *A Theory of Human Action*. Englewood Cliffs, NJ: Prentice-Hall, 1970.

Grandy, Richard E. "Reference, Meaning and Belief." *Journal of Philosophy* 70, 14 (1973): 439-52.

Grant, Ruth W. *Hypocrisy and Integrity: Machiavelli, Rousseau, and the Ethics of Politics*. Chicago: University of Chicago Press, 1997.

Green, Jeffrey. "The Shame of Being a Philosopher." *Political Theory* 33, 2 (2005): 266-72.

Greenspan, Patricia. "A Case of Mixed Feelings: Ambivalence and the 'Logic' of Emotion." In Rorty, *Explaining Emotions*, 223-50.

—. *Emotions and Reasons: An Inquiry into Emotional Justification*. London: Routledge, 1988.

Griffiths, Paul E. *What Emotions Really Are*. Chicago: University of Chicago Press, 1997.

Gross, Daniel M. "Early Modern Emotion and the Economy of Scarcity." *Philosophy and Rhetoric* 34, 4 (2001): 308-21.

Haakonssen, Knud. *Natural Law and Moral Philosophy: From Grotius to the Scottish Enlightenment*. Cambridge: Cambridge University Press, 1996.

Hall, Cheryl. "'Passion and Constraint': The Marginalization of Passion in Liberal Political Theory." *Philosophy and Social Criticism* 28, 6 (2002): 727-48.

—. *The Trouble with Passion: Political Theory beyond the Reign of Reason*. New York: Routledge, 2005.

Halliwell, Stephen. "The Challenge of Rhetoric to Political and Ethical Theory in Aristotle." In Rorty, *Essays on Aristotle's Rhetoric*, 175-90.

Hamburg, D. "Emotions in the Perspective of Human Evolution." In *Expression of the Emotions in Man*, ed. Peter Knapp, 300-17.

Hamilton, Alexander, John Jay, and James Madison. *The Federalist Papers*. Indianapolis, IN: Liberty Fund Press, 2001.

Hampshire, Stuart. *Innocence and Experience*. Cambridge, MA: Harvard University Press, 1989.

Hampton, Jean. "Does Hume Have an Instrumental Conception of Practical Reason?" *Hume Studies* 21, 1 (1995): 57-74.

Harman, Gilbert H. "Knowledge, Reasons, and Causes." *Journal of Philosophy* 67, 21 (1970): 841-55.

Harré, Rom, ed. *The Social Construction of Emotions*. Oxford: Basil Blackwell, 1986.

Harrison, Jonathan. *Hume's Theory of Justice*. Oxford: Clarendon Press, 1981.

Hartmann, H. "Ego Psychology and the Problem of Adaptation." Translated by David Rapaport. *Journal of the American Psychoanalytic Association Series No. 1*. New York: International Universities Press, 1958.

Hartmann, H., E. Kris, and R. Loewenstein. *Papers on Psychoanalytic Psychology*. New York: International Universities Press, 1964.

Herzog, Donald. *Without Foundations: Justification in Political Theory*. Ithaca, NY: Cornell University Press, 1985.

Hirschberg, N. "A Correct Treatment of Traits." Unpublished manuscript, private collection.

Hirschman, Albert. *The Passions and the Interests*. Princeton, NJ: Princeton University Press, 1977.

Hobbes, Thomas. *Leviathan*. Edited by J.C.A. Gaskin. Oxford: Oxford University Press, 1996.

Holmes, Stephen. *Passions and Constraint*. Chicago: University of Chicago Press, 1995.

Homans, George. *Sentiments and Activities*. New York: Free Press, 1962.

Hume, David. "A Dialogue." In *David Hume: Enquiries Concerning Human Understanding and Concerning the Principles of Morals*, ed. P.H. Nidditch, 324-43. Oxford: Clarendon Press, 1975.

—. *An Enquiry Concerning the Principles of Morals*. LaSalle, IL: Open Court, 1966.

—. *Essays: Moral, Political, and Literary*. Indianapolis, IN: Liberty Fund, 1987.

—. *History of England*. Indianapolis, IN: Liberty Fund, 1983.

—. "Of the Coalition of Parties." In *Essays: Moral, Political, and Literary*, 493-501.

—. "Of Commerce." In *Essays: Moral, Political, and Literary*, 253-67.

—. "Of Essay Writing." In *Essays: Moral, Political, and Literary*, 533-37.

—. "Of the Idea of a Perfect Commonwealth." In *Essays: Moral, Political, and Literary*, 512-29.

—. "Of the Populousness of Ancient Nations." In *Essays: Moral, Political, and Literary*, 377-464.

—. "Of Public Credit." In *Essays: Moral, Political, and Literary*, 349-65.

—. "Of the Standard of Taste." In *Essays: Moral, Political, and Literary*, 226-49.

—. "The Sceptic." In *Essays: Moral, Political, and Literary*, 159-80.

—. *A Treatise of Human Nature*. Edited by L.A. Selby-Bigge. Oxford: Clarendon Press, 1968.

Irigaray, Luce. *The Way of Love*. New York: Continuum, 2002.

Izard, C.E. *The Face of Emotion*. New York: Appleton-Century-Crofts, 1971.

James, Susan. "Explaining the Passions. Passions, Desires and the Explanation of Action." In *The Soft Underbelly of Reason. The Passions in the Seventeenth Century*, ed. Stephen Gaukroger, 17-33. London: Routledge, 1998.

—. *Passion and Action*. Oxford: Clarendon Press, 1997.

James, William. *The Principles of Psychology*. Vol. 2. New York: Holt, 1893.

—. "What Is an Emotion?" In Calhoun and Solomon, *What Is an Emotion?* 127-41.

Johnstone, Christopher Lyle. "An Aristotelian Trilogy: Ethics, Rhetoric, Politics, and the Search for Moral Truth." *Philosophy and Rhetoric* 13, 1 (1980): 1-24.

Kahan, Dan M. "The Progressive Appropriation of Disgust." In *The Passions of Law*, ed. Susan Bandes, 63-79. New York: New York University Press, 1999.

Kahn, Charles. "Drama and Dialectic in Plato's *Gorgias*." *Oxford Studies in Ancient Philosophy* 1 (1983): 75-121.

—. *Plato and the Socratic Dialogue: The Philosophical Use of a Literary Form*. Cambridge, MA: Cambridge University Press, 1996.

—. "Plato's Theory of Desire." *Review of Metaphysics* 1 (1987): 77-103.

Kahn, Paul. *Putting Liberalism in Its Place*. Princeton, NJ: Princeton University Press, 2005.

Kant, Immanuel. *Anthropology from a Pragmatic Point of View*. The Hague: Martinus Nijhoff, 1974.

—. "The Contest of Faculties." In *Kant's Political Writings*, 176-90.

—. *Critique of Pure Practical Reason*. In *Philosophy of Kant*, 209-64.

—. *Grounding for the Metaphysics of Morals*. Translated by James W. Ellington. Indianapolis, IN: Hackett, 1981.

—. *Kant's Political Writings*. Translated by H.B. Nisbet, edited by H.S. Reiss. Cambridge: Cambridge University Press, 1970.

—. "On the Relation of Theory to Practice in Morality in General." In *Kant's Political Writings*, 64-72.

—. *The Philosophy of Kant: Immanuel Kant's Moral and Political Writings*. Translated by Carl J. Friedrich. New York: Modern Library, 1949.

—. *Religion within the Limits of Reason Alone*. In *Philosophy of Kant*, 365-411.

Kemp Smith, Norman. *The Philosophy of David Hume*. London: Macmillan, 1964.

Kenny, Anthony. *Action, Emotion and Will*. London: Routledge and Kegan Paul, 1963.

King, Peter. "Aquinas on the Passions." In *Thomas Aquinas: Contemporary Philosophical Perspectives*, ed. Brian Davies, 353-84. New York: Oxford University Press, 2002.

Klein, Melanie. "On the Development of Mental Functioning." In *Envy and Gratitude*, 236-46. New York: Delta, 1975.

Konstan, David. "Shame in Ancient Greece." *Social Research* 70, 4 (2003): 1031-60.

Korsgaard, Christine. *The Sources of Normativity*. Cambridge: Cambridge University Press, 1996.

Kosman, L.A. "Being Properly Affected: Virtues and Feelings in Aristotle's Ethics." In Rorty, *Essays on Aristotle's* Rhetoric, 103-16.

Koyré, Alexandre. *Introduction à la lecture de Platon*. Paris: Gallimard, 1962.

Koziak, Barbara. *Retrieving Political Emotion: Thumos, Aristotle and Gender*. University Park: Pennsylvania State University Press, 2000.

Krause, Sharon R. "Hume and the (False) Luster of Justice." *Political Theory* 32, 5 (2004): 628-55.

Kraut, Robert. "Love." In *Emotion: Philosophical Studies*, ed. G. Myers and K.D. Irani. New York: Haven Press, 1983.

Kripke, Saul. "Naming and Necessity." In *Semantics of Natural Language*, ed. Donald Davidson and Gilbert Harman, 253-355. Boston: Reidel, 1972.

Kristjansson, Kristjan. "Some Remaining Problems in Cognitive Theories of Emotion." *International Philosophical Quarterly* 41, 4 (2001): 393-410.

Lazarus, R.E. "Emotions and Adaptation: Conceptual and Empirical Relations." In *Nebraska Symposium on Motivation*, ed. W.J. Arnold, 175-266. Lincoln: Nebraska University Press, 1968.

Lear, Jonathan. *Open Minded: Working Out the Logic of the Soul*. Cambridge, MA: Harvard University Press, 1998.

Leary, David E. "Fate and Influence of John Stuart Mill's Proposed Science of Ethology." *Journal of the History of Ideas* 43, 1 (1982): 153-62.

LeDoux, Joseph. "Emotion Circuits in the Brain." *Annual Review of Neuroscience* 23 (2000): 155-84.

—. *The Emotional Brain: The Mysterious Underpinnings of Emotional Life*. New York: Simon and Schuster, 1996.

—. *Synaptic Self: How Our Brains Become Who We Are*. New York: Penguin, 2002.

Leighton, Stephen R. "Aristotle and the Emotions." In Rorty, *Essays on Aristotle's* Rhetoric, 206-37.

Levi, Robert. *The Tahitians*. Chicago: University of Chicago Press, 1973.

Liddell, H.G., and R. Scott. *An Intermediate Greek-English Lexicon*. Oxford: Clarendon Press, 2000.

Livingston, Donald. "On Hume's Conservatism." *Hume Studies* 21, 2 (1995): 151-64.

Lloyd, Genevieve. *The Man of Reason: 'Male' and 'Female' in Western Philosophy*. Minneapolis: University of Minnesota Press, 1984.

Locke, John. *Second Treatise of Government*. Indianapolis, IN: Hackett, 1980.

Loewenstein, George. "Emotions in Economic Theory and Economic Behavior." *American Economic Review* 90, 2 (2000): 426-32.

Loughlin, Stephen. "Similarities and Differences between Human and Animal Emotion in Aquinas's Thought." *Thomist* 65 (2001): 45-65.

Lovibond, Sabina. *Realism and Imagination in Ethics*. Minneapolis: University of Minnesota Press, 1983.

Lyons, William. *Emotions*. Cambridge: Cambridge University Press, 1980.

—. *Modern Philosophy of Mind*. London: Penguin, 1996.

MacIntyre, A.C. "Hume on 'Is' and 'Ought.'" In *Hume*, ed. P.H. Nidditch, 242-64. Notre Dame, IN: University of Notre Dame Press, 1968.

Mackie, J.L. *Hume's Moral Theory*. London: Routledge, 1980.

MacLean, Paul. "Sensory and Perceptive Factors in the Emotional Functions of the Triune Brain." In *Explaining Emotions*, ed. A.O. Rorty, 9-36. Berkeley: University of California Press, 1980.

—. "The Triune Brain, Emotion and Scientific Bias." In *The Neurosciences: Second Study Program*, ed. F.O. Schmitt, 336-49. New York: Rockefeller University Press, 1970.

Makus, Ingrid. "The Politics of 'Masculine Openness' and 'Feminine Concealment' in Rousseau." In *Feminist Interpretations of Rousseau*, ed. Lynda Lange, 187-211. University Park: Pennsylvania State University Press, 2002.

Mappes, Thomas A., and David Degrazia, eds. *Biomedical Ethics*. 5th ed. Boston: McGraw-Hill, 2001.

Marcus, George E. *The Sentimental Citizen: Emotion in Democratic Politics*. University Park: Pennsylvania State University Press, 2002.

Marshall, Graeme. "Overdetermination and the Emotions." In Rorty, *Explaining Emotions*, 197-222.

Masters, Roger D. "Rousseau and the Rediscovery of Human Nature." In *The Legacy of Rousseau*, ed. Clifford Orwin and Nathan Tarcov, 110-40. Chicago: University of Chicago Press, 1997.

McClure, Laura. *Spoken Like a Woman: Speech and Gender in Athenian Drama*. Princeton, NJ: Princeton University Press, 1999.

McDowell, John. "Virtue and Reason." *Monist* 62, 3 (1979): 331-50.

McGinn, Colin. "Charity, Interpretation, and Belief." *Journal of Philosophy* 74, 9 (1977): 521-35.

Middleton, John, ed. *From Child to Adult: Studies in the Anthropology of Education*. New York: Natural History Press, 1970.

Mill, John Stuart. *Autobiography*. New York: P.F. Collier and Son, 1909.

—. "Mill on Bentham." In *Mill on Bentham and Coleridge*, ed. G.W. Stewart, 39-98. New York: Harper Torchbooks, 1950.

—. *On Liberty*. Indianapolis, IN: Hackett, 1978.

—. *Utilitarianism*. Amherst, NY: Prometheus Books, 1987.

Miller, Fred D. "Aristotle on Rationality in Action." *Review of Metaphysics* 37, 3 (1984): 499-520.

Miller, William. *The Anatomy of Disgust*. Cambridge, MA: Harvard University Press, 1997.

Monoson, Sara. *Plato's Democratic Entanglements*. Princeton, NJ: Princeton University Press, 2000.

Moreau, Pierre-François. "Les Passions: Continuités et tournants." In *Les Passions antiques et mediévales*, ed. Bernard Besnier, Pierre-François Moreau, and Laurena Renault, 1-12. Paris: Presses Universitaires de France, 2003.

Morrow, Glenn R. "The Significance of the Doctrine of Sympathy in Hume and Adam Smith." *Philosophical Review* 32, 1 (1923): 60-78.

Morton, Adam. "Framing the Psychological." Unpublished manuscript, private collection.

Most, Glenn W. "The Uses of Endoxa: Philosophy and Rhetoric in the *Rhetoric*." In *Aristotle's Rhetoric: Philosophical Essays*, ed. A. Nehamas and Dana J Furley, 167-90. Princeton, NJ: Princeton University Press, 1994.

Murdoch, Iris. "The Idea of Perfection." In *The Sovereignty of Good*, 1-45. London: Routledge and Kegan Paul, 1970.

Needham, Rodney. *Structure and Sentiment*. Chicago: University of Chicago Press, 1962.

Neu, Jerome. "Jealous Thoughts." In Rorty, *Explaining Emotions*, 425-64.

Newell, W.R. *Ruling Passion: The Erotics of Statecraft in Platonic Political Philosophy*. Lanham, MD: Rowman and Littlefield, 2000.

Nichols, James H., Jr. "Introduction." In Plato, *Gorgias*, 1-24.

Nietzsche, Friedrich. *Daybreak*. Translated by R.J. Hollingdale. Cambridge: Cambridge University Press, 1982.

—. *The Genealogy of Morals*. Translated by Walter Kaufmann and R.J. Hollingdale. New York: Vintage, 1989.

Northwood, Heidi. Commentary presented at the 43rd Annual Congress of the Canadian Philosophical Association, Sherbrooke, QC, June 1999.

Norton, David Fate. "Hume, Human Nature, and the Foundations of Morality." In *The Cambridge Companion to Hume*, ed. D.F. Norton, 150-58. Cambridge: Cambridge University Press, 1999.

Nozick, Robert. *The Examined Life: Philosophical Meditations*. New York: Simon and Schuster, 1989.

Nussbaum, Martha C. *Hiding from Humanity: Disgust, Shame and the Law*. Princeton, NJ: Princeton University Press, 2004.

—. "Human Functioning and Social Justice: In Defense of Aristotelian Essentialism." *Political Theory* 20, 2 (1992): 202-46.

—. *Love's Knowledge*. Oxford: Oxford University Press, 1990.

—. "Mill between Aristotle and Bentham." *Daedalus* 133, 2 (2004): 60-68.

—. "Mutilated and Deformed: Adam Smith and the Material Basis of Human Dignity." Talk presented at the 32nd International Hume Conference, Toronto, July 2005.

—. *Sex and Social Justice*. Oxford: Oxford University Press, 1999.

—. *The Therapy of Desire: Theory and Practice in Hellenistic Ethics*. Princeton, NJ: Princeton University Press, 1994.

—. *Upheavals of Thought: The Intelligence of Emotions*. Cambridge: Cambridge University Press, 2001.

O'Connor, John, ed. *Modern Materialism: Readings on Mind-Body Identity*. New York: Harcourt, Brace, and World, 1969.

Ober, Josiah. *The Athenian Revolution: Essays on Ancient Greek Democracy and Political Theory*. Princeton, NJ: Princeton University Press, 1996.

—. *Mass and Elite in Democratic Athens: Rhetoric, Ideology and the Power of the People*. Princeton, NJ: Princeton University Press, 1989.

Ogrodnick, Margaret. *Instinct and Intimacy: Political Philosophy and Autobiography in Rousseau*. Toronto: University of Toronto Press, 1999.

Okin, Susan Moller. *Justice, Gender and the Family*. New York: Basic Books, 1989.

—. "Reason and Feeling in Thinking about Justice." *Ethics* 113, 2 (1999): 229-59.

Orwin, Clifford. "Rousseau and the Discovery of Political Compassion." In *The Legacy of Rousseau*, ed. Clifford Orwin and Nathan Tarcov, 296-320. Chicago: University of Chicago Press, 1997.

Pasnau, Robert. *Thomas Aquinas on Human Nature*. New York: Cambridge University Press, 2002.

Pateman, C. "The Disorder of Women: Women, Love and the Sense of Justice." In *The Disorder of Women: Democracy, Feminism and Political Theory*, 17-32. Palo Alto, CA: Stanford University Press, 1989.

Paul, L.A. "The Worm at the Root of the Passions: Poetry and Sympathy in Mill's Utilitarianism." *Utilitas* 10, 1 (1998): 83-104.

Pears, D.F. "The Causes and Objects of Some Feelings and Psychological Reactions." *Ratio* 4, 2 (1962): 91-111.

Penelhum, Terrence. *David Hume: An Introduction to His Philosophical System*. West Lafayette, PA: Purdue University Press, 1992.

Petit, Philip. *Republicanism*. Oxford: Oxford University Press, 1997.

Phillipson, Nicholas. "Adam Smith as Civic Moralist." In *Wealth and Virtue*, ed. I. Hont and M. Ignatieff, 179-202. Cambridge: Cambridge University Press, 1983.

Pitcher, George. "Emotion." *Mind* 74, 295 (1965): 326-46.

Plato. "Apology." In *The Trial and Death of Socrates*. Translated by G.M.A. Grube, rev. John Cooper. Indianapolis, IN: Hackett, 2000.

—. "Apology." In *Four Texts on Socrates*, trans. Thomas G. West and Grace Starry West, 63-97. Ithaca, NY: Cornell University Press, 1984.

—. *Gorgias*. Translated by James H. Nichols Jr. Ithaca, NY: Cornell University Press, 1998.

—. *Laws*, trans. A.E. Taylor. In *The Collected Dialogues of Plato*, edited by Edith Hamilton and Huntington Cairns, 1225-1513. Princeton, NJ: Princeton University Press, 1961.

—. *The Republic of Plato*. Translated by Allan Bloom. 2nd ed. New York: Basic Books, 1968.

—. *Republic*. Translated by G.M.A. Grube, rev. C.D.C. Reeve. Indianapolis, IN: Hackett, 1992.

Quine, W.V. *Word and Object*. Cambridge, MA: MIT Press, 1960.

Radcliffe, Elizabeth. "Kantian Tunes on a Humean Instrument: Why Hume Is Not Really a Skeptic about Practical Reasoning." In *Hume: Moral and Political Philosophy*, ed. Rachel Cohon, 59-81. Aldershot, UK: Ashgate/Dartmouth, 2001.

Rawls, John. *Lectures on the History of Moral Philosophy*. Cambridge, MA: Harvard University Press, 2000.

—. *Political Liberalism*. New York: Columbia University Press, 1993.

—. *A Theory of Justice*. Cambridge, MA: Harvard University Press, 1971.

Redding, Paul. *The Logic of Affect*. Ithaca, NY: Cornell University Press, 1999.

Roberts, Robert. *Emotions: An Essay in Aid of Moral Psychology*. New York: Cambridge University Press, 2003.

—. "What an Emotion Is: A Sketch." *Philosophical Review* 97, 2 (1988): 183-209.

Robin, Corey. *Fear: The History of a Political Idea*. Oxford: Oxford University Press, 2004.

Robinson, Jenefer. "Startle." *Journal of Philosophy* 92, 2 (1995): 53-74.

Rorty, Amélie Oksenberg. "Introduction." In Rorty, *Explaining Emotions*, 1-8.

—. "Structuring Rhetoric." In Rorty, *Essays on Aristotle's* Rhetoric, 1-33.

—, ed. *Essays on Aristotle's* Rhetoric. Berkeley: University of California Press, 1996.

—, ed. *Explaining Emotions*. Berkeley: University of California Press, 1980.

Rorty, Richard. *Contingency, Irony and Solidarity*. Cambridge: Cambridge University Press, 1989.

—. "Feminism and Pragmatism." In *Philosophical Papers*, vol. 3: *Truth and Progress*. Cambridge: Cambridge University Press, 1998.

—. "Human Rights, Rationality and Sentimentality." In *Human Rights: Oxford Amnesty Lectures*, ed. Steven Smith and Susan Hurley, 111-34. New York. Basic Books, 1993.

—. "On Ethnocentrism." In *Objectivity, Relativism and Truth,* 203-10.

—. *Philosophical Papers*. Vol. 1, *Objectivity, Relativism and Truth*. Cambridge: Cambridge University Press, 1991.

—. "Postmodern Bourgeois Liberalism." In *Objectivity, Relativism and Truth,* 197-202.

—. "The Priority of Democracy to Philosophy." In *Objectivity, Relativism and Truth,* 175-96.

—. "Why Can't a Man Be More Like a Woman, and Other Questions in Moral Philosophy." *London Review of Books* 24 February 1994, 3-4.

Rosen, Frederick. "J.S. Mill on Socrates, Pericles and the Fragility of Truth." *Journal of Legal History* 25, 2 (2004): 181-94.

Rothschild, Emma. *Economic Sentiments: Adam Smith, Condorcet and the Enlightenment*. Cambridge, MA: Harvard University Press, 2001.

Rousseau, Jean-Jacques. *The First and Second Discourses*. Edited and translated by Roger D. Masters and Judith R. Masters. New York: St. Martin's Press, 1964.

—. *Oeuvres complètes de Jean-Jacques Rousseau*, vol. 4: *Emile. Education - Morale - Botanique*, ed. Bernard Gagnebin and Marcel Raymond. Paris: Gallimard, 1980.

—. *Second Discourse on the Origin of Inequality* In *The Social Contract and Discourses,* trans. G.D.H. Cole, 27-113. London: Dent, Everyman's Library, 1973.

Royce, James E. *Man and His Nature. A Philosophical Psychology*. Toronto: McGraw-Hill, 1961.

Ruddick, William. "Hope and Deception." *Bioethics* 13, 3/4 (1999): 343-57.

Russell, Paul. *Freedom and Moral Sentiment: Hume's Way of Naturalizing Responsibility*. New York: Oxford University Press, 1995.

Ryle, Gilbert. *The Concept of Mind*. New York: Barnes and Noble, 1949.

Sabl, Andrew. "When Bad Things Happen from Good People (and Vice Versa): Hume's Political Ethics of Revolution." *Polity* 35, 1 (2002): 73-92.

Sartre, Jean-Paul. *Being and Nothingness*. Translated by H. Barnes. New York: Philosophical Library, 1956.

—. *The Emotions*. Translated by B. Frechtman. New York: Citadel, 1948.

—. *Existentialism and Human Emotions*. Secaucus, NJ: Carol Publishing Group, 1997.

Saxonhouse, Arlene. "Democracy, Equality and *Eidē*: A Radical View from Book 8 of Plato's *Republic*." *American Political Science Review* 92, 2 (1998): 273-84.

—. *Free Speech and Democracy in Ancient Athens*. Cambridge: Cambridge University Press, 2006.

—. "Plato and the Problematical Gentleness of Democracy." In *Athenian Democracy: Modern Mythmakers and Ancient Theorists*, 87-114. Notre Dame, IN: University of Notre Dame Press, 1996.

Schachter, Stanley, and Jerome Singer. "Cognitive, Social, and Physiological Determinants of Emotional State." *Psychological Review* 69, 5 (1962): 379-99.

Searle, John. "Consciousness and the Philosophers," review of *The Conscious Mind* by David Chalmers. *New York Review of Books,* 6 March 1997.

—. *The Rediscovery of the Mind*. Cambridge, MA: MIT Press, 1992.

Self, Lois S. "Rhetoric and Phronesis: The Aristotelian Ideal." *Philosophy and Rhetoric* 12, 2 (1979): 130-45.

Shaffer, Jerome. "An Assessment of Emotion." *American Philosophical Quarterly* 20, 2 (1983): 161-74.

Shaftesbury, Earl of. "An Inquiry Concerning Virtue or Merit." In *Characteristics of Men, Manners, Opinions, Times,* ed. Lawrence E. Klein. Cambridge: Cambridge University Press, 1999.

"A Letter Concerning Enthusiasm to My Lord ***." In *Characteristics of Men, Manners, Opinions, Times,* ed. Lawrence E. Klein. Cambridge: Cambridge University Press, 1999.

Sherlock, Richard, and John D. Morrey, eds. *Ethical Issues in Biotechnology*. Lanham, MD: Rowman and Littlefield, 2002.

Sherman, Nancy. *The Fabric of Character: Aristotle's Theory of Virtue*. Oxford: Clarendon Press, 1989.

—. *Making a Necessity of Virtue: Aristotle and Kant on Virtue*. New York: Cambridge University Press, 1996.

Shklar, Judith. "The Liberalism of Fear." In *Liberalism and the Moral Life*, ed. Nancy Rosenblum, 20-38. Cambridge, MA: Harvard University Press, 1989.

—. *Ordinary Vices*. Cambridge, MA: Belknap Press, 1984.

Shorris, Earl. "Ignoble Liars: Leo Strauss, George Bush, and the Philosophy of Mass Deception." *Harper's Magazine*, June 2004, 65-71.

Smith, Adam. *The Theory of Moral Sentiments*. Indianapolis, IN: Liberty Fund, 1982.

Sokolon, Marlene K. *Political Emotions: Aristotle and the Symphony of Reason and Emotion*. DeKalb: Northern Illinois University Press, 2006.

Solomon, Jon. "Translations of Aristotle's *Rhetoric*." In Calhoun and Solomon, *What Is an Emotion?* 44-48.

Solomon, Robert C. "Emotions and Choice." *Review of Metaphysics* 27, 105 (1973): 20-42. Reprinted in Calhoun and Solomon, *What Is an Emotion?* and in Rorty, *Explaining Emotions*, 251-81.

—. "Getting Angry: The Jamesian Theory of Emotion in Anthropology." In *Culture Theory*, ed. Robert A. Levine and Richard Schweder, 238-56. Cambridge: Cambridge University Press, 1984.

—. "In Defense of Sentimentality." *Philosophy and Literature* 14 (1990): 304-23.

—. "Emotions, Thoughts, and Feelings: What Is a 'Cognitive Theory' of the Emotions and Does It Neglect Affectivity?" In *Philosophy and the Emotions*, Royal Institute of Philosophy Supplements n. 52, ed. Anthony Hatzimoysis, 1-18. Cambridge: Cambridge University Press, 2003.

—. "The Logic of Emotion." *Nous* 11, 1 (1977): 41-49.

—. *Not Passion's Slave: Emotions and Choice*. New York: Oxford University Press, 2003.

—. "On Emotions as Judgments." *American Philosophical Quarterly* 25, 2 (1988): 183-91.

—. *The Passions*. New York: Doubleday, 1976. Rev. ed. Indianapolis, IN: Hackett, 1993.

—. Review of *Modern Philosophy of Mind*, by William Lyons. *Philosophy East and West* 46, 3 (1996): 389-99.

—. *Thinking about Feeling: Contemporary Philosophers on Emotions*. New York: Oxford University Press, 2004.

Spinoza, Benedict de. *Ethics, Preceded by On the Improvement of the Understanding*. Edited by James Gutmann. New York: Hafner Press, 1949.

Spitz, Jean-Fabien. *Le Moment Républicain en France*. Paris: Gallimard, 2005.

Sprute, Jürgen. "Aristotle and the Legitimacy of Rhetoric." In *Aristotle's Rhetoric: Philosophical Essays*, ed. A. Nehamas and David J. Furley, 117-28. Princeton, NJ: Princeton University Press, 1994.

Stewart, John B. "The Public Interest vs. Old Rights." *Hume Studies* 21, 2 (1995): 165-88.

Stich, Steven. "Beliefs and Subdoxastic States." *Philosophy of Science* 45 (1978): 499-518.

Stocker, Michael. "Emotional Thoughts." *American Philosophical Quarterly* 24, 1 (1987): 56-69.

—. "How Emotions Reveal Value and Help Cure the Schizophrenia of Modern Ethical Theories." In *How Should One Live? Essays on the Virtues*, ed. Roger Crisp, 173-90. New York: Oxford University Press, 1996.

—. "Intellectual Desire, Emotion, and Action." In Rorty, *Explaining Emotions*, 323-38.

—. "Psychic Feelings: Their Importance and Irreducibility." *Australian Journal of Philosophy* 61 (1983): 5-26.

—. "The Schizophrenia of Modern Ethical Theories." *Journal of Philosophy* 73 (1976): 453-66.

Straus, Erwin. "Shame as a Historiological Problem." *Phenomenological Psychology* 25 (1979): 222-40.

Striker, Gisela. "Emotions in Context: Aristotle's Treatment of the Passions in the *Rhetoric* and His Moral Psychology." In Rorty, *Essays on Aristotle's* Rhetoric, 286-302.

Strong, Tracy. *Jean-Jacques Rousseau: The Politics of the Ordinary*. Thousand Oaks, CA: Sage Publications, 1994.

Stroud, Barry. *Hume*. London: Routledge, 2000.

Sunstein, Cass. *Laws of Fear*. Cambridge: Cambridge University Press, 2005.

Tanner, Michael. "Sentimentality." *Proceedings of the Aristotelian Society* 77 (1977): 127-47.

Tarcov, Nathan. "The Meanings of Democracy." In *Democracy, Education and Schools*, ed. Roger Soder, 1-36. San Francisco: Jossey-Bass, 1996.

Tarnopolsky, Christina. "Power's Passionate Pathologies." Paper presented at the annual meeting of the American Political Science Association, Washington, DC, 2 September 2006.

—. "Prudes, Perverts and Tyrants: Plato and the Contemporary Politics of Shame and Civility." *Political*

Theory 32, 4 (2004): 468-94.

—. "Response to Green." *Political Theory* 33, 2 (2005): 273-79.

Taylor, Charles. *Human Agency and Language*. New York: Cambridge University Press, 1985.

—. *The Malaise of Modernity.* Concord, ON: Anansi Press, 1991.

—. *Multiculturalism and the Politics of Recognition.* Princeton, NJ: Princeton University Press, 1992.

Taylor, Gabriele. "Justifying the Emotions." *Mind* 84 (1975): 390-402.

Taylor, Jacqueline. "Hume and the Reality of Value." In *Feminist Interpretations of David Hume*, ed. Anne Jaap Jacobsen, 107-36. University Park: Pennsylvania State University Press, 2000.

—. "Hume on Luck and Moral Inclusion." Panel paper presented at the annual meeting of the American Political Science Association, Philadelphia, PA, September 2003.

—. "Humean Ethics and the Politics of Sentiment." *Topoi* 21 (2002): 175-86.

—. "Justice and the Foundations of Social Morality in Hume's Treatise." *Hume Studies* 24, 1 (1998): 5-30.

Thalberg, Irving. "Constituents and Causes of Emotion and Action." *Philosophical Quarterly* 23, 90 (1973): 1-14.

—. *Perception, Emotion and Action*. Oxford: Basil Blackwell, 1977.

Tocqueville, Alexis de. *Democracy in America*. Translated by Harvey C. Mansfield and Delba Winthrop. Chicago: University of Chicago Press, 2000.

Tomkins, Silvan A. *Affect, Imagery and Consciousness*. 2 vols. New York: Springer, 1962-63.

Turner, Frank M. *The Classical Heritage in Victorian Britain*. New Haven, CT: Yale University Press, 1981.

Turner, Jonathan. *On the Origins of Human Emotions*. Palo Alto, CA: Stanford University Press, 2000.

Uffenheimer-Lippens, Elisabeth. "Rationalized Passion and Passionate Rationality: Thomas Aquinas on the Relation between Reason and the Passions." *Review of Metaphysics* 56, 3 (2003): 525-58.

van Fraasen, Bas C. "The Pragmatics of Explanation." *American Philosophical Quarterly* 14, 2 (1977): 143-50.

Viroli, Maurizio. *For Love of Country*. Oxford: Oxford University Press, 1997.

Wallach, John. "Plato's Socratic Problem, and Ours." *History of Political Thought* 18 (1997): 377-91.

Walzer, Michael. "Passion and Politics." *Philosophy and Social Criticism* 28 (2002): 617-33.

—. *Politics and Passion: Towards a More Egalitarian Liberalism*. New Haven, CT: Yale University Press, 2004.

Wardy, Robert. "Mighty Is the Truth and It Shall Prevail?" In Rorty, *Essays on Aristotle's* Rhetoric, 56-87.

Warnick, Barbara. "Judgment, Probability, and Aristotle's Rhetoric." *Quarterly Journal of Speech* 9 (1989): 299-311.

Weithman, Paul J. "Thomistic Pride and Liberal Vice." *The Thomist* 60 (1996): 241-74.

Williams, Bernard. "The Analogy of City and Soul in Plato's *Republic*." In *Plato II*, ed. G. Fine, 255-64. Oxford: Oxford University Press, 1990.

—. "Internal and External Reasons." In *Moral Luck*. Cambridge: Cambridge University Press, 1981.

—. "Morality and the Emotions." In *Problems of the Self*, 207-29. New York: Cambridge University Press, 1973.

—. *Shame and Necessity*. Berkeley: University of California Press, 1993.

Wittgenstein, Ludwig. *Philosophical Investigations*. Oxford: Blackwell, 2002.

Young, Iris Marion. "Asymmetrical Reciprocity: On Moral Respect, Wonder, and Enlarged Thought." In *Judgment, Imagination, and Politics: Themes from Kant and Arendt*, ed. Ronald Beiner and Jennifer Nedelsky, 205-28. Lanham, MD: Rowman and Littlefield, 2001.

Young, P.T. *Motivation and Emotions*. New York: Wiley, 1961.

Zastoupil, Lynn. "J.S. Mill and India." *Victorian Studies* 32, 1 (1988): 31-54.

Contributors

Arash Abizadeh teaches political theory at McGill University. He has published on democratic theory, nationalism, cosmopolitanism, Habermas, and Rousseau. He is currently writing a book on Rousseau's political philosophy in light of his theories of language, music, and aesthetics.

Leah Bradshaw teaches political theory at Brock University. She has written on the subjects of tyranny, Hannah Arendt, the treatment of women in Aristotle and Rousseau, and the political thought of George Grant. She is writing a book comparing ancient and modern understandings of tyranny.

Leonard Ferry is finishing his PhD at the University of Toronto in political philosophy. His work explores the viability of neo-Aristotelian conceptions (the good, virtue ethics, practical wisdom) in the works of Alasdair MacIntyre and Charles Taylor. He is also working on a theory of emotions that draws on semiotics.

Rebecca Kingston teaches political science at the University of Toronto. Her book *Montesquieu and the 'parlement' of Bordeaux* was awarded the Prix Montesquieu, and she has published on French criminal justice history and modern political thought. She is writing a book that explores the idea of public passion in the history of political thought.

Sharon Krause teaches political theory at Brown University. She is author of *Liberalism with Honor*, which investigates the motive of honour as a source of political agency in liberal democracy. She is currently writing about the relationship between reason and passion in democratic deliberation, drawing on the moral sentiment theory of David Hume.

Ingrid Makus is chair of the political science department at Brock University. She has written on Rousseau, citizenship, and the culture of film, as well as the legacy of Hobbes, Locke and J.S. Mill, and is currently writing a book that draws on the thinking of Plato, Aristotle, and Rousseau.

Amélie Oksenberg Rorty, a visiting professor at Harvard University, has published widely in the history of moral psychology, with anthologies on Aristotle's ethics, his poetics and his rhetoric.

Marlene K. Sokolon teaches political theory at Concordia University. She received her PhD from Northern Illinois University and is the author of *Political Emotions: Aristotle and the Symphony of Reason and Emotion.*

Robert C. Solomon was Quincy Lee Centennial Professor and Distinguished Teaching Professor at the University of Texas at Austin. He was the author of *The Passions, In the Spirit of Hegel, About Love, A Passion for Justice, Ethics and Excellence, Up the University, A Short History of Philosophy* (with Kathleen M. Higgins), and most recently *Not Passion's Slave, Spirituality for the Skeptic, The Joy of Philosophy, Thinking about Feeling,* and *Living with Nietzsche.*

Christina Tarnopolsky teaches political theory at McGill University. She is the author of *Prudes, Perverts and Tyrants: Plato and the Politics of Shame,* forthcoming from Princeton University Press. She is currently writing a book on the relationship between the logic of the aesthetic and the logic of emotions.

Index